W9-CRJ-139

GLOBAL CURRENTS IN GENDER AND FEMINISMS: CANADIAN AND INTERNATIONAL PERSPECTIVES

GLOBAL CURRENTS IN GENDER AND FEMINISMS: CANADIAN AND INTERNATIONAL PERSPECTIVES

EDITED BY

GLENDA TIBE BONIFACIO
University of Lethbridge, Canada

United Kingdom – North America – Japan – India – Malaysia – China

Emerald Publishing Limited
Howard House, Wagon Lane, Bingley BD16 1WA, UK

First edition 2018

Copyright © 2018 Emerald Publishing Limited

Reprints and permissions service
Contact: permissions@emeraldinsight.com

No part of this book may be reproduced, stored in a retrieval system, transmitted in
any form or by any means electronic, mechanical, photocopying, recording or
otherwise without either the prior written permission of the publisher or a licence
permitting restricted copying issued in the UK by The Copyright Licensing Agency
and in the USA by The Copyright Clearance Center. Any opinions expressed in the
chapters are those of the authors. Whilst Emerald makes every effort to ensure the
quality and accuracy of its content, Emerald makes no representation implied or
otherwise, as to the chapters' suitability and application and disclaims any warranties,
express or implied, to their use.

British Library Cataloguing in Publication Data
A catalogue record for this book is available from the British Library

ISBN: 978-1-78714-484-2 (Print)
ISBN: 978-1-78714-483-5 (Online)
ISBN: 978-1-78714-943-4 (Epub)

ISOQAR certified
Management System,
awarded to Emerald
for adherence to
Environmental
standard
ISO 14001:2004.

Certificate Number 1985
ISO 14001

INVESTOR IN PEOPLE

Contents

List of Photos

Contributor Biographies

Carly Adams is an associate professor in the Department of Kinesiology and Physical Education at the University of Lethbridge, Alberta, Canada. Her research explores sport, recreation and leisure experiences from the intersections of historical and sociological inquiry with a focus on gender and community. Her work has appeared in, among others, *Journal of Sport History*, *Journal of Canadian Studies* and *International Review for the Sociology of Sport*. Carly is the Editor-in-Chief of *Sport History Review*.

Aylin Akpınar teaches at the Department of Sociology at Marmara University in Istanbul, Turkey. She received her PhD from Uppsala University, Sweden. Her recent works have been published in *Feminist Formations*; *Family, Religion, Law, Cultural Tensions in the Family-Examples of Sweden and Turkey* (2010); *Education in 'Multicultural' Societies: Turkish and Swedish Perspectives* (2007). She is the member of Turkish Sociological Association as well as the European Sociological Association.

Jill Allison holds a PhD in anthropology from Memorial University of Newfoundland. Merging a background in clinical nursing with an interest in global health, social justice, health equity, and health and social values, her work examines the role of health care institutions in shaping identity, gender equity and social equality. Jill is the global health coordinator and a clinical associate professor in Community Health and Humanities in the Faculty of Medicine at Memorial University of Newfoundland in St. John's, Canada. Her current research interests include women's' reproductive health and access to safe birth and contraceptive choice in Nepal and Haiti, the politics of reproduction in Nepal, malnutrition in Haiti, the impact of changing trends in the care of persons living with HIV in Canada, and barriers to access to reproductive technologies. Jill has worked in rural and urban Nepal, Bangladesh, Mexico, Ireland and many communities across Canada. She is the author of *Motherhood and Infertility in Ireland: Understanding the Presence of Absence*; other works have been published in *Medical Anthropology Quarterly*, *The Journal of the Society for the Anthropology of Europe*, and *Aporia* among others. Jill teaches, facilitates opportunities for medical students to work with underserved populations in inner city services and coordinates the InSIGHT programme in Kathmandu, a global health and social justice elective training programme for medical students.

Orly Benjamin is a feminist sociologist at the Sociology and Anthropology Department and at the Gender Studies Program at Bar-Ilan University, Israel. She currently chairs the Poverty Research Unit, studying, among other issues, poverty as shaping occupational development of adolescent girls and young women and mothers' potential contribution to their daughters' occupational efficacy. Her book, *Gendering Israel's Outsourcing: The Erasure of Employees' Caring Skills* (2016) summarizes her research on poverty among women employed in service and care occupations.

Asanda Benya is a lecturer in the Sociology Department at the University of Cape Town (UCT) in South Africa. She is also a research associate at the Society, Work and Development Institute (SWOP) based at Wits University, Johannesburg. Using participant observation, her PhD looked at the construction of gendered subjectivities of underground women mineworkers. In her research, she explores issues of power, bodies, spaces and gendered identities of women in mining. Her broad research interests are: labour studies, gender, labour and social movements, labour geographies, workplace identities, the extractives industry, human rights, social justice in mining communities and ethnography.

Glenda Tibe Bonifacio is associate professor in women and gender studies at the University of Lethbridge, Canada. She completed her PhD in political science at the University of Wollongong, Australia, and Masters in Asian Studies at the University of the Philippines. Glenda is a research affiliate of the Prentice Institute for Global Population and Economy. Her works include a monograph on *Pinay on the Prairies: Filipino Women and Transnational Identities* (UBC Press 2013); editor of *Gender and Rural Migration: Realities, Conflict and Change* (Routledge 2014) and *Feminism and Migration: Cross-Cultural Engagements* (Springer 2012); co-editor of *Canadian Perspectives on Immigration in Small Cities* (Springer 2017), *Migrant Domestic Workers and Family Life: International Perspectives* (Palgrave Macmillan 2015), and *Gender, Religion and Migration: Pathways of Integration* (Lexington Books 2010).

Sonja Boon is associate professor of gender studies at Memorial University, Newfoundland and Labrador, Canada. She has research interests in the areas of identity, citizenship, embodiment, migration, life writing, and feminist theory. Her work appears in *Life Writing*, *Journal of Women's History*, *SubStance*, *International Journal of Communication*, and the *European Journal of Life Writing*, among others. Her second monograph, *Telling the Flesh: Life Writing, Citizenship, and the Body in the Letters to Samuel Auguste Tissot*, was published in 2015.

Catherine Bryan is a PhD candidate in social anthropology at Dalhousie University, Halifax, Canada. Her research interests include feminist political economy, transnationalism, Philippine migration, social reproduction, and regional rural development. Her works have been published in *Refuge: Canada's Journal on Refugees, Anthropologica*, and the *Journal of Immigrant and Refugee Studies*. Other works were included in *When Care Work goes Global: Locating the Social Relations of Domestic Work* (Ashgate 2014) and *Mothering in a Neoliberal Age* (Demeter Press 2014). Catherine holds a BA (honours) in women's studies from the University of Winnipeg, and a Bachelor in Social Work and Masters in Social Work from McGill University.

Panteá Farvid is a senior lecturer in psychology at Auckland University of Technology (AUT). For over a decade her work has examined the intersection of gender, sexuality, power, culture, technology and identity. Most of her research is oriented towards social justice and social change, specifically focused in promoting egalitarianism within heterosexuality. She has worked on projects examining heterosexual casual sex, contemporary heterosexualities, the New Zealand sex industry, men who buy sex, and technologically mediated intimacies via mobile dating, online dating and sugar dating, as well as best practice gender policy for New Zealand. She seeks to promote gender equality as well as gender and sexual fluidity through her ongoing research. She is a frequent media commentator of issues related to psychology, gender, sexuality and other related topics.

Christine Gervais is an associate professor in criminology at the University of Ottawa. Her research and teaching interests are in the areas of human rights, child rights, crimes of the powerful, as well as gender discrimination within religious institutions. She has published in *Signs, Children & Society, Journal of Youth Studies, Canadian Woman Studies, Journal of International Women's Studies, Criminologie, Sociology of Religion, Religions* and *Review of Religious Research*.

Parthiban S. Gopal is a senior lecturer in development studies at the School of Social Sciences, Universiti Sains Malaysia, Penang, Malaysia. He teaches courses in urban and sustainable development and poverty. His special interest and expertise is on urban development particularly related to poverty, Indian studies and labour issues. He has published articles on issues of poverty in Malaysia.

Premalatha Karupiah is an associate professor of sociology at the School of Social Sciences, Universiti Sains Malaysia, Penang, Malaysia. She teaches research methodology and statistics. Her research interests are in the areas of beauty culture, femininity, educational and occupational choices, and issues related to the Indian diaspora. Her articles have been published in leading journals.

Jason Laurendeau is an associate professor in the Department of Sociology at the University of Lethbridge, Alberta, Canada. His research explores intersections of gender, risk and embodiment, and his work has been published in journals such as *Sociological Perspectives*, the *Sociology of Sport Journal*, the *Journal of Sport & Social Issues*, and *Emotion, Space & Society*.

Marlise Matos is an associate professor of political science at the Federal University of Minas Gerais (UFMG). She received her PhD in sociology from the University Research Institute of Rio de Janeiro (IUPERJ). Marlise directs NEPEM, the Center for Studies and Research on Women (UFMG). In the last five years, NEPEM has increased its extension activities in the community and is currently working on a project that monitors human rights programmes and public policies for women in Brazil and Latin America. Her main research interests and publications include gender and politics, feminist theory, identity politics, public policy, sexual and reproductive rights, human rights, and citizenship.

Barbara A. Morningstar has a doctorate in education. She has a wealth of experience working as a patient liaison in the area of mental health, and currently works as a spiritual care professional at the McGill University Health Centre. She has over 20 years of experience in community development and has been actively involved in projects related to diversity, feminism, spirituality, women's learning and advocacy. In 2009, she received the Diversity Scholarship from Argosy University for her contribution to the recognition and development of women leaders in local communities. In 2013, she completed her doctoral studies with a specialization in community and pastoral counselling.

Ebba Olofsson has a PhD in cultural anthropology from Uppsala University, Sweden. She is teaching anthropology and research writing at Champlain Regional College in Saint-Lambert, and she is an affiliate assistant professor of the Department of Sociology and Anthropology at Concordia University, Montreal. She also taught courses in 'Inuit Peoples' at the First Peoples Studies Program at Concordia University and 'Indigenous Women of the North' at the McGill Institute for the Study of Canada at McGill University in Montreal. Her research interests relate to issues about identity, health, gender, kinship, subsistence and colonialism, among the Indigenous peoples in Scandinavia and Canada.

Sigal Oppenhaim-Shachar completed her PhD in gender studies at Bar Ilan University, Israel, in 2012. She is a lecturer and researcher at the Gender Studies Program; the Sociology and Anthropology Department, and the School of Education at Bar-Ilan University, and at Levinsky College of Education. Her work on the topic of adolescent girl's intersectionality and occupational efficacy, has been published (*Hagar Studies in Culture, Policy and Identities*, 2014; *Woman's Studies International Forum*, 2016), and at Israeli academic journals. Her other interests include feminist pedagogy (gender and education) and pedagogy of intervention processes with some population groups. She initiated the 'Daphna Center' in 2010 — a professional development and training centre established by the Bar-Ilan University Gender Studies Program, and managed the programme up to the end of 2014.

Lisa Pasolli is an assistant professor of history and women's and gender studies at St. Francis Xavier University, Canada. Her research explores the contours and dimensions of child care politics in 20th century Canada, and her recent book is *Working Mothers and the Child Care Dilemma: A History of British Columbia's Social Policy* (UBC Press). Her work on the history of child care has also been published in *The Canadian Historical Review* and *BC Studies*.

Beth Pentney studies postfeminist media culture with particular attention to social media, body modification and female celebrity. She is interested in contemporary feminist activism and the ways it emerges in online spaces and through tactile arts such as knitting, especially when they intertwine. She teaches part-time in the Gender Equality and Social Justice program at Nipissing University, in North Bay, Ontario.

Ornit Ramati Dvir is a PhD candidate at the Gender Studies Program at Bar-Ilan University, and holds an MA degree in economics from Tel-Aviv University, Israel. Among her areas of interest include women in the workplace and female adolescents, particularly focused on physical education. Her work in the area of gender and physical education has recently been published in a Hebrew volume, the first of its kind dedicated to various aspects of adolescent girls and their bodies. She works as an advisor for various companies trying to identify barriers and inequality facing women, and runs several empowerment programmes for teenage girls.

Solange Simões has a PhD in sociology from the London School of Economics and Political Science, and an MA in political science from the Federal University of Minas Gerais, Brazil. After earning tenure at the Federal University of Minas Gerais in Brazil, went to the United States as a Fulbright scholar to the University of Michigan's Institute for Social Research/Center for Political Studies, where she became an adjunct faculty associate from 1995 to 2006. In 2006 she joined Eastern Michigan University with a joint appointment in Sociology and Women's and Gender Studies, and has also continued to teach in Brazil as a visiting professor every summer. Her areas of expertise, research and publications include gender and political participation, gender and globalization, racial identity, class structure, environmental values and attitudes, cross-national survey methodology, and global learning. In the period 2006–2014 she was one of the regional representative for United States/Canada in the International Sociological Association's (ISA) Research Committee 32 Women in Society. She is one of the delegates for Sociologists for Women in Society (SWS) at the United Nations' Economic and Social Council.

Ada L. Sinacore is an associate professor in the Counselling Psychology Program at McGill University and the Chair of Women's Studies at the McGill Institute for Gender, Sexuality and Feminist Studies. She has over 20 years of experience working in the United States, Canada and other countries, and is internationally recognized for her expertise and extensive presentations and publications in social justice, career development, migration and immigration, gender equity, pedagogy and feminist psychology. She is actively involved in research, scholarship and programme development addressing social justice concerns at the individual, institutional and policy levels and has particular expertise on workplace abuse and violence. She is the co-editor of a book regarding the teaching of social justice within a multicultural and feminist perspective and is highly sought after for her consultation and programme evaluation skills. In 2010, she received the Oliva Espin Award for Social Justice Concerns in Feminist Psychology: Immigration and Gender, from the Association for Women in Psychology. As well, she is a Fellow of the Canadian Psychological Association. For a list of her publications, awards, and achievements please go to her website at www.mcgill.ca/socialjustice.

Miki Suzuki Him is a lecturer at the Department of Sociology at Ondokuz Mayis University in Samsun, Turkey. Her research interests are gender inequality, rural sociology and women's reproductive and productive labour. Miki studied Kurdish women's struggles for birth control in eastern Turkey for her PhD dissertation. She has also been doing research about female seafood factory workers in rural Black Sea Turkey for the last few years. Her co-authored works on reproductive practices of Kurdish women was published in *Women's Studies International Forum*, and the struggle for birth control of Kurdish migrant women in Van, Turkey in *Health Care for Women International*.

Jocelyn Thorpe is an associate professor in women's and gender studies, and history at the University of Manitoba. Her research examines the history and legacies of colonialism in Canada, focusing particularly on how ideas about gender, race, nation and nature shape human relationships with one another and with the non-human world. She is the author of *Temagami's Tangled Wild: Race, Gender, and the Making of Canadian Nature* (UBC Press 2012) and co-editor, with Stephanie Rutherford and

L. Anders Sandberg, of *Methodological Challenges in Nature-Culture and Environmental History Research* (Routledge, 2017).

Michelle Walks is a queer feminist medical anthropologist and a queer femme Momma. She is a sessional instructor of Anthropology, Sociology, and Gender, Sexuality, and Women's Studies who mainly teaches at Douglas College and the University of British Columbia (Okanagan campus). She completed a postdoctoral fellowship through the University of Ottawa (Nursing), which had her working on an interdisciplinary community-based CIHR-funded project called 'Transmasculine Individuals' Experiences with Pregnancy, Birthing, and Feeding their Newborns: A Qualitative Study'. She guest edited a special issue of *Anthropologica* focused on Queer Anthropology (May 2014), and co-edited the anthology, *An Anthropology of Mothering* (Demeter Press, 2011). She has also written and co-written a variety of chapters and articles on the anthropology of mothering, queer anthropology, and queer/transmasculine reproduction and infant feeding.

Lauren Wallace is a medical anthropologist whose current research addresses issues of family planning in Ghana. She is a PhD candidate in anthropology and a Vanier Scholar at McMaster University. Her PhD research examines gender, changing family size, contraceptive use and marriage in northern Ghana. She has also conducted research on women's nutrition in Cambodia and medical ethics in global health. She has published in *Global Health Perspectives, Education for Health*, the *Asia Pacific Journal of Clinical Nutrition* and *Relational Child and Youth Care Practice*.

Amanda Watson holds a PhD in feminist and gender studies from the University of Ottawa, and is a lecturer at Simon Fraser University, British Columbia, Canada. Her research examines intersections of citizenship, paid and unpaid labour, care, maternal affect, and reproduction. She is also a freelance writer with bylines in the *Toronto Star, Ottawa Citizen*, and *Chronicle Herald*.

Acknowledgements

I am deeply grateful for the following in their heartfelt support to make this book project a reality, and making life beautiful as it unfolds:

Contributors and their collaborators in this collection for the enduring scholarship and commitment;

Staff at Emerald Press, especially Philippa Grand and Rachel Ward, for their assistance from inception to completion of the book;

Ike and our five daughters, Charmaine, Czarina, Charelle, Czyna, and Charithe, for their love and patience through the years of bothering how technology works; of course, Niro and Charly, our pet friends, for the genuine expression of happiness whenever I return home;

My family in the Philippines for understanding the time in between completing the manuscript in the summer of 2017; thank you for the generous hospitality and warmest support, especially to Mana Joy and Mano Yoyoy and family with special mention to Charisse, Mano Butch and Mana Baby, Mana Dayen, Boyen and Lorena, Jack and Chinchin, Athena and Jeffrey, Nanay Babing, Nanay and Tatay, Brandy, Boyboy, Benjie, and Gina;

Friends and colleagues in Lethbridge and elsewhere for the continued affirmation of shared memories and time of unguarded togetherness; Ate Levy, Gemma, Kristy and Chris, Ivy and Barry, Aileen and Brian, Rufa and Doming, Sonya and Rod, Emlou, Anita, Rebecca; the volunteers of ReadWorld Foundation for the inspiration to make a difference; and

Students in women and gender studies for inspiring our work to promote a socially just world.

My blessings are yours.

Glenda Tibe Bonifacio
Editor

Introduction

Glenda Tibe Bonifacio

Abstract

This chapter provides the introduction of the book and argues why gender and feminism matter in theory and praxis in the 21st century. It includes the conceptual interrogation of the meaning of gender and feminism and its practice in western and non-western contexts; global currents in feminist struggles; thematic organization of the book; and the future under 'feminist eyes'. The thread of shared struggles among diverse groups of women based on selected themes — movements, spaces and rights; inclusion, equity and policies; reproductive labour, work and economy; health, culture and violence; and sports and bodies — situates Canada as a western society with avowed egalitarian ideals favouring gender equality and social justice, but with its own issues and concerns like women in other countries facing their own challenges.

Keywords: Cross-cultural; Canada; gender; feminist struggles; global; intersectionality

We live in an increasingly connected world, where issues and events in one place often get transmitted in other areas faster than they used to. Modern communication technologies such as the Internet and its social media applications have somehow facilitated the ease of information sharing, albeit some may not be as credible as other sources. One of the most widely shared information, concerns and discourses across various platforms in the 21st century pertains to gender inequalities, particularly about women's

Global Currents in Gender and Feminisms: Canadian and International Perspectives, 1–18
Copyright © 2018 by Emerald Publishing Limited
All rights of reproduction in any form reserved
ISBN: 978-1-78714-484-2/doi:10.1108/978-1-78714-483-520171001

rights — the 'unfinished revolution' (Worden, 2012) — and transgender rights in both western and non-western societies.

In the age of cyber technology, the status of women around the world tends to claim more friction in popular discourse and inspire movements for change in different scales — local, national and international. The mistreatment of women and girls or gays and lesbians based on cultural practices and religious dogma, for example, has encouraged many individuals and groups to question social regimes, if not, defend existing social orders. Fundamentalism and traditionalist views are not exclusive domains in so-called 'developing countries' (usually in reference to the level of economic development) but also find strong adherents in highly modernized countries with the rise of ultra-right political parties and conservative groups. It is quite perceived that the status of women in economically rich countries is relatively a non-issue, and that they do not face the same struggles as women in economically poor countries. Apparently not. Hence, the interconnectedness of women and feminist struggles for equality and social justice need further scholarly attention at this juncture in human history.

This book collection presents a kind of cross-issue dialogue between Canada and other selected countries. Its approach is based on the idea of 'shared but different' notions of gender and feminism, and shows the seeming interconnections of women's lives and realities. Canada is positioned as a western society with egalitarian ideals favouring gender equality and social justice frameworks, but has its own issues and concerns that connect with women in other regions in the world. The centrality of gender and need for feminist praxis remain significant in our societies today, wherever we are located.

There is no special reason why Canada is selected as the western compass to relate gender and feminism in other countries, except my origin as a Filipino now living in Canada fuses multiple positionalities and subjectivities that seemingly questions privilege and marginality as simultaneous shared realities of women around the world. One may live in the West yet experience the same intersecting discrimination based on gender, class, ethnicity and other markers of difference like those living in Asia, for example. What is special about living in the West? What do we give up by leaving our own countries? In-between transnational spaces, of here and there, are the subtle and direct connections with struggles of women and girls or marginalized groups around the world. After all, following Virginia Wolf (2012 [1938]), 'as a woman, I have no country'.

But perhaps there is something special in Canada in 2017 as it emerges as the leader of multilateralism (Campion-Smith, 2017) with the shift in international relations after the US elections. The renewed liberal policy focus affecting women's lives in Canada and elsewhere by the Trudeau government, especially its support to development programmes empowering women and girls through education and reproductive health, has plausibly made its mark as the most gender-fair country in North America. The United States under Trump's Republican administration, on the other hand, reversed many progressive works of the previous Obama's Democratic administration (Lipton & Lee, 2017; Trotta, 2017). In June 2017, Canada announced the first Feminist International Assistance Policy making it the leader in promoting gender equality in advancing sustainable development goals (Government of Canada, 2017).

This new official feminist stance in Canada, arguably, justifies the significance of situated knowledge (Haraway, 1988; Harding, 1991) of this book coming from Canada on gender and feminism and in other countries. Original works from Canada and case countries are spread throughout the selected themes on movements, spaces and rights; inclusion, equity and policies; reproductive labour, work and economy; health, culture and violence; and sports and bodies. These themes are broad enough to cover various dimensions on the intersections of gender and feminism, but do not discount the importance of other themes like the environment not included in this set. I can only do so much within the limits of available scholarship at the time of working on this book collection.

As a way of providing context for this book, the following sections comprise this chapter: conceptual interrogation of the meaning of gender and feminism and its practice in western and non-western contexts; global currents in feminist struggles; thematic cases and structure; and the future under 'feminist eyes' (cf. Mohanty, 1984). I purposely designed the book as a representation of ongoing concerns and discourses of gender and feminism between Canada and other countries, allowing each chapters to explore these two concepts, and in the process connect them all to the notion of intersectionality, or the idea that varied identities and factors contribute to the production of social realities (Crenshaw, 2012; Hill Collins & Bilge, 2016). An intersectional perspective of and between concepts is, arguably, a better way to look at the complexities of life and our world.

As a threshold concept in women and gender studies, intersectionality, according to Launius and Hassel, is:

> a theoretical framework that posits that multiple social categories (e.g., race, ethnicity, gender, sexual orientation, socioeconomic status) intersect at the *micro* level of individual experience to reflect multiple interlocking systems of privilege and oppression at the *macro*, socio-structural level (e.g., racism, sexism, heterosexism, compulsory heterosexuality, *heteronormativity*, ableism). (2015, pp. 114–115)

Experience is unique and particular to certain situations and realities, and this is a complex layering of factors that a critical lens like intersectionality provide us more sense of understanding *situated knowledge* (Haraway, 1988; Harding, 1991), a feminist epistemological consideration that 'every insight about the world carries traces of the time, place and subject that produced it' (Brenna, 2005, p. 30). In a way, it is an alternative philosophical posturing of the significance of marginal voices in the production of knowledge. When we consider all voices and vantage points in the realities of individuals, groups and even nations in our midst, and the bases in which their realities are explained give us an interconnected dimension of human existence.

I bring further dimension of intersectionality not only from the micro to macro levels among individuals and groups but also among nations or countries. Canada is a country located in North America with a diverse population and a globalized economy. The situated knowledge of indigenous women, immigrant women, women with disability, for example, in Canada maybe similar or different from those in other places. These particularly situated groups in many countries may share similar structural forms of violence that produce gendered inequalities, but are experienced differently. As well, some countries may have unique impact to other countries based on histories of colonialism and trajectories of economic globalization nowadays that contribute to the creation of situated knowledge of diverse groups. This book, however, does not look for the impact of Canadian state policies to other countries, but endeavours to situate the different realities of gendered lives in Canada and those in selected case countries, and claim that gender and feminism still matter.

Constructs: Gender and Feminism

Gender and feminism are perhaps two of the most defining concepts in human interactions since its inception, challenging social norms and transforming institutions and relationships. It is generally accepted that gender is a social construction (Lorber & Farrell, 1991; Ore, 2014), and how it is constructed differently (Zinn & Dill, 1996) in societies is grounded in particular histories and cultures. Gender as the organizing principle (Belkhir & Charlemaine, 2007) in society attached roles, values, attributes and functions of hierarchies or domination primarily based on sexual difference between men and women. As a consequence, women and men are positioned differently with corresponding differential access to power, resources and privileges in organizations and institutions (Akhter, 2014; Hultin & Szulkin, 2003), producing inequalities in social relations and practices.

In regular summer visits to the Philippines in the last seven years mainly for research and training, gender is a tool for mainstreaming policies, practices and activities. There is a GAD (Gender and Development) focal person in almost all offices that attended my lectures and workshops. Philippines is the only Asian country that consistently belongs to the top 10 countries in the Global Gender Gap Index measured in four areas — education, health and survival, economic participation, political empowerment — by the World Economic Forum (WEF). In 2016, Philippines scored 0.786 or ranked 7th out of 144 countries while Canada ranked 35th with 0.729; score of 1 means gender equality and 0 for inequality (WEF, 2016). But there is more to the numbers game. A high rank does not mean gender-equal relations in both policy and practice. For instance, the Philippines is the only country outside of the Vatican that does not grant divorce (Hundley & Santos, 2015). The family gets constitutional protection (Lazo, 2006), civil laws prescribe heterosexual marriage and its sanctified origins become a dictum of marital life (Serrano Cornelio, 2016). Substantive gender equality and enforcement of gender-sensitive policies have yet to be fully realized amidst high economic disparities and socio-political grip of the Catholic Church. The complexities of understanding gender relations and gender equality in different cultural contexts remind us that global measurements are not actual representations of realities.

In the 21st century, gender is not simply about women and men and its deriving identities as gays, lesbians and homosexuals; it has expanded in scope to include transgenders and the intersexed in mainstream discourses (Stein, 2011; Wahlert & Fiester, 2012). According to Rubin (2012), the 'category of intersex was integral to the historical emergence of the category *gender* as distinct from *sex* in the mid-twentieth-century' (pp. 883–884). At this time in our history, the knowledge base and full recognition of them as equals in all aspects of human endeavour remain contested even in most advanced liberal-democratic states. It is fair to assume that our social mindsets have been conditioned, for example, by religion and antiquated interpretations of laws that ingrained binaries: man and woman.

Gender is relational (Baron & Kotthoff, 2001; Bleichmar, 2008; Connell, 2012), and if women become much the focus of this book, it is based on their marginal position relative to men. Having gender as a focus does not require a comparative view of men from their position of privilege. Rather, the perspectives of women and non-conforming gender identified individuals become a critique of patriarchal norms and values that benefited men for ages. The relationships between men and women, notions of masculinity and femininity, and assignment of roles based on sexual difference are some indices of the relationality of gender. Considering the gamut of power and privilege of men in society in general, it is sufficient that we continue to cultivate scholarship coming from the disadvantaged position — then we can see much of the complex web of systems and practices defining the world we live in.

Feminism is a concept that invites varied interpretations and frameworks that to this day there is no universally accepted definition (Thompson, 2001). Rather, we now call it *feminisms* (Bromley, 2012; Humm, 1992). At its core, feminism is about the removal of oppressive social structures and practices that deny the full potential of women, transgender persons and other marginalized groups in society. Feminism is both a theory and praxis that allows for particularistic explanations of gender inequalities and the approach to change them. Because women's concerns are diverse, for example, so does feminism. For the equal participation in the public spheres of work, education, and politics, there is *liberal feminism* with the 'presumption of sameness between men and women' (Beasley, 1999, p. 52); for the fundamental change in social relations where patriarchy is the root of gender inequalities, there is *radical feminism* (Rhodes, 2005); for the class exploitation of women as workers under capitalism, there is *Marxist feminism* (Weeks, 2011); for the oppression of women of colour, there is *multiracial feminism* which views 'race as a basic social division, a structure of power, a focus of political struggle' (Zinn & Dill, 1996, p. 71); for the colonial vestiges of domination and representation, there is *postcolonial feminism* (Lewis & Mills, 2003). And, many more labels to theorize about women's oppression and how to achieve gender justice or social change (Bromley, 2012; Gangoli, 2007; Humm, 1992; Mandell & Johnson, 2017; Zack, 2005).

But gender and feminism appear to have its own silos and are not seen as constitutive of one another. Discussion on gender is great; discussion on feminism is great(er?), too. Why these two concepts are then not acted upon together, even those that embrace GAD as state policy like the Philippines? When gender is said to be mainstreamed, does it mean that feminism is recognized as a theory of action to make those gender-equal claims possible? To gain understanding of gender is to bring insight into gender inequalities and finding ways to change them. Ambiguities and contestations seem to be the norm, and that even critical scholars on gender in different countries will shun the use of *feminism* as a western concept (Roces & Edwards, 2010) riddled with hegemonic assumptions about women in society, and a western export of colonialism.

Word appropriation based on specific contexts is logical. Words such as 'humanism' (Haney, 2014; Johnson, 1994) or 'womanism' (Floyd-Thomas, 2006) may rid feminism of its baggage and the conundrum of its use by different groups of women. These words may mean the same, and one could be used to reflect on the other without inferring negative representations. If understanding gender and the inequalities in society is fundamentally a product of social constructions of natural sexual difference, then it follows that a feminist process is likely to affect needed change. Why is this not so? The general state of affairs is the study of gender and its role and impact in systems of social relationships, progress and development, to which gender-sensitive laws and policies are formulated. Feminism is silenced; it finds its use sidelined by other selectively unpolitical terminologies of the day. Gender appears to be a front matter; feminism a subversive idea. While most countries under the purview of the United Nations lean towards a positive regard of gender mainstreaming, feminisms still must gain a wider ground.

Global Currents in Feminist Struggles

Gender inequality often refers to women 'disadvantaged relative to similarly situated men' and occurs in 'different forms, depending on the economic structure and social organization of a particular society' (Lorber, 2010, p. 4). Gender inequalities and resulting oppression of marginalized groups or communities around the world are causes of action for change. I prefer to use the phrase *feminist struggles* to underscore the critical process of raising consciousness, strategizing actions, solidarity, and building a movement for change towards social justice. In the 21st century, the patterns of feminist struggles are more inclusive of other issues, what I call integrative models of action — economic, political, environmental, etc. — that may start at the centre of women's oppression. In other words, feminist struggles deal with interlocking gender issues that finding a resolution for change require concerted intersectional actions. This find truism in *Transforming our World: 2030 Agenda for Sustainable Development*, the United Nations new global development agenda adopted in 2015 which advocates gender equality as the key to all indicators of human progress (UNESCO, 2016). In this section, five areas of global currents in feminist struggles are highlighted: health and well-being, universal education, economic participation, political empowerment and environmental protection.

Health and well-being are central to feminist struggles around the world. The major thrust is access to information and free or affordable services, particularly related to sexual and reproductive health. 'Women's rights are human rights' (Peters & Wolper, 1995), and this universal phrase includes the right to safe and legal abortion that remain contentious. Women and girls face higher levels of health risks because of discrimination (WHO, 2011), poverty and illiteracy. Control of female bodies in many parts of the world come under state regulation, with punitive outcomes for abortion. Unequal access to basic health services because of class, sexuality and origin is one of the factors that contributes to higher mortality rates. Since the 1960s feminist health activists have raised concerns over the harmful effects of contraceptive drugs, reproductive control, lack of transparency and impact to women of colour (Nelson, 2015; Prescott, 2017). More importantly, gender-based violence is a 'global health epidemic' (WHO, 2013). But health care funding from international development assistance to poor countries depends on the political pendulum that results in discontinuance of effective community health programmes. In many cases, transnational feminism aligns with issues outside national borders, connecting local resources for global action to improve the status of women and girls (Ferree & Tripp, 2006).

Education connects with everything in feminist struggles worldwide — health, economy, politics, etc. It is the key component that forges action, critical awareness and understanding of gender inequalities. Sadly, more girls are out of school than boys, and face far more barriers to continue higher education (UNESCO, 2016). Education for all is a dream to aspire for by governments, yet not accorded utmost national priority based on budgetary allocations (Brown, 2015). Liberal feminism targets the equal participation of women and girls in education, and this is still the focus of many organizations, both national and supranational (Arnot & Weiler, 1993). The Global Partnership for Education (GPE, 2015) identifies leading women advocates, young and mature, for girls' education around the world. When a girl child is educated, the investment transcends beyond the personal to ultimately see its benefits in the community.

Economic participation draws much debate as to what is included in women's work. Feminist struggles point to the unpaid and paid work borne by women, and these remain largely undervalued compared to men. The structuring of economies and equivalent measurements of productivity place that of women at lower scales, if not invisible (Waring, 1999). As half of the world labour force yet having only 10% of income and owning 1% of property, women's economic value is intrinsically connected with patriarchal norms and discrimination (Rutherford, 2011; Singh, 2013). Economic globalization brings unequal distribution and access to resources; the exploitation of human capital many of which borne by female bodies incites varied forms of transnational feminist activism (Hawkesworth, 2006; Rai & Waylen, 2014). The feminization of labour (Lee, 2010) also contributes to the feminization of poverty, and racialized immigrant women in Canada form part of the global picture (Wallis & Kwok, 2008).

Political empowerment of women continues to make significant inroads. The right to vote has far reaching benefits in creating gender-fair laws and policies, with differing levels of enjoyment of rights and freedoms. A considerable high voting turnout among women does not, however, indicate a 'women's vote' (Adams, 2014; Hess, 2016). Or, the election of high-profile women does not translate to progressive stance on gender issues. Formal politics and its institutions such as elections and governance remain a male-dominated sphere (Bjarnegård, 2015), whereas informal politics such as community organizing attracts more women (Lister, 2003). In the 21st century, women's voices are gaining momentum with local, national and transnational solidarity on common issues such as war, violence and changing oppressive laws and practices to be more inclusive and just to women. As it happens, political empowerment is a precondition for achieving social justice amidst all forms of gender inequalities worldwide.

The environment is perhaps the most cause of concern in the 21st century with the call that 'climate change affects everyone' (Fossvik, 2016). The Women's Environmental Network (WEN) whose stated aims are based on feminist principles hosted its first forum at the London School of Economics in 2017 (Lawrence, 2017). For a long time, however, women around the world have shown persistent action to protect the environment. Indigenous communities and local groups, many led by women like Vandana Shiva (Rogers, 2010; Shiva, 2005), are at the forefronts of resistance against environmental destruction from capitalist development: preservation not profit. Ecofeminism connects with ecology and the oppression of women in society where patriarchal domination resonates in the control of the environment (Lee, 2010). But world leaders are still not united in the global consensus proposal, for example, the *Earth Charter* drafted since the 1990s, for a sustainable environment (Wagner, 2008). Even more concerning is the trend towards securing national economic interests at the expense of the environment, as if the air we breathe can be controlled to linger in defined spaces. We see intergenerational bonds in promoting environmental justice from various groups, especially those directly facing peril because of corporate and state neglect or inaction — for example, rising tide levels, oil spills, disrupted food supply, and natural disasters. Climate change has adverse gendered impacts that foster further vulnerability to women's access to livelihood and everyone's survival.

These global currents in feminist struggles demonstrate that *feminism is for everybody* (hooks, 2000), and that working for a better world to live in today and in the future mandates that, according to Chimamanda Ngozi Adichie (2015), 'we should all be feminists'.

Thematic Cases and Structure

This book collection presents 19 diverse original works from interdisciplinary scholars on the selected themes of movement, spaces and rights (Part One); inclusion, equity and policies (Part Two); reproductive labour, work and economy (Part Three); health, culture and violence (Part Four); and sports and bodies (Part Five). These contributions use an intersectional lens to reflect on the state of affairs in gender studies and feminism in Canada and in other parts of the world. A global synthesis is presented for each of the five themes, providing observations to general trends and prospects for change.

Movements, spaces and rights outline the negotiations for equality in contested spaces — from the institutional to the local and global relations. Fusing theory and activism, this theme captures the creative ways of resisting dominance and forging ways to make a difference individually and collectively. Inclusion, equity and policies present the intersections between structures and lived realities. Gendered inequalities are reproduced by policies and legislation, and changing these frameworks could foster better gender-equal relations. Reproductive labour, work and economy demonstrate women's paid and unpaid labour and how their work is largely unrecognized, compensated when unemployed and protected by endemic sexism. Economic globalization and neoliberal affronts on social welfare pose further challenges to a diverse and gendered labour force. Health, culture and violence provide intersecting dimensions of gendered lives, and that the meanings attached to choices are intricately connected to power and access to resources. Sports and bodies reflect on the significance of bodies in representations of masculinity and femininity, and how identities are constructed and experienced relative to them.

In *Part I*, three chapters demonstrate the diverse engagements for empowerment, creative activism, local–global intersections, and theorizing about marginality in institutional religion as sample cases under the theme of movements, spaces and right. *Chapter 1* by Sonja Boon and Beth Pentney reflect on yarn-bombing as craftivism to reveal feminist spaces of learning and doing that give emphasis on collaboration, non-violence and critical self-reflection among undergraduate students working with a community project in Canada. Knitting is not only a form of craft but could also be an 'overtly political activity' depending on its intentions. Following Baumgardner and Richards (2000), the authors weave a discourse that knitting is in itself a form of resistance. *Chapter 2* by Marlise Matos and Solange Simões looks at the emergence of intersectional activist feminism in Brazil since the 1970s. The evolution and transformation of gender and feminism in this part of Latin America resulted in a unique application of the so-called feminist 'wave' developments to counter social and political currents in different decades: fighting the military regime in the 1970s, transition to democracy in the 1980s, democratization in the 1990s, and the ongoing process of institutionalization and policymaking. *Chapter 3* by Christine Gervais and Amanda Watson examines the experiences of the women religious in Canada that includes their unique accounts of marginalization within a renewed patriarchal commitment to gendered hierarchies in the Roman Catholic Church. Their discussion of the seeming regression of gender equality of a global religious institution in the 21st century provides implications for local women. Using critical feminism that seeks to 'decentre and decolonize existing hierarchies of power', this chapter situates the experiences of the women religious at the intersection of colonialism, patriarchy and capitalism.

In *Part Two*, four chapters deal with inclusion, equity and policies in international contexts. *Chapter 4* by Jill Allison examines the intersections of birthright, citizenship and gender in Nepal, and who are included or excluded in its construction of cultural and national identity based on caste, religion and ethnicity. While the country seeks political change in drafting a constitution it is embroiled in a complicated discourse shaped by particulars in history that make certain women's reproductive labour part of its national construct and exclude others. Feminists challenge the private−public dichotomy as women are 'co-opted as part of state projects' that are simultaneously viewed as 'asset and threat' in the fluidity of regional borders or social boundaries. *Chapter 5* by Ebba Olofsson focuses on gender inequality in Swedish legislation of Sámi reindeer herding amidst changing conditions, one of which is the employment of Sámi women that contributes to the continuation and transformation of subsistence practices. Also using the public−private split and the feminist interventions on understanding women's role in indigenous communities, this chapter examines the changes between gender and kinship structures under colonization and modernity together with women's Sámi identity. *Chapter 6* by Aylin Akpınar outlines the importance of woman-friendly policies in Turkey especially for low-income Turkish divorcees. Seeking a divorce is an escape from abusive marriages, but their new status as divorcees make them more vulnerable in a society that constructs it as 'shame' and where women form part of the family, not as individuals, in Turkish law. This is further exacerbated by an Islamic patriarchal imagery of women as 'guardians of morality'; divorcees are socially unacceptable with less access to resources and protection. Akpınar argues that the woman-friendly policies are needed to give these groups of women the capabilities to live in dignity. *Chapter 7* by Panteá Farvid advocates for primary prevention strategies in education and media literacy to address gender inequality in New Zealand. She posits the view that for feminist policies to gain hold, the sexist gender system and problematic versions of dominant masculinity should be the focus of policy interventions especially in introducing gender equality education throughout the school years.

In *Part Three*, five chapters revolve around the theme of reproductive labour, work and the economy. *Chapter 8* by Lisa Pasolli explores child care and feminism in Canada, starting from the 1980s to the present. She outlines the changes in child care advocacy with the disappearance of women in neoliberal discourse, and makes the case for intersectional feminism to allow women more choices, opportunities and rights. *Chapter 9* by Catherine Bryan draws from a multi-sited research to reveal the intersections of reproductive labour with the service economy involving Filipino migrant workers in Manitoba, Canada. She discusses feminist political economy and social reproduction under globalization with critical insights into labour processes and migration trajectories. *Chapter 10* by Ada L. Sinacore and Barbara A. Morningstar analyses sexual harassment in the Canadian workplace through a feminist social constructionist framework. It includes the effect of systemic variables that silence abuse among female workers and leave perpetrators often unsanctioned. A review of policies related to sexual harassment as well as the analysis of organizational responses on reported cases suggest that the workplace environment perpetuates sexism. *Chapter 11* by Asanda Benya demonstrates the continued representation of masculinity of mining work in South Africa resulting in practices that hinder women's inclusion despite legislative changes in the 1990s. Gender still matters as hegemonic masculinity becomes normalized in mine culture and women's fate are sealed with less key stakeholder positions, design of protective equipment and violence underground. *Chapter 12* by Michelle Walks examines the link between femininity and pregnancy among trans and genderqueer individuals in British Columbia, Canada. Walks approaches this chapter using Butler's *performativity* and Halberstam's *female masculinity* and *queer art* as failure among masculine-identified persons experiencing pregnancy.

In *Part Four*, four chapters reflect on the theme of health, culture and violence. *Chapter 13* by Lauren Wallace looks at the reasons why Kassena women in Ghana do not use contraceptives. Their concerns of contraceptive side effects are grounded in practicality that impact family planning. Feminist perspectives on reproduction situate fertility in broader context, but public health practice still 'adopt a narrow lens'. *Chapter 14* by Miki Suzuki Him problematizes fertility decline without women's empowerment in Turkey. It closely reveals the role of men in having smaller families as wage-earners that still indicate men's control over women's bodies. This chapter argues that promoting family planning without women's reproductive rights results in patriarchal control and regulation. Hence, enabling women to assert and control their reproductive capacity could lead to gender equity in relationships. *Chapter 15* by Premalatha Karupiah and Parthiban S. Gopal explores intimate partner violence among poor Malaysian Indian women in Penang. The intersections of gender, violence and poverty reflect embedded patriarchal values in family relationships, particularly hegemonic masculinity and emphasized femininity. *Chapter 16* by Sigal Oppenhaim-Shachar presents a unique study of becoming a 'real man' through a pick-up company and feminism in Israel. It presents the hegemonic masculinity and aggressive seduction techniques employed in course workshops to enhance male dominance in intimate relationships. However, when a modified version is introduced to explore other models of masculinity consistent with feminist perspectives, it failed to attract participants.

It concludes with a positive tone that this modified version facilitated a new 'recognition and sense of worthiness' among male participants.

In *Part Five*, three chapters present the intersections of gender and feminism in sports and construction of female bodies. *Chapter 17* by Carly Adams and Jason Laurendeau provides a feminist poststructuralist discussion on the gains of women in Canadian sports yet continues to be invisible. Using different historical moments with women's narratives, it considers Gordon's 'writing a history of the present' to recognize the 'ghostly (dis)appearances' of women in selected sports. *Chapter 18* by Ornit Ramati Dvir and Orly Benjamin deals with physical education (PE) and teachers' discourse about girl bodies. It exposes the negotiations of PE teachers in the positive or negative views about body shapes and forms of body disciplines among girl students in Israel. *Chapter 19* by Jocelyn Thorpe is a personal account of the meaning of basketball throughout her life as inspired by the writings of Audre Lorde. Basketball becomes a metaphor of the game of life, of the changes we go through to live the process and its effects. It reflects the importance of personal narrative in feminist theory building, especially when the theory itself is about 'creating a different kind of world'.

These thematic cases provide certain depth into the discourse of gender and feminism, with many chapters having overlapping themes that reveal multiple dimensions of issues and concerns affecting gender inequalities and change towards social justice. What these indicate, however, is that gender and feminism are inherently intersectional (La Barbera, 2012; Ngan-ling Chow, Segal, & Tan, 2011; Orr, Braithwaite, & Lichtenstein, 2012). A comprehensive understanding of social inequalities requires gender to be seen in relation with other factors, identities and other aspects creating such realities in given contexts. In postmodern scholarship, feminist claims to truth are subject for consideration and validity.

Future under Feminist Eyes

Currents suggest flows and actions towards a certain direction. In different parts of the world, these currents in gender and feminism are visible and oftentimes lack media and scholarly attention. This book offers a timely resource about gender and feminism in western and non-western contexts. It seeks continuity of understanding the intersectionality of gender and feminist struggles for empowerment. While the backlash continues, this book situates the ways in which feminism is still relevant today and is a necessary engagement for everybody.

Mohanty (1984) examines the hegemonic representation of 'Third world women under western eyes' that denies solidarity among women based on their differences. Following on this approach with a shift, I use 'feminist eyes' to advance a vision of action of the future for all groups of women in whatever language of discourse and however culture-specific this maybe. Individually or collectively, our embodied gendered lives connect us to particular courses of feminist action and direct us to find best options to change or avert oppressive situations. There is no need to push for one voice, one model and one dream for all women; rather, we give recognition to the many ways in which the particularly situated knowledge of gender issues meet feminist action. In doing so, we create simultaneous currents of feminist activism around the world — whether we like it or not.

References

Adams, J. (2014). *Women and the vote: A world history.* New York, NY: Oxford University Press.

Adichie, C. (2015). *We should all be feminists.* New York, NY: Anchor Books.

Akhter, R. (2014). Women's status and fertility differential in the world-system: A cross-national analysis. *Perspectives on Global Development & Technology, 13*(1−2), 246−260.

Arnot, M., & Weiler, K. (1993). *Feminism and social justice in education: International perspectives.* London: The Falmer Press.

Baron, B., & Kotthoff, H. (Eds.). (2001). *Gender in interaction: Perspectives on femininity and masculinity in ethnography and discourse.* Amsterdam: John Benjamins Publishing.

Baumgardner, J., & Richards, A. (2000). *Manifesta: Young women, feminism and the future.* New York, NY: Farrar, Straus and Giroux.

Beasley, C. (1999). *What is feminism?* London: Sage.

Belkhir, J. A., & Charlemaine, C. (2007). Introduction: Race, gender & class as organizing principle. *Race, Gender & Class, 14*(1−2), 153−156.

Bjarnegård, E. (2015). *Gender, informal institutions and political recruitment: Explaining male dominance in parliamentary representation.* London: Palgrave Macmillan.

Bleichmar, E. D. (2008). Relational gender: Compensation of the imbalanced self. *Studies in Gender and Sexuality, 9*(3), 258−273.

Brenna, B. (2005). From science to new knowledge practices. In E. Engelstad & S. Gerrard (Eds.), *Challenging situatedness: Gender, culture and the production of knowledge* (pp. 27−42). Delft: Eburon Academic Publishers.

Bromley, V. (2012). *Feminisms matter: Debates, theories, activism.* Toronto: University of Toronto Press.

Brown, G. (2015). How can we fund education for all? World Economic Forum, May 18. Retrieved from https://www.weforum.org/agenda/2015/05/how-can-we-fund-education-for-all/

Campion-Smith, B. (2017). Canada faces new world order as America reduces leadership role, says Chrystia Freeland. *The Star.com.* Retrieved from https://www.thestar.com/news/canada/2017/06/06/canada-faces-new-world-order-in-the-face-of-dramatic-change-says-chrystia-freeland.html

Connell, R. (2012). Gender, health and theory: Conceptualizing the issue in local and world perspective. *Social Science & Medicine, 74*, 1665–1683.

Crenshaw, K. (2012). *On intersectionality: The essential writings of Kimberle Crenshaw*. Jackson, TN: Perseus Distribution Services.

Ferree, M. M., & Tripp, A. M. (2006). *Global feminism: Transnational women's activism, organizing and human rights*. New York, NY: New York University Press.

Floyd-Thomas, S. M. (Ed.). (2006). *Deeper shades of purple: Womanism in religion and society*. New York, NY: New York University Press.

Fossvik, I. S. (2016). Climate change affects everyone. *Norwegian Refugee Council*, August 15. Retrieved from https://www.nrc.no/expert-deployment/2016/climate-change-affects-everyone/

Gangoli, G. (2007). *Indian feminisms: Law, patriarchies, and violence in India*. New York, NY: Routledge.

Global Partnership for Education. (2015). 15 women leading the way for girl's education. *Global Partnership for Education*, March 8. Retrieved from http://www.globalpartnership.org/blog/15-women-leading-way-girls-education

Government of Canada. (2017). *Canada launches new feminist international assistance policy*. Retrieved from https://www.canada.ca/en/global-affairs/news/2017/06/canada_launches_newfeministinternationalassistancepolicy.html

Haney, K. (2014). Feminism and humanism are equal. Mesa Legend, *University Wire*, February 5. Retrieved from https://search-proquest-com.ezproxy.uleth.ca/docview/1494510052?accountid=12063

Haraway, D. (1988). Situated knowledges: The science question in feminism and the privilege of partial perspective. *Feminist Studies, 14*, 575–599.

Harding, S. (1991). *Whose science? Whose knowledge? Thinking from women's lives*. New York, NY: Cornell University Press.

Hawkesworth, M. E. (2006). *Globalization and feminist activism*. Lanham, MD: Rowman & Littlefield.

Hess, A. (2016). The dream—and the myth—of the 'women's vote'. *The New York Times*, November 15. Retrieved from https://www.nytimes.com/2016/11/15/magazine/the-dream-and-the-myth-of-the-womens-vote.html?mcubz=0

Hill Collins, P., & Bilge, S. (2016). *Intersectionality*. Cambridge: Polity.

hooks, B. (2000). *Feminism is for everybody: Passionate politics*. Cambridge, MA: South End Press.

Hultin, M., & Szulkin, R. (2003). Mechanisms of inequality: Unequal access to organizational power and the gender wage gap. *European Sociological Review, 19*(2), 143–159.

Humm, M. (1992). *Feminisms: A reader*. New York, NY: Routledge.

Hundley, T., & Santos, A. P. (2015). The last country in the world where divorce is illegal. *FP News & Ideas*, January 19. Retrieved from http://foreignpolicy.com/2015/01/19/the-last-country-in-the-world-where-divorce-is-illegal-philippines-catholic-church/

Johnson, P. (1994). *Feminism as radical humanism*. Boulder, CO: Westview.

La Barbera, M. (2012). Intersectional-gender and the locationality of women "in transit'. In G. T. Bonifacio (Ed.), *Feminism and migration: Cross-cultural engagements* (pp. 17–32). New York, NY: Springer.

Launius, C., & Hassel, H. (2015). *Threshold concepts in women's and gender studies: Ways of seeing, thinking, and knowing*. New York, NY: Routledge.

Lawrence, A. (2017). What's feminism got to do with the environment? *Women's Environment Network*, January 28. Retrieved from https://www.wen.org.uk/blog/2017/1/whats-feminism-got-to-do-with-the-environment

Lazo, Jr. R. S. (2006). *Philippine governance and the 1987 Constitution*. Manila: Rex Bookstore.

Lee, W. L. (2010).*Contemporary feminist theory and activism: Six global issues*. Toronto: Broadview Press.

Lewis, R., & Mills, S. (2003). *Feminist postcolonial theory: A reader*. New York, NY: Routledge.

Lipton, E., & Lee, J. C. (2017). Which Obama-era rules are being reversed in the Trump era. *The New York Times*, May 18. Retrieved from https://www.nytimes.com/interactive/2017/05/01/us/politics/trump-obama-regulations-reversed.html

Lister, R. (2003). *Citizenship: Feminist perspectives*. New York, NY: New York University Press.

Lorber, J. (2010). *Gender inequality: Feminist theory and politics* (4th ed.). New York, NY: Oxford University Press.

Lorber, J., & Farrell, S. A. (Eds.). (1991). *The social construction of gender*. Newbury Park, CA: Sage.

Mandell, N., & Johnson, J. (2017*)*. *Feminist issues: Race, class, and sexuality* (6th ed.). Toronto: Pearson.

Mohanty, C. (1984). Under western eyes: Feminist scholarship and colonial discourses. *Boundary*, *2*(12–13), 333–358. doi:10.2307/302821

Nelson, J. (2015). *More than medicine: A history of the feminist women's health movement*. New York, NY: New York University Press.

Ngan-ling Chow, E., Segal, M. T., & Tan, L. (Eds.). (2011). *Analyzing gender, intersectionality, and multiple inequalities: Global, transnational and local contexts*. Bingley: Emerald Group Publishing Limited.

Ore, T. (2014). *The social construction of difference and inequality: Race, class, gender and sexuality* (6th ed.). Boston, MA: McGraw-Hill Education.

Orr, C., Braithwaite, A., & Lichtenstein, D. (2012). *Rethinking women's and gender Studies*. New York, NY: Routledge.

Peters, J., & Wolper, A. (1995). *Women's rights, human rights: International feminist perspectives*. New York, NY: Routledge.

Prescott, H. M. (2017). The pill kills: Women's health and feminist activism. *Nursing Clio*, April 27. Retrieved from https://nursingclio.org/2017/04/27/womens-health-feminist-activism-and-the-pill/

Rai, S. M., & Waylen, G. (Eds.). (2014). *New frontiers in feminist political economy*. New York, NY: Routledge.

Rhodes, J. (2005). *Radical feminism, writing and critical agency: From manifesto to modem*. Albany, NY: State University of New York Press.

Roces, M., & Edwards, L. (Eds.). (2010). *Women's movements in Asia: Feminism and transnational activism*. New York, NY: Routledge.

Rogers, S. (2010). The 20 most influential women in green. *Ecosalon*, December 7. Retrieved from http://ecosalon.com/the-19-most-influential-women-in-green/

Rubin, D. A. (2012). "An unnamed blank that craved a name": A genealogy of intersex as gender. *Sex: A Thematic Issue, 37*(4), 883–908.

Rutherford, S. (2011). *Women's work, men's cultures: Overcoming resistance and changing organizational cultures*. New York, NY: Palgrave Macmillan.

Serrano Cornelio, J. (2016). *Being Catholic in the contemporary Philippines: Young people reinterpreting religion*. New York, NY: Routledge.

Shiva, V. (2005). *Earth democracy: Justice, sustainability and peace*. London: Zed Books.

Singh, S. (2013). *Globalization and money: A global south perspective*. Lanham, MD: Rowman & Littlefield.

Stein, E. (2011). What role for "women", "men", and transpeople/intersex people in gender equality? A commentary. *Pace Law Review, 31*(3), 821–823.

Thompson, D. (2001). *Radical feminism today*. London: Sage.

Trotta, D. (2017). Trump revokes Obama guidelines on transgender bathrooms. *Reuters.com*, February 22. Retrieved from http://www.reuters.com/article/us-usa-trump-lgbt-idUSKBN161243

UNESCO. (2016). *Global education monitoring report 2016. Gender review: Creating sustainable futures for all*. Paris: UNESCO.

Wagner, B. L. (2008). Eco-feminist action in the 21st century. *Feminism, 42*(2). Retrieved from https://canadiandimension.com/articles/view/eco-feminist-action-in-the-21st-century

Wahlert, L., & Fiester, A. (2012). Gender transports: Privileging the "natural' in gender testing debates for intersex and transgender athletes. *The American Journal of Bioethics, 12*(7), 19–21.

Wallis, M. A., & Kwok, S. (Eds.). (2008). *Daily struggles: The deepening racialization and feminization of poverty in Canada*. Toronto: Canadian Scholar's Press.

Waring, M. (1999). *Counting for nothing: What men value and what women are worth*. Toronto: University of Toronto Press.

Weeks, K. (2011). *The problem with work: Feminism, Marxism, anti-work politics, and postwork imaginaries*. Durham, NC: Duke University Press.

Wolf, V. (2012[1938]). *Three guineas*. A Broadview Encore edition. Peterborough: Broadview Press.

Worden, M. (Ed.). (2012). *The unfinished revolution: Voices from the global fight for women's rights*. Bristol: The Policy Press.

World Economic Forum (WEF). (2016). *Insight report: The global gender gap report 2016*. World Economic Forum, Geneva, Switzerland. Retrieved from http://www3.weforum.org/docs/GGGR16/WEF_Global_Gender_Gap_Report_2016.pdf

World Health Organization (WHO). (2011). 10 facts about women's health. *World Health Organization*, March. Retrieved from http://www.who.int/features/factfiles/women/en/

World Health Organization (WHO). (2013). Violence against women: A 'global health problem of epidemic proportions'. *World Health Organization*, June 20.

Retrieved   from   http://www.who.int/mediacentre/news/releases/2013/violence_
against_women_20130620/en/

Zack, N. (2005). *Inclusive feminism: A third wave theory of women's commonality.*
Lanham, MD: Rowman & Littlefield.

Zinn, M. B., & Dill, B. T. (1996). Theorizing difference from multiracial feminism.
Feminist Studies, 22(2), 321–331.

Part One

Movements, Spaces and Rights

Global Synthesis

Glenda Tibe Bonifacio

In different parts of the world, the quest for gender equal rights under the rubric of human rights remains amidst unsupportive social structures, intolerant spaces, repressive political regimes, terrorism and adverse impacts of globalization. The idea that women are equal to men in all aspects of human existence seems unfathomable in patriarchal socialization; that women deserve less rights than men has been entrenched in societies, both western and non-western, but now find new claims for recognition and social justice. Social movements for change, particularly feminist-inspired and regardless of their scale and reach, resonate in many communities among individuals and groups seeking due respect and rightful belonging as citizens and, basically, as human beings. In the 21st century going forward, women's rights as human rights set the premise to embark on continued activism in Asia, Africa, South America and the Middle East, but not to exclude North America and Europe where the rise of conservatism has continued to challenge present feminist gains. Due to differing experiences under colonization and economic globalization, women and other marginalized groups such as the LGBTQI+ around the world advocate for rights within given political systems in accordance with their own particular worldviews and not necessarily anchored in the universal principle of human rights. Non-accommodation of their claims for equality and fair treatment often leads to continued persecution, migration and displacement. But negotiating spaces and finding common grounds among and between diverse groups of women instil hope in a better tomorrow.

Chapter 1

Knitting the Feminist Self: Craftivism, Yarn Bombing and the Navigation of Feminist Spaces

Sonja Boon and Beth Pentney

Abstract

In this chapter, we reflect on the possibilities of craftivism — yarn bombing, specifically — in a fourth-year undergraduate seminar on feminist praxis. We suggest that knitting in the classroom, as an 'everyday [act] of defiance' (Baumgardner & Richards, 2000, p. 283), opens a productive space for complex and challenging conversations, in the process enabling not only different ways of listening, but also different ways of learning. Knitting, as a meditative and embodied practice, encourages and supports critical attentiveness. We also argue that craftivism can operate to make change in a way that emphasizes collaboration, non-violence and critical self-reflection. Social change, in a craftivist framework, happens in the everyday, and perhaps more radically, within the domestic spaces of the normatively feminine. Finally, our project demonstrated that knitting as feminist praxis serves a bridging function: we contend that systems of power may be challenged through knitting-as-protest, and that students may be able to practice engaged citizenship as they navigate the slippery borders between public and private, and academic and community-based feminisms.

Keywords: Craftivism; feminist praxis; social change; yarn bombing; knitting as pedagogy

Global Currents in Gender and Feminisms: Canadian and International Perspectives, 21–34
Copyright © 2018 by Emerald Publishing Limited
All rights of reproduction in any form reserved
ISBN: 978-1-78714-484-2/doi:10.1108/978-1-78714-483-520171004

Sonja: When I handed out knitting needles and yarn on the first day of class, I was met with incredulity and uncomfortable laughter. Knitting, as an embodied practice, was foreign to my students. It was also foreign to their notions of feminism, rooted as they were in understandings of women's access to the public sphere. As student Allison Smith observed: 'Throughout my childhood I always thought knitting was, like, a granny hobby, something you do while you're in a rocking chair' (Tucker, 2014). Knitting, with its links to the domestic, the home, the private sphere (Parker, 2010), was the last thing they expected to be doing in a fourth-year seminar on feminist praxis.

What happens when knitting enters the feminist classroom? In this chapter, we reflect on the possibilities of craftivism — yarn bombing, specifically — in the university classroom. In 2013, we hatched a craftivist project. Developed specifically for an undergraduate seminar on the topic of feminist praxis, it was designed to be collaborative and immersive, a form of experiential learning that could enable students to think through the logics of feminist activism. Beth, an expert in feminist media studies and third-wave feminisms, is also an experienced knitter with research interests in craftivism (Pentney, 2008). Sonja, teaching the seminar for the first time, wanted to move discussions about feminist praxis beyond the students' expected parameters of social justice activism through marching, protests and rallies.

Our conversations started via email.

Monday, 25 November 2013 at 11:11

Hi Beth,

My thought [...] would be to have you come and talk about activisms in the third wave, and if you wanted you could actually stage a knit in or a craftivist act or whatever [...]

Hi Sonja, my immediate thought would be to do a yarn bombing on campus, and then after we've done it, come back to the classroom for hot chocolate and some lively discussion about craftivism and its goals when related to feminism [...]. This would require a bit of prep (getting people to knit, or getting people to get their hands on some knitting pieces) [...].

Over the course of a few months, we worked out a basic plan. We would initiate a yarn bombing project linked to *Red Trench*, one of the most controversial artworks ever created in Newfoundland and Labrador. The students would lead the way in determining the shape and form of the yarn bombing as a form of feminist praxis. Sonja would teach the students how to knit.

Craftivism

Craftivism is a process whereby crafters use their creative skills and energies to comment on and respond to political causes and issues of social concern (Greer, 2008, 2014). Craftivist projects have included the UK-based Craftivist Collective's Jigsaw Project (Craftivist Collective, n.d.), the US-based Wombs on Washington initiative (Pentney, 2008) and Newfoundland-based artist Barb Hunt's project, 'antipersonnel', for which she knitted pink 'replicas of anti-personnel land mines' (Hunt, n.d.). Craftivism emerged out of a resurgence of interest in do-it-yourself (DIY) culture. As Luckman (2013) argues, the notion of the handmade has, in a contemporary, capitalist, mass-produced world, come to be associated with nostalgia and authenticity (pp. 254–255). But it has also taken on a political ethos. Numerous scholars have argued that the DIY phenomenon is a response to and form of resistance against industrial capitalism, capitalist politics of production and environmental concerns (Luckman, 2013; Williams, 2011).

As a mode of activism, craftivism responds to feminist revaluations of notions of 'women's work' (Luckman, 2013), and, more radically, makes public work that was originally designed solely for the domestic sphere (Bratich & Brush, 2011). 'What causes such discomfort about knitting in public? One might put it this way: Knitting in public is out of place.... Knitting in public turns the interiority of the domestic outward, exposing that which exists within enclosures, through invisibility and through unpaid labor: the production of home life. Knitting in public also inevitably makes this question of space an explicitly gendered one' (Bratich & Brush, 2011, p. 237). Indeed, contemporary knitting can challenge historical understandings that have linked craft with the domestic, the utilitarian, and the feminine; that is, with work done in the home, 'usually by women, for "love"' (Parker, 2010, p. 5).

Recent scholarship (Fields, 2014; Groeneveld, 2010; Kelly, 2014; Pentney, 2008) locates knitting in the context of third-wave feminism, a shift that Fields (2014) articulates as a move 'from rocking chair to riot grrrl' (p. 152). This is not to suggest that the feminist reclamation of knitting has been wholly unproblematic. Scholars have pointed to DIY culture's imbrication within the neoliberal consumer culture it simultaneously seeks to disrupt (Solomon, 2013; Springgay, Hatza, & O'Donald, 2011), and the inherent whiteness of DIY culture more broadly speaking. As Solomon (2013) has argued, most DIY websites and texts are 'jarringly apolitical' with neoliberal, consumerist ties (p. 14).

Given all of this, a fourth-year seminar on feminist praxis seemed like an ideal venue to explore notions of gender, craft and social change. Knitting, in particular, was appealing given its role in women's community and social justice organizing in Newfoundland and Labrador (Harling Stalker, 2006; Hunt, n.d.). During World War I, for example, women from across the island of Newfoundland, working under the auspices of the Women's Patriotic Association, knit thousands of pairs of socks to send to soldiers stationed on the front lines (Boon, 2010; Warren, 1998, 2005). The networks developed as a result of this work later proved effective in mobilizing for women's suffrage (Duley, 1993). So, too, has women's knitting served the needs of tiny outport communities in Newfoundland. The work of the Newfoundland Outport Nursing and Industrial Association (NONIA), for example, enabled outport knitters to sell their goods in the urban center of St. John's, in the process raising funds to support the salaries of much-needed nurses in outport communities (Cullum, 1995; House, 1990). Collective knitting projects, in this particular geo-political context, built community by bringing women together to share stories and ideas, facilitated political networks among women in far-flung rural communities, and supported local community initiatives.

Casting on: A Project Begins

The first day was the hardest. Students confident in academic reading, researching, and writing struggled to make sense of casting on and stitching. There was awkward laughter. Computers sat closed as students tried to tame their needles. But slowly they worked it out. By the end of the first class, there were smiles. Now it was time for the hard thinking to begin.

Yarn bombing is not, in and of itself, a feminist activity. Rather, as Kelly (2014) points out, 'the meaning of knitting is dependent on the intention of the knitter and is context-specific' (p. 134; see also Pentney, 2008). Even as many may work with knitting in apolitical ways, it can and has been taken up as an overtly political activity. As a political act, yarn bombing:

> involves using craft, particularly knitting, to alter the physical environment [...] in ways that explicitly challenge cultural norms that embrace or condone psychological violence and

other forms of coercion resulting from hegemonic socialization [...] yarn-bombing ironically suggests by its very name that nonviolent protest is a valuable model of resisting not only physical violence but also systemic (and often identity-based) violence manifested by and resulting from the unequal distribution of material and cultural resources enabling full and equal performances of citizenship. (Williams, 2011, p. 311)

Our site of action? *Red Trench*, one of Newfoundland and Labrador's most controversial works of art.

Red Trench and the Politics of Art in Newfoundland and Labrador

Artist Don Wright's *Red Trench* (1985) remains one of the most contentious pieces of public art ever commissioned in Newfoundland and Labrador (Creates, 1990; Grattan, 1994). Created in 1985, *Red Trench* was installed in the Confederation Building — the site of the provincial government — late that same year. From the outset, it was the subject of derogatory discussion from workmen finishing up renovations to the building, and to intense media scrutiny, with many observing that the work looked like women's genitalia (Grattan, 1994).

As a result of this controversy, *Red Trench* was removed just a few months after its installation and put into storage for eight years. In 1994, it was installed in the Arts Atrium at Memorial University. Again, this installation was not without controversy, as letters sent to the university's publication, *The Gazette*, demonstrate. Alumnus Brian Grant (1994) was vociferous in his critique, writing,

> It was my understanding that universities foster keen inquiring minds, not promote the flashy wares of snake-oil vendors. Your photo leaves little doubt of the origin and intent of this artistic shame; it also leaves little doubt that Memorial deems to denigrate females by displaying such trash [...]. Over the years I have seen numerous odd bits of work masquerading as art and am willing to admit that my taste may not conform to that of others. However, I seriously object to pornographic works blatantly displayed by any university, and am particularly offended that this is happening at Memorial [...]. Trash is trash: if it looks like a pig, smells like a pig and snorts like a pig — it probably is a pig. (p. 9)

Others, however, were more supportive. Faculty member Joan Scott (1994), responding to Grant's letter, linked *Red Trench* with Newfoundland and Labrador as a place, and with the politics of women's bodies:

> [*Red Trench*] is a powerful statement which is very much of this place. It speaks of clean fecund shores, especially at low tide [...]. The portrayal of genitals is not necessarily porno-graphic, and does not necessarily 'denigrate' those whose genitals are portrayed [...]. The Red Trench was hidden away, charged by people like Brian Grant with the crime of looking like a vulva [...]. While patriarchy ruled, what [...] men said and wrote was not merely descriptive, but prescrip-tive. Brian Grant assumes a friendly pose, but in 1994, he is saying that he knows, better than I do, what I think. (p. 4)

Carolyn Emerson (1994), meanwhile, reflected on Wright's artistic prac-tice and inspiration: 'the piece follows on many of the themes, materials and forms of Don's work of a 20-year period, work which depicted the environment around him — sea, sand, waves, and in the last years of his life, his relationship to nature and to death' (p. 2). Wright was powerfully motivated by the ebb and flow of water on sand, and from there, the rela-tionship between humanity and the natural world. Speaking of this project in particular, he explained: 'The image of this sculpture is based on the same trench form which has been foremost in my work over the past two years, my continuing search for my place in nature, my relationship to the forces of sun, sea and land ...' (as cited in Grattan, 1994, n.p.).

Over the years, *Red Trench* had become part of the 'furniture' of the Arts Atrium. Very few students really noticed it. Very few knew its history. It had become dusty, and for a few years, there was a paper airplane sitting on top of it, and an old t-shirt dangling down the side. And yet there was popular lore surrounding it, the lore shared in whispers and giggles by stu-dents across the university: 'Did you know that there's a giant vagina some-where on campus?'

The controversy surrounding the work — and particularly its gendered nature — together with the artist's stated intentions, and the work's posi-tioning within the space of the university, made it an ideal site for contem-porary feminist commentary. How could we, as a class, respond to *Red Trench* in a way that was attentive to the politics of gender, the university and this place? Beth suggested a crotch cozy, something that could respond to the gendered sexualization of this work while also commenting on the contemporary sexualization of women's bodies. One student, playing on the notions of exposure and celebration, suggested a pair of theater curtains to metaphorically symbolize the staging of a 'pornographic' work of art that had been hidden away. Then, another student suggested a bikini, and a spark was lit.

A yarn-bombed bikini bottom can symbolize many things. A bikini is an item of clothing linked with beach, sun, and nature. Designed expressly to expose rather than to hide the body, the bikini is associated with the sexual liberation movement of the 1960s. It also evokes links with *Bikini Kill*, the feminist punk band, and in this way, gestures towards third-wave and Riot Grrrl feminisms and the DIY culture in which these forms of resistance have thrived (Dunn & Farnsworth, 2012). But for this particular group of students, the majority of whom called the Atlantic coastline home, a yarn-bombed bikini bottom symbolized something more: it was a patch-worked piece of yarn-ware designed to cover and comment on otherwise 'pornographic' body parts while also gesturing towards the wild, fertile oceans and beaches of this province and the continuing cycle of life and death that inspired Wright's sculpture. Further, in our response, the bikini bottom was not just something that served to expose, but also something that served to hide; that is, to make what some commentators labelled a pornographic sculpture more proper. Finally, by juxtaposing our collaborative, collectively produced, 'domestic', hand-knitted work with a formally commissioned, professionally created sculpture, we could actively challenge the gendered art/craft divide (Parker, 2010, p. 5).

The student response to the controversy surrounding *Red Trench* took up a number of questions central to feminist conversations about bodies, embodiment, gender, nature and the public sphere: What spaces can bodies inhabit? What forms can nature take? Which body parts are given visibility and voice? Which parts do we silence? And why?

Students brought their knitting to class every week. Knitting accompanied their reading of articles about sexual violence, war, and international surrogacy, and femicide (Denov & Gervais, 2007; Koomen, 2013; Pande, 2010). Later in the term, they knitted to the Feminist Porn Book *(Taormino, Parreñas Shimizu, Penley, & Miller-Young., 2013),* Fat! So? *(Wann, 1998), and writings on 'zines and 'zine culture (Licona, 2005; Piepmeier, 2009; Zobl, 2009). While some knitted throughout class discussions, others knitted sporadically. They knitted between classes. They knitted with friends. And as the weeks progressed, their knitting projects grew longer. One student ended up with a rainbow-coloured scarf. Another, who inadvertently added stitches with every row, ended up with a misshapen triangle.*

Taking the lead, students invited others to participate. The students were clear: they did not need experts or even experienced knitters, they just wanted enthusiasm. Over the next weeks, knitted squares started to appear.

One student's sister gifted the class with a bag of knitted rectangles. Another student's mother experimented and sent along two crocheted vulvas and a nipple cap. We also received a bag of squares crafted by a woman a student met at her sister's church. Beth, working from Nova Scotia, sent squares by mail:

I knit thirteen squares, featuring different patterns in lace, ribbing, cables, and knit/purl motifs. The symbolism of the number thirteen as it is associated with the feminine reproductive cycle resonated with me as I worked on the pieces for the project, including the age when statistically many women begin menstruating, the number of lunar cycles per year, and the number of menstrual cycles statistically most women complete in one year. I also knit the squares in white yarn, picking up on the myth of purity and female sexuality, and the stark contrast of menstrual blood on white fabric. The final square I created for the piece included a gaping knitted cable design, meant to resemble Red Trench, *with the word 'entrenched' stitched below. The demonstration of technical knitting featured in my squares, and others, contrasted with the more organic and 'messy' pieces of knitting included in the final product; this visually reflected the tension between the artist's intent and the reception and controversy surrounding* Red Trench.

The design for the bikini was simple. Sonja and the students laid out the squares to create a giant triangle. And because we had enough, we decided to make two. One side of the bikini would be in pink and purple 'girlie' colors to symbolize normative femininity; the other would be, rainbow-colored and radical. Stitching the individual pieces together was not challenging, but it was labor intensive. Students stitched with their readings. They took a few fieldtrips to figure out the best placement options. They discussed ideas and built arguments to a soundtrack of clicking needles. In the background, Sonja worked with the building management staff and faculty members to figure out where and how to hang it up. The logistics, the students learned, can be daunting. The project ballooned beyond everyone's expectations, and we scheduled extra class time for those who could make it.

Students stitched the crocheted vulvas onto the accidental triangles that marked the crotch. They stitched in the nipple cap. Sonja strengthened the whole by stitching thick fabric between the two sides. We suspended the bikini from a wooden dowel and created poster boards to explain the project purpose and process. Beth's final square — titled 'entrenched' — arrived just in time and Sonja stitched it over the center, positioning it with pink embroidery thread. The finished bikini was 1.7-m wide and 1.3-m tall. Early one morning, we met at the university and hung it in the Arts Atrium, directly facing *Red Trench* (Photo 1.1).

Photo 1.1 Collaboratively Created Yarn-Bombed Bikini Bottom, Arts Atrium, Memorial University, St. John's, Newfoundland and Labrador, Canada (March 2014). *Source*: Sonja Boon.

Measuring Success

The course syllabus asked students to think critically about the notion of success: how would they determine the success of an activist project? Could success be quantified or measured? Or should success be determined in a different way? These kinds of questions were also central to our in-class discussions. During her three-hour guest seminar, Beth asked students to reflect on a number of questions: What was political about the process? The product? The installation? What might resistance to knitting as activism be founded upon? What is craftivism's potential? Is craftivism inclusive? Can it be exclusive? How? What does knitting in public do/mean/ disrupt? Success was also important for us, as facilitators of this project. As we considered the project, we realized that success was something that emerged in the process itself. By this we mean that the journey — from learning to knit, to conceptualizing the bikini, to reading and knitting and thinking — was as important as the eventual bikini. Indeed, the notion of praxis is itself suggestive of this, as it promotes a valuing of process as integral to outcome.

Students indicated that knitting facilitated a process of listening differently, and of opening a space for complex, sometimes difficult conversations, and for processing challenging readings and issues. As student Mary Germaine, interviewed for a campus publication, observed: 'in class we are looking at things that are hard to talk about, like what happens to women in Sierra Leone. We're not socialized to deal with that sort of information. Having our hands busy helped to play out the discussion in a physical way' (cited in Harron, 2014, n.p.). In this way, knitting encouraged and supported critical attentiveness while simultaneously supporting students' affective engagements with the texts they were reading. Put another way, they experienced knitting as a meditative and embodied practice that could facilitate the working out of difficult ideas (Springgay, 2010, p. 119). In the words of Greer:

> By allowing our minds to work through what we're feeling while our hands follow a familiar and comforting rhythm, we allow our emotions to sink in and work their way throughout bodies — from the reluctance of letting our negative feelings settle and root to acceptance of the outcome and the discovery of new paths we can take to make things better [...]. Knitting creates a safe space in which to sit comfortably, whether with our uncomfortable thoughts [...] our anxieties [...] or [...] our joy. (2008, p. 42)

So, too, did knitting encourage students to think critically about inclusions and exclusions. Yarn bombing, student Juls Mack discovered, is not about expertise in craft; rather it is about the process of learning to knit, the process of collaboration and the embodied learning and thinking that emerged as a result: 'We're like riot grrrls. Originally they didn't even know how to play guitar ... We're blurring the lines between professionalism and amateurism' (cited in Harron, 2014, n.p.). Greer (2008), too, links craftivism with her discovery of the Riot Grrrl movement. Riot Grrrl, she writes, made her realize that 'it was okay to be angry and unsure and politically and social aware, and I was finally discovering that I didn't have to be perfect in order to do something. It was acceptable to not be good, because after all I was learning, right? The notion that I could do something and screw it up without apology was novel and liberating' (p. 10).

Students also learned about the challenges of working within a large, often unwieldy bureaucratic structure. It took over a month, for example, for Sonja to get a response from the Facilities Management staff regarding the placement logistics for the project. But they also learned how ideas can spiral and take on lives of their own. The class project inspired a student-developed documentary for another class (Tucker, 2014). So, too, did the project — and its link to *Red Trench* — generate formal media attention, and Sonja did an interview for a Newfoundland-based morning radio show on the CBC (Canadian Broadcasting Corporation). In this way, the project both revived and resituated wider interest in *Red Trench*, and enabled a consideration of pedagogy and feminist praxis in the space of the university.

But the benefits were also of a smaller and perhaps more everyday scale: students learned quite simply that they enjoyed knitting and several continued with personal projects in the aftermath of our yarn bombing project. 'Knitting is really fun', stated Mary Germaine, 'and weirdly addictive ... It's a strange thing that you wouldn't really expect' (Tucker, 2014).

Activism, as Orr (2012) has observed, is a term that is so broad as to have seemingly 'endless elasticity' (p. 88). Indeed, as Baumgardner and Richards (2000) have noted, it is, like feminism itself, 'one of the most confused concepts we know' (p. 282). And yet, activism is also a concept that has been central to the ethos of women's and gender studies; it is through activist work that most women's and gender studies courses, programmes, and departments have come into existence and further, through activism that many programmes have sought to identify themselves (Brown, 2008; Robbins, Luxton, Eichler, & Descarrie, 2008). The questions then become: What counts as activism? Who counts as an activist? And, further, what is the role of activism within the power-laden bureaucratic structure of the university?

The imagery of contemporary activism is that of marches and protests, of individuals coming together in groups and making noise. Women's conventions, suffrage movements, civil rights marches, and more recently, Slut Walks, all share these characteristics. But a craftivist ethos operates from a different starting point. Social change, it suggests, happens in the everyday, and perhaps more radically, within the domestic space of the normatively feminine. Furthermore, craftivism espouses a conversational rather than antagonistic approach; it is playful and often ironic, inviting viewers to engage through humor, wit, and the seeming incongruity of political ideas and craft-making. As Greer (2014) writes, craftivism is an invitation rather than a demand:

> The very essence of craftivism lies in creating something that gets people to ask questions; we invite others to join a conversation about the social and political intent of our creations. Unlike more traditional forms of activism, which can be polarizing, there is a back-and-forth in craftivism. As craftivists, we foment dialogue and thus help the world become a better place, albeit on a smaller scale than activists who organize mass demonstrations. (p. 8)

What, then, ultimately, came of this project? What could we take away? Was it just about play, was it about capitulation to neoliberal imperatives? Was it a moment of transformation, or was it just another opportunity for navel-gazing under the guise of activism? We suggest that knitting in the classroom, as an 'everyday [act] of defiance' (Baumgardner & Richards, 2000, p. 283), opened a productive space for complex and challenging conversations, in the process enabling not only different ways of listening, but also different ways of learning. We also argue that craftivism can operate to make change in a way that emphasizes collaboration, non-violence and critical self-reflection. Finally, our project demonstrated that knitting as feminist praxis serves a bridging function: we contend that systems of power may be challenged through knitting-as-protest, and that students may be able to practice engaged citizenship as they navigate the slippery borders between public and private, and academic and community-based feminisms.

Acknowledgements

Our thanks to the students in the Winter 2014 session of GNDR4005: Feminist Practices, for their enthusiasm, thoughtfulness and commitment to this project. Our thanks, too, to the other knitters — both inside and outside the university — who contributed to the bikini yarn bombing project.

References

Baumgardner, J., & Richards, A. (2000). *Manifesta: Young women, feminism and the future*. New York, NY: Farrar, Straus and Giroux.

Boon, S. (2010). 'Just the kind of girl who would want a chap to be a man': Constructions of gender in the war stories of Tryphena Duley. *Newfoundland and Labrador Studies*, 25(1), 73–90.

Bratich, J. Z., & Brush, H. M. (2011). Fabricating activism: Craft-work, popular culture, gender. *Utopian Studies*, 22(2), 233–260.

Brown, W. (2008). The impossibility of women's studies. In J. W. Scott (Ed.), *Women's studies on the edge* (pp. 17–38). Chapel Hill, NC: Duke University Press.

Craftivist Collective. (n.d.). *Past project — The Jigsaw Project*. Retrieved from https://craftivist-collective.com/blog/2015/04/past-project-the-jigsaw-project/

Creates, M. (1990). Don Wright: The artist as part of the whole. In D. Wright, P. Grattan, M. Creates, R. Mackie, & Memorial University Art Gallery (Eds.), *Don Wright 1931–1988: A retrospective* (pp. 9–54). St. John's: Memorial University Art Gallery.

Cullum, L. (1995). 'A woman's place': The work of two women's voluntary organizations in Newfoundland, 1934–1941. In C. McGrath, B. Neis, & M. Porter (Eds.). *Their lives and times: Women in Newfoundland and Labrador—A collage* (pp. 93–108). St. John's: Killick Press.

Denov, M., & Gervais, C. (2007). Negotiating (in)security: Agency, resistance, and resourcefulness among girls formerly associated with Sierra Leone's Revolutionary United Front. *Signs, 32*(4), 885−910.

Duley, M. I. (1993). *Where once our mothers stood we stand: Women's suffrage in Newfoundland, 1890−1925*. Charlottetown: Gynergy.

Dunn, K., & Farnsworth, M. A. (2012). 'We ARE the revolution': Riot Grrrl Press, Girl empowerment, and DIY self-publishing. *Women's Studies, 41*(2), 136−157.

Emerson, C. J. (1994). In defense of Red Trench artist. *The Gazette, 27*(8), 2.

Fields, C. D. (2014). Not your grandma's knitting: The role of identity processes in the transformation of cultural practices. *Social Psychology Quarterly, 77*(2), 150−165.

Grant, B. (1994). 'A connection with the energy of the sea and sun?' Hogwash! *The Gazette, 27*(6), 9.

Grattan, P. (1994). *Don Wright's Red Trench*. St. John's: Division of University Relations for the Art Gallery, Memorial University of Newfoundland.

Greer, B. (2008). *Knitting for good! A guide to creating personal, social, and political change, stitch by stitch*. Boston, MA: Trumpeter.

Greer, B. (Ed.). (2014). *Craftivism: The art of craft and activism*. Vancouver: Arsenal Pulp Press.

Groeneveld, E. (2010). 'Join the knitting revolution': Third-wave feminist magazine and the politics of domesticity. *Canadian Review of American Studies, 40*(2), 259−277.

Harling Stalker, L. L. (2006). She seeketh wool: Newfoundland women's use of knitting. In L. Cullum, C. McGrath, & M. Porter (Eds.), *Weather's edge: Women in Newfoundland and Labrador. A compendium* (pp. 209−218). St. John's: Killick Press.

Harron, J. (2014). *Gender students get Red Trench beach ready*. Today.Mun.Ca. Retrieved from http://today.mun.ca/news.php?id=8867. Accessed on March 10.

House, E. (1990). *The way out: The story of NONIA in Newfoundland, 1920−1990*. St. John's: Creative Publishers.

Hunt, B. (n.d.). *Antipersonnel*. Retrieved from http://www.barbhunt.com

Kelly, M. (2014). Knitting as a feminist project? *Women's Studies International Forum, 44*, 133−144.

Koomen, J. (2013). "Without these women, the tribunal cannot do anything": The politics of witness testimony on sexual violence at the International Criminal Tribunal for Rwanda. *Signs, 38*(2), 253−277.

Licona, A. C. (2005). (B)Orderlands' rhetorics and representations: The transformative potential of feminist third-space scholarship and zines. *NWSA Journal, 17*(2), 104−129.

Luckman, S. (2013). The aura of analogue in a digital age: Women's crafts, creative markets and home-based labour after Etsy. *Cultural Studies Review, 19*(1), 249−270.

Orr, C. M. (2012). Activism. In C. M. Orr, A. Braithwaite, & D. Lichtenstein (Eds.), *Rethinking women's and gender studies* (pp. 85−101), New York, NY: Taylor & Francis.

Pande, A. (2010). Commercial surrogacy in India: Manufacturing a perfect mother−worker. *Signs, 35*(4), 969−992.

Parker, R. (2010). *The subversive stitch: Embroidery and the making of the feminine.* London: I.B. Tauris.

Pentney, B. A. (2008). Feminism, activism, and knitting: Are the fibre arts a viable mode for feminist political action? *Thirdspace: A Journal of Feminist Theory and Culture,* 8(1). Retrieved from http://journals.sfu.ca/thirdspace/index.php/journal/article/viewArticle/pentney/210

Piepmeier, A. (2009). *Girl 'zines: Making media, doing feminism.* New York, NY: New York University Press.

Robbins, W., Luxton, M., Eichler, M., & Descarrie, F. (Eds.). (2008). *Minds of our own: Inventing feminist scholarship and Women's Studies in Canada and Québec, 1966–76.* Waterloo: Wilfrid Laurier University Press.

Scott, J. (1994). Voicing her opinion about the Red Trench at memorial. *The Gazette,* 27(7), 4.

Solomon, E. (2013). Homemade and hell raising through craft, activism, and do-it-yourself culture. *PsychNology Journal,* 11(1), 11–20.

Springgay, S. (2010). Knitting as an aesthetic of civic engagement: Reconceptualizing feminist pedagogy through touch. *Feminist Teacher,* 20(2), 111–123.

Springgay, S., Hatza, N., & O'Donald, S. (2011). 'Crafting is a luxury that many women cannot afford': Campus knitivism and an aesthetic of civic engagement. *International Journal of Qualitative Studies in Education,* 24(5), 607–613.

Taormino, T., Parreñas Shimizu, C., Penley, C., & Miller-Young, M. (Eds.). (2013). *The feminist porn book: The politics of producing pleasure.* New York, NY: Feminist Press.

Tucker, S. (2014). *Yarnbombing at Memorial University* [Video file]. Retrieved from https://www.youtube.com/watch?v=r2b9YSXcxZ0. Accessed on March 24.

Wann, M. (1998). *Fat! So? Because you don't have to apologize for your size.* Berkeley, CA: Ten Speed Press.

Warren, G. D. (1998). The Patriotic Association of the Women of Newfoundland, 1914–18. *Newfoundland Quarterly,* 33(2), 23–32.

Warren, G. D. (2005). Voluntarism and patriotism: Newfoundland women's war work during the First World War. Unpublished Master's Thesis, Memorial University, St. John's, Canada.

Williams, K. A. (2011). 'Old time mem'ry': Contemporary urban craftivism and the politics of doing-it-yourself in postindustrial America. *Utopian Studies,* 22(2), 303–320.

Zobl, E. (2009). Cultural production, transnational networking, and critical reflection in feminist zines. *Signs,* 35(1), 1–12.

Chapter 2

Emergence of Intersectional Activist Feminism in Brazil: The Interplay of Local and Global Contexts

Marlise Matos and Solange Simões

Abstract

We consider Brazilian society as a case and evidence for a noteworthy transformation — albeit not unique to Brazil — toward gender equality that has resulted from an evolving interplay of transforming gender relations and women's participation in feminist as well as in a wide range of other organizations and social movements, enabled by national as well as global contexts. We claim that the transformations of gender and feminisms in Brazil in the last four decades have been intertwined and closely linked to changes in socio-economic structures and political regimes. Gender equality processes advancing institutional, economic, social, and cultural changes have unequivocally resulted from women's active role in the social and political movements engaged in fighting the military regime in the 1970s, in the transition to democracy in the 1980s (which we call the *second wave*), and in the democratization of the country in the 1990s (the *third wave*), as well as from the ongoing processes of growing institutionalization and policymaking (the *fourth wave*). Throughout the last four decades, feminism has increasingly spread horizontally, creating "horizontal fluxes of feminism," or, in other words, a perspective that highlights the continuity of gender discrimination, but goes beyond that to equally value the principle of non-discrimination based on race, ethnicity, generation,

Global Currents in Gender and Feminisms: Canadian and International Perspectives, 35–47
Copyright © 2018 by Emerald Publishing Limited
All rights of reproduction in any form reserved
ISBN: 978-1-78714-484-2/doi:10.1108/978-1-78714-483-520171005

nationality, class or religion, among others. In fact, we argue that this is a case of increasingly "intersectional feminism."

Keywords: Intersectional feminism; horizontal fluxes of feminism; local and global women's movements

Introduction

Brazil has arguably one of the most well-organized, diverse, and effective women's movements in Latin America. In the last four decades, significant gains have been made in empowering women economically, socially, and politically. The socio-economic and political conditions of Brazilian women have undergone remarkable shifts, with significant gains — especially regarding educational attainment and labor market participation. Initiatives in other crucial areas — such as abortion rights, and political representation, however, have not resulted in significant advancements. Overall, and similarly to trends in both the Global North and Global South, despite important gains, gender inequality persists (United Nations, 2015; World Economic Forum, 2016).

Although not unique to Brazil, it is noteworthy that the progression toward gender equality has resulted from an evolving interplay of transforming gender relations and women's participation in feminist as well as in a wide range of other organizations and social movements, enabled by national as well as global contexts. It is important to highlight that the interactions between Brazilian feminism and the international context can be found early, in a crucial moment for the emergence of transnational feminism: studies about the history of the United Nations (UN) Charter[1] reveal that the Brazilian delegate, Bertha Lutz (a leader of the suffrage movement in Brazil) was a leader in the disputes to incorporate the clause that "re-affirms faith in equal rights for men and women" in the preamble to the UN Charter in 1945. Moreover, Skard (2008) shows that there were two factions regarding the inclusion of women's interests in the United Nations. Delegates from Latin America, Asia, and Europe led by Bertha Lutz fought for the incorporation of women's rights in the UN Charter, while the American, Canadian, and English delegates opposed it. We argue that the interplay between the local and global contexts has been a key enabler of the transformations of gender and feminisms in Brazil.

---

[1]See: "Women in the UN Charter" at http://www.cisd.soas.ac.uk/research/women-and-the-un-charter,7990664.

We also claim that those transformations in the last four decades have been intertwined and closely linked to changes in socio-economic structures and political regimes — ranging from a military dictatorship, that banned and repressed social movements in order to allow capitalist economic growth based on extreme levels of inequality (mainly for black women), to the growing influence and accession to the presidency of a workers' party at least initially rooted in social movements seeking to build greater equality and justice in class, race, sexual, and gender relations by promoting institution building (in the state as well as in civil society) and grass-rooted social policymaking (Alvarez, 1994; Simões, 1985; Simões & Matos, 2008).

We further claim that gender equality processes advancing institutional, economic, social, and cultural changes have unequivocally resulted from women's active role in the social and political movements engaged in fighting the military regime in the 1970s, in the transition to democracy in the 1980s (which we call the *second wave*), and in the democratization of the country in the 1990s (the *third wave*), as well as from the ongoing processes of growing institutionalization and policymaking. We conceptualize the ongoing trends as a *fourth wave*, which we see as defined by a process of "gendered democratic institutionalization" and policymaking, as well as the revitalization, diversification, intersectionalization of a feminist-rights agenda, under the influence of transnational/regional feminism and the globalization of local women's agenda. We claim that the construction of gender relations, gender identities, and intersectional activist feminisms in Brazil are ongoing processes, enabled as well as constrained by domestic and international economic, social, and political contexts.

Although cognizant of the limitations and critique of the "waves" metaphor (Nicholson, 2010), we use it to differentiate the historical, political, and economic contexts in which women's rights and gender equality are conceptualized and advanced by a wide range of actors, organizations, and movements. In our conceptualization, a "wave" does not mean a unified or linear understanding of feminism, nor does it imply particular types of gender activism. We use the "wave" metaphor in Brazil as corresponding to the broader economic, social, and political "context" enabling and constraining the progress of the construction of gender identities, relations, and the related broadening of the gender activism agenda. A "wave," as conceptualized and used in our analysis, encompasses competing views of women's rights and feminisms, disputing strategies, and the interplay of varied political actors and organizations — all enabled and constrained by structural and historical/political factors.

In this chapter, we look at the transformation of gender and feminisms in the interplay between national and global contexts in each of the last "three waves" we address. The *first wave* of the Brazilian feminist movement, similarly to other countries was centered on the right to vote, achieved in 1932, laying the foundations for the last four decades of increasingly intersectional feminism that is the focus of this chapter.

1970s–1980s: The Second Wave

It is curious and relevant to first note that the second wave of the feminist movement in Brazil was preceded by right-wing women's activism. In 1964 Brazilian elite women — the wives, mothers, sisters of the country's top military leaders and entrepreneurs — played a central role in the coordination of "public support" needed to "legitimize" the military coup overthrowing a democratically elected, populist, and reformist government. In close association and under the guidance of those elite men's organizations, the elite women managed to recruit hundreds of thousands of middle and working class women to march in the largest demonstrations the country had seen — the "Marches of the Family with God for Freedom" in support of the 1964 military coup that ousted a democratically elected reformist populist government. These women took to the streets as mothers and housewives, partially transferring to the public sphere their domestic roles. Self-identifying with the "Motherland," they treated the country (the population) as the bigger family they had to save from a supposedly communist threat embedded in the socio-economic reforms promoted by the populist government of President Goulart (Simões, 1985; Simões, Reis, Biagioni, Fialho, & Bueno, 2009).

In sharp contrast to that, in the 1970s, a decade marked by violent repression of popular and left-wing organizations, and in the 1980s, in the context of transition from military rule to democracy, a second-wave feminism emerged out of the resistance and struggle of women against authoritarianism, violence, and lack of citizenship within the military regime. Their struggle against authoritarianism in the state and society extended to the left-wing organizations those feminist activists often originated from. Similarly to second wave women's groups in the Global North, they rejected hierarchical and androcentric practices, and the invisibility and disregard for the need for gender transformations in the general political struggle and within the left-wing organizations.

The international context — the United Nations 1975 Conference on Women and UN Women's Decade — also fostered this organization of middle class women we identified as *feminists*. It is not accidental that 1975 is the year in which the pioneering self-identified feminist organizations emerged in Brazil.

It is noteworthy that in Brazil, the 1970s also gave rise to, besides the *feminist* middle class organizations, a grass-root working class *women's* movement motivated by a new *female* consciousness (concern with family survival) as working class women joined community associations, mothers' clubs, and other social movements opposing the military dictatorship and struggling for social justice (Alvarez, 1990; Simões & Matos, 2008). What was then called the "women's movement" included a wide range of women's groups, not necessarily self-identified as feminist, such as the very active groups linked to the Catholic Church's Ecclesiastic Base Communities. Neighborhood and community associations and housewives' clubs were among the spaces that launched and shaped the political participation of Brazilian women in the public sphere during the 1970s and 1980s.

In this context, the Brazilian women's movements are an example of successful alliances between self-identified *feminist middle class women's groups* with *working class and black women*. And this was not only regarding the struggle against military authoritarianism, but also the struggle for more rights for women. It is also relevant to note that while these *feminist middle class women* also had close links to opposition political parties and left-wing organizations, the *working class and black women's movement* was supported by the Catholic Church and neighborhood grass-roots organizations. Consequently, their issues ranged from a classic feminist rights agenda to demands for the improvement of living conditions for the family (Alvarez, 1990; Simões & Matos, 2008). Whether self-identifying as a feminist movement or as a women's movement, they came together in the opposition to a military dictatorship and its economic models labeled by the left as "savage capitalism," given its oppression of the working classes and extremely high levels of inequality.

Arguably, one of the most important contributions of the feminist movement in the 1980s in Brazil was that it showed the viability of developing new democratic practices (Brabo, 2006). Quite remarkable in this context of democratization and the beginning of demands of institutionalization was the creation of the Women's Rights Councils, the city level Women's Police Stations, and the specific programs related to women's health care and support for victims of sexual and domestic violence. The Women's Rights Councils, which were democratic bodies for public control and civil society participation, created space at the national, state, and city levels for women's participation in elaborating and implementing public policies, as well as in advising and supervising the government's executive actions (Teles, 1993).

There was a special interplay between the *national context* — of a strong women's movement committed to fighting the dictatorship, and social and gender inequality by promoting participatory democracy — and the *international context*. Several international factors came into play: the Brazilian feminists' participation in the UN 1975 Conference on Women; the

1975–1985 UN Women's Decade that led to the ratification of the Convention for the Elimination of All Forms of Discrimination Against Women — (CEDAW) in 1984, which, in turn, was an important tool used by the women's movements to demand the creation of the Women's Right Councils, first at state and municipal levels, and at the national level in 1985. Likewise, the participation of Brazilian women in the UN Conferences, in regional Latin American women's forums, and in the emerging transnational feminists' networks, as well as the ratification of CEDAW, were key factors shaping the progressive and broad conceptualization of women's rights included in the hallmark of the process of democratic transition — the new 1988 Federal Constitution. Among the various constitutional achievements stand out the guarantee of equal rights between men and women, and the establishment of the Brazilian state's obligation to create mechanisms to suppress violence within family relationships. As we have pointed out elsewhere (Simões & Matos, 2008), those rights reflected the movement's local and national organization, in addition to Brazilian women's vigorous participation in the transnational women's movement. According to Alvarez (1990), Brazilian women, actively organized, in what the media called the "lipstick lobby," managed to have about 80% of their proposals passed, ranging from the principle of gender equality to more specific demands such as a four-month paid maternity leave. Alvarez (1994) notes that "with respect to women's rights, Brazil's 1988 Federal Constitution may well be one of the most progressive in the world today" (p. 54).

The 1990s: The Third Wave

It was in the 1990s that several Latin American countries, including Brazil, elected democratic governments. However, on the one hand, the climate of advances for the feminist movement was heavily hit by the adoption of neoliberal policies in Brazil. On the other hand, the emergence on the international agenda of social issues and human rights associated with the various global conferences organized by the United Nations gave a new impulse and new strength to feminism.

According to Pinto (2003), the 1990s was marked by a third wave of feminism, characterized by a "diffuse feminism," focusing on the processes of institutionalization, in the discussion of the differences between women, and new ways to organize collectively. Alvarez (2000) and Vargas (2008) note that feminism in Brazil and in Latin America became more plural with the expansion of shared spaces of feminist politics; with the increased visibility and strength of other identities of feminism — black, lesbian, communitarian, and popular feminisms; organization of women, trade unionists, and rural workers, etc. — with the involvement of feminists who sought to influence and participate in electoral politics; and with the new opportunities for interaction on a range of social and political institutions. Collins and Bilge (2016) note that Brazilian black women experienced gender as closely interconnected with their racial identity and class locations and had a pioneering role in approaching intersectionality as both analytical and praxis. Alvarez (2000) states that "healthy decentralization" of feminism in the region gave rise to an "expansive playing field, polycentric and heterogeneous, encompassing a wide variety of cultural, social and political arenas" (p. 386).

This new reality coincided with the period when Brazil, influenced by the international financial institutions and supported by local elites, began to implement neoliberal policies, which decreased state forms of engagement and sought to strengthen market practices as the arena mediator of social relations. At this stage, some feminist NGOs, increasingly professionalized, advanced in the introduction of issues related to gender in national and international agendas while at the same time distancing from their function of criticizing, pressing, and transforming the state. NGOs gained thus an important role, sometimes even in the preparation and implementation of social policies, while the state experienced a reduction of their social function. According to Alvarez (2000), the NGOs seemed more "neo" than "non"-governmental organizations as they took responsibility for public services that should continue in the government's scope of action (p. 402).

The main differences regarding the relationship of Latin American feminist and women's movements to the state significantly marked the debates among feminists over the 1980s and 1990s, and ended up being polarized around two positions: those known as "institutionalized" and "autonomous." Feminist meetings, especially in the 1990s and during the process of preparation for the 1995 Beijing Conference, were deeply marked by such polarization. While the "institutionalized" feminists were those belonging to organizations that had formal channels of operation with governments and international cooperation agencies (especially non-governmental organizations, for example), those who called themselves "autonomous" (i.e., movements of rural women, blacks, lesbians, and young feminists especially) were part of collective and critical feminist organizations opposing patriarchal institutions. These organizations claimed not to receive funds from the Global North nor negotiate with international organizations, governments, and political parties (Vargas, 2008).

It was in the new millennium that the polarization around the institutionalization of feminism finally cooled down. Some of the "autonomous" group underwent fragmentation and an internal conflict process, and another part started a reflective process of deepening their demands.

Conversely, some of the "institutionalized" groups became self-critical of their performances (Alvarez et al., 2003). In addition, other feminist movements emerged guided by a strong critique of neoliberalism, such as the World March of Women[2] and young feminist movements, reenergizing the political agendas of feminists and building alliance with other social movements, rescuing street and cultural feminist action, which were creative and radical in the context of anti-globalization movements and the establishment of the World Social Forum.[3] According to Nobre and Trout (2008), the World Social Forum transformed the debate climate and political action, and brought up an opportunity for joint action by both "sides" of feminisms. These authors note that the "World Social Forum promoted the rapprochement of both trends and became a fair territory. This new space avoided the isolation of each other and extended the policy agenda" (p. 146).

2000s and on: The Fourth Wave

In 2002 Brazilians elected the Workers' Party to the presidency of the country and to a large representation in congress, inaugurating a new left-wing political and social economic regime. The new government was committed with the implementation of social policies to promote social justice in the country, notorious for being one of the nations with the highest levels of income inequality in the world. The Workers' Party ascension to power resulted from the decades of struggle for democracy and social justice carried out by a large roster of social movements, including the feminist movement. Moreover, this was Brazil's entry point in Latin American "Pink Tide."[4] And it was also in this new context that a fourth wave of feminisms emerged in Brazil (Matos, 2010; Matos & Paradis, 2014).

---

[2]The *World March of Women* is an international feminist action movement connecting grass-roots group and organizations working to eliminate the causes at the root of poverty and violence against women.

[3]According to its Charter of Principles, "The World Social Forum is an open meeting place for reflective thinking, democratic debate of ideas, formulation of proposals, free exchange of experiences and interlinking for effective action, by groups and movements of civil society that are opposed to neoliberalism." The World Social Forum holds annual meetings; the first meeting was held in Brazil in 2001.

[4]In the end of the 1990s, with the election of presidents finally aligned to the left (or to the center-left), Latin America experienced the "Pink Tide." Gradually and with regular elections in place, left-wing opposition forces were consolidated both in the party and government structures. Brazil entered the "Pink Tide" with the election in 2002 of President Lula.

This ongoing phase of the movement has focused on: (a) the institution-alization of women's and feminist demands throughout the elaboration, implementation, and effective monitoring of public policies for women; (b) the creation of new mechanisms for such policies at the national, state, and city levels; (c) the creation and institutionalization of NGOs and femi-nist networks, especially under the influence of transnational feminism and the globalization of feminism; (d) the creation of new spaces and new reper-tories of action that are correlated to the transnational/community frame-work: a renewed activist feminism online, young and autonomous feminists perspectives taking place through the most distinct social media and alternative networks (blogs, Facebook, Twitter, and also through zines, let-ters, audio, photography, video etc.); and (e) and a perspective of feminist struggles that highlights the continuity of gender discrimination, but goes beyond that to equally value the principle of non-discrimination based on race, ethnicity, generation, nationality, class or religion, among others, emphasizing intersectionality; we can call it intersectional activist feminisms (Matos, 2010, 2015).

The fourth wave emerged, among other factors, by two democratizing pressures in Latin America: (1) an endogenous/internal pressure from femi-nist movements and women who brought up their own agenda and demands; and (2) a properly exogenous/external force, the agencies and international organizations linked to the human rights of women. We emphasize here, the influences of international systems of human rights on the Brazilian state, that is, the pressure resulting from the Brazilian ratifica-tion of the various international human rights treaties, including CEDAW and its Committee's critical analysis of the country's reports and recom-mendations for improvements. (Alcântara Costa, 2011; Barsted, 2001).

One key element of this new "wave" — consistent with the Beijing Platform for Action's call for institution building and public policies to promote gender equality — is the centrality of institutionalization pro-cesses. In 2003 a Special Secretariat for Policies for Women was created, and in 2010 it was given ministry status. In July 2004, it organized the first National Conference on Policies for Women, attended by 1787 delegates responsible for drawing the First National Plan of Policies for Women. The whole process should be understood as the beginning of an important public policy of expanding participation that involved more than 120,000 women in all regions of the country. In August 2007, the Second National Conference on Policies for Women was held involving the participation of 200,000 women in city, regional, and the national stages, of whom 2800 made up the delegation responsible for the Second National Plan of Policies for Women. The Third National Conference on Policies for Women took place in 2011, with 200,000 participants nationwide and 2125 delegates at the national level. The result was the 2013−2015 National Plan of Policies for Women, with greater inclusion of gender issues on several fronts of the government. In 2011 the event counted with the participation of the newly elected first woman president of the country, Dilma Rousseff, who expressed a strong commitment to gender mainstreaming as a guiding principle of all public policies.

Another key element of the fourth wave is the fact that it is the first time that one can take seriously the radical (but still recent) existence of feminist diffusion circuits operated from a variety of horizontal currents of feminism (academic, black, lesbian, indigenous, young, rural, male, etc.), which could be called "feminist sidestreaming or horizontal flow of feminism" (Alvarez, 2009; Heilbron & Arruda, 1995). This is a new dynamic in which feminism has spread horizontally, creating the "horizontal fluxes of feminism" or, in other words, a perspective that highlights the continuity of all forms of discrimination. This process refers to the recognition of "other feminisms" that are profoundly intertwined and, sometimes, controversially tangled up in local, national, and global struggles for social, sexual, generational, communitarian, and racial justice. The women's movements and feminisms in Brazil have evolved through various political contexts and diverse activists that demanded multiple commitments and broader alliances — way beyond narrowly defined identity politics. We would like to argue that intersectional identities and corresponding multiple organizational affiliations of activists evolved into what we call intersectional feminism in which generational and racial intersections are strongly marked nowadays.

The Struggle Goes on: Final Remarks

In this chapter, we highlighted the significant gains of feminisms in Brazil. Although important public policies promoting gender equality were established after the approval of the new 1988 Constitution, and powerful women's institutional mechanisms (such as the Special Secretariat for Policies for Women) were created from 2003 onward they did not necessarily imply effective implementation, which many times have been partial and selective.

Moreover, in several crucial areas for gender equality — such as political representation and reproductive rights — Brazilian feminism has been met with insurmountable opposition and has stalled. Although Brazilian women have been very active and effective in political participation resulting in institution building and policymaking, this has not been translated into more women getting elected to political office. After electing Dilma Rousseff as the first woman president in 2010, and one committed to women's rights and gender equality, in 2014 Brazilians reelected Rousseff, but women make up only 9% of the House of Representatives and 12% of the Senate. Although the Brazilian feminist movement is arguably the strongest in Latin America, political representation is far below that of several Latin American countries — for example, Bolivia (53%), Cuba (49%), Mexico (42%), Ecuador (41.6%), Nicaragua (41.3%), Argentina (35.8%), Costa Rica (33%), El Salvador (32%) — and much below the world average (22.9%) (UN Inter-Parliamentary Union, 2016). Several factors explain this very slow growth of women's representation (Simões & Matos, 2008). Among such factors, we point out gender socialization related to Brazilian political culture at large. But equally important are some of the rules and procedures, formal and informal, of Brazilian democracy, which have contributed to keeping women away from decision-making power spheres. These factors include (a) barriers within the political parties, which tend to overlook women candidates; (b) the current Brazilian electoral system — a proportional "open list" system — and ineffective quota legislation; and (c) other sets of adverse factors women face after being elected (Matos, 2006).

Another major area in which significant progress has been halted is reproductive rights. Abortion in Brazil is illegal, except in cases of risk to a mother's life or pregnancy resulting from rape. Debates on decriminalizing abortion have intensified since 2000. During this period more than 50 legislative proposals, both favorable and unfavorable to abortion, have been presented, with a considerable increase in proposals to strengthen the penalties for practice or to suppress the number of legally allowed cases. Although the Brazilian state has been considered secular since the 1891 Constitution, the country's history is marked by a significant influence of Catholic and increasingly Evangelical religious powers on the legislative, executive, and judiciary powers. This is especially visible in court decisions concerning sexual and reproductive rights (Simões & Matos, 2008).

It is also true that in very recent times (especially in the years of 2014, 2015, and 2016) we have seen the emergence of a wave of neo-conservatism in Brazil. It has gained space in the congressional agenda that today clearly has religious traditionalists' touches and setbacks are possible and likely to happen. Despite the persistence of important areas in which gender equality in Brazil needs much improvement, feminist and women's movements, especially from the 1990s on, effectively gained a strong new political form. We can understand them not only as a specific type of "social movement," but, and above all, as a "field": the feminist and gender field where there are heterogeneous, diverse, plural, polycentric forces of organization among women who take to the streets, build specific spaces for self-reflection and critique within trade unions, student movements, universities, NGOs, parliaments, political parties, and the international organizations (Matos, 2008). These activists created networks of activity that have long moved beyond strictly national organization, building up interaction foundations in cyberspace and through transnational networks. One could well argue that in the last decades, feminism in Brazil has experienced continuous transformations, moving beyond narrowly defined identity politics, and leading to a vibrant and increasingly intersectional activism.

References

Alcântara Costa, A. C. (2011). El movimiento feminista en Brasil: Dinámicas de una intervención política. *Hojas de Warmi, 16*, 1–40.

Alvarez, S. (1990). *Engendering democracy in Brazil: Women's movements in transition politics.* Princeton, NJ: Princeton University Press.

Alvarez, S. (1994). The transformation of feminism and gender politics in democratizing Brazil. In J. S. Jaquette (Ed.), *The women's movement in Latin America* (pp. 13–63). Boulder, CO: Westview Press.

Alvarez, S. (2000). A "globalização" dos feminismos latino-americanos: Tendências dos anos 90 e desafios para o novo milênio. In S. Alvarez, E. Dagnino, & A. Escobar (Eds.), *Cultura e política nos movimentos sociais latino-americanos: Novas leituras* (pp. 383–426). Belo Horizonte: Editora UFMG.

Alvarez, S. (2009). Beyond NGO-ization? Reflections from Latin America. *Development, 52*, 175–184.

Alvarez, S., Friedaman, J., Beckman, E., Blackwell, M., Chincilla, N. S., Lebo, N., ... Tobar, M. N. (2003). Encontrando os feminismos latino-americanos e caribenhos. *Revista Estudos Feminista, 11*(2), 541–575.

Barsted, L. L. (2001). Os direitos humanos na perspectiva de gênero. *Colóquio de Direitos Humanos*, I. São Paulo, Brasil. Retrieved from http://www.dhnet.org.br/direitos/textos/a_pdf/barsted_dh_perspectiva_genero.pdf

Brabo, T. S. A. M. (2006). A Pedagogia do movimento feminista na luta contra o preconceito e pelos direitos das mulheres. *Seminário Internacional Fazendo Gênero 7*. Simpósio Temático 15 Políticas Públicas y Movimientos de Mujeres en el Cono Sur desde la Perspectiva de Género. Retrieved from www.fazendogenero7.ufsc.br/artigos/T/Tania_Brabo_15.pdf

Collins, P. H., & Bilge, S. (2016). *Intersectionality.* Malden, MA: Polity Press.

Heilbron, M. L., & Arruda, A. (1995). Legado Feminista e Ongs de Mulheres: Notas preliminares. In *Núcleo de Estudos da Mulher e Políticas Públicas. Gênero e Desenvolvimento Institucional em ONGs.* Rio de Janeiro: IBAM.

Matos, M. (2006). Mecanismos de inclusão de mulheres no poder: A 'corrida de obstáculos' e a experiência das cotas partidárias para mulheres no Brasil. *Seminário Internacional Fazendo Gênero 7*. Florianópolis.

Matos, M. (2008). Teorias de gênero ou teorias e gênero? Se e como os estudos de gênero e feministas se transformaram em um campo novo para as ciências. *Revista Estudos Feministas, 16*(2), 333–357.

Matos, M. (2010). Movimento e teoria feminista: É possível reconstruir a teoria feminista partir do Sul Global? *Revista de Sociologia e Política, 36*(18), 67–92.

Matos, M. (2015). The fourth feminist wave in Latin America. *Sociologists for Women in Society Winter Meeting*, Washington, DC, February 19–22.

Matos, M., & Paradis, C. G. (2014). Desafios à despatriarcalização do estado brasileiro. *Cadernos Pagu, 43*, 57–118.

Nicholson, L. (2010). Feminism in waves: Useful metaphor or not? *New Politics, 12* (4), 48. Retrieved from http://newpol.org/content/feminism-waves-useful-metaphor-or-not

Nobre, M., & Trout, W. (2008). Feminismo en la construcción colectiva de alternativas. *Contexto Latinoamericano, Ciudad de México, Ocean Sur, 7*, 144–151.

Pinto, C. R. J. (2003). *Uma história do feminismo no Brasil*. São Paulo: Ed. Perseu Abramo.

Simões, S., & Matos, M. (2008). Modern ideas, traditional behaviors, and the persistence of gender inequality in Brazil. *International Journal of Sociology, 38*(4), 94–110.

Simões, S., Reis, B. P. W., Biagioni, D., Fialho, F., & Bueno, N. S. (2009). The private motivations of public action: Women's associational lives and political activism in Brazil. In V. Demos & M. Segal (Eds.), *Perceiving gender locally, globally and intersectionally*. Advances in Gender Research (Vol. 13, pp. 203–239). Bingley: Emerald Group Publishing Limited.

Simões, S. D. (1985) *Deus, pátria e família: As mulheres no golpe de 1964*. Petrópolis, RJ: Vozes.

Skard, T. (2008). Getting our history right: How were the equal rights of women and men included in the Charter of the United Nations? *Forum for Development Studies, 1*, 37–60.

Teles, M. A. (1993). *Breve história do feminismo no Brasil*. São Paulo: Brasiliense.

United Nations. (2015). *Progress of the world's women report 2015–2016*. Retrieved from http://progress.unwomen.org/en/2015/pdf/UNW_progressreport.pdf

United Nations. (2016). *Inter-Parliamentary Union, IPU: Women in politics*. Retrieved from http://www.ipu.org/wmn-e/world.htm

Vargas, V. (2008). *Feminismos en América Latina: Su aporte a la política y a la democracia*. Lima: Universidad Nacional Mayor de San Marcos, Colección Transformación Global.

World Economic Forum. (2016). *The global gender gap report 2016*. Retrieved from http://www3.weforum.org/docs/GGGR16/WEF_Global_Gender_Gap_Report_2016.pdf

Chapter 3

Countering Renewed Patriarchal Commitments in the Institutional Catholic Church: Feminist Perspectives among Women Religious in Canada

Christine Gervais and Amanda Watson

Abstract

This chapter argues that feminist inquiries and activism must be pursued considering women's marginalized position within a religious institution in Canada in the 21st century. Drawing on Canadian Catholic nuns' unique accounts of their experiences with the Roman Catholic Church, this chapter brings nuance to the complicated power dynamics navigated by women religious to show how women remain excluded and exploited in various ways in their own religious institutions. We point to the institutionalized Roman Catholic Church's long-standing control over women's reproductive rights, as well as its ongoing prohibition and recent criminalization of women's ordination. We also address recent structural dynamics at play by drawing attention to a recent Vatican investigation and ongoing surveillance of women religious in North America under newly established church doctrine. We view these recent tactics as evidence of the Vatican's renewed commitment to existing gender hierarchies within the Church. Feminist intervention is especially important considering this deepening patriarchal power and how, by extension, the church is regressing rather than progressing towards gender equality, even while it shows evidence of shifting attitudes on other social issues. This

Global Currents in Gender and Feminisms: Canadian and International Perspectives, 49–63
Copyright © 2018 by Emerald Publishing Limited
All rights of reproduction in any form reserved
ISBN: 978-1-78714-484-2/doi:10.1108/978-1-78714-483-520171006

chapter also underscores the implications of a global religious institution for women in Canada.

Keywords: Catholic Church; leadership; reproductive justice; feminist
intervention; women religious

Introduction

From a feminist perspective, there is cause to be critical of the power that
nuns[1] have wielded in their roles[2] as educators, nurses and social workers,
which involved conditioning gendered subservience among generations of
women (Chittister in Bonavoglia, 2005), as well as apprehending Indigenous
children into residential schools in Canada (Finkel, 2006). While that critique is important, nuns in the patriarchal, institutional Roman Catholic
Church have also been subjected to various forms of male violence and
misogyny. They have been relegated to low-status gendered labour, have
been excluded and even criminalized from leadership, and some have been
sexually abused by male clerics (Bonavoglia, 2005; Bouclin, 2006). This
subjugated position of nuns reflects the wider marginalized [dis]location of
women in the Roman Catholic Church, and one that has intensified in the
21st century (Bonavoglia, 2005; Schneiders, 2013).

We argue that feminist inquiries and activism must resist the persistent
marginalization and oppression of women by the Roman Catholic Church
today. First, we describe the women-centred methodological approaches
employed. We then situate our critique within intersectional feminist
approaches before illustrating women's exploitation and abuse in the
Church, their experiences with reproductive injustice, and their exclusion
based on the Catholic Church's recent criminalization of women's ordination. Finally, we detail recent Vatican investigations of women religious in
North America. In doing so, this chapter calls for feminist intervention in
the context of the church's renewed commitment to roll back women's
access to power even while it shows evidence of shifting attitudes on other
social issues.

---

[1]Scholars refer to vowed women in the Catholic tradition as 'women religious'
(Smyth, 2007, p. 8). We use 'nuns', 'sisters' and 'women religious' interchangeably.
[2]Sisters recognize how their own institutional structures were hierarchical and they
have worked for decades to establish democratic governance (Gervais, 2012;
Gervais & Turenne Sjolander, 2015).

Women-Centred Methods

Our analyses are derived from data collected through qualitative interviews, questionnaires and participant observation by Christine Gervais between December 2008 and September 2013. The participants in this study[3] ranged in age from 49 to 91 and consisted of 32 current and former Catholic sisters from eight women's religious communities[4] in the province of Ontario.

Since women religious' experiences have been visibly absent from, and sometimes disparaged in, the androcentric records of the Roman Catholic Church, the consideration of their voices constitutes a valuable contribution to scholarship that seeks to illuminate their spiritual and institutional realities (Chittister, 2004; Gervais, 2012; Johnson, 2002a; Schneiders, 2004; Smyth, 2007). By enabling women religious to tell their own stories, as well as by genuinely consulting and respecting their standpoint, this study has provided women religious with a safe opportunity to relate the concerns and critiques that are significant to them (Johnson, 2002b; Schneiders, 2004).

Our approach resonates with feminist scholars who prioritize women's standpoints and material realities (Harding, 1991; Smith, 1987). In this light, the participants were involved in the realization of this study by providing input on the content and format of the interview guide, by reviewing their interview transcripts, by contributing analytical advice, as well as by reading papers prior to their presentation at conferences and as publications. Such a methodological sensibility offered the women an empowering process through which they could ensure that their own accounts were conveyed and contextualized appropriately and safely.

Critical Feminism

Critical feminists examine overlapping, complex systems of power to challenge what hooks (2013) has called imperialist white supremacist capitalist patriarchy. hooks (2013) reminds us that critical feminism seeks to decentre and decolonize existing hierarchies of power. Our intersectional feminist lens is also informed by Smith's *Native Americans and the Christian Right* (2008) where she troubles normative assumptions about

---

[3]Gervais' study explores sisters' experiences of both gender discrimination and feminist innovation.

[4]To protect the participants' identity, pseudonyms are used and the names of their religious congregations are withheld. Nevertheless, their ages are indicated after their narratives.

right-wing institutional organizations, and advocates unexpected alliances for social justice activism. Building on Smith (2008) and hooks (2000), we situate the experiences and strategies of Anglo-Ontarian Catholic women religious at the intersection of colonial power, patriarchal oppression, misogyny and capitalist configurations of parish and convent life. Some of the women in Gervais' study (2012, 2015) and in others (Barr Ebest, 2003; Winter, Lummis, & Stokes, 1994) report negotiating their feminist and social justice values within the institutional Church despite misogynist attitudes, violence, and intense surveillance, dispelling any myth of Catholic nuns as subservient, and disrupting the notion that the institutional Church is irreconcilable with social justice initiatives (Gervais & Turenne Sjolander, 2015; Gervais & Watson, 2014).

Since we are concerned with the patriarchal power of the institutional Church, our intervention focuses on how gender oppression operates on the inside. But we also recognize the simultaneous exclusion and injustice enacted by the Church on Indigenous peoples, queer and trans folks, and specific migrant and religious groups. Women's experiences with misogyny in the Church, then, exist in the context of imperialism, racism, sexism and heterosexism, where women religious are both complicit in, and subjected to systems of oppression. As Gervais (2012), Gervais and Turenne Sjolander (2015), and others (Chittister, 2004; Holtmann, 2008; Schneiders, 2004) have shown, feminist initiatives within and in the liminal spaces of the institutional Catholic Church are creative and widespread. Yet, feminist values and strategies are as vital as ever in the context of retrenched patriarchal and neocolonial disciplinary tactics by the Church, with implications for women's survival and wellbeing.

Exploitation and Abuse Suffered by Sisters within Their Own Church

Male leadership maintains the patriarchal status quo by keeping women from accessing power and by invalidating their contributions (Schneiders, 2013). In addition to being excluded from organizational and liturgical leadership, women religious had been induced to take on the low-status service work of their parishes. As sisters noted, their exclusion and exploitation have left many sisters in this study feeling undermined intellectually and spiritually, and dislocated institutionally:

> We don't seem to have a place in our church [...] I feel that we haven't received full recognition of who we are as women. (Sister Loretta, 73)

We are ignored completely; we are really [...] put down by the church, by the hierarchy. (Sister Sophie, 82)

Women's exclusion is so flagrant in the church that sisters feel acutely their status as *second class* (Sister Corinne, 74). Responding to the systematically entrenched patriarchy of the contemporary church, women religious contend that it is deteriorating:

> *I think it's getting worse now, it's gone backwards [...] men coming out of the seminary right now are so conservative it's unreal [...] it's very scary.* (Sister Penelope, 62)

> *We as sisters are not involved in the church as we used to be [...] and it disturbs me [...] it's going back to where it's the priest who is the dominant person in the parish.* (Sister Jeanette, 63)

Sister Jeanette notes with fear that priests wielding power have severe consequences for women. Male leadership has also acted out this institutionalized misogyny by sexually abusing women in the church, and then denying it through elaborate cover-ups (Bonavoglia, 2005; Bouclin, 2006). As feminist theorists of rape culture explain, rape is about power and entitlement (Filipovic, 2013; Friedman & Valenti, 2008). It is not difficult to understand, then, that the church's explicit designation of gender roles to subordinate women cultivates an environment where male sexual violence against women is supported (Filipovic, 2008). Men's violent expression of misogyny through rape is not unique to the Church, of course, but the way the Roman Catholic Church has denied and hidden men's abuse of women is telling of their intense hypocrisy (Schneiders, 2013). Sister Colette expands on the inextricably linked forms of exploitation:

> *The priests who have sexually abused [...] it's got to do with the putting down of women again [...] In some of our mother-houses, the person celebrating mass cannot be in a regular parish [because of sexual abuse] so he's with older women. So here's this person up there [on the altar] and we're down here [in the pews]. We're very gifted women who could be celebrating Eucharist, who could be doing wonderful reflections you know [louder].* (Sister Colette, 72)

For Sister Colette, women's exclusion from the altar, their experiences with rape by male priests and their not-so-subtle responsibility to contain abusive priests are part of women's relegation to the margins of power (Gervais,

2018). Carol, a former nun, raises a similar analysis when looking back on incidents of sexual abuse from her earlier days at the convent — incidents that have still not been reconciled:

> *Some of my classmates [...] were told, 'Look it, I will have sex with you and that will help you' by priests that were coming in to run retreats! [...] I mean the gurus! [...] I know of gals that have left because of it and the convent denied them! The nuns themselves, when the sister went and said, 'Father raped me' said, 'It didn't happen. You must have led it on'. [N] is a bad, bad, bad alcoholic. I mean today. I mean she can't even be cured anymore [...] But she was abused by one of the priests [...] From the time she was about 12, 13, 14 years of age; she worked at the rectory and she was abused by [a priest] [...] sad, sad, sad situation [...] I know of [another] one [...] abused by one of the great Spanish priests who'd come from Spain to teach us [...] BUT she got no support from the convent. No. None.*

Male Catholic priests have gravely exploited and abused women (Bouclin, 2006). While clerical sexual abuse of children is more widely known, men's sexual violence against adults, and adult women in particular, 'far exceeds their involvement with minors' (Bonavoglia, 2005, p. 85). In 2001, women's rights advocates called for accountability for 'sexual violence against nuns and other women by Catholic priests worldwide', and especially in mission countries.[5] Rather than assuming its responsibility for the sexual exploitation of nuns, the church deflected attention away from the sexual abuse scandal by condemning sisters for their feminist interventions (Bonavoglia, 2005; Schneiders, 2013). The church's hypocrisy is not limited to censoring nuns; it also involves the sly operation of anti-abortion campaigning alongside secret abortions for women impregnated by priests.

Reproductive Justice: Ongoing Movements against Feminist Initiatives

Whereas the encyclical *Humanae Vitae*[6] forbade all forms of contraception, and the Vatican continues to constrain women's agency regarding sexuality

---

[5]See 'A Call to Accountability' campaign at http://www.womensordination.org/archive/pages/action_pages/AccountabilityPetition.doc
[6]This encyclical was issued by Pope Paul VI in 1968 and has been vindicated by Popes John Paul II and Benedict XVI.

and reproduction (Bouclin, 2006, p. 45), women religious in Gervais' study (2012, 2015) and elsewhere (Bonavoglia, 2005; Kaylin, 2000; Schneiders, 2013) were in favour of contraception and were compassionate about abortion despite having been threatened with sanctions by male church leaders. The sisters touch on issues of women's autonomy, male control and the Church leadership's preoccupation with abortion:

> *I think the church is still taking a stand that goes against the responsibility of the woman herself [...] women who can't really, with their own doctor make a decision of whether or not an abortion is a good thing for their life, or a decision with their family [...] on certain issues ya, I feel that women have been denied.* (Sister Penelope, 62)

> *An explicit example of male clerical control over women's autonomy regarding her reproductive rights is that of a woman who was refused absolution and humiliated by her confessor because she was under doctor's orders to take the 'pill' since her health could not sustain another pregnancy.* (Sister Kelly, 80)

> *The fact that they put so much emphasis on abortion as if it's the only, only sin, the only way in which life is not respected.* (Sister Edith, 76)

One story about a 9-year-old girl in Brazil gives a striking example of the church's misogyny: the girl became pregnant with twins after being sexually abused by her stepfather. Her mother and doctors were swiftly excommunicated from the Catholic Church for having authorized and carried out an abortion (Israely, 2009). The story tells not only of the staunchness of the church's anti-abortion stance, but of the leadership's sustained support of men over women even in cases of obvious abuse. The sisters whom Gervais interviewed in this study were outraged:

> *I'm fed up with the Catholic Church [...] absolutely fed up with it! [...] They are so far away from reality [...] The church is so hard.* (Sister Marian, 80)

> *But that's [...] a good example of power and control and the boys' club [...] the step-father is scott-free and he's a criminal [...] in the eyes of the law.* (Sister Kelly, 80)

After considerable public pressure, including from women's rights advocates, the church recanted its position on the ex-communication of the 9-year-old girl's mother and doctor, which demonstrates how feminist resistance has served women in small ways. Other examples substantiate persistent hypocrisy, though, as in the case of abusive priests impregnating school girls, women and nuns, and forcing them to have abortions or sending them to other countries (to hide them) to give birth to the children they have fathered, most often through abusive relationships (Allen & Schaeffer, 2001; Bonavoglia, 2005; Bouclin, 2006).

The church's stance on abortion is doubly hypocritical in the context of its nuanced doctrine around killing 'life when it is in the hands of men' — which permits killing by the state in self-defence as a sanction (Chittister in Bonavoglia, 2005, p. 134). In contrast, when it comes to abortion, 'when life is in the hands of a woman, it can never, ever, under any circumstances, for any reason whatsoever, be contravened … ' (Chittister in Bonavoglia, 2005, p. 134). Misogyny operates through preventing women from accessing bodily autonomy while condoning acts of violence by men and male leadership as broad-scale 'self-defence'.

Prohibition and Criminalization of Women's Ordination

Progress has certainly been made towards the greater inclusion of girls and women on Catholic altars and in Catholic parishes, as servers, sacristans, pastoral associates, communion servers, readers, committee leaders and council members. However, such gains have been thwarted by what some view (e.g. Cavanagh, 2010) as the example par excellence of the intensification of patriarchal power within the church: the decree[7] released by the Vatican on July 15, 2010 that classified *the attempted sacred ordination of a woman* to the priesthood as a *grave delict* against Canon Law that could result in ex-communication from the Roman Catholic Church. The canonical criminalization and the corresponding sanction of automatic ex-communication apply to both the person who confers the ordination on a woman and she who receives it (*Ibid.*). Thus, Catholics can neither debate, nor request, nor advocate women's ordination, at least not without being punished by their Church (Cavanagh, 2010).

While women's ordination has been prohibited for centuries, controversy flared in 2010 when it was included on the same list of the 'most serious crimes' as clerical sexual abuse and heresy. Thus, through this decree, the Roman Catholic Church made clear its pervasive misogyny: 'in their view, the thought of women fulfilling their calling to the priesthood was as reprehensible as the sexual abuse of a child' (Cavanagh, 2010, p. 14). As the

---

[7]See Article 5 of Substantive Norms enforceable by the Vatican's overseer, the Congregation for the Doctrine of the Faith, available at http://www.vatican.va/resources/resources_norme_en.html

latest of countless misogynist tactics by church authorities to marginalize women, this canonical criminalization further weakens their already profoundly unequal position in the Roman Catholic Church. As such, it reverses gains made by women over the past few decades and it signals a renewed commitment to women's subordination (Cavanagh, 2010).

The long-time prohibition and recent criminalization of women's ordination to the priesthood have angered and saddened women religious who feel that people have been cheated out of the potential benefits of women's organizational and liturgical capacities because of the patriarchal-based barrier:

> *The fact that women are not [...] on an equal footing in the church; I find it a sin [...] women taking their part in liturgy [...] we have a right to be there.* (Sister Marian, 80)

> *I'm still very angry [...] with all the courses we've had [...] all the workshops we've taken [...] I feel that very much [...] my gifts are not welcomed in the Catholic Church [...] I'm a woman, I don't have the right body parts so my gifts aren't used! [...] The Catholic Church seems to be afraid of the gifts of women [...] afraid of their power, their fire, their drive, their passion!* (Sister Colette, 72)

> *I really resent the fact that so many people are being deprived, not only of the Eucharist, but of ministry, because of the limitation of [...] ordination to [...] women.* (Sister Joelle, 67)

As these comments underscore, women's exclusion from organizational and liturgical roles serves to both keep women from accessing power within the church, and exploit women's labour by relegating them to lower-status work. In the Roman Catholic Church, women's exclusion from leadership effectively maintains a gendered division of labour that feminists have long criticized (Acker, 1990; Connell, 2006; Hochschild, 1989).

Many women religious have moved beyond such constraints by organizing their own women-led spiritual celebrations within their own community spaces, which are indicative of their own feminist-informed defiance and resourcefulness (Gervais, 2012; Gervais & Turenne Sjolander, 2015). Yet, as Sisters Marian, Colette and Joelle underscore, the prohibition and criminalization[8] has not only led to the exclusion of women's leadership, but by

---

[8]Pope Francis' willingness in May 2016 to examine the role of female deacons was swiftly constrained by Vatican officials who indicated that the issue would only be studied for clarification purposes, and must not be interpreted as openness to the ordination of women as deacons or priests, which remain criminalized (Vatican Radio, 2016).

extension it has also led to the deprivation of encompassing spiritual experiences for all simply because they cannot be ministered by women (Chittister, 2004; Schneiders, 2013).

Vatican's Investigation and Surveillance of Women Religious

Further attempts by the Church hierarchy to entrench patriarchal power were manifested in an inquiry aimed at pressuring women's orders in the United States to realign with the sanctioned practices of the Church (McElwee, 2013; Murdoch, 2012; Schneiders, 2013; Uebbing, 2013). Extending in its entirety from 2008 to 2015, the controversial inquiry was two-pronged as it involved both an investigation of the Leadership Conference of Women Religious[9] and an Apostolic Visitation of religious orders — both of which were authorized by Pope Benedict XVI for the purposes of scrutinizing the allegedly feminist orientations and practices of sisters who were thought to be disobeying church dogma (Chittister, 2013a; Kristof, 2012; Murdoch, 2012; Schneiders, 2013).

Through the Congregation for the Doctrine of the Faith, the Vatican carried out a multi-year 'Doctrinal Assessment' of the Leadership Conference of Women Religious (LCWR) and determined in 2012 that it found 'a prevalence of certain radical feminist themes incompatible with the Catholic faith in some of the programmes and presentations sponsored by the LCWR' (Congregation for the Doctrine of the Faith, 2012). It further claimed that the LCWR's 'commentaries on "patriarchy" distort ... [and] even undermine [various church] doctrines' (CDF, 2012). Women religious were outraged; renowned author Sr. Joan Chittister (2013b) pointed out the irony of the church calling sisters' commitment to women 'radical feminism' and investigating them for 'heresy', while not mentioning 'male chauvinism or the very structures of patriarchy itself as any kind of concern at all'.

The Vatican subsequently ordered the LCWR collective to revise its priorities and reform its practices. In 2013, adding insult to injury, Pope Francis appointed an overseer to revise LCWR's programmes with the intention of undermining women's abilities to lead their own initiatives (McElwee, 2013; Schneiders, 2013; Uebbing, 2013). The mandate ultimately obliged the LCWR to change its statutes and to commit to being more doctrinally compliant in the content featured in its publications and in its

---

[9]The Leadership Conference of Women Religious is an association of the leaders of Catholic women religious' congregations in the United States. For more information, see https://lcwr.org/

selection of speakers, programmes and award recipients, as well as in its spiritual celebrations (LCWR, 2015a, 2015b).

Of additional concern is the Apostolic Visitation, which was a separate and larger investigation carried out by the Vatican between 2009 and 2012 to scrutinize American nuns' commitment to church doctrine. While the report (released in December 2014) was framed relatively positively, renowned sister-authors Chittister (2014), Schneiders (2014) and Schenk (2014) cautioned that one should not naively be deceived by the positive and appreciative tone of the report given that gender inequality within the church remains entrenched, and that one should recall that such an investigation should never have occurred in the first place. Furthermore, the report on the Apostolic Visitation, like the 2015 report on the LCWR, still identified multiple areas — including their promotion of religious vocations, their forms of prayer, spiritual practices and ministry, community life and financial stewardship — where women religious are expected to re-align their practices to ensure that they are 'in fidelity' with the Church's teachings and with 'Catholic teaching' (Braz de Aviz, 2014, pp. 3, 6). The Vatican's relentless monitoring of such expected re-alignments, and the anti-feminist agenda underpinning it, remain serious concerns given that 15 US orders of sisters were summoned to Rome for further investigation in 2016 (McElwee, 2016).

Such separate yet simultaneous assessments clearly reflect the Church hierarchy's persistent control of women's innovative contributions within both church and societal contexts. While Canadian women religious orders have not been subjected to the same systematic investigation and reprimand as their US counterparts, their actions have not gone unchallenged (Gervais, 2018). Many Canadian women's religious orders, and especially the ones featured in Gervais' (2012) study, have faced more specific targeting, obliging them to negotiate with individual bishops or priests acting within specific diocesan contexts, rather than with representatives of the entire Church hierarchy (Gervais & Turenne Sjolander, 2015).

Women religious in Canada have also been negatively affected by the dual investigation of US women religious and their leaders, as well as by the criminalization of women's ordination — all of which occurred simultaneously in the first decade and a half of the 21st century (Gervais, 2018). This timing is cause for serious concern on several levels, and Chittister (2013b) pointed out the fundamental irony of it all: 'it is [over] 2,000 years after Jesus himself modeled it [the inclusivity and emancipation of women]...', yet the institutional church continues to exclude and restrict women. Thus, it is in this 21st century climate, still closed to women's full participation in leadership within the institutional Roman Catholic Church, that we call on further feminist intervention to propel inclusivity. Such a call is inspired by all women religious affected by this struggle, and particularly by Chittister (2013b) who articulated the rationale so insight-fully: 'It is about bringing to public visibility and public agency the agen-das, the insights, and the wisdom of the other half of the human race'.

Conclusion

Beyond presenting major structural issues facing women religious in Canada, we have pointed to their potentially grave implications for women religious and urged feminist intervention. Acknowledging ongoing feminist initiatives by women religious as complicated movements within and on the outskirts of patriarchal and colonial systems of power, we contend that without increased feminist action in the Catholic Church, women will remain subjected to abuse and coercion by male leaders and doctrine, as well as to unequal and unjust divisions of labour.

The global Catholic Church retains tremendous power to pursue imperi-alist, racist, sexist and heterosexist agendas, diminishing women 'at home' in Canada by ensuring their access to power is systematically restricted in the ways we have shown. Bearing in mind Smith's (2008) call to explore unlikely alliances between conservative and social justice movements, this chapter serves to reinforce the need for cooperation and strategy among feminists who seek a more just position for women religious. In the struggle to advance intersectional feminist, women-centred aims, this chapter has built on our documentation of women's own initiatives and desire to high-light why feminist activism is still necessary. Considering the Vatican's renewed commitment to existing gender hierarchies and deepening patriar-chal power within the Church in the early 21st century, feminist interven-tion is especially vital.

Acknowledgements

We thank Leslie Guldimann and Shanisse Kleuskens for their research assistance, as well as the University of Ottawa's Centre for Academic Leadership for the Women's Writing Days. We extend heartfelt gratitude to the women religious featured in this chapter who generously gave their time, insights and hospitality.

References

Acker, J. (1990). Hierarchies, jobs, bodies: A theory of gendered organizations. *Gender and Society*, 4(2), 139–158.

Allen, J. L., & Schaeffer, P. (2001). Reports of abuse: AIDS exacerbates sexual exploitation of nuns. *National Catholic Reporter*, March 16. Retrieved from http://natcath.org/NCR_Online/archives2/2001a/031601/031601a.htm

Barr Ebest, S. (2003). Evolving feminisms. In S. Barr Ebest & R. Ebest (Eds.), *Reconciling Catholicism and feminism? Personal reflections on tradition and change* (pp. 263–279). Notre Dame: University of Notre Dame Press.

Bonavoglia, A. (2005). *Good Catholic girls: How women are leading the fight to change the Church.* New York, NY: Regan Books, HarperCollins.

Bouclin, M. (2006). *Seeking wholeness: Women dealing with abuse of power in the Catholic Church.* Collegeville, PA: Liturgical Press.

Braz de Aviz, J. (2014). *Final report on the Apostolic Visitation of Institutes of Women Religious in the United States of America.* Rome: Congregation for Institutes of Consecrated Life and Societies of Apostolic Life. Bulletin 0963. Retrieved from https://lcwr.org/sites/default/files/media/files/final_report_of_apostolic_visitation.pdf

Cavanagh, C. (2010). *Women priests: Answering the call.* Brockville, Canada: Butternut Publishing.

Chittister, J. (2004). *Called to question: A spiritual memoir.* Oxford: Sheed & Ward.

Chittister, J. (2013a). Tainted by radical feminism? More like 'living the gospel'. *National Catholic Reporter*, April 24. Retrieved from http://ncronline.org/node/50416/%C2%A0

Chittister, J. (2013b). We are at a crossroads for women in the church. *National Catholic Reporter*, December 11. Retrieved from http://ncronline.org/blogs/where-i-stand/we-are-crossroads-women-church

Chittister, J. (2014, December 17). The ending should have been the beginning. *Global Sisters Report.* Retrieved from http://globalsistersreport.org/column/where-i-stand/ending-should-have-been-beginning-16791

Congregation for the Doctrine of the Faith [CDF]. (2012). *Doctrinal assessment of the leadership conference of women religious*, April 18. Retrieved from http://www.vatican.va/roman_curia/congregations/cfaith/documents/rc_con_cfaith_doc_20120418_assessment-lcwr_en.html

Connell, R. (2006). Glass ceiling or gendered institution? *Public Administrative Review*, 66(6), 837–849.

Filipovic, J. (2008). Offensive feminism: The conservative gender norms that perpetuate rape culture and how feminists can fight back. In J. Friedman & J. Valenti (Eds.), *Yes means yes! Visions of female sexual empowerment and a world without rape* (pp. 13–28). Berkeley, CA: Seal Press.

Filipovic, J. (2013). Rape is about power, not sex. *Guardian.* Retrieved from https://www.theguardian.com/commentisfree/2013/aug/29/rape-about-power-not-sex

Finkel, A. (2006). *Social policy and practice in Canada: A history.* Waterloo: Wilfred Laurier University Press.

Friedman, J., & Valenti, J. (2008). *Yes means yes! Visions of female sexual empowerment and a world without rape.* Berkeley, CA: Seal Press.

Gervais, C. (2012). Canadian women religious' negotiation of feminism and Catholicism. *Sociology of Religion*, 73(4), 384–410.

Gervais, C. (2015). Alternative altars: Beyond patriarchy and priesthood and towards inclusive spirituality, governance and activism among Catholic women religious in Ontario. In B. Cranney & S. Molloy (Eds.), *Canadian woman studies: An introductory reader* (pp. 54–64). Toronto: Inanna Publications.

Gervais, C. (2018). *Beyond the altar: Women religious, patriarchal power and the church.* Waterloo: Wilfrid Laurier University Press.

Gervais, C., & Turenne Sjolander, C. (2015). Interrogating and constructing the 'authentic' Roman Catholic Church: Feminist perspectives among Canadian women religious. *Review of Religious Research, 57*(3), 365–396.

Gervais, C., & Watson, A. (2014). Discipline, resistance, solace and the body: Catholic women religious' convent experiences from the late 1930s to the late 1960s. *Religions, 5*(1), 277–303.

Harding, S. (1991). *Whose science/whose knowledge?* Milton Keynes: Open University Press.

Hochschild, A. (1989). *The second shift.* New York, NY: Penguin.

Holtmann, C. (2008). Resistance is beautiful: The growth of the Catholic Network for Women's Equality in New Brunswick. In M. Beavis (with E. Guillemin & B. Pell) (Eds.), *Feminist theology with a Canadian accent* (pp. 200–219). Ottawa: Novalis.

hooks, b. (2000). *Feminism is for everybody: Passionate politics.* Cambridge: South End Press.

hooks, b. (2013). Dig deep: Beyond lean in. *Feminist Wire.* Retrieved from http://www.thefeministwire.com/2013/10/17973/

Israely, J. (2009). A sequel to the case of the pregnant 9-year old. *Time,* July 18. Retrieved from http://www.time.com/time/world/article/0,8599,1911495,00.html#ixzz1a15q06ta

Johnson, E. A. (2002a). *She who is: The mystery of God in feminist theological discourse.* New York, NY: Crossroad.

Johnson, E. A. (Ed.) (2002b). *The church women want: Catholic women in dialogue.* New York, NY: Crossroad.

Kaylin, L. (2000). *For the love of God: The faith and future of the American nun.* New York, NY: Perennial.

Kristof, N. D. (2012). We are all nuns. *New York Times,* April 28. Retrieved from http://www.nytimes.com/2012/04/29/opinion/sunday/kristof-we-are-all-nuns.html?_r=2&

Leadership Conference of Women Religious [LCWR]. (2015a). *Congregation for the doctrine of the faith concludes mandate regarding LCWR.* Retrieved from https://lcwr.org/media/news/congregation-doctrine-faith-concludes-mandate-regarding-lcwr

Leadership Conference of Women Religious [LCWR]. (2015b). *Statement of the LCWR officers on the CDF doctrinal assessment and conclusion of the mandate.* Retrieved from https://lcwr.org/media/statement-lcwr-officers-cdf-doctrinal-assessment-and-conclusion-mandate

McElwee, J. J. (2013). Pope Francis' LCWR reaffirmation leads sisters to hard questions. *National Catholic Reporter,* April 17. Retrieved from http://ncronline.org/news/sisters-stories/pope-francis-lcwr-reaffirmation-leads-sisters-hard-questions

McElwee, J. J. (2016). Vatican contacting about 15 orders of US sisters for 'serene' dialogue. *National Catholic Reporter,* June 14. Retrieved from https://www.

ncronline.org/news/vatican/vatican-religious-congregation-contacting-15-orders-us-sisters-serene-dialogue

Murdoch, C. (2012). Settle down sisters: American nuns busted for being a crazy bunch of radical feminists. *Jezebel*, April 19. Retrieved from http://jezebel.com/5903343/vatican-pissed-at-american-nuns-for-being-a-crazy-bunch-of-radical-feminists

Schenk, C. (2014). The apostolic visitation report was laudatory, but sisters remain caught in ambiguity. *National Catholic Report*, December 18. Retrieved from http://ncronline.org/blogs/simply-spirit/apostolic-visitation-report-was-laudatory-sisters-remain-caught-ambiguity

Schneiders, S. (2004). *Beyond patching: Faith and feminism in the Catholic Church.* Mahwah, NJ: Paulist Press.

Schneiders, S. (2013). *Buying the field: Catholic religious life in mission to the world.* Mahwah, NJ: Paulist Press.

Schneiders, S. (2014). Engage the future: Reflections on the apostolic visitation report. *Global Sisters Report*, December 18. Retrieved from http://globalsistersreport.org/column/trends/engage-future-reflections-apostolic-visitation-report-17046

Smith, A. (2008). *Native Americans and the Christian right: The gendered politics of unlikely alliances.* Durham, NC: Duke University Press.

Smith, D. (1987). *The everyday world as problematic: A feminist sociology.* Boston, MA: Northeastern University Press.

Smyth, E. M. (Ed.) (2007). *Changing habits: Women's religious orders in Canada.* Ottawa, Canada: Novalis.

Uebbing, D. (2013). Pope backs reform of Leadership Conference of Women Religious. The Congregation for the Doctrine of the Faith issued a Doctrinal Assessment of the LCWR a year ago. *National Catholic Register*, April 15. Retrieved from http://www.ncregister.com/daily-news/pope-backs-reform-of-leadership-conference-of-women-religious

Vatican Radio. (2016). *Fr Lombardi on Pope's remarks about female deacons.* May 13. Retrieved from http://en.radiovaticana.va/news/2016/05/13/fr_lombardi_on_pope%E2%80%99s_remarks_about_female_deacons/1229620

Winter, M. T., Lummis, A., & Stokes, A. (1994). *Defecting in place: Women taking responsibility for their own spiritual lives.* New York, NY: Crossroad.

Part Two

Inclusion, Equity and Policies

Global Synthesis

Glenda Tibe Bonifacio

Diversity is reality. No society or community is ever homogenous, and to claim such is a matter of power dynamics of and between groups. Of course, civilization tells us that the bases for supremacy and normative ideals rest with social construction, history, and reproduction of eschewed knowledge or the preferential discourse to maintain status. In the 21st century, diversity and inclusion continue to rage as issues in both western and non-western contexts. The historical marginalization of women and transgender individuals come to a point where formulation of equity policies provide effective means of inclusion. Legislation becomes the first goal to affect societal change as habits and practices tend to lasts longer, but they do change when hampered by the rule of law. To do this, a concerted action is required at all fronts not only by those affected by exclusivist agenda but with the general allied public to effect genuine change. A cursory survey of what is happening around the world reveals a stark reality among those viewed as 'others' in the community, where rights of citizenship are selectively enjoyed and the sanctity of their life is at the whim of those in authority. To fear based on gender, ethnicity, sexuality and religion, for example, reflect symptomatic social ills that critical and progressive education hold the key in the eventual paradigm shift. Working for equitable distribution of resources, protection of rights and welfare, and the just treatment of all as enunciated by appropriate policies differ across countries based on the level of its social progress and development.

Chapter 4

Preserving Patriarchy: Birthright, Citizenship and Gender in Nepal

Jill Allison

Abstract

Birth and birthright, in relation to citizenship, are entangled in a complex politics of power and patriarchy as well as past and present notions of cultural and national identity in Nepal. The debates highlight how gender inequality intersects historically with social inequality in a highly stratified society based on religion, caste and ethnicity. The constitutional discussion that has been ongoing in Nepal since the end of the 10-year long civil war in 2004 highlights the need for a critical feminist approach that looks at the multi-faceted and intersecting relationship between citizenship, gender, political projects of imagined communities, social inequality and access to political power. Women have become responsible for the containment of attributes, values and identity within nation-state, regional boundaries, and communities or collectivities. They are constituted as both an asset and a threat to the nation-state should there be fluidity in borders or boundaries. With the struggle to produce and promulgate a new constitution in Nepal, we see how women's interests and equality can be sacrificed in the name of protecting idealized social and political values as well as preserving the nation-state itself.

Keywords: Citizenship; birthright; gender; Nepal; patriarchy

Birth and birthright, in relation to citizenship, are entangled in a complex politics of power and patriarchy as well as past and present notions of cultural and national identity in Nepal. Women, as citizens, are caught

Global Currents in Gender and Feminisms: Canadian and International Perspectives, 67–79

Copyright © 2018 by Emerald Publishing Limited
All rights of reproduction in any form reserved
ISBN: 978-1-78714-484-2/doi:10.1108/978-1-78714-483-520171008

between a changing political landscape and the enduring social stratification that has shaped the way citizenship is defined. Since its rapid political transition from an absolute monarchy to constitutional monarchy to republic, Nepal has struggled to write a new constitution. While this process is often an opportunity for nations to acknowledge and account for social and economic change, in the context of Nepal's emergent democracy and rapid political transformation, the promise of citizenship is threatening and uncertain, considering demands for inclusive political recognition from the multi-ethnic population. Discussions in the post-conflict era around drafting of the new constitution provide an opportunity to examine the impact of deeply entrenched patriarchy as women struggle for the right to pass citizenship to their children by descent and to husbands by naturalization. The debates around citizenship in Nepal thus illuminate particular moral, social and reproductive roles for women, and how these roles are constituted, politicized and maintained. More importantly, the debates highlight how gender inequality intersects historically with social inequality in a highly stratified society based on religion, caste and ethnicity. The constitutional discussion in Nepal highlights the need for a critical feminist approach that looks at the multi-faceted and intersecting relationship between citizenship, gender, political projects of imagined communities, social inequality and political power.

This chapter shows how the political discourse around citizenship in Nepal is shaped by its specific historical and social past even as the country moves forward and embraces political change. The chapter is based on media analysis and observations from participation in several public events in Nepal about the drafting of a constitution. It also shows how Tamang's description of a historical shift from 'family to state patriarchy' (2000, p. 127) facilitates the construction of women as the kind of 'boundary keepers' of the imagined nation-state described by Yuval-Davis and Stroetzer (2002, p. 332). This is set against the current backdrop of growing uncertainty and national change as Nepal grapples with its promise to recognize regional autonomy and federalism. The result has been that women's reproductive labour is constituted as producing population and nation but not necessarily producing citizens.

In Nepal, a citizenship certificate based on descent can be obtained at the age of 16 years. To qualify for citizenship, applicants must produce proof of citizenship of their parents or links to land title in the community through family connections. Without a citizenship certificate, people cannot obtain a School Leaving Certificate that qualifies them for higher education, cannot obtain a passport or a driving licence, cannot use banks and other institutions, all of which increases vulnerability and social marginalization. Aryal (2014), in her article on 'Macho Nationalism' published by *Nepali Times*, reports an estimated 4 million Nepali-born children of single mothers or women married to non-Nepali men are without citizenship in Nepal. Women who have been abandoned by husbands or widowed, women who have been raped or cannot name the father of their child cannot pass citizenship, as a right, to their Nepali-born children. Access to citizenship has also been fraught with power relations within communities as the authority to confer citizenship is vested in local government agents who are themselves both products and producers of the stratified and patriarchal political system rooted in both caste and ethnicity.

Gender inequality in Nepal is evident in its relatively low literacy rate for women — 43% as compared to 75% for men — and its rating of .48 on the Gender Inequality Index (United Nations Development Programme).[1] The denial of access to citizenship contravenes the obligations in the Universal Declaration of Human Rights, the Convention on the Elimination of All Forms of Discrimination Against Women (CEDAW), the International Covenant on Civil and Political Rights, and the Convention on the Rights of the Child, all of which Nepal has signed (UN Women, 2014). Nepal is one of the few countries in the world that has not recognized citizenship by descent through mothers.

At the same time, the 2011 census identifies 126 caste and ethnic groups and 123 languages (Government of Nepal National Planning Secretariat, 2011), up from 100 caste and ethnics groups and 96 languages in the 2001 census (Hachhethu, 2003). This indicates the growing pressure for inclusion in a very dynamic political situation. Historically, all of these have been stitched into a hierarchy of caste that has traditionally denied many ethnic groups' access to political leadership and maintained a stratified system in which the majority of the population have little opportunity for social or economic mobility. The stratification of Nepal's social and political system also falls along regional lines, with many ethnic groups living in the region known as the Madhesh near the Indian border. The people living in this area have close ties to India, and marriage and family are porous institutions that transcend national boundaries. This intersection of caste, ethnicity, political region and the politics of nation building loom large in the debates around citizenship and birthright.

The issue has galvanized women's groups to participate in the Citizenship in the Name of the Mother movement and the Collective Campaign for a Women Friendly Constitution in 2015. On one hand, these movements are

---

[1]Gender Inequality Index or GII is based on reproductive health and maternal mortality rates, empowerment (political participation and educational access) and economic status such as labour participation. In the GII 1.0 represents absolute gender inequality and moves down the scale towards 0 which represents a higher level of gender equality (United Nations Development Programme).

fighting for gender equality from a basic human rights' point of view and their arguments are called 'the feminist position' in many of the public events held to discuss the constitution. At the same time, women from disadvantaged communities in regions of Nepal are caught in the deeper debate around inclusion as their ethnicity and cultural identity are bound to their lives in borderlands where marriages, families and communities intersect with Indian communities. These debates revolve around power and the imperative to control national sovereignty over feminist arguments for social equality (Giri & Shrestha, 2015). At the same time, as Abrahams and Varughese (2012) argue that perpetuating patriarchy as a nationalist strategy, leaving millions without citizenship, contributes to potential instability in a nation struggling to build a new constitution and identity.

Feminist Perspectives on Citizenship and Gender

Citizenship, like gender, is a contingent concept with meanings that are socially constructed. The implications of these meanings are bound to what Gururanai (2014) describes as 'overlapping relations of patriarchy, economy, family, community, and state' (p. 39). In addition to this list, history is also significant. Feminists challenge the historical construction of a public—private dichotomy, the binary between the rational and the emotional, opposition between collective and individual concerns and community responsibility in contrast to liberal rights (Fraser, 1995; Isin & Wood, 1999; Mouffe, 1992). Such dichotomies have been employed as obstacles to women's participation as citizens as their roles in reproduction and domestic space are set in opposition to the public domain of decision-making where men exercise political power. Scholars have argued that it is crucial to explore the gendered implications of citizenship and its relationship to the state regarding access to resources, political participation and policy making (Abraham, Hgan-Ling Chow, Maratou-Alipranti, & Tastsoglou, 2010; Pateman, 1992). For feminists who see social transformation as their objective, citizenship presents a paradox in that it promises inclusion and opportunity while also being exclusionary and restrictive (Roseneil, 2013). As feminists seek inclusion, the promise of equality and recognition on one hand, they have to accept the restrictive nature of the system and its potential to obstruct opportunities for social change on the other. Moreover, as Newman (2013) argues, feminist projects around citizenship and rights can be appropriated by states, absorbing them into larger governmentalist projects of modernization, capitalist expansion and consumption, and the moral imperative to participation rather than activism in the new state order.

Women are the reproducers of nations, communities and identities through a host of mechanisms including biological and social processes (Ginsburg & Rapp, 1995; Yuval-Davis, 1997). In their book *Conceiving the New World Order*, Ginsburg and Rapp (1995) explore the ways in which reproduction is co-opted as part of state projects, shaping the ways in which birth and reproductive decision-making are controlled to perpetuate state objectives and ideologies. As a key mechanism for naturalizing gender differences, reproduction holds powerful social and political value for families, communities and nation-states. The meaning of reproduction and the importance of women's reproductive labour to the image of states are described in relation to China's ideal of modernity and quality reflected in control of population and women's reproduction (Anagnost, 1995), and in the banning of abortion in Romania as part of Ceausescu's attempt at extreme paternalist nation building (Kligman, 1995).

States also create mechanisms for identifying and maintaining gendered identities that often rely on specific rules, attitudes and ideas that constitute women as 'boundary keepers' (Yuval-Davis & Stoetzler, 2002, p. 332). Drawing on the work of Anderson (1983), Yuval-Davis and Stoetzler (2002) note that these imagined constructions of nation and community 'involve a paradoxical positioning of women as both symbols and "others" of the collectivity: women symbolize the nation's identity while at the same time they are a non-identical element within the nation' (p. 335). Women thus become responsible for the containment of attributes, values and identity within nation-state, regional boundaries and communities or collectivities. They are both an asset and a threat to the nation-state should there be fluidity in borders or boundaries.

Historical Strata in Contemporary Context: Gender and Identity

We, politicians, women and human right activists and persons engaged in various professions, on 6 July 2015, issue our declaration the following points regarding the draft of Constitution of Nepal, 2072:[2]

1. *Include the word 'Patriarchal' in the Preamble of the draft of Constitution of Nepal, 2072 to accept the reality and ensure the constitutional end to patriarchy in Nepal;*

---

[2]Nepal follows a calendar based on the Bikram Sambat system that differs from the Gregorian calendar.

(Taken from a Declaration presented to government on the occasion of the circulation of a draft constitution. Personal email communication shared by representative of UN Women, July 2015.)

As the inscription above indicates, there is widespread concern that patriarchy must be acknowledged and exposed before its influence and impact can be eliminated. The story of Nepal's political patriarchy is unique in a continent where many nations were colonized. Nepal was never directly colonized by any other country although some would argue it has been colonized by the international NGO and development agencies in recent decades (Tamang, 2002). The significance of the story of Nepal's relationship with outside influences parallels the history of its unique system of social stratification.

Nepal lies between India and China and its political and social landscape have been shaped by its proximity to both. The border with India has always been a more porous one given that the geographic obstacles are less in the plains and the population is denser. Closed to the outside world until the 1950s, the Kingdom of Nepal developed its Hindu-influenced politics through hereditary relations that depend upon patriarchy as a guiding structure. A complex set of laws that were developed in 1854 absorbed non-Hindus into its caste ranking order by assigning the many Tibeto-Burmese peoples a caste that was neither high nor low but succeeded in containing them within the dominant Hindu structure for political purposes (Tamang, 2000). Levine (1987) argues that this system has always been rather fluid, particularly in the more northern and remote regions farther from the Hindu centre of Kathmandu and its politics. People in some communities align and realign their social positions in the caste-based system as political and economic circumstances change. When power was wrested from a lineage-based autocracy and the King was restored to political authority in the 1950s, a system based on promoting local village development emerged. There was an important shift in national focus towards embracing *bikas* — the Nepali word for development — that implies change, progress, modernization and perhaps most importantly, offered wider engagement with the international political and development world (Pigg, 1992; Tamang, 2000).

Development became the mechanism of a form of colonization that permeated multiple sectors of political and social life. As scholars argue, international agencies and foreign governments participated in a process of promoting social change and economic control of resources under the guise of support for the Kingdom's new political philosophy (Kernot, 2006; Pigg, 1992; Tamang, 2002). In reality, however, new forms of dependence and disempowerment occurred as opportunities for economic and political power remained stratified within old caste- and ethnicity-based networks at both the local and national levels. As outsiders worked with the political, social and economic elite, disadvantaged groups remained trapped in a hegemonic system that either exploited or ignored them (Kernot, 2006).

At the same time, uniquely Nepali forms of local governance shifted the system from 'family to state patriarchy' (Boris & Bardaglio, 1983; Tamang, 2000). The state could define the terms around property ownership and inheritance, citizenship, and access to rights and services through localized unelected governance structures that maintained the accepted stratified system of access to power. This state patriarchy has overwritten many traditional social practices that would have given women more autonomy and equality within households and communities. Moreover, it has contributed to a failure to recognize fully, the range of issues and challenges women face in Nepal, in both private and public political spheres.

In the post-1990 shift to constitutional monarchy following a popular movement for democracy, the rewriting of the constitution enshrined gender discrimination. In this new era, hundreds of laws and constitutional clauses discriminated against women through unequal property inheritance laws and only men could confer citizenship to their children (Tamang, 2009). The general tenor of social and economic inequality and the 'failure' of the development agenda fuelled a Maoist led insurgency and 10-year civil war. When the Comprehensive Peace Accord was signed in 2006, elections brought in a Constituent Assembly tasked with writing a new constitution as well as creating a democratic representative government with at least 33% women. The Citizenship Act of 2006 and the Interim Constitution promulgated in 2007 provided for equal access to citizenship by birth based on the mother's or the father's citizenship. However, in the ensuing years, as the interim Constituent Assemblies and governance structures of Nepal attempt to address the demands for federalism and greater regional and ethnic autonomy the meaning of a rights-based citizenship to the central government's control becomes less certain.

Citizenship in the Twenty-first Century: What is at Stake?

The stakes around access to a Citizenship Certificate are high and the larger issues around federalism and a system of governance have yet to be defined. The main issues are discrimination against women through enduring patriarchal political structures, the inequality in access to economic mobility and global employment migration, social equity and equal access to political voice in Nepal, and the issue of boundary keeping and gendered responsibilities for national security and sovereignty. The demarcation of gender distinction in citizenship by descent also highlights the capture of women's reproductive labour by a patriarchal system that seeks to legitimize in the public sphere, only what men acknowledge. In this context, women's political participation as citizens in Nepal is caught between nationalist political desire to control access to citizenship and the constitution of women as agents of an uncertainty that must be controlled.

The most recent draft of the constitution circulated in July of 2015, in the immediate aftermath of the devastating earthquakes in April and May and then promulgated in the Constituent Assembly only a couple of months later, states that both the father and the mother of a child must be Nepali in order for an applicant, at 16 years of age, to acquire citizenship. This means citizenship by birthright is only available to children born in a particular kind of relationship or family formation — one that has been defined by the new 'state patriarchy' (Tamang, 2009). It excludes the children of women who give birth inside or outside the country as a result of a rape, women who have been abandoned by men or in cases where men deny paternity. The state thus naturalizes its patriarchal authority to define the terms of political participation and membership along the lines of gendered social norms around reproduction — both biological and social.

Further discrimination based on gender is enshrined in clauses related to men and women who are married to non-Nepalis. Men who are married to Nepali women must wait for 15 years before they can apply for citizenship and must renounce all claims to their previous national citizenship. Non-Nepali women who marry Nepali men need only wait two years before applying for citizenship, although the same demand for renouncing prior citizenship claims also exists. This means that women have little hope of being able to pass on citizenship to their children at 16 years of age if they marry a non-Nepali. The picture that emerges here is one in which those who currently hold power cannot envision a social system that is organized by any other means than patriarchy.

Nepal is part of the increasing globalization and migratory flow of labour and capital. Citizenship no longer resonates as a purely national issue where the rights and responsibilities can be contained within a nation-state and free of influence and meanings beyond borders. In this era of globalization and with hundreds of thousands of young Nepali men and women seeking employment opportunities abroad, the inability to travel creates obvious disadvantages for those without access to citizenship. More than 20% of the GDP in Nepal now comes from remittances sent home by Nepali migrant labour in the Middle East, India, Malaysia and the West (Sijapati & Limbu, 2012). Access to opportunities locally is also constrained when children who cannot access citizenship are denied the opportunity to take School Leaving Exams and enter higher education programmes. Access to banking services, political participation, voting and property ownership are all dependent on having citizenship. For women, access to marital property can be particularly challenging as they have a more difficult time obtaining a citizenship certificate (Varughese & Abrahams, 2012).

While the debate around citizenship by descent is largely driven by educated women in Kathmandu, there is a larger question about social equality in Nepal. There is in fact, a larger issue of intersectionality in the inequality issue in a context where both gender and caste or ethnicity continue to stratify society. Some have pointed out that the arguments for birthright rather than political equality have only served to deepen the divisions between women in different social circumstances in Nepal, rather than ensuring a unified voice that will also speak for women in disadvantaged Madhesi region along the southern border with India (Rana, 2015). Women in the Madhes who marry Indian men face double discrimination since it is their capacity to provide citizenship to both children and spouses that is being restricted by the new constitution. There is peril in compartmentalizing the debate; the inclusive and exclusive potential of citizenship should be critiqued as a cross-cutting issue rather than simply a gendered one.

At stake for the Nepali political elite is the distribution of political power once federalism is achieved. This is variously described as a security issue and a social one. The social dimension is most evident for the people in the Madhesi region even as their situation is what constitutes the security issue. Their appointment as lower caste in the historical construction of Nepal's stratified community has meant they have been a particularly underserved and disadvantaged, without access to political power or opportunities for political participation in government. Their desire and activism for a greater regional autonomy are also perceived as threatening should members of their large community become eligible to hold political office. The security issue can be linked to growing power and influence from India. The fear of 'Sikhimism' — the annexing of Sikkim by India in 1975 — has been mentioned as a reason for an unfounded but nonetheless present argument for the political reticence around facilitating the citizenship of non-Nepali men (Jha, 2014). The women who marry non-Nepalis, especially at the border sites, are seen by some to pose a risk if they can produce Nepali citizens through marriage or birth.

The following exchange, excerpts taken from the *Nepali Times*, is emblematic of the tenor of the debate. It illustrates how the multiple dichotomies — public and private, individual and collective, rational and emotional — are pressed into service to diminish women's arguments for equality.

> To those who invoke international laws and practices to demand Nepali citizenship to foreigners, are you also ready to follow same rules to manage our border and migration? [...] Even countries like India and the US consider barring

those born elsewhere from reaching the top executive posts, is it logical for Nepal to accept foreigners as heads of constitutional bodies and security forces? It is unfortunate to see some people demanding shortest possible way to grant citizenship to foreigners, that too by descent.

It would be wiser for Nepalis to discuss the citizenship issue as true nationalists. Vested interests and emotion do not bode well for Nepal's sovereign existence. We need a constitution to protect our sovereignty, independence, unity, prosperity and welfare. We cannot allow a constitutional provision that risks our national interests. (Rawal, 2015)

This excerpt identifies the assumption that the state should exert its patriarchal authority as a natural means of protecting the nationalist interests of both the state and the social welfare of individuals within it. The veiled reference to 'vested interests and emotions' in relation to women's demands also harkens to the idea that such arguments are personal and thus less rooted in the rational and logical — the domain of national political interests. This eclipses the long-standing feminist argument that the 'personal is political'.

In response, Nepali feminist political activists and scholars write:

You blame us for demanding citizenship by descent to foreigners. We are demanding citizenship by descent to our children, not to foreigners. How can the children born out of the wombs of Nepali women be foreigners just because their fathers are foreigners? By this same logic, how can the children born out of the wombs of foreign women be Nepalis just because their fathers hold Nepali citizenship certificates? We are concerned about Nepal's sovereignty as much as you are. But we fear the decisions that you politicians make while reaching power-sharingdeals in the constitution making process will lead to foreign intervention in our internal affairs. (Malla & Uprety, 2015)

The impassioned response locates women's power and citizenship in the realm of the biological — something Tamang (2000) argues has, in the past, reduced their political participation as citizens in Nepal. It also implies the clearly divisive hegemony of maintaining boundaries since women who are not Nepali, in this argument, should not be entitled to be producers of Nepalis. The fragmenting of the issue of citizenship, gender and birthright from that of naturalization and family formation across leaky borders and boundaries highlights the complexity and risk associated with women's roles in reproducing citizens. The exchange also exemplifies the way women's social position can be used 'to degrade the men of the "other" side [rather] than as part of a comprehensive egalitarian gender perspective' (Yuval-Davis & Stoetzler, 2002, p. 342). The degradation of men who are part of families at the border with India — men who are constituted as posing a risk to the national integrity of Nepal — is also rooted in patriarchy since men are assumed to be political actors with agency. Thus, the construction of otherness in this debate is clearly about the risk of allowing women to naturalize men as citizens.

Conclusion

The debates around the constitution of citizenship in Nepal highlight the pervasive influence of patriarchy, addressing the intersectionality of social inequality and the way equal access to citizenship is still, at its heart, a restrictive and exclusionary project for women in some regions and ethnic communities. Residual aspects of state patriarchy have been pressed into service in making women responsible for maintaining national and ethnic boundaries against the incursion of socially and politically dangerous others. This is also a compelling feminist issue. The border is open between India and Nepal and the new political imperative to devolve power region-ally means that a potential leaky point where women's capacity to produce citizens must be contained. Women must also maintain boundaries around a particular kind of citizenship — the product of a heteronormative and marriage based family prescribed by dominant social constructions delin-eated by gender roles and status.

Citizenship, as a contested concept, is seen as dangerous and unpredict-able, and at the same time a mechanism for maintaining the stratified social worlds in which Nepal's governance structure have always been comfort-able. With the struggle to produce and promulgate a new constitution in Nepal, we see how women's interests and equality can be sacrificed in the name of protecting idealized social and political values as well as preserving the nation-state itself. Language and fear are the mechanisms by which women can be disempowered even as the role they play in community and family is shaped by their ability to produce children. More importantly, this moment in Nepal's history demonstrates the importance of a gendered and feminist analysis of the political rhetoric around citizenship. The con-stitutional debates expose how women's inequality and denial of rights can be obscured or normalized but also co-opted in a rhetoric that detracts from a much broader discussion on social and political inclusion, national-ism and the impact of globalization.

References

Abraham, M., Hgan-Ling Chow, E., Maratou-Alipranti, L., & Tastsoglou, E. (2010). Rethinking citizenship with women in focus. In M. Abraham, E. Hgan-Ling Chow, L. Maratou-Alipranti, & E. Tastsoglou (Eds.), *Contours of citizenship: Women, diversity and practices of citizenship* (pp. 1−22). Farnham: Ashgate.

Abrahams, P., & Varughese, G. (2012). Stateless in Nepal: Inclusion without citizenship impossible. *The Asia Foundation.* Retrieved from http://asiafoundation. org/2012/05/23/stateless-in-new-nepal-inclusion-without-citizenship-is-impossible/

Anagnost, A. (1995). A surfeit of bodies: Population and the rationality and the post-Mao China. In F. Ginsburg & R. Rapp (Eds.), *Conceiving the new world order* (pp. 22−41). Berkeley, CA: University of California Press.

Anderson, B. (1983). *Imagined communities: Reflections on the origin and spread of nationalism.* New York, NY: Verso.

Aryal, M. (2014). Macho nationalism. Retrieved from http://nepalitimes.com/regular-columns/Interesting-Times/macho-nationalism-in-nepal,252

Boris, E., & Bardaglio, P. (1983). The transformation of patriarchy: The historic role of the state. In I. Diamond (Ed.), *Families, politics and public policy: A feminist dialogue on women and the state* (pp. 70−93). New York, NY: Longman.

Fraser, N. (1995). From redistribution to recognition? Dilemmas of justice in a 'post-socialist' age. *New Left Review, 212,* 68−93.

Ginsburg, F., & Rapp, R. (Eds.). (1995). *Conceiving the new world order.* Berkeley, CA: University of California Press.

Giri, S., & Shrestha, R. (2015). Not everyone is happy about Nepal's Constitution. *Fair Observer,* December 24. Retrieved from http://www.fairobserver.com/region/central_south_asia/not-everyone-is-happy-about-nepals-constitution-31010/

Government of Nepal National Planning Secretariat. (2011). *National population and housing census.* National report of Nepal. Central Bureau of Statistics, Kathmandu, Nepal. Retrieved from http://countryoffice.unfpa.org/nepal/drive/Nepal-Census-2011-Vol1.pdf

Gururanai, S. (2014). "Geographies that make resistance": Remapping the politics of gender and place in Uttarakhand, India. *Himalaya, the Journal of the Association for Nepal and Himalayan Studies, 34*(1), 68−79.

Hachhethu, K. (2003). Democracy and nationalism: Interface between state and ethnicity in Nepal. *Contributions to Nepalese Studies, 30*(2), 217−252.

Isin, E., & Wood, P. (1999). *Citizenship and identity.* London: Sage Publications.

Jha, D. (2014). Citizenship. Paper presented at the Special Constitutional Convention. Nepal Bar Association.

Kernot, S. (2006). Nepal: A development challenge. *South Asia: Journal of South Asian Studies, 29*(2), 293−307. doi:10.1080/00856400600849167

Kligman, G. (1995). Political demography: The banning of abortion in Ceausescu's Romania. In F. Ginsburg & R. Rapp (Eds.), *Conceiving the new world order* (pp. 234−255). Berkeley, CA: University of California Press.

Levine Nancy, E. (1987). Caste, state, and ethnic boundaries in Nepal. *The Journal of Asian Studies, 46,* 71−88.

Malla, S. P., & Uprety, A. (2015). Sacrificial lambs: Fear of foreigners usurping Nepal has made citizenship laws discriminatory. *Nepali Times*, July 21. Retrieved from http://www.nepalitimes.com/blogs/thebrief/2015/07/21/who-will-be-a-nepali/

Mouffe, C. (1992). Feminism, citizenship and radical democratic politics. In J. Butler & J. Scott (Eds.), *Feminists theorize the political* (pp. 369–384). New York, NY: Routledge.

Newman, J. (2013). 'But we didn't mean that': Feminist projects and the government appropriations. In S. Roseneil (Ed.), *Beyond citizenship? Feminism and transformations of belonging* (pp. 89–111). New York, NY: Palgrave MacMillan.

Pateman, C. (1992). Equality, difference and subordination: The politics of motherhood and women's citizenship. In G. Bock & S. James (Eds.), *Beyond equality and difference: Citizenship, feminist politics and female subjectivity* (pp. 17–31). London: Routledge.

Pigg, S. L. (1992). Inventing social categories through place: Social representations and development in Nepal. *Comparative Studies in Society and History*, *34*(3), 491–513.

Rana, K. (2015). No easy way out: We cannot be 'doing feminism' without addressing questions of racism and heterosexism within the citizenship debate. *Kathmandu Post/EKantipur*, June 26. Retrieved from http://kathmandupost.ekantipur.com/printedition/news/2015-06-25/no-easy-way-out-277752.html

Rawal, B. (2015). Who will be a Nepali? *Nepali Times*, July 21. Retrieved from http://www.nepalitimes.com/blogs/thebrief/2015/07/21/who-will-be-a-nepali/

Roseneil, S. (2013). *Beyond citizenship? Feminism and the transformation of belonging*. New York, NY: Palgrave MacMillan.

Sijapati, B., & Limbu, A. (2012). *Governing labour migration in Nepal: An analysis of existing policies and institutional mechanisms*. Kathmandu: Himal Books.

Tamang, S. (2000). Legalizing state patriarchy in Nepal. *Studies in Nepali History and Society*, *5*(1), 127–156.

Tamang, S. (2002). Dis-embedding the sexual/social contract: Citizenship and gender in Nepal. *Citizenship Studies*, *6*(3), 309–324.

Tamang, S. (2009). The politics of conflict and difference or the difference of conflict in politics: The women's movement in Nepal. *The Feminist Review*, *91*, 61–80.

United Nations Development Programme (UNDP). Retrieved from www.np.undp.org/content/nepal/en/home/countryinfo/

UN Women. (2014). Background note on key women's empowerment and gender equality provisions for the Constitution of Nepal, p. 1, para 1.

Varughese, G., & Abrahams, P. (2012). Stateless in Nepal: Inclusion without citizenship impossible. *Nepali Times*, June 8–14, p. 3.

Yuval-Davis, N. (1997). *Gender and nation*. London: Sage.

Yuval-Davis, N., & Stoetzler, M. (2002). Imagined boundaries and borders: A gendered gaze. *The European Journal of Women's Studies*, *9*(3), 329–344.

Chapter 5

Gender Inequality in Swedish Legislation of Sámi Reindeer Herding

Ebba Olofsson

Abstract

This chapter aims to understand how the role and status of Sámi women in kinship system and in reindeer herding were transformed over time in Norway and Sweden. What is the reason for considering men as reindeer herders and not women? Has it always been men who play a more important role in reindeer herding and so have higher status in Sámi society than women? This has not always been the case. Reindeer herding has instead become a dominant male occupation with the implementation of the nation-states' reindeer herding legislation. Gender roles in Sámi communities are changing and new strategies for surviving and maintaining a Sámi identity are being formed. Many women in reindeer herding Sámi communities are now working as wage-labourers and professionals, bringing in money to the family. Their income often facilitates the continuation and transformation of subsistence practices, and power relations. This chapter proposes that the ascribed ethnic identity of Sámi women became linked to the identity of their brothers and husbands with the implementation of modern legislation, and still is, although Sweden is striving to be a gender equalitarian society.

Keywords: Sámi; gender inequality; reindeer herding; legislation; Norway; Sweden

In loving memory of my father Jan Olofsson

— Always encouraging his daughters to
pursue their own choice of career.

Global Currents in Gender and Feminisms: Canadian and International Perspectives, 81–92
Copyright © 2018 by Emerald Publishing Limited
All rights of reproduction in any form reserved
ISBN: 978-1-78714-484-2/doi:10.1108/978-1-78714-483-520171009

Gender Inequality: Swedish Legislation of
Sámi Reindeer Herding

The documentary film 'Sámi Herders' (1974) made by Hubert Schuurman serves as an inspiration for this chapter. In this film, the viewers get to know a reindeer herding family in Norway. The couple has three children — one boy and two girls. The viewers learn that the son — Johan — wants to become a reindeer herder when he grows up and the oldest daughter — Berit — wants to marry a reindeer herder when she becomes an adult. The movie also shows that the Sámi[1] has continued their old ways with reindeer herding at the same time as they are taking part in modern society. A girl cannot become a reindeer herder herself, instead her identity as a reindeer herding Sámi is linked to her future husband. What is the reason for considering men as reindeer herders and not women? Has this always been the case? Is this according to the Sámi traditional worldview? In other words, did men always play a more important role in reindeer herding than women? This chapter argues that this has not always been the case, and that reindeer herding has become a dominant male occupation only with colonization of the Sámi and the implementation of reindeer herding legislation.

This chapter brings together aspects from anthropological kinship studies from a gender perspective, and historical and anthropological research about the changes in the organization of the Sámi society and their subsistence, namely reindeer herding. While the focus is on the Sámi in Sweden, the material also includes Norway and, to a lesser part, Finland, but excludes the Sámi on Kola Peninsula in Russia since they have a different history due to having been subjects of the Soviet Union (Olofsson, 2004). Comparisons are also made to First Nations[2] women in Canada to show similarities among Indigenous women elsewhere affected by colonization. The material for this chapter has been gathered over a longer period of time (1993–2004) with mixed methods using participant observation, literature research, and interviews for the master thesis (Olofsson, 1995) and the doctoral dissertation (Olofsson, 2004), as well as more recent literature and media research (2014–2017).

---

[1]The Sámi have been called Lapps which is a derogatory term and I use it here only in a direct quote or a name for an institution like *lappby*. In English, the name Sámi has been spelled in different ways — Sámi, Sami, Saami and sometimes Saamis in plural — the same with the word *sameby*.
[2]The First Nations have been called "Indians" in the past which is today considered a derogatory term, and First Nations is considered a more appropriate designation in Canada. They are not to be confused with the Inuit. In the United States, they are instead called Native Americans. The term "Indian" is still used to some extent, for example, the Indian Act (the legislation of the First Nations in Canada).

Sámi Reindeer Herding

The Sámi people live in four different nation-states — Norway, Sweden, Finland and Russia. The geographical area that is considered their core area of settlement is called Sápmi, and covers an area over northern Norway, Sweden, northern Finland, and the Kola Peninsula (in Russia). The Sámi is considered both by themselves and by United Nations to be an Indigenous population, and their 'traditional' livelihood is reindeer herding. Before colonization of their land by other European peoples, the Sámi were moving with their reindeer herds in a cyclic pattern depending on the season. Reindeer herding was one subsistence strategy, and some Sámi populations had other subsistence activities, or a combination of reindeer herding with other subsistence activities, such as arctic farming, fishing and Sámi handicraft (Eikjok, 2004).

Today, in Sweden as well in the other countries, most Sámi have incomes from regular jobs. Still, reindeer herding, considered to be the 'traditional' subsistence, continues to play an important role and has become a symbol of Sámi identity (Olofsson, 2004). Contemporary reindeer herding uses modern technology such as trucks, snow-scooters, motorcycles and walkie-talkies. Reindeer herding is organized in *samebyar* (in the singular, *sameby*), which is a territory in which a group of reindeer herders have the right to practice reindeer herding (Beach, 2000).

In Sweden, according to the Reindeer Herding Act of 1971 (revised in 1992/1993), all Sámi have the right to reindeer herding, however, only individuals that are members of a *sameby* can exercise that right. Persons of Sámi descent or persons married to a Sámi have the right to become members of a *sameby* (SOU, 2001, p. 101). Also, in Norway, according to the Norwegian reindeer herding legislation, the Sámi have the exclusive right to reindeer herding (SOU, 1999, p. 25), whereas in Finland both the Sámi and Finns have reindeer-herding rights (Lehtola, 2002).

'Traditionally' reindeer herding was organized in *siida* (sometimes spelled *sii'da* or *sita*) — families connected with each other that worked together tending the reindeer. The *siida* consisted of siblings with their families — different constellations of brothers or/and sisters (Pehrson, 1964). Still today, the extended family (similar to *siida*) is the socio-economic unit for reindeer herding. Reindeer herders with their families work together tending the reindeers, more intensively in the fall and winter (Beach, 2000).

Statistics from 2013 showed that few women were considered reindeer herders in Sweden, especially guardians.[3] In total, there were 2809 male

---

[3]In Swedish modern legislation, a "guardian" is called "*gruppansvarig*" (team leader). It was formerly called "husbanded" which means "head of the household," the word still commonly used today.

reindeer herders of which 837 hold the status as guardians, whereas there were 1829 female reindeer herders but only 184 of them hold status as guardians in 2013. The statistics also showed that women own fewer reindeers than men (Sametinget, 2016). The female guardians own an average of 87 reindeer per person compared to the male guardians with an average of 196 per person (Sjögren, 2016).

Legislation and State Regulation of Reindeer Herding

At the end of the 19th century, the Swedish state legislated reindeer herding with the first reindeer-herding act implemented in 1886. The Sámi women's right to reindeer herding was dependent on the ethnic belonging of her husband. If a Sámi woman married a Swede (or other non-Sámi man), she could lose her right to reindeer herding (Beach, 1982). The Sámi women's right was not based entirely on ethnic heritage, but instead on the patriarchal view that woman's ethnic identity was flexible and tied to her husband's ethnic identity. A Sámi reindeer herding man who married a Swedish woman, however, could confer his reindeer herding rights upon her.

The legislation for Sámi women was comparable to the legislation for First Nations women in Canada until 1985, in which First Nations (Indian) woman lost her status as an Indian when she married a non-Indian, and their children lost Indian status and its rights as well (Jamieson, 1978; Silman, 1994). This gender inequality in reindeer herding legislation was removed in 1971. Since then Sámi women no longer lost their reindeer-herding rights if they married a Swede; instead the Swedish husband could gain the right to reindeer herding, as a Swedish woman could do if she married a Sámi reindeer herder (Beach, 1982). Beach (1982) notes that this policy led to lower numbers of women in the *sameby* since they lost their right to reindeer herding.

The implementation of mandatory schooling for all children in Scandinavia in 1842 had a great impact on reindeer herding (Uppman, 1978). The reindeer herders' children were sent to residential schools especially assigned for them — *nomadskola* — while the other Sámi had their children in regular local public schools (Ruong, 1975). Eikjok (2004) notes that the school year became longer in the 1950s—1960s, which meant that children stayed longer periods at the residential school away from their parents. Many reindeer herding families chose to settle down so that the children could live at home instead of at the residential school. Fathers could continue to attend the reindeer daily, either in the mountains or in the forest, depending on the season. Mothers and children stayed behind in the villages where they had winter land (and still do today) and moved to the summer land when children had their summer holiday from school. Reindeer herding pastures in the mountains and in the forest became the domain of men, while the home and the village became the domain of women (Eikjok, 2004). Eikjok (2004) points out that when the Sámi became more incorporated into the Swedish and Norwegian society, it also meant that the men were considered the head of the family and main provider, following the normative ideal in Europe.

Another change in reindeer herding is the rise of mechanized herding dependent on high technology. Reindeer herders nowadays use snowmobiles, cars, trucks and even helicopters, instead of walking, skiing or using the reindeer as draft animals (Olofsson, 2004). It is, therefore, possible for the reindeer herder to travel every day from the pasture to the village (or town) where he lives with his family (with both Swedish and Sámi neighbours). Many women — Sámi, Swedish or Norwegian — married to Sámi reindeer herders work in the village or town as professionals, for example, in the grocery store, as teachers or at the pharmacy. They often have higher education than men, and their income makes it possible for the family to continue with reindeer herding (Beach, 1982; Eikjok, 2004).

Sámi Reindeer Herding before Modernization

Etienne and Leacock (1980) discuss the anthropological study of economic systems of different societies typically divided into these categories: gathering—hunting (including fishing), horticulture and agriculture, pastoral, and industrial society. Gathering—hunting societies are normally equalitarian societies, where even if there is division of labour by gender, men and women complement each other's work. Not all gathering—hunting societies are or were equalitarian, and there are also examples of equalitarian societies which are not gathering—hunting societies, for example, horticultural societies (Etienne & Leacock, 1980).

Although the Sámi reindeer herding society of the past was a pastoralist society, the division of labour was similar to a gathering—hunting society (Eikjok, 2004; Pehrson, 1964). In the reindeer herding society of the past, some people had more influence and power than others. Sámi reindeer herding organization during the 1930s—1950s went through many changes, but still maintained the similar social organization before colonization. Division of labour was gender-based, but work duties and influence were also based on age. The social organization of reindeer herding units was kinship based, and the genealogical ties lead back to the dominant sibling group. The Sámi traditional society is classified as a bilateral society (tracing descent on both female and male sides of the family). Position in the kinship organization decides a person's duties and influence; depending on the stage in life — sibling, mother, grandmother, wife (often several different positions at the same time) — the person have different roles to play in society. Normally, a reindeer herding unit (*siida*) was headed by an adult man — considered the head of the family — but it does not mean that women and older men alike have no say in the daily operation of reindeer herding (Pehrson, 1964).

Men and women in the older generation who did not have the same physical strength as before mostly give advice on how to practice reindeer herding and tasks of the household. They also take care of children and teach them these tasks. Older men take out young men and boys on the land to teach them about the geography of the landscape and skills in reindeer herding. Older women spend time with young women and girls and teach them sewing, band weaving and other tasks. Adult men do the physical work of the reindeer herding (i.e. collecting and herding the reindeer, castration, slaughter, and marking and so on). Adult women take care of the household and make provisions for herding expeditions of their husbands and brothers (Pehrson, 1964).

Women had the right to own property and normally in charge of family economies. Men and women had different roles — power in different domains — but complement each other (Kuokkanen, 2009; Pehrson, 1964). The Sámi women had a relatively strong status and had an important economic influence. She owned her own reindeer, which she brought with her to the household when she got married (Eikjok, 2004). It was common for a widow to move back to her family and bring her property (Kuokkanen, 2009; Pehrson, 1964). The women had their own reindeer marks, a mark that was cut out in the ears of the reindeer, as a sign of their ownership — a system still in use today (Kuokkanen, 2009; Olofsson, 2004).

Etienne and Leacock (1980) point out that 'equal participation' does not mean that people always do the same work and the same amount of work, instead each one participates in the work according to their skills and interests. This implies a flexible system where sometimes men did women's work and vice versa, either temporary or on a more permanent basis. The equalitarian society is different to the agricultural and the industrial society, which has a more specialized division of labour and is more stratified (Etienne & Leacock, 1980).

The colonization of the Sámi disrupted what Etienne and Leacock (1980) call 'female-male complementarity' in the Sámi society. Like in many other societies which were colonized by Europeans, it caused 'the clash between this egalitarian principle and the hierarchical organization that European colonization brought about in many parts of the world' (Etienne & Leacock, 1980, p. 10). For example, Leacock argues how European colonization with the help of the Jesuit missionaries led to a decline in women's power and influence versus the men's in the Montagnais (today called Innu or Naskapi in Quebec, Canada) society (Leacock, 1980). Etienne and Leacock (1980) describe a similar pattern for other First Nations societies in Canada, even if they still point out that the change of gender roles and status took different forms in different societies (Etienne & Leacock, 1980).

Overall, the national political situation has influenced gender roles and women's status in Indigenous communities today (Lutz, 2006). In Canada, the political and legal rights of First Nations women were restricted by the Indian Act of 1876, which stated that only men could be chiefs and be on the band council, and that the Indian status was dependent on the husband's ethnicity (Lutz, 2006). But changes were made in 1985 in the Indian Act for a more gender equalitarian legislation on Indian status. Even if the women in both First Nations societies in Canada and in Sámi communities in Norway and Sweden have sometimes continued having a high status, or increased their status and gained more economic possibilities versus the men in their societies, they were and are still restricted by their respective national legislations.

'Public Sphere' versus 'Domestic Sphere'

In anthropological kinship studies, it was assumed that there are two domains in society — 'public sphere' and the 'domestic sphere' — used by Morgan and later on developed by Fortes (although the 'public sphere' was called 'political-jural domain') (Collier & Yanagisako, 1987). Typically, women would occupy and have power in the 'domestic sphere' while men in the 'public sphere'. Such assumption is deep-seated and is taught in Anthropology today when describing the division of labour in different societies, and that it is first in our modern western society for women to have power and important roles to play in the 'public sphere' (Collier & Yanagisako, 1987). In this dichotomy, the 'public sphere' typically involved activities with higher prestige such as political leadership, hunting and warfare, while the 'domestic sphere' involved activities with lower prestige such as childrearing, food-preparation, gathering firewood and plants (Rosaldo, 1974).

In feminist anthropology, the opposition between these two domains — the 'public' and the 'domestic' — has been challenged, suggesting that research considers the economic and political context of the 'domestic' sphere (Collier & Yanagisako, 1987). The distinction between 'domestic' and 'public' sphere had its beginnings with the Industrial Revolution (i.e. factory work replacing household production around 1760–1820). Barker (2005) points out that men, as the provider for the family, and women, as the stay-home mothers, became the ideal of the Industrial Revolution. But only women from upper classes could stay home and not work outside the household, while women from the working class or lower social group had to find ways of providing for the family (Barker, 2005).

Sámi Identity in Modern Society

Individual ownership of reindeers in the Sámi reindeer herding society is very different to the principle of collective or no principle of ownership in gathering–hunting societies. Women's right to own property meant that they had a certain economic independence; women in the past could move back to her family at the time of husband's death and bring her reindeer and other property (Pehrson, 1964).

One major change of reindeer herding is brought about by state regulation. Today reindeer herding is regulated by the Swedish state. Reindeer herding both in Norway and Sweden is considered a business enterprise and these states exert pressure on the *sameby* to apply business rationalization to reindeer herding (Olofsson, 2004; SOU, 2001). There are different classes of membership in the *sameby;* the man typically has the status as guardian in the reindeer herding unit (the extended family), and he is a Class 1 member with voting rights. A Class 1 member is someone who participates in reindeer herding on the pastures belonging to that *sameby* (Beach, 1982). Women can own reindeers, work with herding, or do other work that are indirectly linked to reindeer herding, such as taking care of the family business account without being considered a reindeer herder (Beach, 1982). Women are often not registered as members in the *sameby*. Differences in status for men and women imply that women cannot vote in the *sameby*. Men receive the state subsidiaries for reindeer herding. It is problematic for a woman to continue reindeer herding after divorce, or if the husband dies. They risk losing the reindeer, subsidiaries, and right to pasture the reindeer (Kuokkanen, 2009).

Still today the reindeers are individually owned by men, women and even children; however, it is not that easy to claim that property anymore since the reindeer need to be tended by a Class 1 member of the *sameby*. The adult male reindeer herder is most often the guardian of his wife, his children, unmarried sister (if he has one) and older parents' reindeer, which also gives him stronger voting power in the reindeer herding since he gets the votes of others (Beach, 1982).

Reindeer herding in Sweden and Norway has gone from a joint practice of the extended family where not only men and women complement each other but also people from different age groups, with no clear boundary between 'domestic sphere' and 'public sphere,' to a business enterprise where there is a clear distinction between the home (the house) and workplace (pastures in the mountains and forest). Pastures in the mountains and forests become the male arena, while the house and village become the female arena, with men still dominating reindeer herding as head of the household according to reindeer herding legislation (Eikjok, 2004).

Women's work has changed over time. Today, the women, either Sámi or non-Sámi married with a Sámi herder, often contribute both in the 'domestic sphere' and the 'public sphere' inside or outside reindeer herding. Women contribute to the 'domestic sphere' of reindeer herding; women wash clothes, cook meals and take care of reindeer hides and meat (Beach, 1982). Moreover, women are often active in the 'public sphere' of reindeer herding; that is helping with the physical work in reindeer herding — collecting, catching reindeer, building fences, and driving reindeer herders and transporting reindeers. Women work also in the 'public sphere' outside reindeer herding, as professionals (teachers, office clerks, cashiers at the store or at the pharmacy) with their income supporting the continued engagement of the family in reindeer herding (Beach, 1982; Eikjok, 2004).

A distinction between 'domestic' and 'public sphere' is in practice imposed on the reindeer herding families by Swedish legislation, and even if the women are active in the 'public sphere' or reindeer herding, her contribution is not acknowledged by the state. If women work either in the

Photo 5.1   Men and Women Doing Reindeer Herding Work in Sirges (Sirkas) Sameby in Northern Sweden in 1993.

'public sphere' or in the 'domestic sphere,' they are still considered today to be outside reindeer herding and not as reindeer herders. In a study in 2013 of young female reindeer herders in Sweden, the participants describe themselves as being considered as having peripheral roles in the reindeer herding and not being at the centre of reindeer herding as the male reindeer herders, not only in the eyes of the state, but also by other Sámi persons (Kaiser, Näckter, Karlsson, & Salander Renberg, 2015).

Sámi identity is today associated with reindeer herding. Reindeer herding has become a male occupation thus making it easier for men than women to identify themselves as Sámi. If girls wish to keep their Sámi identity they need to marry a reindeer herder. Still, there are Sámi women who are full-time herders but they are facing more difficulties than Sámi men. Sometimes it is too much to overcome these difficulties mostly brought about by legislation that they eventually give up full-time reindeer herding (Olofsson, 2004).

Conclusion

Swedish legislation of reindeer herding failed to recognize the traditional (kinship-based) organization of reindeer herding. When the Sámi became subjects of control of the Swedish legislation, they had to change their organization and gender roles to adapt to the Swedish society. Adaptation and change of gender roles are still problematic for the Sámi women today who want and need to have the connection with reindeer herding to easily identify themselves as Sámi. This situation is similar in Canada where the history of forced adaptation to Canadian legislation of First Nations has led to inequalities for women in their own communities.

When women work in reindeer herding, they are still not considered full status reindeer herders since their work is considered in the periphery of reindeer herding. There are women in reindeer herding who work not only in the periphery, but also in the forest or the mountains working directly with reindeers; however, they are not always considered reindeer herders by legislation. Sámi women who are pushing for an acknowledgement of their work in reindeer herding, and the rights that comes with it, are facing opposition among Sámi men who do not take them seriously (Kaiser et al., 2015; Sjögren, 2016).

The view of women occupying the 'domestic sphere' and men occupying the 'public sphere' imposed by Swedish and Norwegian legislation has thus become internalized in the mindset of many Sámi men and women. Therefore, it is easier for Sámi men to identify themselves as Sámi if they are reindeer herders, and their ascribed identity is Sámi. But Sámi women often find themselves outside of reindeer herding and face more difficulties to be identified by others as Sámi; they are often identified as Swedish or Norwegian.

The resulting division of 'domestic' and 'public' sphere also entails that the work which is done by Indigenous women (as well as other women) is often not only unpaid but also unrecognized. Their work should be counted as part of the economic activities of a nation-state and be included accurately in statistics (Waring, 1990; Eikjok, 2004). Women's work in Sámi society, largely unpaid, is unrecognized in legislation and show that there is still gender inequality in rich and industrialized nations such as Sweden and Norway.

Acknowledgements

I am grateful to Glenda Bonifacio for putting together this book and for her comments on my first draft. I also would like to thank Hugh Beach, Lisbeth and her family, as well as, Apmut Ivar and Sonja Kuoljok for teaching me about reindeer herding.

References

Barker, D. (2005). Beyond women and economics: Rereading "women's work". *Signs: Journal of Women in Culture and Society*, *30*(4), 189−209.

Beach, H. (1982). The place of women in the modern saameby: An issue in legal anthropology. *Antropologisk Forskning, Ymer* (Svenska Sällskapet för Antropologi och Geografi), *102*, 127−142.

Beach, H. (2000). The Sámi. In M. Freeman (Ed.), *Endangered peoples of the Arctic: Struggles to survive and thrive* (pp. 223−246). Westport, CT: Greenwood Press.

Collier, J. F., & Yanagisako, S. J. (Eds.). (1987). *Gender and kinship: Essays toward a unified analysis*. Stanford, CA: Stanford University Press.

Eikjok, J. (2004). Gender in Sápmi. Socio-cultural transformations and new challenges. *Indigenous Affairs: Indigenous Women, International Work Group for Indigenous Affairs (IWGIA)*, *1−2*, 52−57.

Etienne, M., & Leacock, E. (Eds.). (1980). *Women and colonization: Anthropological perspectives*. New York, NY: Praeger Publishers/J.F. Bergin Publishers.

Jamieson, K. (1978). *Indian women and the law in Canada: Citizen minus*. Ottawa: Minister of Supply and Services Canada.

Kaiser, N., Näckter, S., Karlsson, M., & Salander Renberg, E. (2015). Experiences of being a young female Sami reindeer herder. *Journal of Northern Studies*, *9*(2), 55−72.

Kuokkanen, R. (2009). Indigenous women in traditional economies: The case of Sámi reindeer herding. *Signs: Journal of Women in Culture and Society, 34*(3), 499—504.

Leacock, E. (1980). Montagnais women and the Jesuit program for colonization. In M. Etienne & E. Leacock (Eds.), *Women and colonization: Anthropological perspectives* (pp. 42—62). New York, NY: Praeger Publishers/J.F. Bergin Publishers.

Lehtola, V. P. (2002). *The Sámi people: Traditions in transition.* Aanaar-Inari: Kustannus-Puntsi.

Lutz, J. (2006). Gender and work in Lekwammen families, 1843—1970. In M.-E. Kelm & L. Townsend (Eds.), *In the days of our grandmothers—A reader in Aboriginal women's history in Canada* (pp. 216—249). Toronto: Toronto University Press.

Olofsson, E. (1995). *Samer utan samiska rättigheter och icke-samer med samiska rättigheter—en fråga om definition.* Master thesis, Lund University. Published in Northern Series, CERUM, Umeå University.

Olofsson, E. (2004). *In search of a fulfilling identity in a modern world: Narratives of indigenous identities in Sweden and Canada.* Dissertations in Cultural Anthropology, Uppsala University. Published in DICA Series.

Pehrson, R. (1964). *The bilateral network of social relations in Könkämä Lapp District.* Norsk Folkemuseum and Universitetsforlaget, Oslo.

Rosaldo, M. Z. (1974). Woman, culture and society: A theoretical overview. In M. Z. Rosaldo, L. Lamphere, & J. Bamberger (Eds.), *Woman, culture, and society* (Vol. 133, pp. 17—42). Stanford, CA: Stanford University Press.

Ruong, I. (1975). Historisk återblick rörande samerna [Historical perspectives on the Sami]. Samerna i Sverige.

Sametinget (2016). *Statistics.* Retrieved from www.sametinget.se/69263

Schuurman, H. (1974). *Sámi herders.* National Film Board of Canada.

Silman, J. (1994). *Enough is enough: Aboriginal women speak out.* Toronto: Women's Press.

Sjögren, P. (2016). Hur är det att vara kvinna och arbeta i renskogen? *Sametinget.* Retrieved from www.sametinget.se/75801

SOU (Statens offentliga utredningar). (1999). *Samerna—ett ursprungsfolk i Sverige.* Retrieved from http://www.regeringen.se/propositioner/propositioner/index.htm

SOU (Statens offentliga utredningar). (2001). *Renen, renbetet och rennäringen.* Retrieved from http://www.regeringen.se/propositioner/propositioner/index.htm

Uppman, B. (1978). *Samhället och samerna 1870—1925.* Umeå: Umeå universitet.

Waring, M. (1990). *If women counted: A new feminist economics.* San Francisco, CA: Harper San Francisco.

Chapter 6

Turkish Divorcées and Need for Woman-friendly Policies

Aylin Akpınar

Abstract

Gender analysis of the narratives of low-income divorcées in big cities of Ankara, Istanbul and Izmir shows that their lives are under patriarchal domination. Women are subjected to all kinds of violence in their marriage and escape it by getting a divorce. Their lives are vulnerable as the increasing numbers of lone mothers are neither morally nor socially accepted in Turkish society. The patriarchal family ideal exacerbates the situation of lone mothers who become stigmatized as divorcées. Divorce is considered a 'shame' for women, and the ideology of family is used as a political tool where persistent conservative bias ignores wife battering, rape and other types of abuse in society.

Keywords: Turkey; divorcées; family law; policy; gender equality; marriage; conservatism

Introduction

Low-income divorcées may be threatened with death or killed by their ex-husbands in Turkish society. There are far more women who do not dare to seek divorce because they are neither supported by their families nor by the social welfare system. About 53% of women in Turkey have delayed their divorce due to anxiety of being a widow and social control, while

Global Currents in Gender and Feminisms: Canadian and International Perspectives, 93–105
Copyright © 2018 by Emerald Publishing Limited
All rights of reproduction in any form reserved
ISBN: 978-1-78714-484-2/doi:10.1108/978-1-78714-483-520171010

39% were hindered by their parents and kin (T.C. Başbakanlık ASAGEM, 2009).

The so-called 'stability of the family' has been considered important politically, given the unstable situation in Turkey, due to huge gaps between social classes and ethnic as well as religious variations (Kandiyoti, 1991, p. 4). With the establishment of the Republic in 1923, legal reforms have been considered necessary to get rid of tradition-bound control on the lives of the new generation (Kandiyoti, 1995, p. 312). Despite changes that took place, some practices in line with traditional collectivist values survived, such as the code of honour and shame, and the practice of arranged marriages, cousin marriages and early marriages (Akpınar, 2003, p. 429). Although patriarchal domination was challenged in the 1960s with the increase in the educational attainment of women in urban centres, it has continued in new forms of control of women's bodies and their labour (Kıray, 1999, p. 172).

Despite legal reforms in Turkey, getting a divorce is not normatively considered within the framework of women's human rights. This chapter focuses on low-income divorcées and their struggle to get a divorce from their violence-ridden marriages. It is divided into the following sections: background of study and research methodology, impact of neoliberal and neoconservative changes in family law, subordination of women in family and marriage, violence and divorce, struggles in getting a divorce and stigma as divorcées, and women-to-women domination in kinship networks. I conclude with the need for women- and child-friendly family policies in Turkey.

Background and Research Methodology

The family is, in fact, the most dangerous arena of all for women in Turkey. In a survey in 2009, about 36% of women respondents irrespective of marital status explained that they were subjected to physical violence by men in intimate relationships, and 73% among divorcées (T.C. Başbakanlık KSGM, 2009, p. 52). In another research project, which estimated the need of financial support to combat poverty among low-income widowed, divorced or deserted women, 13% were found to be living under the risk of poverty (BÜ Sosyal Politika Forumu, 2011, p. 63). Only 38.6% of divorcées received social support through informal mechanisms such as parents, kin and neighbours. The Ministry of Family and Social Affairs launched a rights-based support programme for 150,000 poor women whose husbands had died. In their case, the family was categorically considered as still existing but without a male. Yet, 20,000 divorcées who lived at the same poverty level were not supported by this programme. The Turkish authorities seem to fear that there will be an increase in divorces if they support divorcées (Özar & Yakut Çakar, 2012, p. 8).

This chapter draws in part from data generated through in-depth interviews with 43 divorcées from September 2014 to February 2015. From this group, 18 participants belonged to low-income families. According to the survey in 2014 conducted by the Turkish Statistical Agency on 'Income and Life Conditions', nearly a quarter of Turkey's population (22.4% households) lived below the poverty line (TÜIK, 2014). The same survey indicated that 30.9% of single-headed households with at least one dependent child lived below the relative poverty line. If we consider that most single-headed households with at least one dependent child are composed of mother-child dyads, lone mothers, despite the lack of statistics in Turkish Statistical Agency Surveys in line with gender, are most vulnerable.

At the time of the interviews, out of 18 divorcées, 4 women were unemployed after having worked sporadically in various jobs, such as textile industry and services. Three other women had small clerical jobs; 4 were cleaning ladies; 1 cooked food at home for catering; and 2 worked at home as manicure-pedicurists. Two women had married again, and 2 have retired and are surviving by retirement benefits.

The aim of the study was to explore the diversities as well as similarities in women's lives. Ages of participants range from 34 to 59, with a mean of 43. Majority of them had high school education ($n = 8$) and some had primary education ($n = 4$). A lesser number had completed their junior high school education ($n = 2$) or were junior high school dropouts ($n = 2$). One woman had never been to school but was literate, and another woman was studying at the Open University. All but one woman had one or two children. Only one woman had a third child from her second marriage. Their narratives are included in this chapter using assigned pseudonyms.

Neoliberal and Neoconservative Trends on Family Policies

In Turkey, conservative family policies based on clientelism found support mainly among migrant families that were easily integrated into informal support networks by the rising Islamist party politics conducted under the guise of social municipality approach (Urhan & Urhan, 2015, p. 241). Clientelist social networks were produced and reproduced because of widespread poverty. Social facilities as well as health services for the economically disadvantaged and mother care services to promote women's fertility were provided to these families.

While low-income families were trying to survive under deteriorating economic circumstances, the conservative circles considered the nearly two-fold increase in crude divorce rates from 0.84 in 1994 to 1.33 in 2008 as a risk factor for the stability of the family (T.R. Prime Ministry Directorate General of Family and Social Research, 2009, p. 292). Family Courts were established to deal mostly with protective and social aspects of family life, and to provide expert advice, when necessary, in cases of divorce.

The ideal family in Turkey is defined by conservative circles as the nuclear family annexed to an extended family. It has been considered as an institution where raising children and caring for the sick and elderly are undertaken by women/wives who are the main caregivers. Since the establishment of the Turkish Republic in 1923, women have never been considered independent actors. They are primarily regarded as mothers responsible for the reproduction of the Turkish family and population. Women gained the right to abortion and birth control not because they were considered agents capable of controlling their own bodies, but because women's fertility has been instrumentalized to realize population policies (Öztan, 2014).

The year 2023, the 100th anniversary of the Turkish Republic, has been considered as the target year to realize a strong state. The motto is: "strong family leads to strong nation and strong nation leads to strong state" (T.C. Başbakanlık ASPB, 2013, p. 3). Women have been targets of these conservative state programmes. The Purple Roof Foundation for women's shelter has pointed to the fact that changes in abortion law have practically meant denial of the right to abortion especially for low-income women who hardly receive service at public hospitals and cannot access abortion without the consent of authorities and/or their husbands (Mor Çatı, 2015). The most recent programme launched with the title 'The Package to Support Family and Dynamic Population Structure' in March 2015 involves several measures to increase family building in early ages based on heterosexual norms. Both males and females are encouraged to build up families before the age of 27 by the promised 15% state subventions if either or both partners manage to spare bride and/or groom price up until that age. Increasing women's employment up to 35% has also been the target which means pushing the majority of female labour into unsecure work (KEIG, 2015).

Turkey is still counted in the category of societies with the lowest divorce rates even if divorce rates which was 1.67 in thousand in 2013 is expected to increase to 1.93 in thousand in 2023 (T.C. Başbakanlık ASPB, 2014, p. 48). Feminists have interpreted the claims not supported by data as pointing to the construction of divorce as a social problem. Feminist organizations were critical of the parliamentary commission's report of May 2016 on the investigation of divorces which reflected men's interests. They argued that women's and children's rights were not considered, whereas counselling by religious authorities in cases of divorces was suggested (EŞITIZ, 2016).

Changes in Family Law: Path to Gender Equality?

Turkish Family Law was secularized in 1926 with the adoption of the Swiss Civil Code in which the husband was considered as the head of the family. The principle of equality of the sexes has been guaranteed by the 1961 and 1982 constitutions. Yet, gender equality is a legal rhetoric rather than a social reality (Örücü, 2010, p. 299). In 1991, the State Ministry responsible for Women, Family and Social Services was established. In 1998, Turkey adopted the Family Protection Law. Turkey also ratified the Convention on the Elimination of all Forms of Discrimination against Women (CEDAW) and withdrew all reservations in 1999. Together with the new Family Law which took effect in 2002, the family was redefined as an institution established by 'equal partners' who should decide together in almost every marital question. Partners should contribute to marital expenses in relation to their resources. The concept of 'family residence' was introduced and the regime of 'joint ownership of property' was accepted (Moroğlu, 2000). The minimum age of matrimony for both men and women became 17, or in exceptional cases 16. Feminists have argued that this legal provision has not only legitimized but also motivated early marriages. Even the 2002 Civil Code upheld equality only as a rhetoric. For example, by tying the right of spouses to work outside the home 'to the condition of not adversely affecting the well-being of the family', the dominant position of the husband is supported (Örücü, 2010, p. 304).

Turkey follows the covenant marriage regime whereby divorce requires proof of fault and judges have ultimate authority to give their consent by weighing evidence. In contrast, Switzerland has adopted the contractual nature of marriage in 2000 (Çiftçi, 2015, p. 1793). Recently, almost all European nations have made reforms in their legal systems to unify and harmonize their family laws. However, Örücü (2010, p. 312) points out that the German Constitutional Court, The British House of Lords and the Dutch Supreme Court share the tendency in accepting the weaker party in family relationships. But in Turkey, Örücü (2010) warns that demanding alimony from respective partner regardless of financial status, as it was accepted under the 2002 Civil Code, could in fact be against women who comprise most of the poor in Turkey.

In 2011, the government restructured the State Ministry for Women and renamed it as the Ministry of Family and Social Policies. Such move of the government confirmed the social reality that Turkish women were perceived and treated as components of the family, rather than as individuals with equal status (KadınMedya, 2011).

Subordination of Women in Family and Marriage

In Turkey, one out of four marriages are conducted as cross-cousin marriage, 60.1% being from the father's side. This practice, however, seems to be waning nowadays, with only 14.4% agreeing with kin marriages (T.C. Başbakanlık ASPB, 2011, pp. 214–219). Marrying outside the kin group appears to be the trend in Turkish society.

All the 18 women in the study shared about their feelings of subordination in their natal families. There were stories of son preference or stories of parents who were indifferent to their daughters' need to receive higher education. Naciye, age 48, said:

> My father's friends had told him, 'Your daughter is not going to study anyhow' […] My mother had tried hard to convince my father, by saying 'she is still too young' […] They never thought that I might have had bad grades because of their fault […] I was a teenager […] My father had decided to give me in marriage with the first person who would ask for me […] He was 38, I was only 16.

The narrative represents masculine domination whereby daughters, because of their sexualities, were considered as nuisance in the family and were given away in marriage. Alternatively, young women opted to marry to get rid of the pressure exerted on them. Sündüz, age 51, said:

> My mother was very tough. We, the children could not share anything with her. I had my period, my breasts grew. I could not buy underwear. It was a sin. I did it in secret […] My father used to beat my mother up and my sister too. For him everything was shame, he always said 'do not wear this, do not walk like that, and do not flirt' […] After having been subjected to all that pressure, you get married with the first man who shows a little sympathy for you.

Nermin, age 39, told me that she was raped by her half-brother when she was 13. Her mother, instead of informing the father, tried to give her away in marriage to get rid of the 'shame'. She had hoped that her father might rescue her from being given away in marriage so young, and said:

I did not want to get married, I wanted to study. My father said 'I will not invest in a girl's education for the sake of a stranger who is going to get her'. I was punished for what I did not do [...] They could not kick the boy from home who raped me but gave me in marriage with the first person available.

Aysu, age 49, confided that she was forced to marry a distant relative when she was 12 years old. It was her elder sister who forced her to marry to migrate with her own family to Istanbul. The man who was 20 years older than her owned a flat and they could all stay in his house if she married him. That was the deal Aysu understood it later.

Being forced to marry as a child was not only an instance of gender discrimination but also a violation of the Convention on Children's Rights which took effect in Turkey in 1995. Women married under 18 years old comprised 29.2% compared to men at 6.5% (T.C. Başbakanlık ASPB, 2011, p. 181). The final backlash was the proposal that the perpetrators of rape could get married to girls under the age of 15 on the condition that marriages functioned successfully up to five years. Also, the perpetrators of rape, if under the age of 15, would not be considered criminals. Feminist advocates have pointed out that this proposal was against the integrity of the child-woman, and questioned who decides how marriages functioned successfully or not (EŞITIZ, 2016).

Spiral of Violence: Common Reason for Divorce

In a representative research on family structure in Turkey in 2011, the most common reasons for divorces among low-income women were their spouses' irresponsible and unconcerned attitudes (28.8%), followed by their spouses' economic incapacity (14.7%) and violence in the family (13.9%) (T.C. Başbakanlık ASPB, 2011, p. 231).

Women were already socialized in violent families and violence continued when they got married. As Sevcan, age 37, states:

My father would find any simple reason to hit children all the time [...] My girl-friends in the school had boy-friends, I also wanted to have one [...] As a fourteen-year old girl I did not know anything about men. He was eight years older than me [...] One day he grappled me from my arm and we went to the village of his friend. I remember that he battered me there. [Question: 'Did he have sex with you there?'] Yes, he said that my family would not otherwise give me in marriage. So, I agreed [...] Then, I married with the permission of my father. I left school and started working in textile atelier [...] Meanwhile, my husband continued beating me up.

Turkish women's narratives revealed continued discrimination against daughters in families by parents. Even parents with better education still held patriarchal values whereby the female sex was undervalued. As Özge, age 35, states:

My father was a faculty graduate [a well-educated man]. My mother had graduated from teacher training college [...] Yet, I was raised in a loveless family. They said that I had food to eat and I had pocket money [...] They never asked me what happened in the school. My father only complained about my friends and swore.

In the end, Özge decided to 'escape' into marriage but her husband started beating her up after a month, too, and she tried to commit suicide. When she wanted to file a divorce, her father said that it was her decision to marry and was not welcome back home. In some other cases, since women had already children when they had decided to divorce, their coming back home was considered a burden on families who lived at subsistence levels. These considerations were reasons for delaying divorce.

Struggling for Divorce, Stigmatized as Divorcée

Data reveal that low-income divorcées put up with various kinds of abuse and violence. Men do not want to divorce as they want to live within the comfort of a family life and to maintain the 'family image'. The idea of having a family gives men the power to possess the sexuality of their women (Bourdieu, 2001). Even after divorce, families hardly accept that a divorcée could have a separate life as a single parent. Saygül, age 43, said:

After I divorced [...] my brother who was four years older than me started living with me. In the week-ends I would have loved to take my son to the park but even that was not possible. My brother tried to control my life indirectly by asking to my four-year-old son 'What did you do today? Did you meet anyone in the park?' This repression even played a role in my decision for a second marriage!

When low-income women decide to divorce, this is considered as their proclamation of individuality. As Mernissi (1996, p. 110) comments, 'Individualism, ...is an alien concept and fatal to heavily collectivist Islam...I would suggest, however, that the woman, identified in the Muslim order as the embodiment of uncontrolled desires and undisciplined passions, is precisely the symbol of heavily supressed individualistic trends'.

As such, if women claim their own individuality by getting divorced, they are viewed as agents of disruption of the social order. Divorcées are regarded with suspicion in the patriarchal imagery as neither man nor 'real' woman, or as creatures apart. Within Islamic circles in Turkey, it is debatable whether a woman has the right to divorce, but a husband can give his consent to his wife. In this case, the woman should claim the right to divorce as a condition already set in the marriage contract from the beginning and that the husband should accept this condition (Topaloğlu, 1995, p. 155). The man is considered the partner who should initiate divorce if necessary as he is given the responsibility as 'the head of the family'.[1]

Divorce is considered as the last resort for women, and, in a survey of Islamic journals on family life conducted by Demir (1998, p. 45), divorcées have metaphorically been likened to persons who have been exposed to a sinking ship in the middle of the night; in other words, as women who have lost the anchor in their lives. Yet, some Islamic women respondents interviewed by Demir (1998, p. 46) have also pointed out that 'the end of love' or 'lack of share' in family life could be counted as some of the most important reasons for divorce today. These contradictory positions suggest that there is a difference between Islamic thought and Islamic conduct. It seems that in the patriarchal imagery of a woman fed by Islamic thought as well as in traditional Islamic conduct, she is considered dependent on her father as maiden, and on her husband upon marriage. However, the existence of Islamic women who find it legitimate to get rid of marriages which are not based on love and sharing a family life shows the possibility of discrepancy between conduct of women and Islamic patriarchal imagery.

The May 2016 proposal by the government on compulsory mediation in divorce processes including cases of violence 'to protect the family' was

---

[1]Karaman has pointed out that divorce is obligatory in cases where both partners demand solution due to severe family conflicts, and if referees who can be relatives of respective partners or a religious authority find it necessary. Furthermore, both husband and wife can also seek divorce at the court, and the woman who has appealed to the court can divorce by the decision of the judge and this would be religiously approved if the reasons of her divorce were suitable. She is also expected to pay back her 'mehr', i.e., bride price she has received from her husband upon marriage (see Karaman, 1995).

considered as another backlash in combatting violence in the family. One cannot fight against violence in the family while at the same time upholding the ideal of a patriarchal and/or Islamic family where a woman is expected to obey her husband's authority. Feminist scholars and legal practitioners pointed out that majority of divorcées in Turkey were in fact victims of violence. Furthermore, they emphasized the fact that compulsory mediation in divorces was forbidden by the 2011 Council of Europe Convention on preventing and combating violence against women and domestic violence, also known as Istanbul Convention as it took place in Istanbul on 12 April 2011. All forms of violence against women and domestic violence were condemned in the Istanbul Convention by 'recognising that the realisation of *de jure* and *de facto* equality between women and men is a key element in the prevention of violence against women'. The Istanbul Convention was also ratified by Turkey and went into effect on 1 August 2014 (Eşitiz, 2016).

Other Side of Patriarchy: Women-to-Women Domination

Like mothers who had given their daughters in marriage to 'avoid shame', there were women who yielded to patriarchal oppression. Aycan, age 45, said:

> My mother-in-law did not want me to divorce. She tried to hinder me from going to the hearing in court [...] She said, 'Aren't you married with him anyhow? Let him do whatever he wants, every man behaves like him' [pointing to the fact that he was adulterous].

In this narrative, Aycan's mother-in-law is trying to practice her power over the bride by referring to the implicit acceptance of her son's sexual domination in marriage. Sevil, age 51, had put up with her husband who was used to cheating with several women for more than 20 years. When she finally decided to divorce, her elder sister tried to hinder her. She said:

> My sister said that she was beaten by her husband all through her marriage. Moreover, she was married to a cousin [...] I said that we did not live in the past when divorcing one's husband was considered a shame, things were different now and she would open her eyes [...].

Sevil's elder sister could not acknowledge her own subordination as she was socialized to take part in patriarchal familial relationships only through the men (Bourdieu, 2001, p. 79).

Within the context of patriarchal relations, domestic femininity is celebrated and divorce is considered a shame because the family is called upon to bring morality. In Islamic patriarchal imagery, women as mothers and wives are considered guardians of morality. Divorcées are out of the norm because they are not a part of a family. In the patriarchal familial relationships where males set the rules, women must find their primary self as familial for men to exercise and sustain a sense of themselves. Men are considered superior to women because of their role as providers. In the case of several low-income families, husbands are not able to function well in this expected role due to their excessively immoral and selfish habits, like cheating or drinking, while domestic femininity is celebrated. Thus, the male provider role for them is a myth.

The married woman's role is to carry the heavy burden of the patriarchal family honour by not dissolving the family, the backbone of the patriarchal gender regime (Sancar, 2004). Low-income women in Turkish society are not able to divorce because of the fear of violence, be it from their parents or kin, or especially from the husband and/or husband's family. Thus, it is important to unveil gender-based masculine violence implicit in the structural inequalities in Turkish family life which not only stem from the domination of parental authority on daughters, but from the economically powerless position of wives and the idealized dominant position of husbands in marriages as well.

Conclusion

Narratives of low-income divorcées in Turkish society show that women are not given the possibility to develop their capabilities and live their lives with human dignity (Nussbaum, 2000). Many women who are forced into marriages are obliged to put up with abusive relationships. Low-income Turkish women have legal right to marriage and divorce, but they have no access to choose and, thus, lack the capability to exercise agency as they are forced into marriages and are threatened with violence should they dare to divorce.

As getting a divorce is not considered simply getting rid of a bad marriage, Turkish women are expected to sacrifice themselves for the sake of 'protecting the family'. Women's empowerment as individuals is neither supported by their families nor by the society at large and, hence, the idea of 'single parent household' is not widely acknowledged in Turkey. Even if lone mothers usually receive the custody of their children, they face difficulties receiving alimony from ex-husbands due to complexities in legal procedure and male bias of the system.

Therefore, there is a need to evolve a woman and child friendly policy to support divorcées by acknowledging them as individuals belonging to a disadvantaged group. Policy makers should recognize their capability and assist this marginalized group of women develop themselves and their children for a better future. This goal cannot be accomplished without feminist organizations and activists who steadily fight for women's human rights, including the acceptance of lone mothers as decent citizens of Turkish society who can take care of their children, given the necessary financial, social and moral support.

Acknowledgement

This project was supported by the Marmara University Scientific Research Committee, Project no. SOS-A-050614-0253, 2014.

References

Akpınar, A. (2003). The honour/shame complex revisited: Violence against women in the migration context. *Women's Studies International Forum*, *26*(5), 425−442.

Bourdieu, P. (2001). *Masculine domination*. Cambridge, MA: Polity Press.

BÜ Sosyal Politika Forumu. (2011). *Eşi Vefat Etmiş Kadınlar için Bir Nakit Sosyal Yardım Programı Geliştirilmesine Yönelik Araştırma Projesi Final Raporu.* Retrieved from http://www.spf.boun.edu.tr/content_files/SPF-SYDGM_Nihai Rapor.pdf

Çiftçi, P. (2015). Boşanma Sisteminin Yargılamada Doğurduğu Temel Hak Ihlalleri ve Ispat Sorunları. *Dokuz Eylül Üniversitesi Hukuk Fakültesi Dergisi*, *16*, Özel Sayı 2014, 1741−1821.

Demir, H. (1998). *Islamcı Kadının Aynadaki Sureti.* Istanbul: Sel Yayıncılık.

EŞITIZ. (2016). *Eşitiz'den Boşanma Komisyonunun Önerilerine Tepki*, May 16. Retrieved from http://www.bianet.org/bianet/insan-haklari/174845-e sitiz-den-bosanma-komisyonunun-onerilerine-tepki

KadınMedya. (2011). *Kadın Bakanlığı Kaldırılmasın*, June 10. Retrieved from http://www.kadinmedya.com/haber/esitlik-mekanizmaları-kadin-platformu-mucadelede-kararlı.php

Kandiyoti, D. (1991). Introduction. In D. Kandiyoti (Ed.), *Women, Islam and the state* (pp. 1−21). Philadelphia, PA: Temple University Press.

Kandiyoti, D. (1995). Patterns of patriarchy: Notes for an analysis of male dominance in Turkish society. In Ş. Tekeli (Ed.), *Women in modern Turkish society: A reader* (pp. 306−318). London: Zed Books.

Karaman, H. (1995). *Islam'da Kadın ve Aile.* Istanbul: Ensar Neşriyat.

KEIG. (2015). *Ailenin ve Dinamik Nüfus Yapısının Korunması Paketine Itirazımız Var! Aileye Köle Sermayeye Kul Olmayacağız*, January 28. Retrieved from http://www.keig.org/gundemimiz.aspx?id=25

Kıray, M. (1999). Türkiye'de Kadının Rolü Nasıl Değişmiştir. In *Seçme Yazılar* (pp. 168−178). Istanbul: Bağlam Yayınları.

Mernissi, F. (1996). *Women's rebellion & Islamic memory*. London: Zed Books.

Mor Çatı. (2015). *Ücretsiz, Güvenli, Erişilebilir Kürtaj Hakkının Takipçisiyiz*, February 26. Retrieved from https://www.morcati.org.tr/tr/301-ucretsiz-guvenli-erisilebilir-kurtaj-hakkinin-takipcisiyiz

Moroğlu, N. (2000). *Yasalarda Kadın Erkek Eşitliğinin Sağlanması ve Uygulanmasında Karşılaşılan Aksaklıkların Giderilmesi için Kadın Avukatların İşbirliği*. Retrieved from http://www.barobirlik.org.tr/dosyalar/duyurular/2015/20150620_tubakkom-kitap.pdf

Nussbaum, M. (2000). Women's capabilities and social justice. *Journal of Human Development, 1*(2), 220–247. doi:10.1080/14649880020008749

Örücü, E. (2010). The rhetoric of equality juxtaposed to family realities: The wife – an equal partner or a protégé? In A. Singer, M. Jäntera-Järeborg, & A. Schlytter (Eds.), *Familj, Religion, Rätt. En Antologi om Kulturella Spänningar i Familjen – Med Sverige och Turkiet som Exempel* (pp. 295–317). Uppsala: Iustus Förlag.

Özar, Ş., & Yakut Çakar, B. (2012). *Aile, Devlet ve Piyasa Kıskacında Boşanmış Kadınlar*. Retrieved from http://www.spod.org.tr/turkce/wp-content/uploads/2013/06/Özar-ve-Yakut-Çakar-Feminist-Yaklaşımlar-Şubat-2012-2.pdf

Öztan, E. (2014). Türkiye'de ailecilik, biyosiyaset ve toplumsal cinsiyet rejimi. *Toplum ve Bilim, 130*, 176–188.

Sancar, S. (2004). Otoriter Türk Modernleşmesinin Cinsiyet Rejimi. *Doğu-Batı, Kasım 2004*, 197–211.

T.C. Başbakanlık ASAGEM. (2009). *Boşanma Nedenleri Araştırması*. (N. Türkarslan Ed.), Ankara: ASAGEM.

T.C. Başbakanlık A.S.P.B. (2011). *Türkiye'de Aile Yapısı Araştırması*. Ankara: A.S.P.B.

T.C. Başbakanlık ASPB. (2013). *T.C. Aile ve Sosyal Politikalar Bakanlığı 2013 Yılı Faaliyet Raporu*. Retrieved from http://www.aile.gov.tr/duyurular/aile-ve-sosyal-politikalar-bakanligi-2013-yili-idare-faaliyet-raporu

T.C. Başbakanlık A.S.P.B. Aile ve Toplum Hizmetleri Genel Müdürlüğü. (2014). *Türkiye Boşanma Nedenleri Araştırması* (M. Turğut Ed.). Istanbul: Araştırma ve Sosyal Politika Serisi, 23.

T.C. Başbakanlık K.S.G.M. (2009). *Türkiye'de Kadına Yönelik Aile İçi Şiddet*. Ankara: K.S.G.M.

T.R. Prime Ministry Directorate General of Family and Social Research. (2009). *The researches on family*, In: M. Turğut & A. Abduşoğlu (Eds.). Ankara: Directorate General of Family & Social Research Publications.

TÜIK. (2014). *Gelire Dayalı Yoksulluk İstatistikleri*. Retrieved from http://www.tuik.gov.tr

Urhan, G., & Urhan, B. (2015). AKP Döneminde Sosyal Yardım. In M. Koray & A. Çelik (Eds.), *Himmet, Fıtrat, Piyasa AKP Döneminde Sosyal Politika* (pp. 229–258). Istanbul: İletişim.

Chapter 7

Gender Equality Education and Media Literacy: Primary Prevention Strategies in New Zealand

Panteá Farvid

Abstract

Gender inequality in New Zealand, and globally, remains a social justice and human rights issue despite decades of feminist activism and scholarship as well as social and political interventions. This chapter outlines the strides in gender equality in New Zealand, and the continued manifestations of gender *inequality* within the country. It argues that to address persistent patterns of gender inequality, a primary prevention approach that deals with gender polarity and then sexism is needed *before* it takes hold. New Zealand considers best practice from other countries in implementing gender equality education and better media literacy in schools. Drawing on existing Scandinavian policies and other empirical work, this chapter explores how such gender equality education policy is outlined.

Keywords: Gender equality; education; media literacy; sexism; policy; gender roles

As the first country in the world to grant women the vote in 1893, New Zealand has a long way to go to achieve genuine equality across all genders. As a relatively affluent and ostensibly democratic and egalitarian nation, with a rich history of women's rights achievements, there is an

Global Currents in Gender and Feminisms: Canadian and International Perspectives, 107−125
Copyright © 2018 by Emerald Publishing Limited
All rights of reproduction in any form reserved
ISBN: 978-1-78714-484-2/doi:10.1108/978-1-78714-483-520171028

alarming (and growing) rate of *inequality* between genders. The domains of this inequality span gender-based violence, women's public participation and leadership, the continued gender pay gap, minority and immigrant women's deteriorating status, among others. Such trends have led to one of New Zealand's major women's organisations, the National Council of Women (NCWNZ), to state: 'women's development and advancement has stalled and is sliding backwards' (2016). Many scholars, feminists and community organisations have similarly voiced concerns over the current state of gender affairs in New Zealand (NCWNZ, 2016; Redstall, 2016; Rotherham, 2013).

In this chapter, I first examine the current and continued manifestations of gender inequality in New Zealand, and the deteriorating social and economic position of women. Drawing on empirical research, academic theorising and examples of successful gender policies, I offer a way forward in terms of primary prevention strategies to create a more gender egalitarian society. My main argument is that for gender equality or feminist policies to get mass buy-in in the contemporary sociocultural context, be taken up *and* be successful, we need to move away from a focus on women to a focus on *gender* (as well as masculinity). This statement, which might seem obvious to some but controversial to others, denotes the need to debunk gender polarity with a focus on dismantling the current *gender system* (including dominant versions of masculinity and femininity) which creates gender inequality (Farvid, 2016a). We need to move away from seeing gender inequality as solely a 'women's issue'. Women are heavily disadvantaged as a group due to the shape of the current gender system, but the problem does not sit with women alone. Rather, it is a part of an enduring sexist gender system — and problematic versions of dominant masculinity — which in many ways are the source of gender-based difficulty women (and men) experience in daily life (Farvid, 2016a).

To bolster women's position, we need to address the sexist gender *system* which produces particular ways of being a man and a woman as better than others. We need to broaden the conversation and address the *primary* causes of gender inequality — which starts with dismantling a polarised heterosexual gender system. In a sociocultural context rife with neoliberal ideology, so-called postfeminism and changing femininities and masculinities, a critical analysis of *gender* relations is not only desperately needed, but also essential.

In what follows, I outline the current state of gender inequality in New Zealand, and then move on to suggest primary prevention strategies for preventing gender-based inequality. That is, the introduction of gender equality education, that includes better media literacy, in schools across the country. Considering that gender inequality results in a myriad of public health, social justice and other social issues, which are hugely costly, the government needs to make gender equality education a primary goal in future educational policy. Much like the attention given in schools to environmental issues, dietary health and safety from 'stranger danger', teaching children that gender is fluid and that both boys and girls have the capacity to take on and perform any roles or identities that are available is desperately needed.

Gender and In/Equality in New Zealand

Genuine gender equality means that everyone, regardless of gender, should have the same access, rights, privileges and burdens in daily life (Farvid, 2014a). This means that everyone should have the capacity to work, support themselves financially, be supported by the state if they are not able to earn a living via paid work, live free from violence, have control over their bodies, have autonomy in daily decision-making and take on an equal share of unpaid labour. Greater equality also means sharing power and influence within society.

In New Zealand, and globally, considerable strides have been made towards gender equality since women were granted the vote albeit invariably between developed and developing countries. Some of the gains in New Zealand include increased participation in paid labour; better access to primary, secondary and tertiary education; abortion rights and better access to birth control; tightening of sexual assault and rape laws; and wider participation in politics and governance. In politics, Marilyn Waring, for example, is a prominent feminist scholar who was elected into the New Zealand Government in 1975 at the young age of 23. She was the 15th elected women member of the New Zealand Parliament, and one of only two women elected that year. Since then women's participation in public and political life has grown considerably.

However, these feminist strides seem to have remained stagnant for some time and there are clear signs of regression when it comes to overall gender parity in New Zealand (NCWNZ, 2016; Redstall, 2016; Rotherham, 2013). According to the 2016 Global Gender Gap report produced by the World Economic Forum, New Zealand ranked 9 out of 144 countries, having dropped considerably from number 7 in 2012 (and steadily from 6 in 2012/2011 and 5 in 2010/2009), and regained its standing from number 13 in 2014 and number 10 in 2015. The drop in ranking since 2009 coincides with a change in a left-centrist Labour Government to the right-centrist National Government, mostly critiqued for holding policy positions that are less woman-centred or concerned with gender equality. New Zealand currently lags behind Nordic countries (Iceland, Finland, Norway,

Sweden), as well as Rwanda, Ireland, Philippines and Slovenia. When it comes to the tested categories in the gender equality index, New Zealand ranks 30 in economic participation and opportunity, 1 (joint with many others) on educational attainment, a shocking 105 on health and survival and 15 on political empowerment. The state of affairs is not improving fast enough for women in New Zealand and that the overall picture in the specific measured domains is mixed.

The central manifestations of gender inequality in New Zealand are manyfold. They span gender-based violence, including sexual violence, intimate partner violence (IPV), family violence, online and offline harassment and men's violence against boys or with other men. Gender pay gap and women's lack of participation in society, including holding powerful positions, also remain. The following section examines these forms of inequalities and provides the bases to embark primary prevention strategies in education.

Male Violence: Women and Children

The term gender-based violence denotes all forms of physical and non-physical violence perpetrated against women and girls, such as 'physical, sexual or mental harm or suffering … including threats of such acts, coercion or arbitrary deprivation of liberty, whether occurring in public or in private life' (World Health Organisation, 2016). It is typically girls and women who experience this sort of violation, but 16% of New Zealand males will also experience sexual abuse before the age of 18 (typically from a family member) (New Zealand Family Violence Clearinghouse [NZFVC], 2016). Although the abuse of men by other men is more common, a small percentage of male survivors have been offended against by a woman. The eradication of violent masculinity thus not only requires men's active involvement, but will also directly benefit them (Katz, 2012). Gender-based violence is a major public health concern, a violation of human rights and comes at an extremely high cost to New Zealand society.

Much of the acute violence experienced by women and children is within the family home. In New Zealand, one in three women (35%) report having experienced physical and/or sexual IPV in their lifetime (NZFVC, 2016). When psychological or emotional abuse is included, this increases to half of the female population (55%) (NZFVC, 2016). As the New Zealand Family Violence Clearinghouse (2016) reports, in 2015, the police recorded six homicides by an intimate partner and all the offenders were men. There were 110,114 family violence investigations by New Zealand Police — there were 7406 recorded male assaults female victimisations and 4629 proceedings against offenders for breaching a protection order (NZFVC, 2016). In the same year, 5264 applications were made for protection orders: 4857 (89%) were made by women and 513 (9%) by men, with a corresponding 4774 (89%) of respondents being men and 543 (10%) women (NZFVC, 2016). Over 80,000 crisis calls were made to New Zealand Women's Refuge, with almost 5000 women accessing advocacy services in the community and just under 3000 women and children staying in safe houses (National Collective of Independent Women's Refuges [NCIWR], 2015). Between 2009 and 2012, an average of 13 women, 10 men and 9 children were killed each year because of family violence — with 76% of intimate partner violence-related deaths perpetrated by men and 24% perpetrated by women (Family Violence Death Review Committee [FVDRC], 2014; Statistics New Zealand, 2016).

When considering adult sexual assault, one in five women will be a victim of rape or attempted rape in her lifetime (Ministry of Justice, 2015) and about 17% of New Zealand women report having experienced sexual violence by an intimate partner in their lifetime (Fanslow & Robinson, 2011). An alarming 'rape culture' is increasingly evident in New Zealand (and abroad), and it is becoming more and more difficult to get convictions in sexual assault cases. This was recently demonstrated by the infamous Roast Busters case where a group of young New Zealand men systematically and repeatedly planned to intoxicate (typically) underage girls at parties and gang rape them or engage in lewd acts with them (Bilby, 2015). These instances were boasted about on a private Facebook page, sometimes with accompanying videos or pictures of the incidents. The New Zealand police were massively criticised for taking little action, misleading the public, as well as not being able to secure any convictions, even though they had been following the case for some time and multiple complaints were made by different girls (e.g. Hunt, 2015). The horrific nature of this event and the inaction of the police, the boys' school and the victim blaming that ensued saw this case in New Zealand media for months. Many touted it as evidence of an enduring and entrenched rape culture that seems to be escalating (e.g. Marvelly, 2015) with no immediate remedy.

Male Violence: Other Men and Boys

It is now well documented that men's violence and aggression against other men is one of the biggest killers and producers of harm for boys and men (Katz, 2000, 2012, 2013). Men on average physically assault other men at far greater rates than they assault women, and men make up 90% of the prison population for violent assaults (Department of Corrections, 2015). Physical violence is not only normalised as part and parcel of heterosexual manhood, but displaying aggression that results in dominance or control provides men with greater status among their peers (Connell, 2005). We live in a society where there are highly contradictory messages about men's violence. On the one hand, violence is touted as inappropriate or to be avoided, and, on the other hand, media portrayals of idealised masculinity portray men as extremely aggressive, controlling or powerful. Within movies and popular television series, any conflict resolution by men is typically done so by fists or guns. Men are taught to supress their emotions, besides perhaps anger, and that the only appropriate expression of any internal affect is those that are aggressive in nature (Farvid, 2016a).

Furthermore, there are many high impact and high contact sports that are celebrated within our culture, even though they directly depict, glorify and reward male aggression and violence (e.g. boxing, martial arts sports, ultimate fighting championships [UFC], rugby, ice hockey, American football). The continued prevalence and glorification of war and armed conflict also feed into an idealisation of violent masculinity. Although boys are taught that violence is technically socially acceptable, the cultural messages surrounding men's violence is not only mixed but also seen as an enticement and inducement to violence. Dominant or hegemonic forms of masculinity teach men that to be a man one should be able to exert power, either physically or otherwise (Connell, 2005), not only over other men, but especially over women (Farvid, 2016a).

In New Zealand, one in five sexually abused children is a male, and the majority of this abuse is carried out by male family members (or is deemed incest) (Rape Prevention Education [RPE], 2016). While one out of three girls are sexually abused before she turns 16 years old, it is one in seven for boys by the time they reach adulthood (HELP, 2016). Male survivors of rape are often younger than females, and a man is more likely to be gang raped, and with more force (RPE, 2016). While the abuse of men by other men is more common, a small percentage of male survivors have been offended against by a woman (RPE, 2016). Hence, boys and men, along with girls and women, will hugely benefit from curbing violent, aggressive and abusive masculinity (Katz, 2012).

Women's Participation: Public and Economy

Although women in New Zealand make up more than half of the population and workforce, and two thirds of university graduates (Masselot & Brand, 2015), they are still poorly represented in high-paying public, political, governance and executive positions (Humane Rights Commission [HRC], 2012). Leading scholars, social commentators and activists continue to note that the glass ceiling is still existent in New Zealand and globally (Masselot & Maymont, 2015).

Three key factors that create barriers to women's career progression and taking on leadership roles include: sexist attitudes (unconscious bias based on gender stereotypes), taking career breaks (the requirement for women to be the main caregivers of children) and accessing low status but flexible work (where women trade down their skills to gain flexibility) (Ministry of Women's Affairs [MWA], 2013). Although women in New Zealand make up more than 50% of the population and workforce, they are still poorly represented in high-paying executive positions (HRC, 2012). The state of affairs is much better for women in the government and public sector, but the private sector is still largely male dominated. The New Zealand Government continues to have about 30% women members — a statistic that remained stable since 1996. In the public sector, statistics from the Human Resource Capability Survey carried out by the State Services Commission in 2012 indicated that women make up 59% of the Public Service workforce, but that only 42% of senior roles were held by women (Sanderson, 2013). Furthermore, when the top tiers were examined separately, for that same year, only 4% of chief executives were women, with 38% in the second tier and 44% in the third tier (Sanderson, 2013). In the 2000s, women held some of the highest positions in New Zealand (such as prime minister, governor-general, attorney general and chief justice), and the current numbers have led researchers to note that when it comes to the public sector, the 'percentage of women decreases as seniority increases' (Sanderson, 2013, p. 9). In the public sector, Sanderson (2013) states:

> Of the top 100 companies listed on the New Zealand Stock Exchange, the proportion of female board members is just over 9%, and only 4% of these companies have women chief executives — leaving New Zealand behind Australia, the United Kingdom, the United States and a number of European countries. (p. 8)

There is a persistent gender gap in the New Zealand labour market and this refers to occupational segregation based on gender, both horizontal and vertical, pay equity and work and family life balance (Casey, Skibnes, & Pringle, 2011). For the last five years, women on average have earned 10 cents less than men per dollar (MWA, 2015), and spent twice as long on unpaid work. Unlike some Nordic countries (e.g. Norway), New Zealand policymakers and employers as well as employees tend to not favour direct policies or a quota system to address gender issues in the workplace (Casey et al., 2011; Masselot & Brand, 2015). Even self-regulatory models favoured by United Kingdom and Australia that require reporting gender composition of companies to the government have not been adopted. Instead, an indirect approach has been taken since the 1990s, and this has so far had 'very limited effectiveness in advancing gender equality' in all areas of the labour force (Casey et al., 2011, p. 628) and has even been touted as completely 'failing' (Masselot & Brand, 2015). In New Zealand, the Equal Employment Opportunities (EEO) trust was established in 1992, which sought to promote the benefits of EEO to businesses. However, along with others, former EEO Commissioner Judy McGregor noted that EEO legislation itself does not go far enough in achieving gender equality and gets caught up dealing with complaints instead of developing mandates and legislation (McGregor, 2011). Furthermore, as Powell (2011) points out, 'the legal requirement of equal opportunities for men and women in the workplace is not equivalent to a societal commitment to ensure that they will be similarly oriented to take advantage of such opportunities' (p. 2). Such commitment would require a shift in mind-set when it comes to gender equality in the workplace.

Inadequate legislation, ongoing discrimination, a lack of workplace flexibility and other organisational factors are said to inhibit female progression through the ranks of management. Other factors include male-dominant cultures in the workplace, negative stereotyping and preconceptions of women, a lack of developmental opportunities for women, inflexible workplaces in job design and career paths, and gender-based harassment (McPherson, 2010). The dominance of male values and a belief that women do not make good leaders are also seen as major barriers to women's advancement, ahead of conflict with family obligations (McPherson, 2010). In professions that do offer some flexibility, the outcome is not much better. For example, although there are relatively equal number of postgraduate graduates in New Zealand, only 25% of professorial positions are held by women across the country.

In terms of health and well-being, young women in New Zealand are twice as likely to be hospitalised for intentional self-harm, present with much higher rates of eating difficulties across all ages, and rates of anxiety and depression are also much higher in adult women than men (Farvid, 2016a). New Zealand's indigenous female population, Maori women, do much more poorly when it comes to health, well-being and victims of gender-based violence.

Within this context, surprisingly, it is still very difficult for feminists or politicians to argue that gender provides a 'structural disadvantage' in New Zealand (Simon-Kumar, 2011, p. 75). Many argue this is part of a backlash towards feminism since the 1980s where the New Zealand context has become quite hostile to addressing specific interests of women, with many men and women, especially in government not accepting a 'feminist position' (Curtin, 2008). The sociocultural context of New Zealand at present does not lend itself easily to feminist policies or women-centred approaches to dealing with gender inequality. For example, popular opinion research on women CEOs and academic analyses all indicate that introducing a gender quota system in the private sector would not be well-received (Casey et al., 2011). Although a quota system could be exactly what is needed, considering not much has changed for about 40 years, such initiatives directly conflict with prevalent notions of the importance of an individualist work ethic and dislike for anything that positions the government as treating New Zealand as a 'nanny state'. For example, in 2013 when the Labour Party of New Zealand attempted to introduce a gender-based quota system to ensure 45% of its MPs would be women in future elections, it was met with hostility by the public and branded as implementing a 'man ban' by local media (Trevett, 2013).

Although a targeted quota system seems to be exactly what New Zealand needs when it comes to equal representation of women in the public and private sector, popular buy-in is difficult under the current sociocultural conditions. One way to address such forms of sexism which manifests in widespread gender inequality is to focus on a primary prevention approach that seeks to stop the formation of sexism and sexist attitudes before they are formed. To address the issues stated above, I outline a way forward for New Zealand in terms of primary prevention vision that needs to be transformed into policy to ensure gender equality in the future.

Primary Prevention Strategies

(Re)dismantling the Link between Sex and Gender

> One is not born, but rather becomes, a woman [or man].
> (de Beauvoir, 1953, p. 301)

This powerful and renowned statement refers to the notion that *sex* and *gender* are different. Sex refers to the biological characteristics that distinguish one as boy or girl and gender denotes the moulding of boys and girls into masculine or feminine beings. Research and theorising has long indicated that gender inequality exists primarily due to the idea that there are two separate and vastly different 'genders', with men and women positioned as having different skills or capabilities (de Beauvoir, 1953; Millett, 1970; Oakley, 1972; Rubin, 1975).

Gender is not biological or 'naturally' tied to bodies; it is a cultural artefact that constitutes women and men as inherently different (Butler, 1990). This gendered socialisation has long been identified as a problem because (traditional) masculine traits (i.e. assertiveness, rationality, aggressiveness) were, and are, more highly regarded and given to dominant social roles, whereas (traditional) feminine traits (i.e. nurturance, sensitivity, intuitiveness) were, and are, associated with submission/dependence and given to less socially valued roles (Lohman, 1981). Historically, women's (financial) dependence on men, as well as the cultural ideology that women were inferior to men, had cast women into servicing men's supposed needs (e.g. sexual, domestic upkeep) (Lohman, 1981). Women's worth has often been contingent on how she looked, and much energy has gone into women constructing themselves into visual objects of desire for men (Wolf, 2002), as well as her role as mother or caregiver (Rutman, 1996), at the expense of mass participation in public or political life. Women's sexuality (i.e. the avenues within which women have been legally or socially allowed to 'express' or make visible female sexuality) have been theorised as intertwined with a sex/gender system that only allows for very limited versions of acceptable femininity and female sexuality (Rubin, 1984), based on binaries such as chaste/moral or promiscuous/depraved (Ussher, 1989).

Owed much to the activism of second-wave feminism in the West, these categories and dichotomous understandings of men and women as vastly different and suited to different roles within society have softened greatly over the years. Even very recent and extensive contemporary reviews of the literature within the biological, psychological and social sciences has indicated that:

> There is little evidence that gender identity is fixed at birth or an early age. Though biological sex is innate ... gender is ... defined or expressed in ways that have little or no biological basis. (Mayer & McHugh, 2016, p. 87)

It is now well understood by most in academia, even from the most traditional disciplines, that gender is a social construct. For example, the American Psychological Association (APA) has extended de Beauvoir's definition in recent years to read:

> Sex is assigned at birth, refers to one's biological status as either male or female, and is associated primarily with physical attributes such as chromosomes, hormone prevalence, and external and internal anatomy. Gender refers to the socially constructed roles, behaviours, activities, and attributes that a given society considers appropriate for boys and men or girls and women. These influence the ways that people act, interact, and feel about themselves. While aspects

of biological sex are similar across different cultures, aspects
of gender may differ. (APA, 2016, p. 1)

Furthermore, multiple reviews and meta-analyses of the psychological
literature over the last 30 years have consistently found that men and
women are more similar than they are different when it comes to a whole
host of psychological traits and mental functioning (Hyde, 2007; Petersen
& Hyde, 2011). These include cognitive functioning, mathematical abilities,
personality traits, social behaviours, temperament, emotions, aggression
and leadership as well as psychological well-being (Hyde, 2007; Petersen &
Hyde, 2011). Some minor differences have been found when it comes to
3D mental rotation, the personality dimension of agreeableness/tender-
mindedness, sensation seeking, the expression of physical aggression, some
sexual behaviours like masturbation, pornography consumption and attitudes about casual sex (Petersen & Hyde, 2011). However, such differences
can also be explained by the cultural expectations we have of men and
women, and the effect disappears the more gender-neutral the social or
experimental context (Hyde, 2007; Petersen & Hyde, 2011). In countries
with greater gender equality, there are much smaller gender gaps in mathe-
matics performance and sexual behaviours (Petersen & Hyde, 2011). Such
evidence has prompted some scholars to promote *a gender similarity
hypothesis*, rather than the gender *differences* discourse that we typically
hear of (Hyde, 2005, 2007; Petersen & Hyde, 2011).

But the common approach to understanding gender, within popular culture, the media, the education system and mass psyche still needs immediate reworking. Such a reworking is needed not only to address gender
inequality but also to allow for a diversity of identity formations and
greater gender fluidity (Farvid, 2016a). A fluid approach also captures
those who identify as transgender, intersex and non-gender conforming.
The source of many so-called 'women's issues' stem from a polarised
gender system and aggressive or domineering versions of macho masculinity (Farvid, 2016a). The focus needs to shift from being mostly on women
to changing the nature of gender relations, debunking gender polarity and
promoting softer masculinities that do not only seek to dominate or be
powerful. To do this, primary prevention strategies addressing how gender
is socially and culturally understood, as well as constructed, are needed to
address the covert and overt sexisms that lead to gender inequality.

Beyond the Gender Binary: Gender Equality Education in Schools

New Zealand needs to introduce gender equality education throughout the
school years, beginning at primary school, to address gender equity issues

within our society. There are three different ways of understanding gender equality education. The first is gender equality in terms of *access* to schooling where both boys and girls get that same rights and access to education (United Nations Children's Fund [UNICEF], 2015). The second is in parity and treating boys and girls the same at school as well as offering them the same opportunities and subjects (United States Agency for International Development [USAID], 2008). The third is educating boys and girls about the cultural, social and political history of gender inequality as well as the socially constructed nature of gender roles and norms (Richardson, 2015). The latter is the type of gender equality education I am referring to for implementation in New Zealand schools.

Although still a problem in other countries (Baker & Wiseman, 2009), boys and girls in New Zealand have what is considered gender equality and parity (Subrahmanian, 2005) when it comes to educational access and treatment within the educational system. What we do not have is specific educational curricula that addresses the history and nature of gender inequality, gender role stereotyping and sexism, which provide students with the tools to dismantle rigid gender binaries (including sexism) and offer them more options for gender identification and expression.

In other countries, Sweden has implemented some strategies to provide boys and girls the opportunity to take on diverse roles and have the capacity to be who or what suites them individually, rather than fitting into pre-defined categories and expectations (Farvid, 2014a). The Swedish government strongly emphasises gender equality in their educational laws, stating that 'gender equality should reach and guide all levels of the Swedish educational system' (Sweden, 2015). From pre-school level onwards, their aim is to give 'children the same opportunities in life, regardless of their gender, by using teaching methods that counteract traditional gender patterns and gender roles' (Sweden, 2015). This gender equality approach is weaved into the educational system with both the teaching and the curricular reflecting these policy aims.

Recently, research within the United States (US) has interrogated the public schooling system, calling for an urgent deinstitutionalisation of what is referred to as 'sextyping' (the reifying of gender norms through the education system) (Richardson, 2015). By doing some extensive research into the culture, curriculum and teaching styles in US public schools, Richardson (2015) argued that the current system was not only reifying traditional gender binaries, but also subtly upholding patriarchal values. He argued that schools need to better understand the complexities of gender and 'adopt policies and curriculum, train teachers, and interrogate their practices so that they might produce and serve a better, more well-rounded citizenry' (p. 182). In addition, schools could become much more interested and invested in gender equality and equity, seeking a shift 'toward a more radical space of supporting students' actualisation of individual desires and capabilities' (Richardson, 2015, p. 183).

Based on my own research on gender and (hetero)sexuality for over a decade (Beres & Farvid, 2010; Farvid, 2014b, 2015; Farvid & Aisher, 2016; Farvid & Braun, 2006, 2013, 2014, 2017; Farvid & Glass, 2014; Farvid, Braun, & Rowney, 2016) the Swedish model of gender equality education (Sweden, 2017) and some of the suggestions made by Richardson (2015), I then make the following recommendations on gender equality education for New Zealand policymakers and educators:

- Gender equality education needs to guide all levels of the New Zealand educational system.
- From primary school onwards, the tenets of a gender equality approach (debunking rigid gender norms and gender polarity) needs to be incorporated into the school curricula.
- The training of teachers needs to incorporate gender theory and gender equality at tertiary institutions and teacher training colleges.
- Teachers need to understand the flexible spectrum of gender, and interpretations of performativity and socialisation housed within feminist and gender theory.
- At school, students need to be seen as more than just the sum of their gender, but as complex citizens of the school and the world, and from a *holistic* perspective.
- Each student needs to be approached as a sophisticated individual who is capable of embodying and desiring several changing gendered identities.
- School curricular needs to include lessons on the social production of gender, gender roles, gender norms and categories.
- Schools need to incorporate curricular on contemporary and global ethical citizenship, which includes an awareness, acceptance and celebration of diversity and the promotion of egalitarianism and equality for all humans (Biesta, 2010; Gardner, Cairns, & Lawton, 2000).
- Schools need to include lessons on ethical sexual and relational practices towards all (Carmody, 2005, 2009), regardless of their gender or sexual orientation (including in online communication).
- The education system and curricular need to identify and interrupt heteronormative, heterosexist and patriarchal practices that are part of society at large as well as at times part of the school culture.
- Schools need to introduce the use of gender neutral language that challenges the boy/girl binary.
- Schools should provide gender inclusive bathrooms for transgender and non-gender conforming students.

These primary prevention strategies for gender equality in education work in conjunction with media literacy. That is, media literacy curricula (Potter, 2014; Thoman & Jolls, 2003) promoting critical thinking around gender, identity, sexuality, relationships and representation should be more thoroughly integrated. At present, New Zealand teaches some media literacy within the subject of media studies, but only if the subject is offered in secondary schools.

However, we live in a society saturated with idealised media images that portray gender, sexuality, relationships and stereotypical male and female roles. Furthermore, rapid technological developments (e.g. smartphones, Internet, social networking) have led to mass media becoming widespread, and one of the main forums for relaying information and cultural messages (Abreu & Yildiz, 2016). Young people today are interacting with and navigating media (often via personal technology) in unprecedented rates (Statistics New Zealand, 2011). The current media saturated environment increasingly depicts extremely narrow definitions of appropriate womanhood and manhood, including highly sexualised and gendered themes. Girls and boys need the tools from an early age to critically dismantle stereotypical, violent and unrealistic media content. As the use of online media increases, so has online harassment and 'trolling' (the deliberate attempt to cleverly and often secretly upset people, usually via the Internet), which can have a gendered element (Farvid, 2016b). Ethical digital citizenship education, as part of media literacy curricula, can help young people when it comes to navigating the online world and battling new forms of gender-based harassment.

Conclusion

The basis of gender inequality is the idea that there are two discrete and distinct genders and that one of these genders is inferior to the other. Feminist thought, theorising, research and activism have for decades sought to dismantle and rework this unegalitarian approach. To address ongoing manifestations of gender inequality in New Zealand, we need some new and radical feminist inspired approaches — located in education and schooling.

In this chapter, I have argued that the way forward for New Zealand is a new form of policy intervention that focuses on *primary prevention* in the form of gender equality education at school. As a primary prevention strategy, we not only need to teach our boys and girls that gender is much more fluid than that, but that besides a few anatomic differences, there is very little else that differentiate males/females. If boys/men and girls/women are virtually the same socially, psychologically and cognitively, then there is no need to try and fit young people into predefined gender-specific categories. By opening the possibilities of gender identity performativity, young boys and girls have a greater opportunity to choose from a range of possible outcomes for who or what they can or want to be. The loosening of gender polarity and the promotion of gender fluidity not only allow for the greater diversity, but also make more difficult for gender-based violence and discrimination to take hold. Hence, my argument regarding primary prevention involves three main tenets. Through education, we need to:

1. Dismantle the binary gender system that results in various forms of sexism.
2. Teach boys and girls about the history of gender and gender inequality for them to understand that traditional gender, gender roles and gender expectations are social and cultural products, and that gender is much more fluid and changeable.
3. Material regarding ethical social, sexual and digital relating needs to be incorporated into the health curricula.
4. Engage with global ethical citizenship.

Such primary interventions seek to stop the manifestations of sexism and gender inequality before they occur. For example, we know that violence and gender-based violence are preventable. But preventing gender-based violence requires changing enduring norms and beliefs about the nature of gender and men's and women's roles within relationships and society (MWA, 2013). Gender equality education and media literacy, with the teaching of ethical global citizenship, are fresh directions that can seek to address these enduring, entrenched and unchanging patterns of gender inequality. As long as gender inequality remains in New Zealand, and elsewhere, we need feminism and fresh policy perspectives to redress such patterns of ongoing sexism.

References

American Psychological Association (APA). (2016). *Being transgender*. APA.com. Retrieved from http://www.apa.org/topics/lgbt/transgender.aspx

Baker, D., & Wiseman, A. W. (2009). *Gender, equality and education: From international and comparative perspectives*. Bingley: Emerald Group Publishing Limited.

Beres, M. A., & Farvid, P. (2010). Sexual ethics and young women's accounts of heterosexual casual sex. *Sexualities*, *13*(3), 377–393.

Biesta, G. J. J. (2010). *Good education in an age of measurement: Ethics, politics, democracy*. Boulder, CO: Paradigm Publishers.

Bilby, L. (2015). Warnings for Roast Busters II. *The New Zealand Herald*. Retrieved from http://www.nzherald.co.nz/nz/news/article.cfm?c_id=1&objectid=11541781

Butler, J. (1990). *Gender trouble: Feminism and the subversion of identity*. New York, NY: Routledge.

Carmody, M. (2005). Ethical erotics: Reconceptualizing anti-rape education. *Sexualities, 8*(4), 465–480.

Carmody, M. (2009). *Sex and ethics: The sexual ethics education program for young people*. South Yarra: Palgrave Macmillan.

Casey, C., Skibnes, R., & Pringle, J. K. (2011). Gender equality and corporate governance: Policy strategies in Norway and New Zealand. *Gender, Work & Organization, 18*(6), 613–630.

Connell, R. W. (2005). *Masculinities* (2nd ed.). Berkeley, CA: University of California Press.

Curtin, J. (2008). Women, political leadership and substantive representation: The case of New Zealand. *Parliamentary Affairs, 61*(3), 490–504.

de Abreu, B. S., & Yildiz, M. N. (2016). *Global media literacy in a digital age: Teaching beyond borders*. New York, NY: Peter Lang.

de Beauvoir, S. (1953). *The second sex*. Harmondsworth: Penguin Books.

Department of Corrections. (2015). *Trends in offender population 2014/2015*. Department of Corrections. Retrieved from http://www.corrections.govt.nz/__data/assets/pdf_file/0007/835693/Trends_in_the_Offender_Population_201415.pdf

Family Violence Death Review Committee. (2014). *Fourth annual report: January 2013 to December 2013*. Wellington, NZ: Health Quality and Safety Commission.

Fanslow, J. L., & Robinson, E. M. (2011). Sticks, stones, or words? Counting the prevalence of different types of intimate partner violence reported by New Zealand women. *Journal of Aggression, Maltreatment & Trauma, 20*, 741–759.

Farvid, P. (2014a). The Internet Mana Party Gender Policy Position. *The Internet Party of New Zealand*. Retrieved from http://piratetimes.net/gender-policy-from-the-internet-partys-gender-spokesperson/

Farvid, P. (2014b). "Oh it was good sex!": Heterosexual women's (counter)narratives of desire and pleasure in casual sex. In S. McKenzie-Mohr & M. Lefrance (Eds.), *Women voicing resistance: Discursive and narrative explorations* (pp. 121–140). New York, NY: Routledge.

Farvid, P. (2015). Heterosexual psychology. In M. Barker & C. Richards (Eds.), *The psychology of sexuality and gender* (pp. 92–108). Houndmills: Palgrave.

Farvid, P. (2016a). Saying goodbye to binary gender. *TEDx Auckland*. New Zealand. Retrieved from https://www.youtube.com/watch?v=DW5YctpK7pM

Farvid, P. (2016b). *The adaption of misogyny to 'new media': Examining the online harassment of women*. Public Lecture, Auckland Women's Centre Forum, Auckland, New Zealand.

Farvid, P., & Aisher, K. (2016). "It's just a lot more casual": Young heterosexual women's experiences of using Tinder in New Zealand. *Ada: A Journal of Gender,*

New Media, and Technology, *10* (Online journal). Retrieved from http://adanewmedia.org/2016/10/issue10-farvid-aisher/

Farvid, P., & Braun, V. (2006). 'Most of us guys are raring to go anytime, anyplace, anywhere': Male and female sexuality in *Cleo* and *Cosmo*. *Sex Roles*, *55*(5–6), 295–310.

Farvid, P., & Braun, V. (2013). Casual sex as 'not a natural act' and other regimes of truth about heterosexuality. *Feminism & Psychology*, *23*(3), 359–378.

Farvid, P., & Braun, V. (2014). The "sassy woman" and the "performing man": Heterosexual casual sex advice and the (re)constitution of gendered subjectivities. *Feminist Media Studies*, *14*(1), 118–134.

Farvid, P., & Braun, V. (2017). Unpacking the 'pleasures' and 'pains' of heterosexual casual sex—Beyond singular understandings. *The Journal of Sex Research*, *54*(1), 73–90.

Farvid, P., Braun, V., & Rowney, C. (2016). 'No girl wants to be called a slut!': Women, heterosexual casual sex and the sexual double standard. *Journal of Gender Studies*, 1–7. Retrieved from http://www.tandfonline.com/doi/abs/10.1080/09589236.2016.1150818

Farvid, P., & Glass, L. (2014). "It isn't prostitution as you normally think of it. It's survival sex": Media representations of adult and child prostitution in New Zealand. *Women's Studies Journal*, *28*(1), 47–67.

Gardner, R., Cairns, J., & Lawton, D. (2000). *Education for values: Morals, ethics and citizenship in contemporary teaching*. London: Kogan Page.

HELP. (2016). Information statistics. *HELP Organisation*. Retrieved from http://helpauckland.org.nz/get-info/statistics

Human Rights Commission (HRC). (2012). *New Zealand census of women's participation*. Retrieved from https://www.hrc.co.nz/files/2314/2360/5171/web-census.pdf

Hunt, E. (2015). New Zealand police apologise to Roast Busters' victims. *The Guardian*. Retrieved from https://www.theguardian.com/world/2015/mar/19/new-zealand-police-apologise-to-roast-busters-victims

Hyde, J. S. (2005). The gender similarities hypothesis. *American Psychologist*, *60*(6), 581–592.

Hyde, J. S. (2007). New directions in the study of gender similarities and differences. *Current Directions in Psychological Science*, *16*(5), 259–263.

Katz, J. (2000). *Tough guise: Violence, media and the crisis in masculinity*. Documentary film. Retrieved from http://shop.mediaed.org/tough-guise-p163.aspx

Katz, J. (2012). Violence against women—It's a men's issue. *TEDxFiDiWomen*. Retrieved from https://www.ted.com/talks/jackson_katz_violence_against_women_it_s_a_men_s_issue

Katz, J. (2013). Tough Guise 2: Violence, manhood and American culture. Documentary film. Retrieved from http://shop.mediaed.org/tough-guise-2-p45.aspx

Lohman, C. P. (1981). The social origins of femininity. *Smith College Studies in Social Work*, *51*(3), 162–191.

Marvelly, L. (2015). Roast Busters II: Does New Zealand have a rape culture problem? *The New Zealand Herald*. Retrieved from http://www.villainesse.com/culture/roast-busters-ii-does-new-zealand-have-rape-culture-problem

Masselot, A., & Brand, T. (2015). Diversity, quotas and compromise in the board-room: Tackling gender imbalance in economic decision-making. *New Zealand Universities Law Review*, 26(3). Retrieved from http://www.nzulr.com/archives/vol26no3.htm

Masselot, A., & Maymont, A. (2015) Gendering economic and financial governance through positive action measures: Compatibility of the French real equality measure under the European Union framework. *Maastricht Journal of European and Comparative Law*, 22(1), 57–80.

Mayer, L. S., & McHugh, P. R. (2016). Special report—Sexuality and gender: Findings from the biological, psychological and social sciences. *The New Atlantis: A Journal of Technology & Society*, 50. Retrieved from http://www.thenewatlantis.com/docLib/20160819_TNA50SexualityandGender.pdf

McGregor, J. (2011). Women in management in New Zealand. In M. J. Davidson & R. J. Burke (Eds.), *Women in management worldwide: Progress and prospects* (pp. 211–224). Farnham, Surrey: Gower Publishing.

McPherson, M. (2010). Women in senior management—Why not? Labour, employment and work in New Zealand. *Equal Employment Opportunities Trust.* Retrieved from http://ojs.victoria.ac.nz/LEW/article/view/1718

Millett, K. (1970). *Sexual politics.* New York, NY: Doubleday.

Ministry of Justice. (2015). *2014 New Zealand crime and safety survey: Main findings.* Retrieved from http://www.justice.govt.nz/assets/Documents/Publications/NZCASS-201602-Main-Findings-Report-Updated.pdf

Ministry of Women's Affair's (MWA). (2013). Realising the opportunity: Addressing New Zealand's leadership pipeline by attracting and retaining talented women. *MWA.* Retrieved from http://women.govt.nz/sites/public_files/Realising%20the%20opportunity.pdf

Ministry of Women's Affair's (MWA). (2015). Gender pay gap. *MWA.* Retrieved from http://women.govt.nz/work-skills/income/gender-pay-gap

National Collective of Independent Women's Refuges (NCIWR). (2015). *Annual report: July 2014-June 2015.* NCIWR, Wellington.

New Zealand Council of Women New Zealand (NCWNZ). (2016). Data summaries. Retrieved from http://www.ncwnz.org.nz/

New Zealand Family Violence Clearinghouse (NZFVC). (2016). Data summaries. Retrieved from https://nzfvc.org.nz/sites/nzfvc.org.nz/files/Data-summaries-snapshot-2016.pdf

Oakley, A. (1972). *Sex, gender and society.* London: Maurice Temple Smith.

Petersen, J. L., & Hyde, J. S. (2011). Gender differences in sexual attitudes and behaviors: A review of meta-analytic results and large datasets. *Journal of Sex Research*, 48(2–3), 149–165.

Potter, W. J. (2014). *Media literacy* (7th ed.). Thousand Oaks, CA: Sage.

Powell, G. N. (2011). *Women and men in management* (4th ed.). Los Angeles, CA: Sage.

Rape Prevention Education (RPE). (2016). *Rape prevention education NZ.* Retrieved from http://rpe.co.nz/information/sexual-violence-against-males/

Redstall, S. (2016). *Trade Me data shows gender inequality in New Zealand employment.* Retrieved from http://www.newshub.co.nz/home/money/2016/07/trade-me-data-shows-gender-inequality-in-new-zealand-employment.html

Richardson, S. (2015). *Gender lessons: Patriarchy, sextyping and schools*. Rotterdam: Sense Publishers.

Rotherham, F. (2013). *Women still behind in gender equality*. Retrieved from http://www.stuff.co.nz/national/women-of-influence/8860246/Women-still-behind-in-equality

Rubin, G. (1975). The traffic in women. In R. R. Reiter (Ed.), *Toward an anthropology of women* (pp. 157–210). New York, NY: Monthly Review Press.

Rubin, G. (1984). Thinking sex: Notes for a radical theory of the politics of sexuality. In C. S. Vance (Ed.), *Pleasure and danger: Exploring female sexuality* (pp. 267–319). Boston, MA: Routledge and Kegan Paul.

Rutman, D. (1996). Child care as women's work: Workers' experiences of powerfulness and powerlessness. *Gender and Society, 10*(5), 629–649.

Sanderson, L. (2013). Gender balance in the New Zealand Public Service. *Luminous Consulting Limited*. Retrieved from http://www.luminousconsulting.co.nz/resource-list/

Simon-Kumar, R. (2011). The analytics of "gendering" the post-neoliberal state. *Social Politics, 18*(3), 441–468.

Statistics New Zealand. (2011). *Time use survey 2009/2010*. Retrieved from http://www.stats.govt.nz/~/media/Statistics/Browse%20for%20stats/TimeUseSurvey/HOTP2009-10/TimeUseSurvey2009-10HOTP.pdf

Statistics New Zealand. (2016). Annual recorded offences for the latest calendar years. Retrieved from http://nzdotstat.stats.govt.nz/wbos/Index.aspx

Subrahmanian, R. (2005). Gender equality in education: Definitions and measurements. *International Journal of Educational Development, 25*, 395–407.

Sweden. (2015). *Gender equality in Sweden*. Retrieved from https://sweden.se/society/gender-equality-in-sweden/

Sweden. (2017). Retrieved from https://sweden.se/society/genderequality-in-sweden/

Thoman, E., & Jolls, T. (2003). *Literacy for the 21st century: An overview and orientation guide to media literacy education: Center for Media Literacy*. Retrieved from http://www.medialit.org/sites/default/files/mlk/01_MLKorientation.pdf

Trevett, C. (2013). Labour backs away from man-ban plan. *The New Zealand Herald*. Retrieved from http://www.nzherald.co.nz/nz/news/article.cfm?c_id=1&objectid=10895712

United Nations Children's Fund (2015). *Girls' education and gender equality*. Retrieved from https://www.unicef.org/education/bege_70640.html

United States Agency for International Development (USAID). (2008). *Education from a gender equality perspective*. Retrieved from http://www.ungei.org/resources/files/Education_from_a_Gender_Equality_Perspective.pdf

Ussher, J. M. (1989). *The psychology of the female body*. London: Routledge.

Wolf, N. (2002). *The beauty myth* (2nd ed.). New York, NY: Harper Collins.

World Health Organisation (WHO). (2016). *Violence against women: Intimate partner and sexual violence against women fact sheet*. Retrieved from http://www.who.int/mediacentre/factsheets/fs239/en/

Part Three

Reproductive Labour, Work and Economy

Global Synthesis

Glenda Tibe Bonifacio

Women comprise half of the world's labour force, yet their contribution remains undervalued in both productive and reproductive labour. They provide the backbone of the 'service' industry in homes, communities and nation-states. Essentialism remains at the core of women's primary role in society — as caregivers — and this continues as an added responsibility with paid work even in most advanced countries. The international transfer of care work, from the global South to the global North, in the service economy created a class of vulnerable migrant workers with less access to rights and protection in host countries. Globalization also ushered labour mobility within and across borders with differing levels of employment benefits, often those in developing states are sources of cheap labour to manufacture goods for international distribution, while those found in host countries tend to provide the necessary labour to maintain the comfort of a middle-class lifestyle. The supply of skilled labour from many developing countries with younger populations to developed countries with ageing populations brings social realities quite different than before. For women workers across the board, sexism and the glass ceiling continue to deny equal standing with men. Closing the gender pay gap remains a struggle henceforth. Until new measures of accounting women's full contribution in the economy, to include unpaid work, becomes a standard could we affirm global gender fair play. But there is progress in sight to eliminate barriers for women's full participation in the economy with many traditionally male-oriented occupations now open to women.

Chapter 8

Child Care and Feminism in Canada

Lisa Pasolli

Abstract

This chapter considers the interwoven history of child care advocacy and feminism in Canada. It begins by examining the efforts of second-wave feminists to make child care part of national political discussions. It then moves into the 1980s and 1990s, when, as part of broader neo-liberal reforms, feminist demands were no longer foregrounded in child care advocacy. Instead, 'social investment' and childhood development rationales took centre stage. This chapter considers the implications of the 'disappearing woman' from child care advocacy, and concludes by making a case for the ongoing relevance of intersectional feminism to the child care landscape, to ensure that all women are offered mean-ingful choice, opportunities and rights when it comes to their roles as caregivers and workers.

Keywords: Child care; feminism; Canada; neoliberalism; social policy

On a blustery weekend in November 2014, more than 600 early childhood education and care (ECEC) advocates from across the country converged in Winnipeg for *ChildCare 2020: From Vision to Action*, Canada's fourth national child care conference. After almost a decade of stagnation on child care policy under Stephen Harper's Conservative government, and with a federal election on the horizon, a feeling of optimism suffused the conference. If *ChildCare 2020* offered a snapshot of the Canadian child care advocacy movement in 2014, it painted a multifaceted picture. Unions,

Global Currents in Gender and Feminisms: Canadian and International Perspectives, 129–140
Copyright © 2018 by Emerald Publishing Limited
All rights of reproduction in any form reserved
ISBN: 978-1-78714-484-2/doi:10.1108/978-1-78714-483-520171011

ECEC workers and associations, parents, academic researchers, politicians, bureaucrats and even corporate interests were represented. Delegates heard that more and better child care services would promote economic prosperity, foster healthy child development, create inclusive workplaces, cultivate cultural sensitivity and strengthen Canadian families. Clearly, that weekend in Winnipeg reflected a mature and broad-based advocacy movement, one that has drawn together child care champions from many sectors of Canadian society (Halfon & Macdonald, 2014/2015).

But what about women's interests and gender equality? What was the place for feminism at *ChildCare 2020*? Certainly, the feminist framing of child care — that access to affordable and comprehensive child care services is a necessary cornerstone for women's equality in the workforce and the family — ran implicitly through the weekend. But explicit discussion of feminist objectives and *women's rights* to publicly funded child care services did not take centre stage in Winnipeg. When we step back and view the child care landscape through a wider lens, nor does the feminist framework feature prominently in national advocacy campaigns. The Child Care Advocacy Association of Canada (CCAAC), for example, proclaims its commitment to 'promote the shared vision of a universal, pan-Canadian child care system that meets the needs of all children and parents', and insists on the 'right of all children to access a publicly funded, inclusive, quality, non-profit child care system' (2016). The rights of *women*, however, do not get prominent play in their messaging and advocacy work. Perhaps this reflects the taken-for-granted importance of child care to women's interests and opportunities. More worryingly, it is a sign of the 'temper[ing] of feminist demands' in response to neoliberal shifts in policy-making since the 1980s, and of the political relegation of women's rights to 'special interests' (Collier, 2010, p. 4). Not only is this a significant deviation from the deeply entwined history of child care and feminism, but it raises concerns about the woman-friendliness of child care policy moving forward (Hernes, 1987). This chapter considers that interwoven history of feminism and child care and examines the recent disappearance of women from child care debates. It concludes by making a case for the ongoing relevance of intersectional feminism to child care policy, to ensure that all women are offered meaningful choice, opportunities and rights when it comes to their roles as caregivers and workers.

Feminism and Child Care: A Brief Late-20th Century History

As the 'second-wave' women's movement exploded into Canadian consciousness and society in the late 1960s and early 1970s, child care took centre stage on the feminist agenda. Feminists disagreed on a lot of things, of course, but the need for publicly funded, universal, high-quality child care programmes as a cornerstone of women's equality was an issue of remarkable consensus. Perhaps most famously, the federal government-appointed Royal Commission on the Status of Women, when it reported in 1970, called for a national, universal day care programme. Such a programme was a necessary replacement, the commissioners argued, for the welfare-oriented approach to day care that had characterized government policy up to that point, mostly in the form of targeted subsidies to low-income and 'needy' mothers (Mahon, 2000). Though the Commission recommendations did not result in any substantial policy changes, it did serve as a catalyst for sustained child care advocacy. In the aftermath of the Royal Commission, liberal feminist groups like the National Action Committee on the Status of Women committed themselves to the cause of child care as a central plank of their fight for women's workplace opportunities. At the grassroots level, too, child care demands were passionate and energetic. Women's groups on university campuses, for example, occupied administration buildings and established day care co-operatives, framing their actions as part of broader efforts to free women from the constraints of patriarchal families. Socialist feminists allied with welfare rights organizations in calling for more and better day care services that would allow low-income women and mothers on social assistance to achieve meaningful economic autonomy. Feminist unions, such as Vancouver's Service, Office, and Retail Workers' Union of Canada (SORWUC), insisted that child care provisions should be built into collective agreements, and fought for better wages and working conditions for child care workers (Adamson, Briskin, & McPhail, 1988; Pasolli, 2015).

Feminist analyses, strategies and tactics remained important to child care advocacy into the 1980s, the decade when a distinct child care movement began to take shape in Canada. The Canadian Day Care Advocacy Association (now the CCAAC) was established in 1982, for example, as was the Ontario Coalition for Better Day Care, an organization imbued with socialist-feminist analyses and tactics (Prentice, 1999). The Katie Cooke Task Force on Child Care, which was appointed by the Liberal government in May 1984 and reported in 1986, recommended a universal child care programme, and in the 1984 Royal Commission on Equality in Employment, Rosalie Abella called the provision of child care 'the ramp that provides equal access to the workforce for mothers' (Timpson, 2001, p. 122).

But there were also signs by the 1980s that feminism and women's rights were being relegated to the sidelines in child care politics. Instead, children's interests were emerging as a policy priority, and one that had been 'driven apart' from concerns about women's employment equity and thus a

feminist framework. In her important study about child care and employment policy, Timpson (2001) outlines multiple reasons for this, including jurisdictional challenges and fiscal restraints that left the federal
government reluctant to intervene in child care but more willing to
develop employment equity policies. Just as importantly, the prevention of child poverty and the enhancement of child development had
become more salient political issues, represented mostly obviously by
the House of Commons' 1989 resolution to eliminate child poverty by
the year 2000. The Conservative federal government also replaced the universal Family Allowance with the Child Tax Benefit in 1993 — one of
several policy reforms that were designed to target low-income and disadvantaged families and their children. Advocacy groups responded to
these shifting political currents by de-emphasizing the 'women's issue'
angle on child care and focusing on child care's potential as an anti-pov-
erty and early years' development measure (Dobrowolsky & Jenson, 2004,
pp. 167–170).

The shift from women's rights to children's interests in the 1980s also
needs to be understood in the broader political context of neoliberalism.
The election of Brian Mulroney's Progressive Conservative government in
the fall of 1984 firmly ushered in the Canadian version of neoliberalism,
with its emphasis, in social policy terms, on a minimal role for the state,
privatization of services, and an emphasis on personal responsibility, self-
sufficiency through participation in the labour market, and individualiza-
tion (Dobrowolsky, 2009). One indication of neoliberal rationales making
their way into child care was Bill C-144, the Canadian Child Care Act
proposed by Mulroney in 1987 (after rejecting Katie Cooke's calls for a
universal programme). Bill C-144 focused on tax deductions and relied on
the for-profit sector to create new child care spaces. Though the bill died
on the order paper in 1988, it was a sign of things to come. By the 1990s,
under the Liberals, neoliberalism came to define the Canadian social policy
approach — with significant implications for women, for gender equality
and for child care politics.

Child Care as 'Social Investment' in the 21st Century: Considering Costs

Neoliberalism is defined, in part, by a suspicion of social spending because
of its potential to 'conflict with economic prosperity'. Any social spending
must be considered 'productive' — it should represent a 'social investment'
(Jenson & Saint-Martin, 2003, p. 82). By the late 1990s, the federal
Liberals' spending rationales were clearly geared towards this social

investment paradigm (Dobrowolsky, 2009). Social programmes were reoriented towards labour market 'activation' and enhancing employability. For adults, this meant that stricter eligibility and reduced benefits were applied to income security programmes to get people out of welfare. In the social investment paradigm, people are meant to earn their own way. That included mothers with children, whose labour force activation came under scrutiny through federal and provincial welfare reforms in the 1990s to an extent not seen for decades. Their child care needs, though, were rarely given serious consideration (Jenson, 2009; Little & Marks, 2010). Instead, child care had become most closely associated with children — and children were the social investment target *par excellence*. Targeted investment in the early years, according to this logic, was the best way to enhance human capital and ensure a society filled with well-educated, well-trained, productive and prosperous workers.

The social investment perspective, and particularly the focus on investing on young children as human capital, came to dominate the universe of Canadian child care politics as the 20th century turned into the 21st. Quebec, however, was an exception. In 1997, a $5-a-day universal child care programmes was introduced in that province (today, the costs range from $7.55 to about $20 daily, depending on family income). Jenson (2009) has argued that there was 'less emphasis on 'investing in children' in the Quebec context (p. 31). Instead, that province's day care programme was embedded in feminist-influenced family policy that included generous parental leave for women and men as well as targeted family allowances. Quebec, Jenson (2009) argues, 'did not write gender out' and thus 'there continued to be political space for women's groups of all kinds to defend gender-based and equality claims' and to justify putting money towards such objectives (p. 31).

But in the realm of federal policy-making, human capital investment was the order of the day. We need only look to the introduction of the National Child Benefit (NCB) in 1998. It offered an income-based tax benefit as well as a low-income supplement that was meant, as Mahon (2008) explains, to be an 'incentive for social assistance recipients to work — or for the working poor to keep at it, despite low rates of pay' (p. 353). But provinces could claw back part or all of the NCB and 'reinvest' the money in children's services (Mahon, 2008, p. 353). According to the government, the NCB fulfilled the interlocking objectives of directing investments to disadvantaged children and enhancing mothers' employability. A few years later, the logic of human capital investment in young children was reflected in the language of the bilateral agreements-in-principle negotiated in 2005 between the federal government and all provinces except Quebec. The focus was on the crucial importance of the 'early years', and the 'social, emotional, and cognitive development' of children (Jenson, 2009, pp. 33–34).[1]

Prentice (2009) has traced the efforts of late-20th and early-21st century child care advocacy movements to keep pace with the shifting political currents. Advocates have largely adopted what Prentice (2009) calls the 'business case' for child care to have their lobbying resonate in the political milieu that is now so concerned with the economic returns on social investments (p. 687). Examples of this economic reframing abound. Cleveland and Krashinsky's 1998 report, *The Benefits and Costs of Good Child Care*, is an early example that famously argued that for every dollar spent on a comprehensive child care programme, two dollars would be generated. The Quebec experience has also given fodder to this kind of framework, with reports from that province suggesting that dramatic economic benefits have accrued from their child care programme, particularly in the form of women's higher labour force participation (Prentice, 2009). Even banks and corporate interests have jumped on board: economists from the Royal Bank of Canada, the Toronto-Dominion (TD) Bank and the Bank of Canada have published reports touting the economic benefits of child care investments. According to TD Bank's Craig Alexander and Dina Ignjatovic, ECEC programmes can 'unlock the potential of individuals' through education and 'skills development' at an early age, which will 'help reduce poverty, address skills shortages, improve productivity and innovation, and a host of other national priorities', contributing to an overall healthier and more prosperous economy (Alexander & Ignjatovic, 2012, p. 1).

For those who have committed themselves to the implementation of good child care policy, this economic reframing of child care offers potential benefits. As Prentice (2009) points out, it is encouraging that long-time child care advocates have influential new allies from the business, corporate and population health worlds. But Prentice (2009) and others (Michel, 2015) also caution advocates about setting aside feminist rationales for ECEC in favour of economic frameworks that comply with the social/human capital investment policy paradigm. Michel (2015), who is tracking similar patterns in the United States, warns that implementing child care programmes on the basis of lowering crime rates and deviance and ensuring

---

[1]The bilateral agreements followed the 2003 Multilateral Framework on Early Learning and Child Care, and the federal government's 2004 promise to implement a national early learning and care strategy based on the principles of quality, universality, accessibility and developmental programming. This promise included $5 billion over five years to see the plans through. These plans were cancelled in 2006 when Stephen Harper's Conservative government was elected.

productive future workers is not a sound moral or philosophical basis for child care. Children, she argues, are not 'human capital', but 'human', and should not be treated simply as a potential return on investments (Michel, 2015, p. 375). ECEC programmes built around human capital principles may be much more limited and punitive in scope than gender-justice-based programmes. They may, for example, be more likely to be targeted as 'disadvantaged' children, running counter to goals of universalism as well as further pathologizing and justifying state intrusion into the lives of poor families. Moreover, programmes may be more likely to be offered only as part-day and part-year programmes, or limited to three-to-five-year olds only, on the basis that social investment goals can still be met while also being cost-effective. Such programmes would not necessarily be useful or convenient for working mothers. The investment rhetoric also largely ignores child care workers; feminists would say that workers' wages and working conditions need to be considered as part of a comprehensive approach to child care policy because at the heart of child care is the 'revaluing of carework' (Prentice, 2009, p. 700). Finally, there is the very real concern that reducing child care to questions of economic return can play into the hands of the for-profit, commercial child care sector, which is lower in quality and exerts downward pressure on standards and regulations of child care services as a whole (Prentice, 2009).

Clearly, emphasizing the feminist framing of child care is a perilous proposition in a political climate that is not receptive to gender-equality priorities. But Prentice (2009), Michel (2015) and others caution that abandoning the feminist framework altogether is a 'high-stakes' gamble for women in the 21st century (Michel, 2015; Prentice, 2009, p. 704). History reminds us that the feminist vision of child care took into consideration the needs, rights, and interests of children, mothers and workers who provided care. If feminist claims are not part of advocacy, then policymakers will continue to prioritize children over their mothers, failing to consider that both women *and* children — as well as the economy, families and society as a whole — can benefit from universal, accessible and comprehensive child care policies.

Continuing Relevance of Feminism to Child Care in the 21st Century

Despite these prevailing trends, the landscape of child care advocacy in Canada has not abandoned feminism. Though the Harper years (2006–2015) put something of a damper on national child care advocacy, we can look to the provinces for evidence of ongoing innovation and sustained energy in ways that foreground equality objectives for women. In British Columbia, for example, the Coalition of Child Care Advocates of British Columbia (CCCABC), in cooperation with the Early Childhood Educators of British Columbia (ECEBC), has developed a plan for '$10-a-day' universal child care. Based on principles long-established in the advocacy movement — universality, high quality and affordability — the plan is sold as an economic booster and a benefit to child poverty and development. Supporters also emphasize that the plan will have positive effects on women's labour force participation, and the plan includes a proposal for a $25/hour minimum wage for child care workers (Coalition of Child Care Advocates of British Columbia, 2016). The plan highlights, in other words, women's equality as one of the primary goals of good child care policy. Public, political and corporate support for the plan continues to grow in British Columbia, demonstrating that feminism still has resonance.

As 21st-century Canada faces new child care challenges, intersectional feminism also offers the analytical tools that allow us to examine the layers of inequality and privilege built into our social and political organization of care. It allows us to imagine ways to create more equitable and inclusive care relationships based on women's ability to make meaningful choices. Feminism gives us the tools, in other words, to think about relations of care in a country confronting ongoing inequities not only in gender, but also in class, race, ethnicity, nationality and other kinds of social difference.

Take, for example, Canada's Caregiver Program. This programme was formerly known as the Live-in Caregiver Program (LCP), which was formed in 1992 as part of the Temporary Foreign Worker Program. Under the LCP, foreign-born workers who lived with Canadian families providing child care and elder care services could apply for permanent residency status after 24 months of live-in work. In the late 2014, changes to the programme removed the live-in requirement (though living-in is still an option). Women from the Philippines comprise the majority of workers in the Caregiver Program. Besides being encouraged by their own government to migrate in search of work opportunities and thus provide an important source of economic stability to the Philippines through their remittances, these caregiving women provide a desperately needed service for Canadian families, who face chronic child care space shortages and ballooning fees that can reach upwards of $1500 per month in some parts of the country (Friendly, 2015; Parreñas, 2002).

To say that the LCP, and the reformed Caregiver Program, has been an imperfect solution to Canada's child care crisis is an understatement, however. The alleviation of middle-class Canadian mothers' care crises occurs at the expense of the rights, opportunities and well-being of Filipino (and other migrant) women, whose migration renders them 'socially and politically invisible' (Brickner & Straehle, 2010, p. 311). Researchers, caregivers' advocates and caregivers themselves have compiled a long list of problems these programmes have. Filipina caregivers are vulnerable to abuse, lack of privacy, unpaid overtime and even food insecurity (Brickner & Straehle, 2010). They are put in positions where they are unable to protest contract violations or breaches of employment regulations, and their path to permanent residency is often plagued by delays. Transitioning out of the Caregiver Program and into the labour market, furthermore, can be challenging because of unrecognized credentials, low pay and lack of resources to pursue educational opportunities (Tungohan et al., 2015). Moreover, the 2014 reforms that removed the live-in requirement also restricted the pathways to permanent residency, making workers even more vulnerable to abuse. Finally, many caregivers pay high emotional costs: pursuing opportunities in Canada often means leaving behind children and families of their own, and studies have shown that family reunification can be fraught with procedural and emotional difficulties (Pratt, 2012). Canadian families benefit, in other words, from the exploitative international division of reproductive labour and a 'global care chain' that Hochschild (2002) has called a 'new emotional imperialism' (p. 27). To build equity-based child care policy moving forward means, then, considering not just the so-called liberation of middle-class women for participation in the labour force, but the full range of citizenship rights, economic opportunities and social inclusion to which *all* women, including marginalized caregivers, are entitled. Intersectional feminist frameworks give us the tools to keep these objectives in sight. As the Canadian Research Institute on the Advancement of Women (CRIAW, 2006) explains, when it comes to feminist activism, a 'focus on gender-based discrimination alone fails to recognize and address the multifaceted causes and impacts of marginalization on the lives of women most adversely affected by poverty and exclusion locally and globally' (p. 9). It is necessary, in other words, to consider how relations of power such as class, race, ethnicity, citizenship and immigration status intersect with gender to structure oppression in the lives of migrant caregivers. Intersectional feminism not only offers frameworks for 'unravel[ling] how social categories of difference intersect', but also ways to 'crack open oppressive dialogues, structures and practices', thus offering path for change and equality for those who require care as well as those who provide it (CRIAW, 2006, p. 10).

Finally, feminist analysis should prompt us to think about the full range of women's choices when it comes to designing care policy. The Conservative government, when they introduced the Universal Child Care Benefit in 2006, maintained that they were offering choice in child care, but critics have pointed out the obvious fact that $100 per month offers very little choice at all, especially in a time when child care costs are rising and welfare supports are collapsing. While a universal child care programme is certainly a necessary cornerstone of support for women's full and equal worker-citizenship rights, once again historical lessons remind us that choice in child care should also include the choice to care for one's own children. We need only think of the 'Wages for Housework' movement of the 1970s, when welfare mothers insisted that they did not need to be rehabilitated through wage work. Instead, they demanded compensation that would allow them to stay home and care for their children (Dalla Costa & James, 1972). There are important parallels here with the activism of Black women, for example, who argued for the 'right to care' as a reaction to a long history of being relegated to the low-wage workforce and the devaluing of their mother-work (Boris & Kleinberg, 2003). Today, feminist scholars like Kershaw (2005) suggest that our social policy infrastructure should include mechanisms that value caregiving equally with wage-earning through much more generous parental leaves and pensions, revised employment standards, and, of course, greater public commitment to child care. Such reforms, Kershaw (2005) argues, should also include carer-citizen obligations for men as part of a much broader societal re-valuing of care work.

Valuing care is an especially important consideration as we begin to think about reconciling the long history — and ongoing conditions — of colonialism in Canada. The recently released Truth and Reconciliation Commission of Canada Report (2015) includes calls for action on child welfare and education, including providing adequate resources to enable communities and welfare organizations to keep Indigenous families together and to make sure children can stay in culturally appropriate environments that include good ECEC programmes. For Indigenous women, caregiving is a political act, one that is crucially important to counteract the obstruction of care within Indigenous families that resulted from residential schools and racist child welfare practices. Caregiving, in other words, can serve decolonization and community development efforts. For these reasons, policies to support caregiving need to include generous and well-designed parental leave benefits, well-resourced local family services and accessible, affordable child care services that serve community interests (Kershaw & Harkey, 2011).

This feminist analysis of caregiving should remind us that the way we organize and distribute care between states, markets and families; between women and men; and between women of different class, race, ethnic and national identities has a fundamental bearing on all women's equality, inclusion, opportunities, citizenship and rights. Feminists have conceived of the care of children as a burden, a privilege, as a source of oppression and a source of empowerment; feminism reminds us that the care of children has multiple, and sometimes paradoxical, meanings for women. This perspective is needed more than ever as families and labour markets continue to evolve and as we move forward with creating a child care policy that secures all women's rights in a changing world.

References

Adamson, N., Briskin, L., & McPhail, M. (1988). *Feminist organizing for change: The contemporary women's movement in Canada*. Toronto: Oxford University Press.

Alexander, C., & Ignjatovic, D. (2012). *Early childhood education has widespread and long lasting benefits*. TD Economics Special Report. Retrieved from https://www.td.com/document/PDF/economics/special/di1112_EarlyChildhoodEducation.pdf

Boris, E., & Kleinberg, S. J. (2003). Mothers and other workers: (Re)conceiving labor, maternalism, and the state. *Journal of Women's History, 15*(3), 90–117. doi:10.1353/jowh.2003.0061

Brickner, R. K., & Straehle, C. (2010). The missing link: Gender, immigration policy and the Live-In Caregiver Program in Canada. *Policy and Society, 29*, 309–320. doi:10.1016/j.polsoc.2010.09.004

Canadian Research Institute for the Advancement of Women (CRIAW). (2006). *Intersectional feminist frameworks: An emerging vision*. Retrieved from http://www.criaw-icref.ca/images/userfiles/files/IntersectionalFeministFrameworks-AnEmergingVision(2).pdf

Child Care Advocacy Association of Canada. (2016). Retrieved from https://ccaac.ca/

Cleveland, G., & Krashinsky, M. (1998). *The benefits and costs of good child care: The economic rationale for public investment in young children – A policy study*. Retrieved from http://childcarecanada.org/sites/default/files/bc.pdf

Coalition of Child Care Advocates of British Columbia. (2016). *10aday.ca*. Retrieved from www.10aday.ca

Collier, C. N. (2010). The disappearing woman? Locating gender equality in contemporary child care and anti-violence policy debates in Canada. Unpublished manuscript.

Dalla Costa, M., & James, S. (1972). *The power of women and the subversion of the community*. Bristol: Falling Wall Press.

Dobrowolsky, A. (2009). Introduction: Neo-liberalism and after? In A. Dobrowolsky (Ed.), *Women and public policy in Canada: Neo-liberalism and after?* (pp. 1–24). Toronto: Oxford University Press.

Dobrowolsky, A., & Jenson, J. (2004). Shifting representations of citizenship: Canadian politics of "women" and "children". *Social Politics, 11*(2), 154–180. doi:10.1093/sp/jxh031

Friendly, M. (2015). Taking Canada's child care pulse: The state of ECEC in 2015. In E. Shaker (Ed.), *Our schools/our selves. Moving beyond baby steps: Building a child care plan for today's families* (pp. 7–24). Toronto: Canadian Centre for Policy Alternatives.

Halfon, S., & Macdonald, L. (2014/2015). From vision to action: ECEs role in the Canadian child care movement. *Association of Early Childhood Educators Ontario*. Retrieved from https://d3n8a8pro7vhmx.cloudfront.net/aeceo/pages/753/attachments/original/1430416439/FromVisionToAction.pdf?1430416439

Hernes, H. M. (1987). *Welfare state and woman power: Essays in state feminism*. Oslo: Norwegian University Press.

Hochschild, A. R. (2002). Love and gold. In B. Ehrenreich & A. R. Hochschild (Eds.), *Global woman: Nannies, maids, and sex workers in the new economy* (pp. 15–30). New York, NY: Owl Books.

Jenson, J. (2009). Writing gender out: The continuing effects of the social investment perspective. In A. Dobrowolsky (Ed.), *Women and public policy in Canada: Neo-liberalism and after?* (pp. 25−47). Toronto: Oxford University Press.

Jenson, J., & Saint-Martin, D. (2003). New routes to social cohesion? Citizenship and the social investment state. *Canadian Journal of Sociology, 28*(1), 77−99. doi:10.2307/3341876

Kershaw, P. (2005). *Carefair: Rethinking the responsibilities and rights of citizenship.* Vancouver: University of British Columbia Press.

Kershaw, P., & Harkey, T. (2011). The politics and power in caregiving for identity: Insights for Indian residential school truth and reconciliation. *Social Politics, 18*(4), 572−597. doi:10.1093/sp/jxr015

Little, M., & Marks, L. (2010). Ontario and British Columbia welfare policy: Variants on a neoliberal theme. *Comparative Studies of South Asia, Africa and the Middle East, 30*(2), 192−203. doi:10.1215/1089201x-2010-004

Mahon, R. (2000). The never-ending story: The struggle for universal child care policy in the 1970s. *Canadian Historical Review, 81*(4), 582−622.

Mahon, R. (2008). Varieties of liberalism: Canadian social policy from the 'golden age' to the present. *Social Policy & Administration, 42*(2), 342−361. doi:10.1111/j.1467-9515.2008.00608.x

Michel, S. (2015). Wall Street meets the day nursery: A new rationale for early education and care in the United States in the twenty-first century. *Social Politics, 22*(3), 360−380. doi:10.1093/sp/jxv025

Parreñas, R. S. (2002). The care crisis in the Philippines: Children and transnational families in the new global economy. In B. Ehrenreich & A. R. Hochschild (Eds.), *Global woman: Nannies, maids, and sex workers in the new economy* (pp. 39−54). New York, NY: Owl Books.

Pasolli, L. (2015). *Working mothers and the child care dilemma: A history of British Columbia's social policy.* Vancouver: University of British Columbia Press.

Pratt, G. (2012). *Families apart: Migrant mothers and the conflicts of labor and love.* Minneapolis, MN: University of Minnesota Press.

Prentice, S. (1999). Less, worse, and more expensive: Child care in an era of deficit reduction. *Journal of Canadian Studies, 43*(2), 137−158.

Prentice, S. (2009). High stakes: The 'investable' child and the economic reframing of childcare. *Signs, 34*(3), 687−710. doi:10.1086/593711

Timpson, A. M. (2001). *Driven apart: Women's employment equality and child care in Canadian public policy.* Vancouver: University of British Columbia Press.

Truth and Reconciliation Commission of Canada. (2015). *Honouring the truth, reconciling for the future: Summary of the final report of the Truth and Reconciliation Commission of Canada.* Retrieved from http://www.myrobust.com/websites/trcinstitution/File/Reports/Executive_Summary_English_Web.pdf

Tungohan, E., Banerjee, R., Chu, W., Cleto, P., de Leon, C., Garcia, M., ... Sorio, C. (2015). After the Live-in Caregiver Program: Filipina caregivers' experiences of graduated and uneven citizenship. *Canadian Ethnic Studies, 47*(1), 87−105. doi:10.1353/ces.2015.0008

Chapter 9

Service Work as Reproductive Labour: A Feminist Political Economy of Filipino Migrant Hotel Workers in Rural Manitoba

Catherine Bryan

Abstract

Drawing on multi-sited ethnographic fieldwork conducted in rural Manitoba and throughout the Philippines with temporary foreign workers employed at a small inn and conference centre and their non-migrant kin, this chapter offers an introduction to and expansion of feminist engagements with social reproduction and global care chains. This chapter illustrates the importance of feminist analysis of migration trajectories and labour processes that fall outside of the conventional purview of gender and migration studies. To this end, it suggests that in addition to interrogating the conditions and rational under which *reproduction* comes to be articulated and experienced as labour, consideration of how divergent forms of labour also constitute and shape *reproduction* can provide significant insight into the social consequences of neoliberal capitalism, while revealing the ways in which the gendered and racialized parameters of reproductive and intimate labour come to be reproduced.

Keywords: Manitoba; Philippines; service and hospitality; social reproduction; transnationality; migration

Global Currents in Gender and Feminisms: Canadian and International Perspectives, 141–153
Copyright © 2018 by Emerald Publishing Limited
All rights of reproduction in any form reserved
ISBN: 978-1-78714-484-2/doi:10.1108/978-1-78714-483-520171013

Introduction

Between 2009 and 2014, 71 Filipino migrant workers arrived in a small town in Manitoba's central-west. They were service workers recruited by a small hotel and conference centre, hereafter called the Inn. Their arrival in the town signals several histories and globalized processes, including (though not limited to) the ongoing reconfiguration of social reproduction under capitalism. While they are not reproductive workers in the conventional sense, as these migrant workers tend to the daily needs of the hotel's guests, their labour assumes a decidedly reproductive quality. Broadly, the purpose of this chapter is to reveal the reproductive characteristics of this labour. More precisely, however, it aims to capture and articulate the practices and mechanisms through which their work comes to be constituted as reproductive, and in so doing to simultaneously review and contribute to the ongoing feminist engagement with social reproduction.

To open new space from which to conceptualize the entanglement of production, reproduction and commodification, this chapter offers an initial formulation of a framework that links hospitality production with reproduction. It draws on ethnographic fieldwork conducted in Manitoba and in the Philippines between 2012 and 2014. During this time, I met with 50 of the Inn's migrant workers, and approximately 100 of their family members, still residing in the Philippines. Although questions varied from site-to-site, all interviews were intended to elicit information about histories of migration, social reproductive and livelihood strategies and labour conditions. In Manitoba, participant observation was conducted to document the physical and relational labour of the Inn's Filipino workers across departments. In the Philippines, focusing on the family lives of participants, a similar method of observation was deployed. Here, the objective was to connect the paid labour of the Inn's migrant workforce to the lives of their non-migrant relatives. From the data generated by this multi-faceted and multi-sited research process, the explicit, as well as implicit, reproductive qualities of this labour came to be revealed.

This chapter unfolds in two sections. The first offers insight into the theoretical framing of the ensuing analysis, offering a sketch of feminist political economy's engagement with social reproduction, and more recently, the globalizations of social reproductive labour. Through an interrogation of the processes that operationalize and commodify intimacy and reproduction in the context of service and hospitality work, the second section explores the shifting and continuous dynamics of reproduction. This chapter illustrates the importance of feminist analysis of migration trajectories and labour processes that fall outside of the conventional purview of gender and migration studies. It suggests that in addition to interrogating the conditions and rationale under which *reproduction* comes to be articulated and experienced as labour, consideration of how divergent forms of labour also constitute and shape *reproduction* can provide significant insight into the social consequences of neoliberal capitalism, while revealing the ways in which the gendered and racialized parameters of reproductive and intimate labour come to be reproduced. Given its capacity to illuminate the otherwise unseen, feminist political economy offers a vital means of moving us beyond 'the domestic' to consider the manifold permutations of reproduction, and its associated labour.

Feminist Political Economy of Social Reproduction

Social reproduction encompasses a variety of relationships and activities intended to sustain individuals and groups as physical, social and cultural beings on daily basis, as well as generationally (Bakker, 2007). In its simplest form, it refers to biological reproduction and the tasks required to sustain life: finding food, building shelter, making clothes and providing care. Despite its consistent and necessarily embodied qualities, reproduction is 'secured through a shifting constellation of sources encompassed within the broad categories of the state, the household, capital, and civil society' (Katz, 2001, p. 711). As a result, reproduction is variable. It assumes its form in accordance with the socio-cultural, political, ideological and economic context in which it unfolds. These can transform reproduction, to direct the labour associated with it, to shape the relationships constituted within the parameters of that labour and to establish its relative value.

Social reproduction also refers to the reproduction of social relations (Mackintosh, 1981). More than procreation, the processes associated with reproduction reinforce and naturalize the systems in which biological survival occurs. Under capitalism, these processes are in one way or another dependent on the ability of individuals to sell labour for wages, which are, in turn, exchanged for the necessities of life. This dependency prompts the reproduction of particular kinds of labour. Not only biologically, speaking to the reproduction of labouring bodies, but also structurally and ideologically, speaking to the reproduction of forms of social organization, and their adjoining and supporting ideological systems. This occurs in large part through socialization, which includes the intergenerational transmission of gendered practices and behaviours. These reflect and reinforce the sexual division of labour. Under capitalism, the sexual division of labour follows a functional, spatial and ideological separation of reproductive and productive labour (Benston, 1969; Coulson, Magaš, & Wainwright, 1975; Youngs, 2000). This has direct consequences for social relationsand the organization of gender, as reproduction and production come to be centred in different social spaces (one fulfilling the biological needs of sexuality, reproduction and care; the other, the site of industrialized production, history, progress, economics and politics), and systematized according to perceived biological differences — the domestic and gendered coding of reproductive labour as essentially female, reinforcing its practical devaluation and its conceptual peripheralization (Federici, 2012; Waring, 1988).

Feminists, across disciplines, have long challenged women's position within the sexual division of labour (Federici, 2012; Friedan, 1963). Early feminist intervention into the sexual division of labour sought to liberate women from their domestic lives through education and labour market participation. And indeed, for *some* women, liberation was (if only partially) secured through those means. Feminist anthropologists have long pointed to the socially constructed and culturally variable nature of gendered configurations of labour (see Sanday, 1973). And beginning in the 1970s, Marxist feminists have argued that the sexual division of labour is, itself, an artifice: an ideological sleight of the capitalist class (Molyneux, 1979). Reduced to natural inclination and intuitive duty, women's reproductive labour is trivialized and obscured. It is made to *appear* valueless (Mackintosh, 1981), despite its inherent value. Here, the argument goes that largely unpaid and systemically unacknowledged, reproductive labour diverts the cost of sustaining and reproducing labour away from capital, redirecting it to the domestic sphere. There, women become primarily responsible for reproduction and the unending physical and emotional labour associated with it — labour that necessarily underpins all other forms of labour and productivity (Mies, 1986). Reflecting the economic aim of capitalism — the generation of profit — this highly gendered duality enables the capitalist mode of production to operate at a much higher level of productivity relative to other earlier modes of production as two workers (one 'productive', the other 'reproductive') come to be exploited with one wage (Fortunati, 1995).

Gender is, of course, not the only axis along which reproductive labour is divided, nor, is the sexual division of labour, the only division of labour upon which capital depends. Arrangements of productive and reproductive labour are furthered complicated by intersecting identities with constructs of race, ethnicity, nationality, legal status (immigrant vs. locally born) informing the extent to and manner in which women participated in paid labour, at a given time and in each place (Glenn, 1992). This speaks to the uneven distribution of reproductive labour, not simply between women and men, but amongst women themselves. More recent theorizations of the sexual division labour have furthered this analysis through an engagement with globalized processes of racialization and hierarchy. This work emphasizes the transformation of social reproduction in the wake of contemporary globalization and neoliberal restructuring as reflected in the rapid emergence of global care labour markets (Andersen, 2000; Gamburd, 2000; Sassen, 2000).

Although highly racialized domestic labour markets have long existed in North America and Europe (see Glenn, 1985), the incorporation of migrant labour into these markets since the 1980s has brought into focus the extent to which the division of domestic labour is unevenly distributed amongst women globally (Parreñas, 2000). This has received considerable academic attention, following in large part from Hochschild's formulation of the 'global care chain' (2000). The 'global care chain' is made up of three groups of women who meet their reproductive responsibilities in connected yet divergent ways: those who employ care labour migrants, those who migrate as care labourers and those who assume the socially constituted reproductive responsibilities of migrants in their absence (Mattingly, 2001; Misra, 2006; Sarvasy & Longo, 2004). The global care chain reflects the persistence of the sexual division of labour. Indeed, in most of the analysis to date, women remain responsible (in one way or another) for social reproductive labour. Drawing attention to *who does what for whom where*, this body of work highlights the emotional, social and relational consequences of global inequality, as 'care' is redirected away from those who are (by familial relation and social convention) 'entitled' to it towards those who can pay for it.

In the last several years, feminist scholars have attempted to push beyond the somewhat linear account of care transfer offered by the 'global care chain'. Yeates (2005, 2009), for example, situates the global transfer of care in transnational labour networks comprised of a variety of actors in a diverse range of settings, including home-based care, but also the many institutional settings that employ migrant care labour. Care labour, thus, comes to encompass the high-tech, the low-tech, the high-status, the low-status, the formal and the informal, and it includes a wide range of actors, including state and non-state intermediaries, and different kind of migrants (not only care labour migrants, and not only those with dependents). Bringing into sharper focus the invariable combination of caring and commodification that characterizes reproductive work both inside and *outside* of households (Peterson, 2010), this scholarship moves us closer to a conceptualization of service work as reproductive labour. It reminds us that 'care' — the dominant analytical framework in much of the research — can be commodified in several ways in a number of settings. And moreover, that while central, 'care' is but one element of a broader process; vital to, but not alone in, ensuring the reproduction of human bodies and social systems over time. The following section begins charting an initial theory of service work as reproductive labour — encompassing the reproduction of daily life, of labour and of social hierarchy. It concludes with an expansion of the 'global care chain' thesis, through a focus on the ways in which the commodified reproductive labour of the Inn's migrant Filipino workers articulates globally in supporting the daily reproductive needs and intergenerational reproductive projects of non-migrants in the Philippines.

Service and/as Reproduction

At the Inn, many reproductive cycles are initiated. These unfold in different ways, responding to the immediate physical needs of human bodies, both in Manitoba and in the Philippines, and to the needs of the Inn vis-à-vis its client base and workforce. These needs are connected; indeed, they are mutually constitutive. In its simplest and perhaps most obvious form, reproduction at the Inn plays out in the daily tasks performed by the workers employed there. Sitting at the intersection of three highways, 3400 vehicles are estimated to pass the hotel's expansive complex each day (Manitoba Transportation and Infrastructure, 2011). A combination of tourists, mobile workers (seasonal construction crews, trades people and truckers), travellers transiting the region and local residents make up the hotel's client base. Some stop for a coffee, a meal or a drink after work, while others arrive for a night's rest or longer term accommodation. For those who make use of the Inn's amenities, the efforts of individual workers (who cook, serve, clean and care) blend together in the service of daily reproduction. While much of this work is visible, much is performed behind closed doors: the preparation of food, the cleaning of rooms, the washing of bed sheets and towels, etc. — all go largely unnoticed by those who benefit from them. This is particularly true of housekeeping.

Although the reinstatement of guest rooms is one of the most important services offered by hotels (Powell & Watson, 2006), there is a remoteness to housekeeping. Housekeeping activities typically occur in the absence of guests, in the seclusion of individual rooms. Moreover, guest interactions with housekeeping staff, while not uncommon, tend to be brief and/or mediated through the front desk. The outcome of housekeeping labour contributes to its remote, or almost invisible, quality. An undoing or re-doing, the work of the Inn's housekeeping staff is rarely noticed unless it goes uncompleted. Manny, a Filipino worker from Iloilo, began working at the Inn in 2013. Having worked as a hotel housekeeper in Manila for over ten years, he is precise and exacting in his work. He begins with the beds. He vacuums. He dusts, disposing the occupant's garbage as he goes. He steps into the hallway, returning moments later with several spray bottles and a rag, elbow-length, yellow rubber gloves covering his hands and forearms. Turning his attention to the bathroom, he scrubs the counter-tops, the bathtub, the floor and the toilet. Finishing one room, he moves onto the next. And so, while guests rotate in and out — their temporary dependency on Manny's labour, the labour itself is highly repetitive and consistent.

For Manny and his co-workers, each day begins with a review of the room schedule — every housekeeper is assigned a set number of rooms in a section of the Inn. This number fluctuates, corresponding to the hotel's occupancy rate. The housekeepers, relative to their co-workers in other departments, are more vulnerable to the seasonal operations of the hotel. While open year-round, peak seasons (winter and summer) tend to see an additional influx of guests and therefore longer hours. In contrast, down-times (spring and fall) see fewer guests (generally) and therefore, fewer hours. For housekeepers, regardless of their residency status, this causes con-siderable stress. The experiences of the housekeeping staff most explicitly reflect the devaluing of reproductive labour, and the generally low-status afforded to cleaning work. Relative to other departments, housekeepers earn less, and are more frequently called upon to work outside of their assigned department, replacing janitorial and custodial staff, and being shuf-fled between the Inn and its satellite operations.

From this assemblage of isolation, repetition, precarity and flexibility, a particular continuity becomes clear — a persistent devaluing of reproduc-tive labour regardless of its organization and despite its commodification. Underwriting the devaluation of service and hospitality work are the funda-mental contradictions of domestic labour under the capitalist mode of pro-duction (Youngs, 2000). In the first instance, it speaks to women's socially constituted roles as caregivers — a role strategically devalued and natural-ized to ensure its ongoing fulfilment. In the second instance, and stemming from the foundations of the sexual division labour, are gendered discourses and practices that position men as 'breadwinners' and women as 'depen-dents', relegating the latter to the status of labour-reservists within paid labour markets (Mies, 1986). Regarded as supplemental, women's earnings traditionally have been lower than those of men. Within the service and hospitality sector, these characteristics of women's labour (both paid and unpaid) converge: the reproductive contours of the labour itself preclude the possibility of decent wages, while the history of the service and hospitality labour market (traditionally an enclave of female-employment) means that even as a growing number of men enter the sector, it remains low-status, poorly paid and insecure.

While differently configured and compartmentalized (no one worker is responsible for all aspects of a client's stay), the labour performed at the Inn resembles domestic work — both paid and unpaid. This is reflected in the reproductive contours of the work, its modest remuneration *and* in its interactive condition — that is the requirement that workers interact directly with customers, and that these interactions will produce a particular effect of hospitality. In the setting of a hotel, hospitality runs akin to care commodified. It requires workers to manage their feelings (often profound and fraught) so as to manage those of the client. As paying customers, guests are entitled to *feel* welcome, safe, appreciated, liked and taken care of. To this end, the Inn's workers engage in a variety of affective performances, intended to 'create, reinforce, or change the emotional and experiential states of customers on behalf of the organization that employs them' (Otis, 2012, p. 11). Such performances demand of the worker a particular, and at times, disingenuous, emotional output and display. And as such, they are predicated on the suppression of ones' own feelings and on the production of, a proper state of mind (Hochschild, 1983), one conducive to ensuring the emotional well-being of others.

Despite her frustrations at work and her ongoing anxiety concerning her family in the Philippines, Elizabeth — when at the front desk — is rarely without a smile. Manny, the primary breadwinner for his family, making his way through the halls (yellow gloves back on), offers guests a 'ma'am' or a 'sir' with every smile and every nod. Having just received word of a flood in her home town in the Philippines, Violet cheerfully prepares a customer's sandwich, one eye on the task at hand, the other (discretely) on the clock. At the Inn, such performances and acts of affective regulation are ubiquitous. Indeed, they are central to the mode of production undertaken there. If the Inn is to remain profitable, guests need to return, and so workers must meet their physical needs and their expectations. Put differently, guests must be satisfied; an outcome, not only of the provision of goods and services, but of the ways those goods and services are delivered, and importantly, by whom. Much like in other work places, stereotypes concerning gender and ethnicity shape the assumptions held by hotel management concerning worker suitability. These influence hiring and promotion decisions, and they structure the relationship between management and staff, as well as between workers and guests. These stereotypes further affect the labour performances (both bodily and affective) produced by workers, who, to meet the expectations of management (and guests), conform to the characteristics, attributes and skills associated with them.

At the Inn, perceptions of who is best suited to 'take care' of customers are additionally, and increasingly shaped by the characteristics of Philippine labour migration to Canada, and as such, they are mediated by the conditions of the Temporary Foreign Worker Program (TFWP), and by the vulnerabilities engendered by those conditions (Goldring, 2010). Once in Canada, temporary foreign workers (TFWs) must sell their labour in accordance with the conditions of the TFWP. These include restrictions on employment and housing, and they exclude workers from the normative legal frameworks that, following the Charter of Rights and Freedoms (1982), dictate labour standards and ensure resident-workers freedom of mobility. Because their residency is dependent upon their ongoing employment, TFWs are often reluctant to report maltreatment, breach of contract and abuse when it happens (Vosko, 2000). The extent of TFW dependency becomes more salient when one considers the reasons for which Filipino workers seek out temporary overseas employment: the ongoing reproduction of kin groups in a social and political context (that of the Philippines) fraught with insecurity.

At the same time, drawing on Philippine workers in particular, the Inn can access the high levels of competency engendered by their post-secondary education (Barber, 2008). For example, Violet, Elizabeth and Manny each hold degrees in hotel and restaurant management. While this is not an education that Canadian-born workers are likely to possess, it is what qualifies Philippine workers for employment at the Inn. This existing value is further augmented by practices and expectations of deference and respect, which while common-place in hotels generally, underpin hotel and hospitality work in the Philippines far more explicitly than they do in rural Manitoba. In their staging of hospitality, the Inn can capitalize on this combination of vulnerability, dependency, education and training to ensure higher than normal productive and affective outputs. In turn, the Inn (as an employer) decreases in desirability amongst local workers, who take up employment in other sectors. And so, a feedback loop comes to be established. In the absence of willing Canadian-born or naturalized workers, the Inn's use of the TFWP allows for the reproduction of its workforce, and of those qualities typical of the service and hospitality sector that have the tendency to dissuade local workers from taking up employment.

This cycle of reproduction is further reinforced through the dynamics of dependency connecting these workers to their non-migrant kin in the Philippines. Manny is his family's primary earner. He pays for his brother's education, and he provides for sister, mother, father and grandparents — all of whom live in the family's ancestral village. Without Manny's remittances, his family would struggle to survive. To improve the quality of their life and to redress some of the precarity they experience, Manny has been funding the construction of a concrete house. The project has been put on hold twice. In the first instance, following a fire that left the initial structure in ruins, and more recently, following an increase in his brother's tuition. Violet assumed the role of primary breadwinner for her family when her mother — who had worked in Malaysia as a domestic worker for 12 years, retired. Violent now supports her mother, her father, her two brothers and her sister. They share a small house in a congested subdivision. With her earnings from the Inn, Violet pays the bills, makes improvements on the family's home (including, most recently, the additional of a second floor where the family sleeps), and she pays for her youngest brother's school. From the Inn, Elizabeth also has assumed responsibility for her family's financial well-being and future. She has three children in the care of her husband (their father) and the family's helper, Shelly, in the Philippines. In Elizabeth's absence, both tend to the immediate needs of the children, providing them with emotional and material care, and tending to the myriad domestic tasks required for the functioning of the household. With her small earnings as a helper, Shelly supports her parents in Pangasinan, a province in the north-eastern part of the Philippines, and provides her cousin with a small salary to help them.

From the Inn, Elizabeth ensures the ongoing viability of their family's social reproductive project, as well as Shelly's. Relative to Manny and Violent, her reproductive labour and efforts reflect more precisely those of the 'migrant mothers' so frequently depicted in gender and migration scholarship (Bryan, 2014; Constable, 1997; Ehrenreich & Hochschild, 2003; Parreñas, 2001, 2005). Motivated by a desire to provide a different kind of future for her children, and following from new configurations of motherhood in the Philippines, international migration emerged as a viable option. Similarly, the ways in which 'care' has been distributed between Elizabeth, Shelly, and Shelly's cousin reflect the parameters of the global care chain as formulated by Hochschild and taken up within the gender and migration literature. And yet, Elizabeth is not a 'care worker', nor are the hotel's guests 'receivers of care', in the conventional sense. At the same time, Shelly's salary goes towards supporting her parents, as opposed to her children, of which she has none. Similarly, Manny and Violet support their parents and siblings in the Philippines. They do this while tending to the commodified reproductive needs of the hotel's clients who by virtue of their own mobility (be it short term or more permanent, corresponding to their own work lives), require that those needs be met on the market. Rather than transferred from woman to woman along gendered lines of affinal responsibility, then, reproduction, and the labour associated with it, is dispersed amongst an expansive circuitry that incorporates a variety of people and relationships — commodified in some corners, kin-based in others; at times, visceral and immediate; other times, stretched and abstracted; corresponding to gendered expectations, but also reflecting the increased incorporation of men in labour (both paid and unpaid) conventionally coded as a female.

Conclusion

Globally, the last 30 years have seen a dramatic redirection and redistribution of reproduction, and its associated intimate labours. While at the same time, there remains a certain kind of consistency — a tendency to devalue reproductive labour and to undervalue those who preform it regardless of its shape and/or delivery. Reflecting on the very permeable, yet consistent, parameters of reproductive labour, feminist scholars have noted that, rather than tangential (an outcome of economic restructuring), these transformations are central to strategies of capital accumulation, historically (Mies, 1986), as well as in the contemporary moment (Barber & Bryan, 2012). Following its commercial purpose, the Inn constructs a space that is intended to invoke the comforts, conveniences and services of 'home'. This is most immediately revealed through the Inn's provision of food, shelter and comfort — services rendered through the labour and physical efforts of the Inn's, largely migrant workforce. And yet, there is more to their labour than cooking, cleaning and engaging in pleasantries. Indeed, not unlike commodified care giving, the migrant workers at the Inn engage in emotional labour, constantly and consistently altering their affective states to produce hospitality — an effect central to the ongoing viability of the Inn.

The Inn's success is contingent upon the availability of specific kinds of workers: those regarded as most conducive to the manifold reproductive labour undertaken at the Inn. This labour is shaped, in large part, by the inequalities that characterize reproductive work and women's work (paid and unpaid) more generally. Indeed, underwriting the relative low status of service and hospitality work (at the Inn as elsewhere) is its historic and ongoing connection to the gendered division of labour. And so, despite the integration of a growing number of men in this work (e.g. Manny), it has remained feminized in both content and structure. These inequalities, however, do not simply run along an axis of gender. Indeed, reflecting the history of service work, racialized asymmetries underpin the labour of the Inn's migrant workforce as well. These are further compounded by the logistics of migrant worker recruitment, the local—global interface through which these workers are mobilized, and the social and economic hierarchies that demand the transnational distribution of reproduction.

References

Andersen, B. (2000). *Doing the dirty work? The global politics of domestic labour*. London: Zed Books.

Bakker, I. (2007). Social reproduction and the constitution of a gendered political economy. *New Political Economy, 12*(4), 541−556.

Barber, P. G. (2008). Cell phones, complicity and class politics in the Philippine labour diaspora. *Focaal: European Journal of Anthropology, 51*, 28−42.

Barber, P. G., & Bryan, C. (2012). "Value plus plus": Housewifization and history in Philippine care migration. In P. G. Barber & W. Lem (Eds.), *Twenty-first century migration: Political economy and ethnography* (pp. 86–116). New York, NY: Routledge.

Benston, M. (1969). The political economy of women's liberation. *Month Review, 21*(4), 13–27.

Bryan, C. (2014). Multiplying mothers: Migration and the work of mothering. In M. Vandenbeld Giles (Ed.), *Mothering in a neoliberal age* (pp. 35–50). Bradford, ON: Demeter Press.

Constable, N. (1997). *Maid to order in Hong Kong: Stories of Filipina workers.* London: Cornell University Press.

Coulson, M., Magaš, B., & Wainwright, H. (1975). The housewife and her labour under capitalism—A critique. *New Left Review, 1*(89), 59–71.

Ehrenreich, B., & Hochschild, A. R. (2003). *Global woman: Nannies, maids, and sex workers in the new economy.* New York, NY: Macmillan.

Federici, S. (2012). *Revolution at point zero: Housework, reproduction, and feminist struggle.* Oakland, CA: PM Press.

Fortunati, L. (1995). *The arcane of reproduction: Housework, prostitution, labour and capital.* New York, NY: Autonomedia.

Friedan, B. (1963). *The feminine mystique.* New York, NY: W. W. Norton & Company, Inc.

Gamburd, M. G. (2000). *The kitchen spoon's handle: Transnationalism and Sri Lanka's migrant housemaids.* Cornell: Cornell University Press.

Glenn, E. N. (1985). Racial ethnic women's labor: The intersection of race, gender and class oppression. *Review of Radical Political Economics, 17*(3), 86–108.

Glenn, E. N. (1992). From servitude to service work: Historical continuities in the racial division of paid reproductive labor. *Signs, 18*, 1–42.

Goldring, L. (2010). Temporary worker programs and precarious status: Implications for citizenship, inclusion and nation building in Canada. *Canadian Issues: Special Issue of Temporary Foreign Workers*, (Spring), 50–54.

Hochschild, A. (1983). *The managed heart: Commercialization of human feeling.* Berkeley, CA: University of California Press.

Hochschild, A. R. (2000). Global care chains and emotional surplus value. In W. Hutton & A. Giddens (Eds.), *On the edge: Living with global capitalism* (pp. 130–146). London: Jonathan Cape.

Katz, C. (2001). Vagabond capitalism and the necessity of social reproduction. *Antipode, 33*(4), 709–728.

Mackintosh, M. (1981). Gender and economics: The sexual division of labor and the subordination of women. In K. Young, C. Wolkowitz, & R. McCullogh (Eds.), *Of marriage and the market: Women's subordination internationally and its lessons* (pp. 3–18). London: Routledge.

Manitoba Transportation & Infrastructure. (2011). *Traffic on Manitoba Highways.* Retrieved from http://umtig.eng.umanitoba.ca/mhtis/printedreports/2011%20MHTIS%20Traffic%20Report.pdf

Mattingly, D. J. (2001). The home and the world: Domestic service and inter-national networks of caring labour. *Annals of the Association of American Geographers, 91*(2), 370−386.

Mies, M. (1986). *Patriarchy and accumulation on a world scale: Women in the international division of labour.* London: Zed Books.

Misra, J. (2006). The globalization of care work: Neoliberal economic restructuring and migration policy. *Globalizations, 3*(3), 317−332.

Molyneux, M. (1979). Beyond the domestic labour debate. *New Left Review, 116,* 3−27.

Otis, E. (2012). *Markets and bodies: Women, service work, and the making of inequality in China.* Stanford, CA: Stanford University Press.

Parreñas, R. S. (2000). Migrant Filipina domestic workers and the international division of reproductive labor. *Gender and Society, 14*(4), 560−580.

Parreñas, R. S. (2001). Mothering from a distance: Emotions, gender, and intergenerational relations in Filipino transnational families. *Feminist studies, 27*(2), 361−390.

Parreñas, R. (2005). Long distance intimacy: Class, gender and intergenerational relations between mothers and children in Filipino transnational families. *Global Networks, 5*(4), 317−336.

Peterson, V. S. (2010). Global householding amid global crisis. *Politics and Gender, 6*(2), 271−281.

Powell, P. H., & Watson, D. (2006). Service unseen: The hotel room attendant at work. *Hospitality Management, 25,* 297−312.

Sanday, P. (1973). Toward a theory of the status of women. *American Anthropologist, 75,* 1682−1700.

Sarvasy, W., & Longo, P. (2004). The globalization of care. *International Feminist Journal of Politics, 6*(3), 392−415.

Sassen, S. (2000). Women's burden: Counter-geographies of globalization and the feminization of survival. *Journal of International Affairs, 53*(2), 503−524.

Vosko, L. (2000). *Temporary work: The gendered rise of precarious employment.* Toronto: University of Toronto Press.

Waring, M. (1988). *If women counted: A new feminist economics.* London: Harper & Row.

Yeates, N. (2005). A global political economy of care. *Social Policy and Society, 4*(2), 227−234.

Yeates, N. (2009). *Globalizing care economies and migrant workers.* Basingstoke: Palgrave.

Youngs, G. (2000). Breaking patriarchal bonds: Demythologizing the public/private. In M. H. Marchand & A. S. Runyan (Eds.), *Gender and global restructuring: Sighting, sites, and resistances* (pp. 27−43). London: Routledge.

Chapter 10

Endemic Sexism in the Canadian Workplace: Systematic Support for Sexual Aggression

Ada L. Sinacore and Barbara A. Morningstar

Abstract

The aim of this chapter is to apply a Feminist Social Constructionist (FSC) epistemological stance to the analysis of the literature on sexual harassment and aggression in the workplace. Research demonstrates that institutions and their policies are ineffective in addressing sexual harassment and that, for the most part, perpetrators are not sanctioned. This chapter deconstructs the ways in which Canadian policies and systemic variables serve to silence victims of workplace abuse and, consequently, protect perpetrators. To this end, we review the definition, legislation and policies related to sexual harassment. Next, factors that lead to risk, reporting and silencing are assessed. As well, organizational responses are analysed to identify institutional factors that result in creating environments that serve to perpetuate sexism, and the resulting victimization of workers with little to no change in the number of perpetrators being implicated.

Keywords: Sexual harassment; workplace harassment; sexism; workplace abuse; policy; victimization

In Canada, the Ghomeshi case brought to the forefront the topic of sexual harassment and assault in the workplace resulting in a groundswell of response from the media and public (Tucker, 2014). Moreover, within this groundswell, the media has focused predominantly on women's reporting

Global Currents in Gender and Feminisms: Canadian and International Perspectives, 155–167

Copyright © 2018 by Emerald Publishing Limited

All rights of reproduction in any form reserved

ISBN: 978-1-78714-484-2/doi:10.1108/978-1-78714-483-520171015

giving rise to the social media movement "#beenrapedneverreported". However, little to no attention has addressed why workplace sexual harassment and assault exists. A recent Angus Reid poll (2014) indicated that over 28% of Canadians report having been sexually harassed and more than 14% report having been sexually assaulted at work with women being targeted at a significantly higher rate than men. On whole, in a span of two years, greater than 1,000,000 Canadians, mostly women, will have experienced sexual aggression at work (Angus Reid Institute, 2014). However, these statistics do not represent if these victims have filed formal complaints against their aggressor or the consequences they may have experienced because of the aggression (e.g. leaving job, trauma, medical complaints). The endemic and pervasive nature of sexual harassment was recognized by the Canadian Human Rights Commission which reported,

> We at the Commission believe, in fact, that sexual harassment in the workplace is under-reported. Filing a complaint takes courage. In some organizations, there could be fears of stigma or retaliation. For many, complaining is a last resort. It's often easier just to quit or to remain silent and take it. And there are gaps in our understanding. (Langtry, 2012, p.1)

As well, research indicates that for the most part men are the perpetrators of sexual harassment and aggression with little attention given to why men commit the offense and why they are rarely sanctioned (Johnson, 2012). Further, the media's focus on reporting or lack thereof only serves to perpetuate the myth that women are somehow responsible for the sexual aggression and, therefore, responsible for its prevention (Weiss, 2010). Research demonstrates that institutions and their policies are endemically sexist resulting in the re-victimization of the victim, in effect exonerating the perpetrator (Hart, 2012).

Accordingly, in this chapter, we aim to analyse the literature on sexual harassment and aggression in the workplace through the lens of feminist social constructionist (FSC) theory to highlight how institutions and their policies are constructed, such that endemic sexism is perpetuated resulting in the victimization of workers, while perpetrators go unsanctioned.

FSC Theory

FSC theory proposes that there are multiple valid truths, and views language as a means for constructing and maintaining a reality that benefits certain individuals and groups (Sinacore & Enns, 2005). Gender is a central construct of FSC, whereby, gender is viewed as performative and socially constructed. As such, FSC addresses the hegemonic links between gender performance and biological sex. Further, this theory, deconstructs and questions accepted truths and dualistic constructs (Sinacore & Enns, 2005). Thus, FSC as an analytic tool requires an examination of how multiple social identities (e.g. women, worker) are shaped across time and contexts. Therefore, employing FSC as an epistemological stance to analyse the literature on sexual harassment allowed us to identify the ways gender, social identity and marginalization influences women's experiences and negotiation of victimization. Deconstructing the dualities within the sexual harassment literature allowed for an assessment of how systems of power and oppression serve to silence victims of sexual harassment and aggression and highlighted the discourses that maintain and create contexts wherein women continue to be victimized and blamed for that victimization.

Defining Sexual Harassment

To understand and critically address the social construction of sexual harassment it is necessary to define this phenomenon. A commonly used and foundational definition of sexual harassment was put forward by Louise F. Fitzgerald in 1988. She proposed a three-fold definition which includes; (a) a hostile environment with negative attitudes, (b) unwelcome sexual attention and sexual coercion and (c) threat regarding the target's work (e.g. denying access to information or opportunities for promotion).

However, for the most part, the definition used by employers is embedded in the legislation that evolved to address sexual harassment in the workplace. That is, sexual harassment is a workplace problem that was, predominantly, ignored until the emergence of the feminist movement in the 1970s in North America, wherein feminist groups raised a range of issues regarding workplace discrimination (e.g. equal pay for equal work, sex-based discrimination) and pressed governments to bring about legislative changes (Cohen, 1992). Resultantly, Parliament passed the *Canadian Human Rights Act* in 1977; yet at that time sexual harassment was not included as a form of discrimination in this Act. In fact, it was not until the 1980s that sexual harassment became recognized as a workplace problem (Haiven, 2006). That is, in 1983 sexual discrimination was added to the *Canadian Human Rights Act* (Langtry, 2012). In 1989, the Supreme Court of Canada confirmed the definition in the decision *Janzen v. Platy Enterprises Ltd.* with the ruling "that sexual harassment is sex discrimination" (Canadian Human Rights Reporter, 2013).

Subsequently, provincial legislation followed suit. For example, in the *Ontario Human Rights Code*, sexual harassment is explicitly defined and prohibited. The Ontario Human Rights Commission (OHRC) legally defines sexual harassment as "unwanted or unwelcome physical and verbal behaviours of a sexual nature" (OHRC, 2007, Para. 2), and these behaviours can include exposure to images, language or touching. While in other provinces, notably Nova Scotia and Alberta, sexual harassment is considered to be included in legislation that prohibits discrimination based on sex (Haiven, 2006). In Quebec, the labour standards include sexual harassment within the criteria of psychological harassment. Those standards state that "psychological harassment at work is vexatious behaviour in the form of repeated conduct, verbal comments, actions or gestures: that are hostile or unwanted that affect the employee's dignity or psychological or physical integrity and that make the work environment harmful" (CNESST, 2016).

Risk Factors for Sexual Harassment

In addition to legislative definitions, researchers have tried to understand the problem of sexual harassment beyond its mere definition. Scholars posit that sexual harassment is a form of violence that results from hierarchal relationships and a misuse of power therein. Dionsi, Barling, and Dupré (2012) suggest that "harassment is a means of social control that objectifies and forces women into positions of subordination — all characteristics reflected in rape and domestic violence" (p. 399). Similarly, McDonald (2012) describes sexual harassment as, "one of a range of abusive or counterproductive workplace behaviours which have hierarchical power relations at their core" (p. 2). Given these power dynamics it is not surprising that the most frequent type of harassment is women being targeted by heterosexual men (McDonald, 2012).

In Canada, statistics reveal that, "in nearly all the incidents of sexual violence against women (99%), the accused perpetrator was male. In 2009, 81% of sexual assault incidents against women involved unwanted sexual touching…" (Sinha & Statistics Canada, 2013, p 31). Statistics reveal that perpetrators of sexual harassment in the workplace are predominantly male (Barling, Clegg, & Cooper, 2008) and several sources indicate that approximately 85% of complaints are filed by women with about 15% filed by men (Angus Reid, 2014; Langtry, 2012; McDonald, 2012). However, these statistics represent complaints that are filed, and therefore, it is difficult to assess how many actual incidents of sexual harassment and aggression occur within the workplace due to underreporting (Langtry, 2012). For example, in a 2016 landmark case, where class actions were brought forward for victims of sexual harassment in the Royal Canadian Mounted Police (RCMP), it was estimated that, since the inclusion of women in the ranks in 1974, over 20,000 past and current employees could be eligible for compensation which could cost upwards of $100 million. In fact, the RCMP acknowledged and offered an apology for the systemic harassment suffered within their institution (Harris, 2016). This case clearly exemplifies the long term, on-going and pervasive nature of workplace sexual harassment.

Further, studies that have attempted to identify variables that may put individuals at risk for sexual harassment and/or aggression, for the most part, do not indicate that there is a psychological profile that leads to victimization (Schneider, Pryor, & Fitzgerald, 2011). The few studies that successfully identify variables that may lead to victimization such as low-esteem and high levels of negative affect were conducted after the abuse occurred, and consequently, it is difficult to assess as to whether these attributes led to victimization or were a result of victimization (Aquino & Thau, 2009).

In addition to psychological variables, some studies have examined demographic variables. For men, risk factors for victimization include being from an ethnic minority, gay and/or young. However, risk factors that may lead to a woman being the target include divorce or separation, holding a non-traditional job, having a disability, being a sexual minority and/or being an ethnic minority (McDonald, 2012; Schneider et al., 2011). As well, women who are temporary or contract workers are more likely to be targeted (McDonald, 2012). Additionally, the risk of sexual harassment increased for women who took on positions of authority within the workplace (McLaughlin, Uggen, & Blackstone, 2012). Finally, research indicated that the likelihood of being harassed increased with the number of risk factors an individual holds (McDonald, 2012).

Embedded in the definition of sexual harassment is an abuse of power. In addition to this power differential, sexual harassment is connected to the hegemonic link between gender role expectations and biological sex. For example, McLaughlin et al. (2012) posit that women who are bosses, "create a paradox of power in a gender system that continues to subordinate women. In taking on positions of authority, they also take on a greater risk of sexual harassment" (p. 642). These authors suggest that some men who must listen to a woman boss feel threatened and, to exert their masculinity, they become aggressors. Similarly, McDonald (2012) suggests that to maintain the social power connected to heterosexual male masculinity, women must perform in their prescribed feminine roles. Thus, as a means to maintaining their male heterosexual privilege, some men may become harassers as a way of 'putting women in their place' thus threatening women into submission. Concurrently, effeminate men (gay or heterosexual) and gay men may be at risk for harassment due to their rejection of either masculinity or heterosexuality; again, threatening the power associated with the hegemonic links between heterosexuality, masculinity and privilege (Barling et al., 2008).

Hence, sexual harassment in the workplace is a manifestation of societal power dynamics, whereby individuals who are situated on the margins are vulnerable to abuse. While oftentimes victims of sexual harassment are accused of attracting the behaviour (Sekreta, 2006), these individuals are not acting in any way to invite sexual harassment; they are simply targeted for stepping outside of the social constructed power relations linked to their gender or biological sex that threatens constructions of masculinity and heterosexuality.

Reporting and the System's Response

Institutions, family members and coworkers are all negatively impacted by sexual harassment (Lim & Cortina, 2005). Specifically, once an individual is targeted for sexual harassment the victim's response, or lack thereof, reverberates through the system (Cortina & Berdahl, 2008). Given that the victim's response may over time have many different and evolving components (e.g. ignoring, denying, reporting), how information about incident(s) becomes known and how the system responds both formally and informally may serve to ostracize the victim (Benavides & Cunningham, 2010; Butler & Chung-Yan, 2011; Johnson, 2012; Salin, 2009). This impacts a range of interpersonal relationships including those with coworkers and family members (Clarke, 2014; Lim & Cortina, 2005; Rospenda, Fujishiro, Shannon, & Richman, 2008).

Overall, victims do not report the harassment. In fact, in Canada, it has been found that four out of five individuals surveyed, who state that they have been harassed or worse at work never made a complaint (Angus Reid, 2014). This non-response is due to a range of factors such as age, personal characteristics (e.g. multiple minority identities), severity of harassment and the role or status of the perpetrator (e.g. supervisor, popular with peers). In addition, research indicates that when a woman is harassed she is decentralized and at first may minimize the incident and try to manage it on her own depending on how she perceives the severity of the harassment. According to the Angus Reid poll (2014), reasons for not reporting included, (a) being afraid, (b) shame, (c) fear for job or career, (d) minimizing the incident, (e) fear of not being believed, (f) thinking they can handle the incident on their own and (f) not wanting to revisit the incident. This avoidance of reporting may be exacerbated by living in a society wherein women are socialized to be passive and to avoid conflict (Sekreta, 2006). As such, women may choose not report to 'toe the line', and to avoid being blamed or ostracized. Ironically, women who do not report or wait to report are accused of either having consented, invited or fabricated the story (Cortina & Berdahl, 2008). Consequently, women are in a double bind situation, because whether or not women report they run the risk of being further traumatized through the process as they are blamed for their victimization as perpetrators are, typically, not held accountable.

This assessment of whether or not to report is further complicated by organizational factors that deter or discourage reporting. In organizations where employees are under the impression that sexual harassment is tolerated and that there are no consequences for harassers, the likelihood of reporting is low (Benavides & Cunningham, 2010; Butler & Chung-Yan, 2011; Salin, 2009). Salin (2009) and Johnson (2012) suggest that in most cases, minimal, if any, consequences are imposed on perpetrators leaving victims and observers with the sense that the negative behaviour is tolerated. The 2014 Angus Reid poll highlights that victims both believe that the organization will not respond, and that in fact this lack of response was the case. Moreover, reporting procedures that put the burden of proof on the victim alone results in an environment where it is dangerous for a victim to report, especially when the reporting process starts with the employee's manager or supervisor. That is, managers may be in a position of conflict of interest, as well they may not have the requisite skills (e.g. conflict resolution) to address the complaints rendering their response ineffectual.

In addition, researchers have examined the many negative outcomes for victims of sexual harassment that reverberate throughout the system. That is, victims of sexual harassment experience a range of physical and psychological consequences including, a lack of life satisfaction, disengagement from family (Lim & Cortina, 2005) and the development of negative coping mechanisms such as addiction (Rospenda et al., 2008). In addition, victimization negatively influences the employee's engagement with work compromising their performance, productivity and relationships with colleagues (Clarke, 2014).

However, if the victim pursues compensation (e.g. paid sick leave) for the injuries resulting from the sexual harassment, this process of reporting may result in additional hardship and suffering for the victim. For example, Makela (2006) argues that since most workplace compensation schemes are constructed for identifiable physical injury or psychological diagnoses, victims are then required to submit themselves to physical and/or psychological evaluations, thus, declaring themselves ill, while perpetrators are viewed as healthy functioning individuals. One could even argue that it is the perpetrator who is 'sick', yet only the victim must receive a diagnosis. Makela (2006) laments that this problem is a, "reflection of a society that has yet to eliminate the underlying prejudices and presuppositions that accompany the systemic devaluation of women and their experiences (p.46)".

Moreover, reporting does not mitigate these negative outcomes. Oftentimes for those victims who put forth the effort to report and denounce the perpetrator, the negative effects of the victimization are amplified if there is an insufficient response by the employer (Clarke, 2014). Reporting may result in fears of, or actual victim blaming resulting in further mistreatment such as not being believed, being bullied by coworkers to renege and an increasingly negative work environment (Bergman, Fitzgerald, & Cortina, 2002; Dionisi et al., 2012). In addition, employers (regardless of size of organization) may dissuade individuals from reporting due to the legal implications for the institution. That is, although laws in Canada prohibit sexual harassment with the goal of promoting a safe working environment, oftentimes employers are less interested in the impact of harassment on the environment or other employees, but rather they are more interested in the legal risks for the organization. If the harassment were to become public, employers are concerned about how this information, once known, will affect the reputation of the institution. As such, policies, procedures and enforcement may appear to be appropriate on paper but, in reality, maybe constructed such that there is little to no change to the suffering of the victims (Perry, Kulik, & Field, 2009).

As well, when the aggressor is perceived by the employer (and coworkers) to be more important to the institution than the victim, employers may be more likely to protect the perpetrator to benefit the institution. Thus, any laudable goal such as providing a safe workplace or protecting the rights of workers falls away when the 'cost benefit analysis' cuts out the victim and prioritizes the aggressor, while coworkers observe the process. In this type of institutional climate, the victim oftentimes leaves the organization due to illness or dismissal, while the perpetrator remains in the institution without sanctions (Hubert, 2003).

Furthermore, within a unionized work environment reporting may be complicated when both employees involved are members of the same union. Specifically, the role of the union is to represent all its members, however, unions are also mandated to protect their members from losing their job or being sanctioned. Resultantly, when both the victim and perpetrator are members of the same union, unions tend to fight to reinstate alleged harassers, aggressors and abusers regardless of the cost to the victims. According to Haiven,

> Unions are so tied up in defensive mode with the employer that not much attention is paid to the union member who was aggrieved. Either she is cast in the role as witness for the company and a *stool pigeon* not to be spoken to, or she

leaves the workplace — sometimes at high personal and financial cost ... In these cases, unions have rarely concerned themselves as much with the victim as with the perpetrator. (2006, pp. 199−200)

Similarly, Hart (2012) argues that unions in their support of male aggressors demonstrate a lack of understanding of sexual harassment. She contends that the gendered arguments applied by unions "ignored the underlying cause of gendered organizational hierarchy and also ignored available arbitral jurisprudence on sexual harassment as involving the abuse of sexual and economic power" (p. 277). Through supporting the interests of male grievers, unions serve to continue to marginalize women's experiences, while, keeping male workers interests at the forefront (Hart, 2012). If the union were to litigate on behalf of the victim, the costs could be quite significant. For example, it is estimated that taking up a legal case for a victim could cost the union upwards of $150,000 in Quebec (Tremblay, 2007). Thus, there may be a financial benefit to the union to exonerate the perpetrator.

Therefore, when the system's response aims to both elevate the image of the organization and minimize liability and exposure to the public justice or arbitration systems, the interests of the victims are often lost in both pursuits. Caught between the interests of unions and the interests of corporations or government employers, victims can be viewed as a problem. The most common means for victims to report sexual harassment is through a complaint or grievance procedure; however, the procedures in place for reporting sexual harassment are inadequate as they do not attend to the structural inequities within the institution resulting from the conflicting duality between the need for legal compliance and protecting the interests of the corporation (McDonald, 2012). Handy (2006) suggests that management may collude with harassers against the interests of the victims when this collusion is perceived to be in the interests of the employer. Ironically, when an organization is responsive to reports of sexual harassment signalling that perpetrators will be sanctioned, victims are less likely to seek out redress through the legal system (Clarke, 2014). Thus, strategies that serve to protect the perpetrator in the interest of protecting the organization may ultimately backfire as sexual harassment negatively affects both victims and observers. While the organization may, in the short run, believe they are protecting their interests; in the long run, the collateral damage resulting from the negative effect of harassment combined with organizations ineffectual responses to both victims and bystanders can ultimately result in a less productive and committed workforce in the long run.

FSC Analysis

Using the lens of FSC analysis highlighted that policy and procedure surrounding sexual harassment serves to protect the societal privilege ascribed to being male, heterosexual and masculine. Thus, women who take on roles outside of what is socially prescribed and men who are effeminate or gay are at risk of being sexual harassed; clearly taking on these non-traditional social locations fundamentally challenges heterosexual male privilege. Additionally, the FSC analysis indicated that there are systemic variables that continue to serve to oppress women workers, and ultimately support environments in which sexual harassment is likely to occur. These systemic variables, such as victim blaming, poor policy construction, lack of response on part of the organization and ineffectual union responses result in victims being afraid to report and perpetrators going unsanctioned. Moreover, when organizations put their reputation above the safety of employees, not only does this phenomenon create an environment ripe for sexual harassment but is likely to reduce employees' loyalty to the institutions. Consequently, these discourses result in the silencing of victims, such that perpetrators and the organization's reputation are protected at the expense of the victims' health, security and professional development.

Feminism Still Matters

Feminism implores us to examine the multiple social locations in which people reside to address the power, privilege and oppression related to those locations regardless of biological sex. Yet, for women, the workplace remains a dangerous environment due to sexual harassment and aggression. Resultantly, women's physical and psychological health is compromised and they are economically disadvantaged due to loss of job and occupational status. In fact, the primary way in which women cope with being sexually harassed is to leave their job, and many leave the workforce entirely due to the resulting physical and psychological challenges (Chafetz, 1999; Sims, Drasgow, & Fitzgerald, 2005). Sexual harassment results in the loss of a significant amount of potential and talent in the workforce, as women are pushed out ensuring that heterosexual male masculinity remains privileged and in positions of power. Sadly, in the 1970s feminists raised the issue of workplace inequities and these inequities still exist. Thus, until inequities in the workplace are truly addressed and policies and procedures are put in place that support all employees' rights to a safe and productive work environment feminism still matters.

While steps to address sexual harassment through developing provincial and federal legislation in Canada is laudable, this legislation will remain ineffective until policies and procedures are in place that actually support a victim's right to pursue redress when they are sexually aggressed at work. Reconstruction of how sexual harassment is mitigated is necessary such that victim blaming is ameliorated and safe reporting is the norm. In sum, the goal of feminism is to develop a just society which translates into a safe workplace, wherein all employees can meet their potential, regardless of their social locations.

References

Angus Reid Institute/Public Interest Research. (2014). *Three-in-ten Canadians say they've been sexually harassed at work, but very few have reported this to their employers.* Angus Reid Institute/Public Interest Research. Retrieved from http://angusreid.org/wp-content/uploads/2014/12/2014.12.05-Sexual-Harassment-at-work.pdf

Aquino, K., & Thau, S. (2009). Workplace victimization: Aggression from the target's perspective. *The Annual Review of Psychology, 60,* 717–741. doi:10.1146/annurev.psych.60.110707.163703

Barling, J., Clegg, S., & Cooper, C. L. (2008). *The Sage handbook of organizational behavior.* Los Angeles, CA: Sage.

Benavides, E. C., & Cunningham, G. B. (2010). Observers' reporting of sexual harassment: The influence of harassment type, organizational culture, and political orientation. *Public Organization Review: A Global Journal, 10*(4), 323–337. doi:10.1007/s11115-009-0109-4

Bergman, M. E., Fitzgerald, L. F., & Cortina, L. M. (2002). The (un)reasonableness of reporting: Antecedents and consequences of reporting sexual harassment. *The Journal of Applied Psychology, 87*(2), 230–242.

Butler, A. M., & Chung-Yan, G. A. (2011). The influence of sexual harassment frequency and perceptions of organizational justice on victim responses to sexual harassment. *European Journal of Work and Organizational Psychology, 20*(6), 729–754.

Canadian Human Rights Reporter (2013). *Sexual harassment is sex discrimination.* Retrieved from http://www.cdn-hr-reporter.ca/hr_topics/sexual-harassment/sexual-harassment-sex-discrimination

Chafetz, J. S. (1999). *Handbook of the sociology of gender.* New York, NY: Kluwer Academic/Plenum Publishers.

Clarke, H. M. (2014). Predicting the decision to report sexual harassment: Organizational influences and the theory of planned behavior. *Journal of Organizational Psychology, 14*(2), 52–65.

CNESST/Commission des Normes, de l'Équité, de la Santé et de la Sécurité du Travail (2016). *Psychological harassment at work.* Retrieved from http://www.cnt.gouv.qc.ca/en/in-case-of/psychological-harassment-at-work/index.html

Cohen, M. G. (1992). The Canadian women's movement and its efforts to influence the Canadian economy. In C. Blackhouse & D. H. Flaherty (Eds.), *Challenging times: The women's movement in Canada and the United States* (pp. 215−224). Montreal, QC: McGill-Queen's University Press.

Cortina, L. M., & Berdahl, J. L. (2008). Sexual harassment in organizations: A decade of research in review. In J. Barling, S. Clegg, & C. L. Cooper (Eds.), *The Sage handbook of organizational behavior* (pp. 469−497). Los Angeles, CA: Sage.

Dionisi, A. M., Barling, J., & Dupré, K. E. (2012). Revisiting the comparative outcomes of workplace aggression and sexual harassment. *Journal of Occupational Health Psychology, 17*(4), 398−408.

Fitzgerald, L. F. (1988). The incidence and dimensions of sexual harassment in academia and the workplace. *Journal of Vocational Behavior, 32*(2), 152−175.

Haiven, J. (2006). Zero tolerance: Can it work in a unionized environment? *Labour/ Le Travail, 58,* 169−202.

Handy, J. (2006). Sexual harassment in small-town New Zealand: A qualitative study of three contrasting organizations. *Gender, Work and Organization, 13*(1), 1−24.

Harris, K. (2016). Mounties offer apology and $100M compensation for harassment, sexual abuse against female members. *CBC News,* October 6. Retrieved from http://www.cbc.ca/news/politics/rcmp-paulson-compensation-harassment-1.3793785

Hart, S. M. (2012). Labour arbitration of co-worker sexual harassment cases in Canada. *Canadian Journal of Administrative Sciences/Revue Canadienne Des Sciences De L'Administration, 29*(3), 268−279.

Hubert, A. B. (2003). To prevent and overcome undesirable interaction: A systematic approach model. In S. Einarsen, H. Hoel, D. Zapf, & C. L. Cooper (Eds.), *Bullying and emotional abuse in the workplace: International perspectives in research and practice* (pp. 299−311). London: Taylor & Francis.

Johnson, H. (2012). Limits of a criminal justice response: Trends in police and court processing of sexual assault. In E. Sheehy (Ed.), *Sexual assault in Canada: Law, legal practice and women's activism* (pp. 613−634). Ottawa: University of Ottawa Press.

Langtry, D. (2012). Canadian Human Rights Commission. Presentation to the House of Commons Standing Committee on the Status of Women: Sexual harassment persists in Canada, October 16. Retrieved from http://www.chrc-ccdp.gc.ca/eng/content/sexual-harassment-persists-canada

Lim, S., & Cortina, L. M. (2005). Interpersonal mistreatment in the workplace: The interface and impact of general incivility and sexual harassment. *Journal of Applied Psychology, 90,* 483−496.

Makela, F., (2006). Tell me where it hurts: Workplace sexual harassment compensation and the regulation of hysterical victims. *McGill Law Journal, 51*(1), 27−46.

McDonald, P. (2012). Workplace sexual harassment 30 years on: A review of the literature. *International Journal of Management Reviews, 14*(1), 1−17.

McLaughlin, H., Uggen, C., & Blackstone, A. (2012). Sexual harassment, workplace authority, and the paradox of power. *American Sociological Review, 77*(4), 625−647.

Ontario Human Rights Commission (OHRC) (2007). *Sexual and gender-based harassment: Know your rights.* Retrieved from http://www.ohrc.on.ca/en/issues/sexual_harassment

Perry, E. L., Kulik, C. T., & Field, M. P. (2009). Sexual harassment training: Recommendations to address gaps between the practitioner and research literatures. *Human Resource Management, 48*(5), 817—837.

Rospenda, K. M., Fujishiro, K., Shannon, C. A., & Richman, J. A. (2008). Workplace harassment, stress, and drinking behavior over time: Gender differences in a national sample. *Addictive Behaviors, 33*, 964—967. doi:10.1016/j.addbeh.2008.02.009

Salin, D. (2009). Organizational responses to workplace harassment. An exploratory study. *Personnel Review, 38*(1), 26—44.

Schneider, K. T., Pryor, J. B., & Fitzgerald, L. F. (2011). Sexual harassment research in the United States. In S. Einarsen, H. Hoel, D. Zapf, & C. L. Cooper (Eds.), *Bullying and emotional abuse in the workplace: International perspectives in research and practice* (pp. 245—266). London: Taylor & Francis.

Sekreta, E. (2006). Sexual harassment, misconduct, and the atmosphere of the laboratory: The legal and professional challenges faced by women physical science researchers at educational institutions. *Duke Journal of Gender Law and Policy, 13*, 115—137.

Sims, C. S., Drasgow, F., & Fitzgerald, L. F. (2005). The effects of sexual harassment on turnover in the military: Time-dependent modeling. *Journal of Applied Psychology, 90*, 1141—1152.

Sinacore, A. L., & Enns, C. Z. (2005). Diversity feminisms: Postmodern, women-of-color, antiracist, lesbian, third-wave, and global perspectives. In A. L. Sinacore & C. Z. Enns (Eds.), *Teaching and social justice: Integrating multicultural and feminist theories in the classroom* (pp. 41—68). Washington, DC: American Psychological Association.

Sinha, M., & Statistics Canada. (2013). *Measuring violence against women: Statistical trends.* Ottawa: Ministry of Industry. Retrieved from http://www.statcan.gc.ca/pub/85-002-x/2013001/article/11766-eng.pdf

Tremblay, J. (2007). Harcèlement: Les syndicats coincés. *La Presse.* February 12. Retrieved from http://affaires.lapresse.ca/economie/200901/06/01-679062-harcelement-les-syndicats-coinces.php

Tucker, D. (2014). Timeline: Jian Ghomeshi charged in sex assault scandal. *Global News Online,* December 3. Retrieved from globalnews.ca/news/1647091/timeline-sex-assault-allegations-arise-after-cbc-fires-jian-ghomeshi/

Weiss, K. (2010). Too ashamed to report: Deconstructing the shame of sexual victimization. *Feminist Criminology, 5*(3), 286—310.

Chapter 11

Excluded While Included: Women Mineworkers in South Africa's Platinum Mines

Asanda Benya

Abstract

In 1994 South Africa transitioned from apartheid — a system of racial segregation and oppression — to a democracy. After the transition, legislations which had prohibited women from working underground in mines were repealed and replaced by gender sensitive ones. These legislative changes were crucial in the entrance of women in mining, especially underground occupations. Yet, while legislative changes have taken effect women continue to feel like outsiders and invaders in mining. They face many challenges and their experiences at work continue to be mediated by their gender. While some argue that legislative changes in mining symbolise a shift towards a gender inclusive mining industry, this chapter demonstrates a gendered structural resistance to the inclusion of women and argues that more changes are required if mining is to be seen as gender sensitive and inclusive.

Keywords: Women mineworkers; mining; masculinity; feminism; occupational culture

Introduction

The South African mining industry employs close to 1.3 million people, about 500,000 directly and 800,000 indirectly. According to the Department of Mineral Resources' (DMR) annual report (2014), only 52,000 of these

Global Currents in Gender and Feminisms: Canadian and International Perspectives, 169–180
Copyright © 2018 by Emerald Publishing Limited
All rights of reproduction in any form reserved
ISBN: 978-1-78714-484-2/doi:10.1108/978-1-78714-483-520171016

workers are women or roughly 10.9% of the total mining workforce. These figures are novel 'highs' since women in South Africa (SA) have largely been absent from mining. Their exclusion was legislated from as early as the 1911 Mines and Works Act No. 12 and as recent as the South African Minerals Act of 1991.[1] The transition[2] from apartheid to post-apartheid led to legislative changes which covered the mining industry. They sought to facilitate and accelerate women's inclusion in mining (Benya, 2009; Simango, 2006). These include the Mine Health and Safety Act (1996), the Mineral and Petroleum Resources Development Act (MPRDA 2002) and the Broad-Based Socio-Economic Empowerment Charter (also known as the Mining Charter 2002).[3] The Mining Charter, for instance, sets six specific targets with time frames.[4] One of these is a 10% participation of women in mining.[5] Progress on targets is monitored by the Commission on Gender Equality, an independent Chapter Nine Institution[6] which promotes gender equality and ensures the protection of gender rights. These policies and targets, which were supposed to be strictly enforced with severe penalties (e.g. possibilities of withdrawal of a mining licence if not implemented), were the bedrock of women's inclusion in mining (Benya, 2009).

While the inclusion of women in mining is legislated and women can now work underground, in practice it was not a welcomed change, it produced 'a state of disorientation and ontological anxiety' (Puwar, 2004, p. 13) in the industry with some male workers and some in management claiming that women negatively affect productivity, mining traditions,

---

[1]The banning of women from mining in South Africa was partly prompted by the British Mines Act of 1842. Other countries which also banned women from mining were Sweden in 1900, Russia in 1917, Japan in 1928 and India in 1929 (Alexander, 2007; Lahiri-Dutt & Macintyre, 2006).

[2]Von Holdt (2003) and Webster and Von Holdt (2005) have called the transition a 'triple transition' (p. 4); political, economic and social, while earlier work by Adler and Webster (2000) saw it as a 'double transition' mainly focusing on the political and economic transition.

[3]Gender equality is enshrined in the Constitution of the Republic of South Africa, and the Bill of Rights (1996). Other general labour legislations adopted after 1994 include, but is not limited to, the Labour Relations Act of 1996, the Basic Conditions of Employment Act of 1997 and the Employment Equity Act of 1998.

[4]To ensure empowerment of the previously excluded and disadvantaged, the industry has committed to human resources development which is based on the Skills Development Act 97 of 1998, to the Employment Equity Act 55 of 1998, addressing migrant labour through the Immigration Act 13 of 2002, mine community development, housing and living conditions, amongst many others (Mining Charter Impact Assessment Report, October 2009).

[5]The Bill has been revised twice since 2004; first in 2009 and again in 2014.

[6]Chapter Nine Institutions are institutions established in terms of Section 187 of the SA Constitution (1996) to safeguard the country's democracy.

morals, families and ultimately society (Benya, 2009). As such, the position of women in mining is tenuous and contested. While mining has transformed legislatively, this transformation has not produced structural changes; men continue to dominate and masculinity remains the norm.

The aim of this chapter is to lay bare the normalised ways in which masculinity continues to be the norm in mining and a hindrance to the inclusion of women in mining. This chapter builds on work done by feminist scholars (Acker, 1990; Britton, 2000; Kelan, 2009; Lahiri-Dutt, 2006; Puwar, 2004; Sasson-Levy, 2007) in masculine workplaces and occupations where women disrupt masculine naturalisation and assumptions and, despite inclusive legislation, demonstrate the deeply entrenched hegemonic masculinism and maleness of these industries and occupations. In this chapter, I demonstrate how the entrance of women in mining jobs makes visible the hegemonic position of masculinity in the mines and in mine culture. I argue that maleness and masculinity remain; the taken for granted norm, the naturalised and invisibilised, yet hegemonic masculine occupational culture. I draw on a few examples; the representation of women in key occupations in mining, the gendered design of personal protective equipment (PPE) and the gendered violence women are subject to underground, yet ignored by different stakeholders such as the mine, the Chamber of Mines and the union. The ways in which occupations are allocated and the violence that women face illustrate how gender still matters and why feminism continues to be key in ensuring not only legislative but structural gender inclusivity and a full incorporation and recognition of women as equal workers in the masculine mining industry and not support workers who are only brought in to fulfil a legislative demand.

Disrupting Masculinity: Women in Mining

The recent entrance of women into mining is seen in three ways. First, as unfeminine or 'unnatural', and an insult to women who must now go labour underground under conditions that should only be endured by men. This view, which has sought to maintain the status quo and promote 'appropriate' gender roles and thus women's domesticity, argues that women's participation in mining, a 'naturally' masculine industry, will negatively impact on their femininity, safety and production underground.[7] It has been used to legitimise the slow integration of women in mining.

The second perspective, mainly from liberal feminists and politicians, argues that the inclusion of women in mining symbolises an air of change,

---

[7]See evidence of these views by mineworkers, unionists and mine management in Simango (2006) and Benya (2009, 2013).

a breakdown of gender barriers which have historically prevented women from entering the mines, and therefore represents an advance for equality. The third and more critical perspective argues that women's inclusion in the mines disrupts 'gender regimes' (Connell, 2002, p. 53), masculine normativity and hegemony, but does not necessarily alter the gender order or challenge masculine hegemony.[8] The premise is that, while women's entrance disrupts somatic norms and highlights the ways in which spaces are gendered, it has not led to a reimagining of gender and gender order, relations and regimes, but seems to reinforces them (Irvine & Vermilya, 2010; Puwar, 2004; Sasson-Levy, 2007). This chapter draws from and builds on the third premise. I provide a more nuanced historically grounded picture of how gender operates in mining and why feminism matters.

It is undisputed that women's inclusion, especially in underground occupations that typify masculinity, is a significant challenge and a disruption in how we have imagined mining. Women's inclusion in mining brings to focus and makes visible what has long been considered a natural affiliation between men and mines, masculinity and mining productivity, mine culture and the ideal mineworker. The presence of women in mining, therefore, challenges and changes the eternalised and naturalised 'coupling of particular spaces with specific types of bodies' (Puwar, 2004, p. 8). It also raises questions about gender and feminism and what would constitute equality in spaces that have been marked as masculine.

The data presented in this chapter were collected through participant observation, life histories, formal interviews, focus group discussions and day-to-day conversations and observations underground which were all carried out between 2011 and 2012 when I worked in the mines and lived with mineworkers. The research was conducted in a platinum mine (Mine A) in the North-West province of South Africa. While the results are specific for Mine A, they can be generalised and applied to the platinum industry as a whole, and mining in South Africa.

Mines and Masculinity

South African constructions of mineworkers as exclusively male included workers in occupations that were considered feminine such as nurses, administrators and cooks (Benya, 2013). Mines explicitly preferred male

---

[8]The third notion has been supported by studies that argue that when women enter masculine workplaces they tend to assimilate to masculine norms and values and distance themselves from femininity (Czarniawska, 2013; Kvande, 1999; Pyke & Johnson, 2003; Sasson-Levy, 2003).

workers (Breckenridge, 1998; Moodie & Ndatshe, 1994). Breckenridge (1998) argues that only three out of a dozen hospitals and clinics servicing the mines had female nurses. Data from the 1927 survey of the gold mines show that, out of a labour force of well over 100,000 men, only 2750 were women and children. Mines in South Africa from their inception, were 'a world without women' a world where men, and by extension masculinity, ruled (Breckenridge, 1998, p. 975). This was reinforced by depicting the mines and mine life as physically demanding, the conditions as inconceivably hot, humid and not suitable for the 'fragile' female bodies, and the place as dangerous where only 'strong men' could survive (Dennis, 1956; Gouldner, 1954; Moodie & Ndatshe, 1994; Stewart, 2013; Timothy Phakathi, 2013; Webster et al., 1999). Studies on mine culture depict and characterise it as thriving on masculinity, collective disregard for dangers and discomforts, valorising risk taking behaviour, putting themselves in harm's way, tacit knowledge (which is transferred through gendered networks), racial and gender solidarity and male camaraderie (Connell & Messerschmidt, 2005; Webster et al. 1999). The solidarity, according to Gouldner (1954) and Moodie and Ndatshe (1994), was a result of the high levels of danger that (male) workers contended with daily. With minimal to no presence of women in the mines, mine culture has been depicted as quintessentially masculine (Gouldner, 1954; Webster et al., 1999).

Alexander (2007) cites reasons as to why South African mines, as Breckenridge argues, were 'a world without women' (Breckenridge, 1998, p. 675). He argues that the historical trajectory of mining in South Africa was informed by Victorian attitudes of the British colonisers; apartheid legislation, which restricted movement of and residency for Africans; the advanced mechanisation levels of South African mines; the type of minerals mined and deep level mining which required a trained workforce, which according to the Mine and Works Act No. 25 of 1926's restrictions, could only be white men — not black men, let alone women; the geographical location of mines and later the migrant labour system which guaranteed the exclusion of women (Alexander, 2007; Alverson, 1978; Bezuidenhout & Buhlungu, 2011; Burawoy, 1976; Moodie & Ndatshe, 1994; Wolpe, 1972).[9] Scholars also point to the myths, superstitions and cultural beliefs that were used to justify and legitimise the absence of women from the gold and

---

[9]The 1911 Mines and Works Act No. 12 and the South African Minerals Act of 1991, for instance, had racially prohibitive pass laws which ensure that husbands did not bring their wives to towns, and housing of mineworkers in single sex hostels with strict controls of entry and exit (Moodie & Ndatshe, 1994), the job reservation policies which ensured that jobs and competency certificates were only issued to white males only.

diamond mines (Addei & Amankwah, 2011; Lahiri-Dutt, 2006; Machipisa, 1999; Moodie & Ndatshe, 1994; Ralushai, 2003).[10] Additionally, unlike many places where the legislative bans were lifted during war periods and re-instated upon soldiers' return, in South Africa, with the reserve army of labour from the homelands and from other countries in southern Africa, mining remained mainly masculine (Alexander, 2007; Moodie & Ndatshe, 1994; Morrell, 1998; Wolpe, 1972).

Gender and Feminism Still Matters

Despite recent legislative shifts, mines continue to be masculine bastions. This is demonstrated in several ways. I focus on a few of the factors below.

Representation of Women in Key Occupations

While women are now included in mining they remain a minority in some occupations if not totally absent. In the mine where I conducted this research there were 27,606 workers in total. In 2014, males were the majority at 25,508 and females the minority at 2098, thus constituting only 7.5% of the total workforce. When the numbers above are disaggregated by occupation and gender the 'exclusion while included' reality facing women becomes clearer. The quota system which ensures that women enter mining jobs has only served to open spaces, they largely remain male preserves. For example, at Mine A where I conducted the research, out of the 27,606 workers, about 5500 were rock drill operators (RDOs) and not a single woman worked as a rock drill operator. This occupation was reserved for men; only men were trained to be RDOs and only men were sourced to occupy the RDO positions. Women were effectively barred from it from recruitment, at the training centre and in the work teams.

While barred from working as RDOs women could work as winch operators. In total the mine where I conducted my research had 6925 winch operators and only 88 of them were women and the rest — 6837 — were men in 2014. While 88 women were hired as winch operators very few of them operated winches because their teams did not trust that women could be productive winch operators. Most of women who were licensed to operate winches were often informally reallocated domestic tasks far from men

---

[10]Some workers believed that the presence of women underground could lead to fall of ground, or seismic events or even cause the minerals to disappear (Hoecke, 2006).

and far from the stopes, instead of operating their winches. Those who operated winched remained a minority. The same mine also had 1566 miners (holders of a blasting certificate), the highest occupation underground, of these, 1516 were men and only 50 women, and they, too, faced distrust and other challenges because they are women.

While women could be found in some of the occupations in mining, they were often prevented from doing the work and even removed from teams because the occupations were considered 'masculine'. In these 'masculine' occupations women tended to be treated like second class citizens, reduced to assistants who fetch water and clean; working and waiting places and reallocated informal tasks that reinforce domesticity. While officially these women were hired for a particular occupation, for example winch operators, unofficially they worked in another, often with a lower status and with domestic responsibilities. There was thus informal gendered job reallocation which strategically and systematically excluded women while it pretended to include and protect them.

Exclusion of women in mining happened through alienation from their work, spatial separation and isolation from their teams. It was therefore not explicit. It resulted in exclusion from the day-to-day team interactions and relationships where solidarities were forged and nourished, where tacit knowledge was informally passed from one worker to the other and thus enable workers to develop abilities and tacit knowledge and skills that help them to navigate mine work and master their underground work as legitimate mineworkers.

Women were excluded because their female bodies did not render them automatically trustworthy as mineworkers where the mining ideology has insisted on a male body. Their gender rendered them illegitimate mineworkers. To 'preserve' and 'protect' the legitimacy of the 'real' mineworkers and their masculinity, which are both associated with productivity, women were thus kept far from some occupations (and teams) which are seen as quintessentially masculine. Instead of having teams which properly integrate women, there are teams which exclude and isolate women based on their gender. Due to women's 'exclusion while included' strategy adopted by underground work teams, they cited feeling like outsiders; they do not belong in their teams or in mining, and that underground or mining was not their space. They felt and were viewed as intruders, nuisances and 'the unwanted'.

The isolation and resulting exclusion further reinforce the idea that women do not belong underground and are not capable of doing mine work. This was the insidious part of mine culture; the mine occupational culture which is rooted in masculinity, gendered solidarities, which casts women as the other, excluding them and positing them as non-core and non-workers. Shifts in legislation do not necessarily help facilitate inclusion, but gender does. Legislation opens doors, but in mining it is gender which marks some bodies as legitimate while marking others as illegitimate and, thus, facilitate inclusion or ensure exclusion.

Design of Mining Machines and Personal Protective Equipment

It is not only the job allocations which mark some bodies as legitimate and others as illegitimate using gender and sex, but also the machines and work-suits. The design of the machines used and work-suits worn in the mines still reflect exclusively male bodies with all their masculine and cultural sensibilities, and 'capitals'. As I argue elsewhere, the work-suits are mainly one piece and that makes it difficult for women to take them off underground when they want to use the toilet. To take them off they must remove hard hats, lamps and then take off the top part of their work-suits. Not only is this process time consuming but it is also dangerous. Rocks can — and do — fall any time underground without warning. Hard hats are meant to protect workers from, amongst many other underground hazards, rock falls. A trip to the toilet, however, can leave them vulnerable to rock falls since they must take off the hard hats and all their clothes before they can use the toilet. The one-piece design of the suits makes it impossible for women to simply take off the bottom part. This makes one wonder if the worker in mining is truly imagined as neutral or if indeed the male body continues to be the default body despite legislative changes.

Gender Violence Underground and Mine's Masculine Health and Safety Conceptions

Sexual harassment continues to occur in mines. This seems to be the case across the entire industry. In the past few years it has moved from sexual harassment to incidents of rape and murder of women underground (COSATU Press Statement, 2014; Masondo, 2012; Wanneburg, 2014). Cases of rape are hard to count as not all of them are reported due to fear and intimidation. While a serious threat to the safety and even health of women mineworkers, none of these, whether rape or sexual harassment are recognised by the Mine Health and Safety Act of 1996 as workplace health and safety issues. The Chamber of Mines argues that since they are 'not' related to the work process, meaning production, they cannot do anything about them, only the individual mining companies can. With women dying underground and others subjected to rape and sexual harassment, stakeholders such as unions insist on distancing themselves from and refuse to put on their agenda the rape and murder of women underground.

Gendered atrocities have been on the rise since Binki Mosiane's rape and murder underground in 2012. Yet, the cases have been treated with light-heartedness and dismissed by key players which are tasked with ensuring the health and safety of workers underground. The Chamber of Mines argues that sexual harassment and rape of women do not fall under their health and safety mandate because these are 'gender issues'. The *City Press* 'Death in the Pit of Sexism' (2013) reported that 'For the Chamber of Mines women's safety is not of particular concern'. This newspaper noted that the spokesperson for the Chamber, Mr Jabu Maphalala, after Binki's murder had said 'safety in the mines is an issue, but the chamber deals with safety issues such as rock falls, dust and noise and does not deal with gender specific safety issues'. Conceptual limitations of the Health and Safety Act means that the figures of rape and murder of women underground, are not included in the 'injuries and fatalities' statistics. This is not to argue that rape is an 'accident', but it *is* a workplace safety issue which concerns women. It would therefore seem fitting that their killings and rape be included in these figures. Labour unions, besides the rhetoric after the murder and rape, have also been stalling and not effectively dealing with perpetrators of these crimes within their membership and leadership ranks, at times leaving women completely defenceless.

These factors expose the power of gender as currency in mining, the necessity to continue to critically engage with masculinity. Gender specific challenges that women face underground and in mining show why gender and feminism continues to matter, especially in workplaces previously constructed as masculine.

Conclusion

The numerical upsurge of women in mining in South Africa has not necessarily radically changed how mines operate, how they are imagined and function, how work is allocated and who and what is protected under existing health and safety legislations. Mine culture, how life is patterned in the mines, the workplace practices, the division of labour, the work-suits, ideologies, the distribution of power, resources and transfer of skills favours men. Similarly, the subtext and undertones, the logics and assumptions circulating, whether through job allocations, conceptions of what constitutes health and safety, depict masculinity as a norm (Acker, 1990; Kelan, 2009). Gender influences occupational allocations and organisational hierarchies. It is the mining masculine culture which influences the 'authorised' versions of workplace practices, the 'doings and sayings' of the mines (Hauser, 2011; Irvine & Vermilya, 2010; Lahiri-Dutt, 2006; Martin, 2003).

Legislative shifts and numerical changes of the workforce do not necessarily always correspond with organisational culture in South Africa. Mining interactions and daily practices underground all reflect the hegemony of masculinity and marginalisation of femininity and female bodies. Whichever way one look at the mines, gender continues to matter.

References

Acker, J. (1990). Hierarchies, jobs, bodies: A theory of gendered organizations. *Gender & Society, 4*(2), 139–158.
Addei, C., & Amankwah, R. K. (2011). Myths and superstitions in the small-scale gold mining industry of Ghana. *Research Journal of Environmental and Earth Sciences, 3*(3), 249–253.
Adler, G., & Webster, E. (Eds.). (2000). *Trade unions and democratization in South Africa, 1985-97.* Basingstoke: St. Martin's Press.
Alexander, P. (2007). Women and coal mining in India and South Africa, c1900-1940. *African Studies, 66*(2–3), 201–222.
Alverson, H. (1978). *Mind in the heart of darkness: Value and self-identity among the Tswana of Southern Africa.* New Haven, CT: Yale University Press.
Anonymous. (2013). Death in the pit of sexism: Women working in the belly of the Earth face a double battle. *City Press,* September 1. Retrieved from http://www.news24.com/Archives/City-Press/Death-in-the-pit-of-sexism-20150430
Benya, A. (2013). Gendered labour: A challenge to labour as a democratizing force. *Rethinking Development and Inequality, 2*(Special Issue). Retrieved from http://www.andir-south.org/rdi/index.php/rdi/article/view/11
Benya, A. P. (2009). *Women in mining: A challenge to occupational culture in mines.* Masters dissertation, University of the Witwatersrand, Johannesburg, South Africa.
Bezuidenhout, A., & Buhlungu, S. (2011). From compounded to fragmented labour: Mineworkers and the demise of compounds in South Africa. *Antipode, 43*(2), 237–263.
Breckenridge, K. (1998). The allure of violence: Men, race and masculinity on the South African goldmines, 1900–1950. *Journal of Southern African Studies, 24*(4), 669–693.
Britton, D. M. (2000). The epistemology of the gendered organization. *Gender & Society, 14*(3), 418–434.
Burawoy, M. (1976). The functions and reproduction of migrant labor: Comparative material from Southern Africa and the United States. *American Journal of Sociology, 81*(5), 1050–1087.
Connell, R. W. (2002). *Gender: Short introductions.* Cambridge: Polity Press.
Connell, R. W., & Messerschmidt, J. W. (2005). Hegemonic masculinity rethinking the concept. *Gender & Society, 19*(6), 829–859.
COSATU Press Statement (2014). Retrieved from http://www.cosatu.org.za/show.php?ID=9782

Czarniawska, B. (2013). Negotiating selves: Gender at work. *Tamara Journal of Critical Organisation Inquiry*, *11*(1), 59−72.

Dennis, N. (1956). *Coal is our life: An analysis of a Yorkshire mining community* (vol. 50). London: Eyre & Spottiswoode.

Department of Minerals (2014). *2013−2014 Annual report*. Pretoria, South Africa: Government Printers.

Gouldner, A. W. (1954). *Patterns of industrial bureaucracy*. New York, NY: Free Press.

Hauser, O. (2011). "We rule the base because we're few": "Lone girls" in Israel's military. *Journal of Contemporary Ethnography*, *40*(6), 623−651. doi:10/11.77/0891241611412959.

Hoecke, E. V. (2006). The invisible work of women in the small mines of Bolivia. In K. Lahiri-Dutt & M. Macintyre (Eds.), *Women miners in developing countries: Pit women and others* (pp. 265−287). Aldershot: Ashgate Publishers.

Irvine, L., & Vermilya, J. R. (2010). Gender work in a feminized profession: The case of veterinary medicine. *Gender & Society*, *24*(1), 56−82.

Kelan, E. (2009). *Performing gender at work*. New York, NY: Palgrave Macmillan.

Kvande, E. (1999). "In the belly of the beast": Constructing femininities in engineering organizations. *European Journal of Women's Studies*, *6*(3), 305−328.

Lahiri-Dutt, K. (2006). Mining gender at work in the Indian collieries: Identity construction by *Kamins*. In K. Lahiri-Dutt & M. Macintyre (Eds.), *Women miners in developing countries: Pit women and others* (pp. 163−179). Aldershot: Ashgate Publishers.

Lahiri-Dutt, K., & Macintyre, M. (Eds.). (2006). *Women miners in developing countries: Pit women and others*. Aldershot: Ashgate Publishing.

Machipisa, L. (1999). *Rocky path for women miners*. Retrieved from http://www.ips.fi/koulut/199751/6.htm

Martin, P. Y. (2003). "Said and done" versus "saying and doing": Gendering practices, practicing gender at work. *Gender & Society*, *17*(3), 342−366.

Masondo, S. (2012). Female miner, killed underground. *Times Live*, February 14. Retrieved from http://www.timeslive.co.za/local/2012/02/14/female-miner-killed-underground

Moodie, T. D., & Ndatshe, V. (1994). *Going for gold: Men, mines and migration*. Johannesburg: Witwatersrand University Press.

Morrell, R. (1998). Of boys and men: Masculinity and gender in Southern African studies. *Journal of Southern African Studies*, *24*(4), 605−630.

Puwar, N. (2004). *Space invaders: Race, gender and bodies out of place*. New York, NY: Berg.

Pyke, K. D., & Johnson, D. L. (2003). Asian American women and racialized femininities: "Doing" gender across cultural worlds. *Gender & Society*, *17*(1), 33−53.

Ralushai, M. (2003). *Experiences of women working on the mines: A case study from Rustenburg Platinum Mines*. University of Johannesburg.

Sasson-Levy, O. (2003). Feminism and military gender practices: Israeli women soldiers in "masculine" roles. *Sociological Inquiry*, *73*(3), 440−465.

Sasson-Levy, O. (2007). Contradictory consequences of mandatory conscription: The case of women secretaries in the Israeli military. *Gender & Society*, *21*(4), 481−507.

Simango, K. B. (2006). *An investigation of the factors contributing to failure of heat tolerance screening by women at Impala Platinum.* Unpublished MA dissertation, The Da Vinci Institute for Technology Management, South Africa.

Stewart, P. (2013). 'Kings of the mine': Rock drill operators and the 2012 Strike Wave on South African mines. *South African Review of Sociology, 44*(3), 42–63.

Timothy Phakathi, S. (2013). "Getting on" and "getting by" underground: Gold miners' informal working practice of making a plan (planisa). *Journal of Organizational Ethnography, 2*(2), 126–149.

Von Holdt, K. (2003). *Transition from below: Forging trade unionism and workplace change in South Africa.* University of KwaZulu Natal Press.

Wanneburg, G. (2014). *Murder trial highlights the plight of women miners.* Retrieved from http://www.enca.com/south-africa/murder-trial-highlights-plight-woman-miners

Webster, E., & Von Holdt, K. (2005). *Beyond the apartheid workplace: Studies in transition.* University of KwaZulu Natal Press.

Webster, E., Moodie, D., Stewart, P., & Psoolis, C. (1999). *Deep Mine Collaborative Research Programme: The impact of ultra deep mining on the occupational culture of miners.* Johannesburg: Sociology of Work Unit (SWOP), University of the Witwatersrand.

Wolpe, H. (1972). Capitalism and cheap labour-power in South Africa: From segregation to apartheid 1. *Economy and Society, 1*(4), 425–456.

Chapter 12

The Gender of Pregnancy

Michelle Walks

Abstract

This chapter focuses on the culturally assumed link between femininity and pregnancy. It situates itself using the feminist theories of performativity (Butler, 1990), female masculinity (Halbertstam, 1998) and the queer art of failure (Halberstam, 2011). The chapter is based on ethnographic research with butch lesbians and genderqueer individuals in British Columbia, Canada. It focuses on these individuals' desires to experience pregnancy, find appropriate clothes to wear when pregnant, and not being simultaneously socially recognized as both pregnant and masculine. It argues that feminism is still needed to broaden how we gender pregnancy, and to challenge the assumptions and social pressures that link individuals with uteruses to female to femininity to pregnancy and motherhood.

Keywords: Queer; pregnancy; butch lesbians; performativity; trans men

Pregnancy made me a dad. — wallace (2010, p. 192).

Since the 1980s there has been an increased visibility of lesbian mothers, and legal rights for queer parents have subsequently passed in many countries including in Western Europe and North America (Agigian, 2004; Epstein, 2009; Kelly, 2011; Lewin, 1995; Luce, 2010). This has been accompanied by a cultural shift in recognizing gay men and lesbians as good

Global Currents in Gender and Feminisms: Canadian and International Perspectives, 181–194
Copyright © 2018 by Emerald Publishing Limited
All rights of reproduction in any form reserved
ISBN: 978-1-78714-484-2/doi:10.1108/978-1-78714-483-520171017

(potential) parents. Thus, the assumption and social recognition of only heterosexual parents being good parents have been challenged. Limited attention, however, has been given to the link between femininity and pregnancy.

In Canada and other Western countries, there is an assumed link between femininity and pregnancy. In fact, when a baby is seen as having a vulva and subsequently identified as female, the social expectation is that that child will grow up to be feminine, and a heterosexual mother is established. Given these social pressures, I was curious to know what experiences and desires existed outside of these norms. Thus, I studied the pregnancy and infertility experiences and expectations of butch lesbians, trans men and genderqueer individuals, from a queer feminist medical anthropological perspective.[1] This chapter considers the pregnancy desires and experiences of butch lesbians, trans men and genderqueer individuals. It is based both on my doctoral research in British Columbia, as well as published materials by butch lesbians and trans men who have experienced pregnancy.

I chose to do my research in British Columbia (BC) because, like researchers Kelly (2011) and Luce (2010), I recognized BC as a leader for queer individuals and families, due to its social and political climate. British Columbia, and East Vancouver more specifically, have earned notoriety for being a lesbian and queer mecca, especially for those interested in parenting. From the 1995 Human Rights Tribunal decision that made it illegal to deny lesbians access to fertility services in BC (Luce, 2010), to the 2001 Human Rights Tribunal regarding the recognition of two women on their child's Registration of Live Birth and birth certificate (Kelly, 2011; Luce, 2010), and the queer family planning events organized by various Vancouver-based midwifery clinics today, Vancouver and the rest of BC have worked to make queer families feel welcome.

Research Methods and Theory

Between February 2011 and April 2012, I conducted research that involved questionnaires, interviews and participant observation in southern British Columbia. The questionnaires and interviews were conducted both with various types of health care professionals, as well as butch lesbians, trans men and genderqueer individuals. I inquired about expectations, social

---

[1]This chapter is based on my doctoral research, 'Gender Identity and In/Fertility' (see also Walks, 2013a, 2013b, 2015).

pressures, attitudes, desires and experiences related to pregnancy, infertility, and parenting. As no previous research had specifically considered these experiences and attitudes, my project was exploratory and attempted to start recognizing some of the experiences and attitudes that people have.

I approached this research with queer and feminist critical lenses, engaging most explicitly with Butler's *performativity* and Halberstam's *female masculinity* and *queer art as failure*. Butler's *Gender Trouble* (1999), originally published in 1990, is often cited as the foundational text of Queer Theory. In this book, Butler (1999[1990]) calls attention to what she labelled the 'performativity' of gender, not as a way of making the 'doing' of gender fun or unimportant, but instead to bring awareness to the way 'gender is manufactured through a sustained [culturally constructed and expected] set of acts' (p. xvi). What was particularly new about this approach was how Butler explicitly explained and demonstrated how 'under certain conditions of normative heterosexuality, policing gender is sometimes used as a way of securing heterosexuality' (p. xii). Halberstam expanded from this notion in *Female Masculinity* (1998), in which he exemplifies how female masculinity is a 'queer subject position that can successfully challenge hegemonic models of gender conformity' (p. 9). Moreover, in *The Queer Art of Failure* (2011), Halberstam argues that *failure* is not equal to a lack of success, per se, but rather it is found through the unsuccessful maintenance or contribution to the neoliberal, patriarchal, heteronormative *status quo* or 'refusing to acquiesce to dominant logics of power and discipline and [used] as a form of critique' (p. 88). Whereas failure is ordinarily feared, Halberstam illustrates that engaging in the *queer art of failure* allows us to 'revel in and cleave to all of our own inevitable fantastic failures' (p. 187). As is evidenced below, by partaking in pregnancy as masculine-identified individuals, the individuals I interviewed engaged in *female masculinity*, and *failed* to meet normative standards regarding gender *performance*.

Desiring Pregnancy

> I confess that I have this womanly desire, an animal urgency,
> to make a baby. Would they [the other butches] see me as
> less of a butch? (Jiménez, 2011, p. 161)

While pregnancy is socially expected of all who are born with a uterus, individual agency is important to consider. People do not get pregnant just because it is expected or 'it just happens', many also get pregnant because they desire it. The people I spoke with were all aware of the culturally assumed connection between femininity and pregnancy, and yet all but one of the butch lesbians and genderqueer individuals with whom I spoke who had experienced pregnancy expressed their feelings of tension or awkwardness with its typical *performance* being so tied to femininity. While they each desired to experience pregnancy, they did not tie their individual desires to gender.

Instead of their desire for pregnancy being a feminine one, the people I spoke with *failed* to make this link, but instead listed other reasons. They linked their desire to their love of children, or felt that their desire was rooted in what can be described as human biology (as in DNA or the biological clock/'yearning'), or simply that their innate desire could not be explained. Lou[2] noted that becoming a mother or parent was always expected of *hir*.[3] Despite that, there was a time when Lou did not think parenting was a possibility for *hir*.

> It was an expectation [of my parents and society] right from day one, but I always wanted to have kids and I remember in my grade nine yearbook we had a photo and the grade nines were able to write a little blurb about ... And my greatest ambition was to have 10 kids, and it's something I always wanted, not just from external pressure, just a really strong desire from within to have a [close-knit] family, and be close to my kids ... [But] when I came out, it was 1983/84, and I thought I could never get married, I could never have kids just because nobody was doing it. And then people started doing it. I remember my friend was talking to me one day and she just said, 'I wanna have a baby'. And I thought, 'That's great, but how? You can't do that!' And she said, 'Yes I can. I'm gonna do it'. She was single at the time even, and she just got together with a friend, and she had a baby, who's now a beautiful teenager. So I think she kind of opened the door for everyone in Vancouver. (Lou)

While being a parent in a close-knit family was key to Lou's explanation of wanting to be a parent, Bryn explained having the desire to have children play a central role in her life.

Bryn had always loved children, and figured that she would be a parent, although not likely a biological one. In fact, Bryn did not feel a desire to experience pregnancy until she had experienced the role of being a co-parent

---

[2]All names of participant are pseudonyms.
[3]'Hir' is a pronoun alternative to her or his, often used by genderqueer and some trans individuals. It is pronounced like 'here' or 'hear'.

in a multi-parent family. She loved her role as a parent, but when a job offer had her heading geographically away from that family and those children, Bryn was torn and disappointed about having no say in whether the children could come live closer to where she would be. She explained the job offer and situation.

> I decided to take it up, and I could no longer live with them [the kids] ... And that is a lot of why I wanted to biologically have a kid. I never want to be trumped again.

Bryn noted that she would not use her biological connection to her child to trump her wife (Kait) either, but her fear of being trumped was likely significant in their decision regarding which of them would experience pregnancy.

For Vanessa, Bryn, and Joy, as well as the other butch lesbian and genderqueer parents who came to experience a pregnancy, their decisions were not about gender. They were comfortable with the idea of experiencing pregnancy, as it did not present itself as a uniquely feminine experience to them, but they still had to negotiate their own sense of how to fit their gender (identity and expression) together with a *performance* typically thought of as feminine. For Joy this realization happened when reading Epstein's article entitled 'Butches with Babies' (2002).

> When I read [that article], it started making me think about my own [future] experience. I was quite a bit younger then, and I wanted a child. I wanted to carry a child ... And it got me thinking about [my gender] presentation. And the fact that I was very comfortable with who'd I'd become, and very comfortable with my body, but knowing this would raise issues for me in the future. So, whenever I think about — [the topic of your research] — I mean, I think about my own experience as well — but it often goes back to that moment of realization, that there was going to be dissonance there for me at some point.

Clearly, the fact that butch lesbians and genderqueer individuals are not 'feminine' presented a challenge to their thoughts about and experiences of pregnancy. It, of course, also presented a challenge to those they encountered, as their *performances* of pregnancy did not fit the social norm.

The individuals I spoke with were sometimes surprised by the reactions of others to their desires and experiences of pregnancy, as well as frustrated by their need to justify and prove themselves. Bryn talked at length about needing to justify her desires for pregnancy with her butch/genderqueer identity. Bryn told me, 'I've always been clear to my family and friends that I wanted kids', and yet before conceiving, she felt she had to weigh her desire to experience a pregnancy against her need to be recognized and accepted as a 'butch' by fellow queers:

> It's not acceptable in the queer community to have trans people, butch people, all these people who are not feminine to be pregnant — I have to feel people ... think weird of me, I mean if we are supposed to be a community that is about accepting ... and yeah, I do this thing, and it is like, 'Why would you do that?'

Once she was pregnant, Bryn found her friends and family critical of her experience, and committed to the discordance between being butch and pregnant.

The individuals I spoke with are, by far, not the only butch lesbians, trans men or genderqueer individuals to have experienced a pregnancy. While many people see butches, trans men and genderqueer individuals as being in opposition to experiences of pregnancy, Rubin (2006) explains otherwise — at least with respect to butch lesbians — noting that:

> Butches vary in how they relate to their female bodies. Some butches are comfortable being pregnant and having kids, while for others the thought of undergoing the female component of mammalian reproduction is utterly repugnant. (p. 474)

Moreover, some trans men have written about their experiences and desires of pregnancy noting that their desire is for the end product — a baby, a family — rather than for the pregnancy itself.

For some trans men, such as wallace (2015) and Surkan (2015), their desire for children was what led them to experience pregnancy, rather than the desire for pregnancy itself. Surkan (2015) notes:

> I hadn't thought much about *pregnancy* itself; my focus had been on the larger questions of whether to have a child and how to add that new person to our relationship, taking us from being a couple to a family ... [P]regnancy per se had never been on my bucket list of somatic experiences ... Given the biological realities of my conventional female embodiment and reproductive system, pregnancy seemed to me to be a necessary nine-month expedition I would take, a temporary transformation of the body that would be a mere blip on the larger road trip of life. (p. 59)

wallace (2015) notes a similar sentiment in his blog which was written after both a miscarriage and the safe birth of his youngest child:

> I don't like being pregnant, but I sure like being a parent.
> I did the former for the latter. I did the former for a year.
> I hope very much I get to do the latter for the rest of my life.

Pregnancy, however, is not just about desire, whether for the experience itself or the outcome. In Canadian society, it is also about the public experience, being recognized as pregnant, which includes dressing the part.

Dressing the Part: Gender Policing

Pregnancy is a public experience. 'The everyday behaviours of pregnant women tend to be policed by strangers ... People frequently regard themselves as societal supervisors of pregnant women's behaviour' (Longhurst, 2000, p. 468). Thus, people who are pregnant experience gender policing, a critique of their pregnant *performance*. Every person in Canadian society or elsewhere experiences and partakes in gender policing. Gender policing is the surveying and responding to violations of gender norms. One common example of gender policing is the scrutinizing of individuals going into or being in, particularly the women's washroom — 'Are they really a woman? Do they really belong here?' For those who I interviewed, gender policing was engaged in both with those they had established relationships with, as well as strangers.

Bryn provided examples relating to how friends and family could not fathom pregnancy as anything other than feminine; she commented on how people made inaccurate assumptions about her pregnancy and her gender identity. For example, Bryn revealed to me that her parents were convinced that her being pregnant meant that she was *finally* embracing femininity. She explained that her family had always been accepting of her being gay, but her masculinity *dumbfounds them*; they continued to say,

> 'Your hair would be so much nicer if you grew it out ...' [Thus,] when they found out I was pregnant, it was a big hurray! ... It was like, 'you are finally acting like you should be acting'.

Similarly, she noted how her friends were sometimes unable to see beyond the *status quo* and imagine pregnancy as something someone 'butch' could do. Part of this might be tied to what pregnant people are supposed to wear.

Before engaging in this research, I was quite aware of the overtly feminine nature of maternity clothes, yet I gained a new perspective on maternity clothes from the research participants. When I asked Tracy about her reaction to finding out she was pregnant — after she inseminated with a little semen that was left in the syringe after her girlfriend tried inseminating at home — she noted: 'I was shocked. What was I going to wear? ... [There is] nothing that I'm going to freakin' wear!' Only one of the seven interviewees who had experienced pregnancy noted that she felt comfortable in the available maternity wear. The six others either endured being uncomfortable in maternity wear, or wore larger sizes of the typical men's wear they were used to, or a mix of both.

Before becoming pregnant, and early in her pregnancy, Bryn was unsure about what she was going to wear when she was visibly pregnant, and if she would still be recognized by others in the queer community.

> I was very apprehensive about my body changing, and very apprehensive about how people were going to see me in the [queer] community. I think I was still in their [butch] club. I was still wearing a plaid shirt [just] extra, extra large.

While for most of her pregnancy Bryn wore the same clothes as before she became pregnant, just in larger sizes, at a certain point she needed maternity pants. At this point she found that not only were the men's pants not comfortable, but they were not staying up either. Thus, she had to concede, and change into the more feminine maternity wear.

> Yeah, I actually ended up going to the men's section and wearing those, but at the end, the pants — but the pants, eventually you are going to need something that is going to stay up. No matter how wide of a belt you get — you need, those elasticky pants. They really work. You know what I mean? The elastic band at the front, they really work, but they all had these flair bottoms! ... So, I had to go modify all my maternity pants — 2 pairs of jeans and 2 pairs of cords. Like I had to cut out the bottom, and unflair them. But damn those things were comfy!

While Bryn felt she had to concede at the end, Tracy, Quinn and Cathy *failed* to find maternity clothes as a choice for them at all. Instead, they opted to wear larger sizes of men's clothing. Part of this lack of choice, at least for Cathy, was the fact that she could not get the help she needed when she did enter a maternity wear store.

Choices of what to wear, thus, were not just about comfort, but also about being able to access clothes that fit. While Vanessa turned to the internet for appropriate maternity wear, Cathy, Bryn and Joy attempted to find appropriate clothes at local maternity stores. There, however, each of them was ignored by the sales associates. Being ignored or not recognized as (potentially) pregnant it turns out was not limited to sales associates, but due to a *failure* of *performing* pregnancy in a socially normative manner. In the last few years there have been at least two or three attempts by different individuals to start businesses focusing on masculine maternity clothes, unfortunately none have yet produced items for sale. Thus, butch lesbians, trans men and genderqueer individuals' choices remain: feminine maternity wear or larger sizes of the so-called men's clothes. With these choices, and given the gendered social norms, it should come as no surprise that often masculine and queer experiences of pregnancy are not recognized.

Invisiblity and Erasure: Failing to Be Seen

> [Thomas] Beatie says in his book that he went public with his story because it would have been impossible for a guy to hide a pregnancy. Well, we did. Kind of. Friends and family and colleagues knew because we told them. Our neighbours didn't have a clue until we introduced them to our two week old baby. I don't think strangers ever really gave me a second glance. Or if they did they were too polite to ever say anything. I wore somewhat baggy sweaters and that took care of things. (MacDonald, 2011)

Just as MacDonald (2011) was not recognized as a pregnant man, all the research participants in my study who had experienced pregnancy *failed* to be recognized as a pregnant masculine individual. Sometimes this was a result of what they wore when they were pregnant, but they felt there was more to it than that. Their invisibility might be explained by the fact that, as questionnaire respondent, Isabella, noted with regards to Thomas Beatie being 'a pregnant man': 'Pregnancy seems discordant to being masculine. [Pregnancy] seems contradictory the idea of a trans man. In this light, the title "the pregnant man" seems inaccurate' — pregnancy must be performed as feminine. Surkan (2015) notes of his own experiences as a pregnant man:

> The pregnant man was an oxymoron; either I could be read as pregnant, or male, but never both simultaneously. As my belly grew bigger around my gestating fetus, paradoxically,

> my pregnancy became in some contexts more invisible;
> I could only be seen as a fat man. (p. 60)

In contrast to Isabella's perspective and the cultural norm expressed in Surkan's (2015) narrative, Bryn, Cathy, Joy, Imogen, Quinn, Vanessa and Lou did not see pregnancy as something innately feminine, but rather something they wanted to experience, despite their butch/genderqueer identity, and thus something to *fail* at.

Not being recognized for who one is can be a matter of safety (and thus positive), gratitude (and thus positive), as well as erasure (and thus negative). None of the research participants noted that they felt safer because they were not recognized as simultaneously pregnant and masculine, nor did they express gratitude for this lack of visibility. Instead, they were surprised that even those they knew could not conceive of them being simultaneously masculine and pregnant. While femme lesbians are often invisible as lesbians in their daily life, and thus it is not surprising that when pregnant they are recognized as 'straight', even I was surprised to find out during the interviews that none of the interview participants felt that they were recognized as lesbians or queer during their pregnancy. This was despite the fact that almost every one of them lived in East Vancouver during their pregnancy or pregnancies. Tracy, Quinn and Cathy, who wore larger sizes of men's clothes, each noted that publicly they were very rarely, if ever, recognized as pregnant, but instead perceived as men with a beer belly. Tracy noted: 'I still got called man or sir — [people thought I had a] beer belly'. Similarly, Cathy and Tracy noted how even at 8-months pregnant, their co-workers could not fathom that they were pregnant. Their embodied masculinity denied any possibility of pregnancy.

In contrast, those who wore typical maternity wear were continuously recognized as 'straight'. Imogen noted that pregnancy was the first time in many years that she was perceived as a straight woman. Bryn and Gayle noted similar experiences.

> When I was pregnant, people just assumed that I was straight, and it was the weirdest thing to be seen as straight .... I am sure everyone experiences that — everybody assumed that there was a husband waiting at home for me. (Bryn)

Likewise, Gayle, a butch questionnaire respondent in her 40s noted,

> When [I was pregnant and out] with my wife I was constantly frustrated with people trying to figure out our relationship cause being a lesbian couple didn't make sense to them. We were sisters or friends or something else.

While strangers had a hard time seeing Gayle, Bryn and Imogen as anything but straight, Bryn's friends could not understand her being pregnant.

Bryn noted that her friends not only questioned why her wife was not the one who was pregnant, but also could not fathom that she, in fact, was pregnant.

> We were at a friend's dinner party — I even said, 'oh I am pregnant', and [my friend] said, 'oh that's great', and later she offered me a drink. When I said 'no', she said, 'So big of you not drinking when your partner is pregnant'.

Another example demonstrated Bryn's awkward position due to her friends' disbelief and questioning.

> Even when I was showing, one of my best friends didn't get that it was me [who was pregnant, so I said to them,] 'Like do you see that it is me?'
>
> 'Like, what? It is you?!? I thought it was Kait! I just thought you were getting stuffier'.
>
> Like over and over again with my friends, they just wouldn't get it ... 'What, you're pregnant?!? Oh there must be something wrong with Kait'.
>
> And I felt awkward about it too ... Cause then, when they realized there is nothing wrong with Kait — that I fought for this — I felt like I had to get into the details of the relationship that I wasn't even comfortable talking about ... But no, thank you very much, Kait is okay. They just assumed there [are] fertility issues there.

Bryn's awkwardness is definitely a result of macroaggression, even if her friends did not necessarily or explicitly want to hurt her feelings or invade the privacy of her relationship with her wife. As Sue et al. (2007) explain:

> Microaggressions are often unconsciously delivered in the form of subtle snubs or dismissive looks, gestures, and tones. These exchanges are so pervasive and automatic in daily conversations and interactions that they are often dismissed and glossed over as being innocent and innocuous. Yet ... microaggressions are detrimental ... because they impair performance in a multitude of settings by sapping the psychic and spiritual energy of recipients and by creating inequities. (p. 273)

It is important, however, to also understand that microaggressions also relate to erasure, and that erasure to the need of feminism today.

Conclusion: Meaning for Feminism Today

> The idea of erasure is important to feminist and postcolonial-ist literary theory and cultural studies. Erasure is not exactly oppression or suppression, but rather being eliminated from the field of language, not being heard. Certain narratives are told over and over, making some realities visible while erasing others. This process is at the heart of political struggles over defining the canon and who gets to be part of the official story and who does not. (Agigian, 2004, p. 51)

The social context in which masculine pregnancy is erased through seeing pregnancy as exclusively a feminine desire, making available only feminine maternity clothes, and the lack of recognition of the possibility of masculine pregnancy, is the one in which my research participants experienced pregnancy. I have elsewhere referred to this as a cultural fetish of feminine pregnancy (Walks, 2013a). It is important for us to challenge the cultural assumption that pregnancy is ultimately and exclusively feminine. Moreover, queer folks are not the only ones to experience a masculine pregnancy, or have desire for maternity wear that is not overtly feminine. In fact, many heterosexual women also are not comfortable with the pressures they face to present themselves as blatantly feminine, especially when they are pregnant. They too struggle with finding maternity clothes that suit their personality, work environment and comfort.

Additionally, some transmasculine folks find that they have a supportive community that revels in gender fluidity, and *fails* to meet social norms. wallace (2010) found himself in such a community. Of his experience as a trans father-to-be, he explains

> I became a dad through pregnancy and birth. Along the way, people who love me created the language of 'bearing father' and 'seahorse papa'. We're queers, and we are well versed in creating the language we need to describe our realities. We will bring our world into being through words, as we bring babies into being through our bodies. (wallace, 2010, p. 193)

This creating of language and identities that respects the fluidity of gender, and reproductive desires and experiences is important as we move forward in a world where more reproductive opportunities exist, given the technology we have available.

Some people argue that we are in a post-feminist society, one where equality has been reached between the sexes, and there is no longer a need for feminism. Feminism is, however, still needed. It is needed for many reasons, including but not limited to the fact that pregnancy is so closely tied to femininity. Straight cis women still face a social expectation to desire pregnancy, to get married and to be feminine. All the while trans folks are pressured to fit a binary that results in trans men being made fun of or rendered invisible when they desire or experience pregnancy. Butch lesbians, trans men and genderqueer individuals' desires and experiences are important to consider, regardless of how common their experiences are. Feminism helps us to see and hear from those who are marginalized, not just those who have had the privilege and power to write history, and to recognize the intersecting forces at play including gender identity, sexuality, class, race, dis/ability, citizenship status and even parenthood status. Most of all, feminism helps us all to see how we are pressured to live up to certain gender expectations, and how hard it can be to challenge those expectations.

Acknowledgement

Research was partially funded through a four-year Social Sciences and Humanities Research Council of Canada (SSHRC) doctoral grant.

References

Agigian, A. (2004). *Baby steps: How lesbian insemination is changing the world*. Middleton, CT: Wesleyan University Press.
Butler, J. (1999[1990]). *Gender trouble* (2nd ed.). New York, NY: Routledge.
Epstein, R. (2002). Butches with babies. *Journal of Lesbian Studies, 6*(2), 41–57.
Epstein, R. (Ed.). (2009). *Who's your daddy*. Toronto: Sumach Press.
Halberstam, J. (1998). *Female masculinity*. Durham, NC: Duke University Press.
Halberstam, J. (2011). *The queer art of failure*. Durham, NC: Duke University Press.
Jiménez, K. P. (2011). *How to get a girl pregnant*. Toronto: Tightrope Books.
Kelly, F. (2011). *Transforming law's family: The legal recognition of Planned Lesbian Motherhood*. Vancouver: UBC Press.
Lewin, E. (1995). On the outside looking in the politics of lesbian motherhood. In F. D. Ginsburg & R. Rapp (Eds.), *Conceiving the new world order* (pp. 103–121). Berkeley, CA: University of California Press.
Longhurst, R. (2000). "Corporeographies" of pregnancy: "bikini babes". *Environment and Planning D: Society and Space, 18*, 453–472.

Luce, J. (2010). *Beyond expectation: Lesbian/bi/queer women and assisted conception.* Toronto: University of Toronto Press.

MacDonald, T. (2011). The first pregnant man. *Milk Junkies*, December 30. Retrieved from http://www.milkjunkies.net/2011/12/first-pregnant-man.html

Rubin, G. (2006). Of calamities and kings: Reflections on butch, gender, and boundaries. In S. Stryker & S. Whittle (Eds.), *The transgender studies reader* (pp. 471–481). New York, NY: Routledge.

Sue, D. W., Capodilupo, C. M., Torino, G. C., Bucceri, J. M., Holder, A. M. B., Nadal, K. L., & Esquilin, M. (2007). Racial microaggressions in everyday life: Implications for clinical practice. *American Psychologist, 62*(4), 271–286.

Surkan, K. J. (2015). The fat man is giving birth: Gender identity, reproduction and the pregnant body. In N. Burton (Ed.), *Natal signs* (pp. 58–72). Bradford: Demeter Press.

Walks, M. (2013a). Feminine pregnancy as cultural fetish. *Anthropology News, 54*(1–2), 12.

Walks, M. (2013b). Gender identity and infertility. Unpublished PhD Dissertation. University of British Columbia.

Walks, M. (2015). Masculine pregnancy: Butch lesbians', trans men's & genderqueer individuals' experiences. In N. Burton (Ed.), *Natal signs* (pp. 41–57). Bradford: Demeter Press.

wallace, i. (2015). Last year I was mostly pregnant. *Visibly Transparent*. Retrieved from http://ishai-wallace.livejournal.com/2015/08/07/

wallace, j. (2010). The manly art of pregnancy. In K. Bornstein & S. B. Bergman (Eds.), *Gender outlaws: The next generation* (pp. 188–194). Berkeley, CA: Seal.

Part Four

Health, Culture and Violence

Global Synthesis

Glenda Tibe Bonifacio

Gender is intrinsically connected with health, culture and violence. In general, women tend to face more health hazards simply because of their gender — sexual harassment, rape and others. Direct exposure with harmful chemical agents at home and in different workplaces make women prone to particular diseases compared to men. Lack of access to safe and legal abortion and other reproductive health services contribute to high mortality rates among women and girls especially in poor countries. Even reproductive choices come with a price in countries with strict penalties and strong religious lobby. Women and girls are positioned unfairly in societies to experience high levels of gender-based violence in their lifetime: sex-selective abortion, female infanticide, child bride, intimate partner abuse, to name a few. Men and boys do experience violence in masculinist cultures and practices, but women and girls suffer the gravest and most numerous counts around the world to lay claim to systemic patriarchal violence. In times of war, men and boys are counted most in the frontlines while women and girls face the spoils of hate from enemies and at the hands of their own compatriots. However, women and girls, both in times of war and in peace, continue to experience higher levels of gender-based violence from many fronts. Violence is the single most unifying experience that women and girls share around the world. Activism and advocacy are markers of dynamism to change the culture of violence in many countries. When there is persistent action and support against gender-based violence, gradual change comes close in our midst.

Chapter 13

'It Doesn't Match My Blood': Contraceptive Side Effects and Kassena Women in Northern Ghana

Lauren Wallace

Abstract

Concern about side effects is one of the most commonly cited reasons for women's non-use of contraceptives in sub-Saharan Africa, and the most common reason why women discontinue family planning. While studies find that some of women's worries about contraceptives are based on distressing side effects, such as menstrual disruption, nausea, weight gain and delays in fertility, researchers frequently focus on mis-information spread by rumour. These studies decontextualize women's concerns from the larger gendered context of their lives. Drawing on ethnographic field research carried out in northern Ghana with a feminist approach to understanding reproduction, this chapter examines women's concerns about side effects, and the impact of these concerns on family planning practice. I show that despite anxiety about side effects, and their real physical, social and economic consequences, some women's conceptions of the action of contraceptives on their bodies are pragmatic. Ethnogynecological perceptions of the importance of blood matching, combined with the importance of having small families for economic success, often encourage contraceptive use and mitigate the action of side effects rather than prompt non-use or discontinuation.

Keywords: Family planning; contraceptives; side effects; Ghana; West Africa

Global Currents in Gender and Feminisms: Canadian and International Perspectives, 197–209
Copyright © 2018 by Emerald Publishing Limited
All rights of reproduction in any form reserved
ISBN: 978-1-78714-484-2/doi:10.1108/978-1-78714-483-520171019

Prudence is 33 years old with four children. Today she looks extremely tired and stressed, her head hanging and posture stooped as she sits in the yard of her compound. As the conversation turns to her children, she confides that she does not want to give birth any more. When I ask why, she explains that her husband has stopped providing her with things that she needs. He has left for a neighbouring community to farm with his second wife, leaving Prudence in a state of constant stress and despair. She tells me that, given her current economic and marital situation, she will go to the family planning clinic soon to avoid giving birth again. A few months later, I saw Prudence walk into the clinic. She greeted me quickly, shyly and uncomfortably and then stood by the nurses and whispered: 'I have just taken the injection, that was eleven days ago when I was bleeding. Now I am still bleeding. I am worried that I have not experienced this before'. The nurses took Prudence into another room to ensure the bleeding was not too heavy.

Prudence's case demonstrates that fears about side effects of contraceptives in northern Ghana are very real, and that family planning is perceived to pose great risks to women's health and fertility. Drawing on ethnographic field research carried out in northern Ghana, and a feminist view of reproduction, this chapter examines women's concerns about side effects and the impact of these concerns on family planning practice. I argue that despite anxiety about side effects, and their real physical, social and economic consequences, Kassena women's conceptions of the action of contraceptives on their bodies are pragmatic and promote contraceptive switching rather than discontinuation.

Family Planning and Feminist Perspectives on Reproduction

Rather than recognizing reproduction as a one-time, biological event, feminists view reproduction as a socially constructed phenomenon that is impacted by a larger gendered social and cultural environment. In feminist analyses, reproduction is influenced by power struggles at various levels, including at the locus of the family and community, and in the realm of national and international policy-making (see Greenhalgh, 1994; Maternowska, 2006). Some of the most important feminist studies of reproduction document women's loss of control over reproduction and the dominance of biomedical knowledge about women's bodies through the rise of medicalized reproductive policies and practices (Jordan, 1997; Martin, 1987). For instance, anthropologist Brigitte Jordan's (1997) work on 'authoritative knowledge' shows how women's ideas about their bodies and the birth process are supressed by the biomedical system. According to Jordan (1997), medical knowledge privileges professional and medical expertise, while occluding women's knowledge about their bodies. Feminist perspectives on reproduction are extremely useful for situating fertility within the larger gendered context of women's lives. Unfortunately, public health studies of women's contraceptive use continue to adopt a narrow lens for understanding reproduction (Chipeta, Chimwaza, & Kalilani-Phiri, 2010).

Family Planning in Ghana

I conducted ethnographic research in Ghana in 2013 and 2014. Knowledge of contraceptive use in Ghana is almost universal, with 99% of women having heard of at least one family planning method (GHS & GSS, 2015). Twenty-seven per cent of married women use contraceptives. However, national-level statistics for Ghana mask large local and regional differences in rates of contraceptive use. One third (32%) of women in the Greater Accra Region (South) use contraceptives, compared to only 11% in the Northern Region and 24% in the Upper East region (North) (GHS & GSS, 2015).

Researchers and family planning programme administrators consider these results to be discouraging signs of resistance to contraceptive use or the failure of family planning programmes. This resistance has been attributed to women's fear of side effects (GHS & GSS, 2015), especially to concerns about infertility, which is the most common reason reported in national demographic surveys for non-use of contraceptives. In one of the few qualitative studies examining community perspectives on contraceptive use in Ghana, Adongo et al. (2014) argue that popular misconceptions about contraceptive side effects are impediments to contraceptive use, and call for improved access to qualified counselling. Drawing on ethnographic data, which allow for an in-depth understanding of gender, I examine contraceptive use in the Upper East region of northern Ghana, a region with one of the lowest rates of contraceptive use in the country.

Family Planning in Sub-Saharan Africa

Contraception and family planning are important components of reproductive health services and have demonstrated positive effects on maternal and newborn health, including preventing unintended pregnancies and lowering rates of death associated with complications of pregnancy, childbirth and illegal abortions. Yet in 2014 an estimated 225 million women worldwide who wanted to avoid a pregnancy were not using a contraceptive method (UNFPA, 2014).

Rates of contraceptive use vary considerably. In sub-Saharan Africa, an estimated 28% of married women of reproductive age are currently using contraception; this rate is lower than levels reported in Latin America and Asia (UNFPA, 2016). Although much of the family planning literature assumes that the main barrier to family planning in sub-Saharan Africa is access to contraceptives, surveys suggest that fear of side effects may influence family planning decision-making even more than supply issues (Campbell, Sahin-Hodoglugil, & Potts, 2006). Concern about side effects is one of the most commonly cited reasons for women's non-use of contraceptives in sub-Saharan Africa, and the most common reason why women discontinue family planning, aside from contraceptive failure (GHS & GSS, 2015; USAID, 2009).

While studies find that some of these women's worries about contraceptives are based on uncomfortable or distressing side effects, such as menstrual disruption, nausea, weight gain and delays in fertility, researchers frequently focus on misinformation spread by rumour and hearsay, rather than on side effects themselves (Chipeta et al., 2010). Some studies indicate that health programmes on the African continent should target eliminating misinformation and strengthening factual information about family planning by directing more resources toward providing high-quality counselling and education (Adongo et al., 2014; Castle, 2003; Chipeta et al., 2010).

Studies of perceptions of family planning often narrowly focus on identifying 'incorrect knowledge' women hold about their bodies and about contraceptives (Chipeta et al., 2010). While understanding women's negative perceptions about side effects of contraceptives is important, these studies decontextualize women's concerns from the larger gendered context of their lives. Such decontextualization draws attention away from the real physical, social and economic implications that side effects and worries about them have; less attention is paid to gender issues than to fertility itself. Without consideration of the larger gendered context of women's lives, the impact of side effects of contraceptives on women's bodies, and family planning practice is difficult to discern, and recommendations for family planning programming and policy may fall short.

While some side effects discussed by women fall into the category of 'myths and rumours', women are equally concerned about the impacts of commonly experienced physical symptoms, such as nausea, irregular bleeding and weight fluctuations (Rutenberg & Watkins, 1997). Conversations with women in sub-Saharan Africa reveal that they are often more worried about the impact of side effects on their relationship with their husbands than about physical consequences (Castle, 2003). For example, after using an injectable contraceptive, a woman's normal menstrual cycle may be delayed by several months and she may experience temporary difficulties conceiving. While biomedically speaking temporary infertility is considered trivial, to many women in sub-Saharan Africa it is a major concern. Women's daily lives are grounded in a cultural reality in which temporary and permanent infertility is socially abhorrent, and a woman's adult status and marital security is largely the product of her children. In addition, in much of West Africa, the practice of polygyny is commonplace. Owing to competition between co-wives, it is paramount that women remain fertile and sexually desirable to their husbands. Infertility or a husband's loss of affection can contribute to the impoverishment of a woman through loss of child labour and by undermining her position in her marriage relative to her co-wives (Feldman-Savelsberg, 1999).

Just as temporary infertility can be socially and economically problematic for African women, so too are menstrual irregularities that can be caused by some hormonal contraceptives such as the pill and the injectable. Castle's (2003) ethnographic work with adolescents in Mali demonstrates that prolonged bleeding that can result from using hormonal contraceptives affects women's sexual and marital relationships. An Islamic woman who is menstruating, for example, is considered unclean and cannot pray, cook or have sex with her husband. Excessive bleeding may jeopardize a woman's relationship with her husband, who may fear that he will become ill from having sex with his wife or assume that she is infertile. Such fears may, in turn, prompt him to divorce her or to favour another wife or mistress emotionally or economically (Castle, 2003). In Mali and Kenya, prolonged bleeding may also reveal a woman's secret use of contraceptives to her husband or other prying family and community members (Castle, Kani Konate, Ulin, & Martin, 1999).

Research into women's beliefs about contraceptive side effects often concludes that women's culturally informed knowledge about their bodies may lead to non-use or discontinuation of family planning since it is inconsistent with biomedical understandings of the body (Chipeta et al., 2010). However, the direct link between women's perceptions of their bodies and non-use of family planning has been questioned. For example, Bledsoe's (2002) work in The Gambia shows that women's biosocial understandings of their bodies facilitate the use of contraceptives. Gambian women understand that their reproductive capacity is affected by reproductive mishaps such as miscarriages and negative social relationships, and these views prompt them to use contraceptives for spacing pregnancies rather than for limiting the number of children they bear. These practices encourage women to bear as many children as possible in a social and economic climate in which large numbers of children are welcome and necessary (Bledsoe, 2002). In this chapter, ethnographic research with Kassena women also highlights the gendered consequences of contraceptive side effects, and the importance of women's ethnogynecological knowledge for contraceptive practice.

Kassena-Nankana West District

I conducted ethnographic research in two villages in the Kassena-Nankana West District of Ghana's Upper East region, the second smallest region in Ghana and the poorest in the country. Both rural communities involved in this study are Kassena. Families involved are predominantly small-scale peasant farmers, with farming complemented by retail and petty trading. Few adult women or men have high levels of education or regular sources of income through wage employment. Villages are arranged in extended family compounds of about seven regular residents, comprising one or more nuclear families with a common male head. Descent among the Kassena is patrilineal and patrilocal, and payment of bride wealth recognizes the future birth of children to the patrilineage. Polygynous relationships represent a minority of unions. The practice of formal polygyny has declined considerably, although some men continue to have 'outside wives', owing to the popularity of Christianity and the cost of raising and educating a large family, which increase rivalry between wives.

Family planning programmes in northern Ghana are funded by the Ministry of Health, but contraceptives are provided by the United Nations Population Fund at affordable prices. In the public sector, contraceptives are readily available at numerous venues, including district and regional hospitals and health clinics. In rural areas, community health nurses provide family planning services through the Community-Based Health Planning and Services Initiative, which places nurses in rural clinics to provide basic curative and preventative primary health services. Clinics provide one-on-one counselling as well as home visits (Phillips et al., 2012). Family planning education is also provided by nurses and community-based volunteers during child welfare clinics and community outreach.

Infertility and Fertility Control

In rural northern Ghana, as in much of West Africa, fertility is understood as a bodily resource that is the basis of women's economic and social power and security. Children provide a wide range of social and economic benefits, especially in rural areas. Children ensure perpetuity of the lineage, serving as a memory of and perpetuating their parent's reputation in their absence or after death. Perhaps most importantly, children are vital for completing tasks in the home and on the farm, and for the overall development of the community. In a context where few individuals have formal, salaried jobs with pensions and benefits or social insurance, remittances children provide to families are significant and essential for survival, especially when children become well educated and are employed in government work.

While sterility is problematic for men, the social consequences of infertility for women continue to loom larger (Tabong & Adongo, 2013). For women, who continue to be disproportionately blamed for infertility, even temporary infertility is problematic and can lead to marital discord, divorce and consequently economic struggle. Barrenness is not only linked to poverty but has serious social consequences, evoking pity, gossip and insults such as accusations of witchcraft. While local and national development discourses emphasize risks *from* motherhood, women in my study were equally concerned about risks *to* motherhood (cf. Allen, 2002).

Although Kassena women and men are concerned about infertility, they are also worried about having too many children. Women's discussions about the ideal number of children frame family planning as a helpful strategy to care for children considering changes in the rural economy. A positive view of family planning exists among the Kassena because it is necessary to limit family size to afford education for every child. Over the past few decades, declining agricultural yields have diminished the usefulness of children's farm labour. In view of these economic insecurities, it is not surprising that 72% of married women of reproductive age who participated in my study reported that they were currently using some form of contraception other than natural methods such as abstinence, rhythm or withdrawal. This is considerably higher than the estimate of 24% for contraceptive use among married women in the Upper East Region generated by the most recent Demographic and Health Survey (GHS & GSS, 2015).

Gendered Nature and Social Costs of Fertility Control

The majority of couples I interviewed separately discussed the need to adopt family planning together. However, Prudence's case, and focus group exchanges between young women, demonstrate that most women feel it is appropriate for them to use contraceptives secretly when communication and economic transactions between spouses are precarious, such as when a husband fails to provide for a woman or her children, favours another wife, spends his money on alcohol or concubines (instead of his wife and children) or wants to have more children than he and his wife can care for.

Even in good marital relationships, women are usually responsible for practicing contraception. Although male condoms are available and inexpensive, few married couples use them because married men believe 'ko ba yoma': that they reduce the pleasure of sex. As one middle-aged man exclaimed, using a condom is like putting meat in a bag and then trying to eat and enjoy it. Dislike of male condoms, coupled with the abundance of methods for women, means that family planning falls within the domain of women, an assertion that nurses often encounter while educating couples on home visits. Various types of family planning, including injections, implants, birth control pills, female condoms and emergency contraception are available to women. The most popular method is the injectable Depo-Provera. It is popular because it only requires visits to the clinic every three months, and because its use can be hidden more easily from community members, and husbands, where necessary: it requires no visible bandages or packages of pills. Adopting contraceptives and navigating physical and economic consequences of resulting side effects is thus another responsibility faced by rural Kassena women in addition to a long list of other chores and tasks that includes childcare, cooking, farming and often trading.

Perceived Dangers of Contraceptive Use

Although programme strategies have actively addressed concerns about side effects, women's worries about the impact of contraceptives on their fertility and sexual desirability continue. Today, Kassena women and men argue that family planning is beneficial, owing to the economic importance of small families, but still express concern that contraception can lead to infertility, a delay in return to fertility, or other side effects that could jeopardize women's health. About one third of patients at clinics in the region are not new or continuing clients but rather women reporting concerns about side effects from a new contraceptive method.

Among married interlocutors, young women express the most concern about side effects. One young mother in a focus group expressed the typical female view that while family planning is positive, contraceptives can also have negative effects:

> To me family planning is very good because it has helped us to decide on the number of children that we want to have. Also, it has bad effects. Why? Because it can cause a problem of destroying your womb or delaying your childbirth. At the time, you want give birth you may not get pregnant.

The most popular form of family planning, the injectable contraceptive, Depo-Provera, generates considerable unease among women because of side effects such as delays in fertility, nausea, pain, and amenorrhea or excess bleeding. Delayed menses is believed to cause health problems or infertility and is, thus, perceived as a risk to a woman's health. Menstrual blood is thought of as a dirty waste product that must be removed every month, and menstruation is thus envisaged as a process through which the womb is cleansed of impurities. One phrase for menstruation, 'a wo achana zare ne', literally translates to 'I'm doing my monthly washing'. Amenorrhea is considered to lead to an accumulation of dirty blood inside the womb that takes time to be discarded for the womb to be clean enough for conception. In contrast, having too little blood in the body is linked to infertility.

In a social climate in which suspicions of infertility can be grounds for divorce or taking another wife (polygyny), and where children ensure continued emotional and financial support from husbands, amenorrhea and delayed fertility are yet another stress rural women face in addition to their daily worries about money and food. These side effects may also cause anxiety for women who wish to hide their use of contraceptives from husbands or other community members, or who fear their difficulties may interrupt important activities such as trading, carrying firewood, fetching water and farming, which are important for the social and economic well-being of women and their families (cf. Rutenberg & Watkins, 1997).

Women also have particular concerns about the injectable contraceptive because of associated weight gain, as focus group discussions revealed.

> *Moderator:* What do you think of family planning?
>
> *Young woman:* The injection can make you gain excess fat and that is not good.
>
> *Elder:* ...You know some contraceptives they have side effects. For instance, you can grow fat. Some men they don't want fat women, so they leave the women and go in for another one.

Weight gain is a side effect that produces anxiety for both men and women because slimness is an important aspect of feminine beauty. Women are concerned that, if they gain too much weight, they will no longer be attractive to their husbands. Women's discussions reflect sexual and marital double standards, in which a wife should satisfy her husband sexually and remain desirable to him, otherwise she might cause his extramarital relationships. Women's ongoing concerns about infertility and the stability of their marriages reveal that while health programming has increased communities' acceptance of contraceptives, gender inequality and poverty persist.

Nurses are aware of women's fears about side effects, and do their best to reassure their clients that they are not permanent or serious. Women's conversations and observations of nurse—client interactions suggest that nurses usually take the necessary time to counsel patients and to create a comfortable and flexible environment in which women are encouraged to present troubling side effects early and to switch to a method with minimal side effects or those that are acceptable. Although investigation of reported side effects is thorough, women can end up paying as much as an additional 15 cedis (US$4) for treatment of amenorrhea or breakthrough bleeding, and these costs are not covered by health insurance. Clients with amenorrhea are first tested for pregnancy at the cost of 4 cedis. To correct irregular bleeding, women may receive one cycle of birth control pills at the cost of 1 cedi, or may be sent for an ultrasound scan to check for ovarian cysts or fibroids at the cost of 10 cedis. These costs are significant for women, considering the daily average expenditure per person on food in northern Ghana is less than 0.5 cedis per day (see GSS, 2008); unexpected healthcare fees may lead women to make trade offs, which can lead to neglect of other needs essential for daily survival, such as food (cf. Nanda, 2002).

'It Doesn't Match My Blood'

Married Kassena women understand that side effects of drugs, such as hormonal contraceptives, result from incompatibility between medication and their individual body or blood. In fact, when women not using contraception are asked which method they would like to use in the future, they often reply '*kulo na wo ma de amo jana to*', the one that matches my blood or the one that matches my system. Fit between contraceptives and the unique bodily constitution of an individual woman is used to explain why a family planning method is effective for her, but not for another person. Side effects are often interpreted by women as a sign of drug incompatibility. Christie, a forty-year-old woman with four children, commented on the importance of a family planning drug matching with a woman's system:

> [...] it is based on the way it will be within your system. For instance, with this one I bleed normally, I don't feel any pain and I do my normal activities well. So, it has really matched with my system.

In other words, although several options are available, there is often one contraceptive that matches best with each woman's body. While family planning methods are considered risky, side effects are understood as a risk that can easily be mitigated.

Women believe that blood tests may help determine whether a particular method will match their bodies. Elaborating on the concept of blood compatibility, a young woman in a focus group discussion of benefits and consequences of family planning said:

> [...] to me they [the nurses] ask us to go for a blood test to determine the one [contraceptive] that is suitable for our systems and if care is not taken, it harms the individual.

Women's descriptions of the importance of blood tests may reflect nurses' practice of measuring new clients' blood pressure prior to administering hormonal methods such as injections and birth control pills; women with high blood pressure who use hormonal methods may have an increased risk of cardiovascular events. The practice of testing blood pressure may reinforce women's ideas about the link between blood and finding the right method of contraception.

Worries about side effects can prompt some women to delay returning for their next family planning appointment, which can result in a lack of protection, unintended pregnancy or even abortion. Fortunately, like Prudence, the majority of women interviewed in this study who experienced side effects returned to the clinic soon after experiencing them to discuss their concerns and to have them treated or switch to a method more compatible with their body. Kassena women's concepts of the body serve their interests by providing the opportunity to avoid unpleasant physical, economic and emotional experiences associated with side effects from contraception, while at the same time achieving a small family size necessary for economic success in a changing political economic climate. Women's ethnogynecological perceptions of 'blood matching' can actually facilitate rather than block contraceptive use, by encouraging them to practice contraceptive switching rather than compelling them to stop altogether.

Conclusion

The use of a feminist approach to reproduction to examine family planning in northern Ghana highlights real physical and economic costs of family planning. Rather than being simply a benign or primarily agency-promoting activity, contraceptive use has tangible, often hidden, negative effects on Kassena women's emotional, physical, social and economic security. Despite observable and hidden costs of contraceptive side effects, and worries about their physical impact, Kassena women continue to choose to adopt contraceptives. Local gynecological perceptions of the importance of blood matching, combined with the importance of having small families for economic success, often encourage contraceptive use and mitigate the action of side effects rather than prompt non-use or discontinuation.

A feminist approach to understanding family planning reveals ways in which women's culturally informed knowledge about their bodies can be mobilized. Family planning programmes in northern Ghana should recognize and address women's concerns that contraceptive methods match with their individual bodies. Programmers could incorporate into their counselling and education activities contraceptive users from local communities who have successfully 'matched' their family planning method.

Yet, perhaps most importantly, Kassena women's worries about side effects reflect much deeper social and economic concerns that cannot be addressed by family planning education or counselling. The typical technical approach, which emphasizes increasing contraceptive prevalence by improving nurse–client interactions, sidelines the real crux of the problem: socioeconomic and political dimensions of existing gender hierarchies and marriage arrangements. Ultimately, these concerns underlie women's worries about side effects from contraceptives and point to the need for a strategic agenda aimed at reducing gender inequality.

Acknowledgements

I thank the women and men of Kassena-Nankana West who opened their communities and their hearts to me. The stories they told me are invaluable and I am forever indebted to their kindness and warmth. Aurelia Abapali is also owed special gratitude for her contributions of time and knowledge as my research assistant.

References

Adongo, P., Tabong, P., Adongo, T. B., Phillips, J. F., Sheff, M. C., Stone, A. E., & Tabsoba, P. (2014). A comparative qualitative study of misconceptions associated with contraceptive use in southern and northern Ghana. *Frontiers in Public Health*, 2(137), 1–7.

Allen, D. R. (2002). *Managing motherhood, managing risk: Fertility and danger in West Central Tanzania*. Ann Arbor, MI: University of Michigan Press.

Bledsoe, C. (2002). *Contingent lives: Fertility, time and aging in West Africa*. Chicago, IL: University of Chicago Press.

Campbell, M., Sahin-Hodoglugil, N. N., & Potts, M. (2006). Barriers to fertility regulation: A review of the literature. *Studies in Family Planning*, 37(2), 87–98.

Castle, S. (2003). Factors influencing young Malians' reluctance to use hormonal contraceptives. *Studies in Family Planning*, 34(3), 186–199.

Castle, S., Konate, M., Ulin, P. R., & Martin, S. (1999). A qualitative study of clandestine contraceptive use in urban Mali. *Studies in Family Planning, 30*(3), 231–245.

Chipeta, E. K., Chimwaza, W., & Kalilani-Phiri, L. (2010). Contraceptive knowledge, beliefs and attitudes in rural Malawi: Misinformation, misbeliefs and misperceptions. *Malawi Medical Journal, 22*(2), 38–41.

Feldman-Savelsberg, P. (1999). *Plundered kitchens, empty wombs: Threatened reproduction and identity in the Cameroon Grassfields.* Ann Arbor, MI: University of Michigan Press.

Ghana Health Service (GHS) & Ghana Statistical Service (GSS). (2015). *Ghana demographic and health survey 2014.* Retrieved from https://dhsprogram.com/pubs/pdf/FR307/FR307.pdf

Ghana Statistical Service (GSS). (2008). *Ghana living standards survey: Report of the fifth round.* Retrieved from http://statsghana.gov.gh/docfiles/glss5_report.pdf

Greenhalgh, S. (1994). Controlling births and bodies in village China. *American Ethnologist, 21*(1), 3–30.

Jordan, B. (1997). Authoritative knowledge and its construction. In R. E. Davis Floyd & C. F. Sargent (Eds.), *Childbirth and authoritative knowledge: Cross-cultural perspectives* (pp. 55–79). Berkeley, CA: University of California Press.

Martin, E. (1987). *The woman in the body.* Boston, MA: Beacon Press.

Maternowska, C. (2006). *Reproducing inequities: Poverty and the politics of population in Haiti.* New Brunswick, NJ: Rutgers.

Nanda, P. (2002). Gender dimensions of user fees: Implications for women's utilization of health care. *Reproductive Health Matters, 10*(20), 127–134.

Phillips, J., Jackson, E., Bawah, A., MacLeod, B., Adongo, P., Baynes, C., & Williams, J. (2012). The long-term impact of the Navrongo Project in Northern Ghana. *Studies in Family Planning, 23*(3), 175–190.

Rutenberg, N., & Watkins, S. (1997). The buzz outside the clinics: Conversations and contraception in Nyanza Province, Kenya. *Studies in Family Planning, 28*(4), 290–307.

Tabong, P., & Adongo, P. B. (2013). Understanding the social meaning of infertility and childbearing: A qualitative study of the perception of childbearing and childlessness in Northern Ghana. *PLOS One, 8*(1), e54429.

United Nations Population Fund (UNFPA). (2014). *Adding it up: The costs and benefits of investing in sexual and reproductive health 2014.* Retrieved from http://www.unfpa.org/sites/default/files/pub-pdf/Adding%20It%20Up-Final-11.18.14.pdf

UNFPA. (2016). *Universal access to reproductive health: Progress and challenges.* Retrieved from http://www.unfpa.org/publications/universal-access-reproductive-health-progress-and-challenges

United States Agency for International Development (USAID). (2009). *Levels, trends, and reasons for contraceptive discontinuation.* Retrieved from http://pdf.usaid.gov/pdf_docs/Pnadq639.pdf

Chapter 14

Problematizing Fertility Decline without Women's Empowerment in Turkey

Miki Suzuki Him

Abstract

This chapter examines men's involvement in birth control from a feminist political-economic perspective. Fertility, and hence women's body, is still a focus of political struggles today. In the late 1990s, the international community of population policy recognized a concept of women's reproductive rights and adopted a rights-based discourse in place of a language of economic efficiency. At the same time, they advocated for men's participation in family planning and burden sharing between couples. This gender-sensitive new policy was effective in achieving more successful contraception in patriarchal societies where men are decision-makers in many aspects of social life. Yet, from a feminist perspective, such a policy could threaten women's reproductive rights if gender relations remain patriarchal. A close examination of Turkey's fertility decline suggests that the process was led by men who increasingly aspired to have small families which they could manage to look after as wage-earning fathers. In other words, it was realized without women's empowerment. A case study of Kurdish women conducted in Eastern Turkey where fertility rate was significantly higher than the national average indicates a positive impact of men's involvement on effective birth control. Yet this study also suggests a risk of undermining women's empowerment and autonomy. The promotion of men's involvement in family planning can reinforce men's control over women's bodies

Global Currents in Gender and Feminisms: Canadian and International Perspectives, 211–224
Copyright © 2018 by Emerald Publishing Limited
All rights of reproduction in any form reserved
ISBN: 978-1-78714-484-2/doi:10.1108/978-1-78714-483-520171020

and endorse birth control without women's empowerment again, unless it is consciously designed in the context of reproductive rights.

Keywords: Birth control; patriarchy; empowerment; fertility; Kurdish women; Turkey

Introduction

Feminism still matters because we still live in a patriarchal society. Patriarchy is a social system which organizes human relations into gendered relations that privilege men, rather than women, in various ways (e.g. Connell, 1987; Johnson, 2005; Kandiyoti, 1988; Walby, 1990). Reproduction is one of the foremost areas where human relations are deeply gendered. Since Firestone's (2003) problematization of reproduction as a key arena upholding patriarchy, many feminist studies have attempted to reveal the ways in which human reproduction is organized patriarchally. O'Brien (1981) conducted a historical materialist analysis of biological reproduction while socialist feminism generally studied the issue of women's unpaid labour for social reproduction in relation to capitalism. O'Brien (1981) asserts that it is men's, not women's, physiology and reproductive consciousness that underlie patriarchal gender order. In their effort to resist alienation in reproduction, men historically strived to appropriate women's reproductive labour power. Biological paternity was thus ingeniously invented and substantiated by creation of such institutions as patrilineality, heterosexual monogamous marriage and gendered public/private distinction. Rich (1986) also argues that it is not women's reproductive body but patriarchally organized relations of reproduction which subordinate women. Women's capacity to bear and nourish human life is alienated labour under patriarchy. Mothers are expected to be endowed with 'maternal "instinct"' rather than intelligence, selflessness rather than self-realisation, and relation to others rather than the creation of self' (Rich, 1986, p. 42). Patriarchy institutionalizes motherhood in a way of ensuring that women devotedly labour for 'larger purposes' (Rich, 1986, p. 159). Only when patriarchally institutionalized motherhood is destroyed, women could be empowered from creative mothering and achieve not just sexual liberation, but also genuine emancipation (Rich, 1986, p. 184).

O'Brien (1981) and Rich's (1986) historical insights deny the inevitability of patriarchy. Until the late 1980s, however, many feminist studies treated reproduction as the possible fundamental cause of patriarchy or a site of feminine experience shared by all women (e.g. Daly, 1978; Firestone, 2003). When such universalistic and essentialist approaches came to be attacked by postmodern currents in the 1990s, reproduction became an unpopular

subject to study despite enduring patriarchal control over women's reproductive capacity across societies. Recurrent backlash and persistent reluctance to recognize women's bodily integrity confirm that feminist projects
are unfinished. More tangible and nuanced understanding of patriarchal
organization of reproduction is required not to be drawn back to such
patriarchal universals as biological causes of women's dependency, as well
as to avoid feminist universalism which often ends up magnifying patriarchy rather than uncover its contradictions and strenuous efforts to uphold
male domination (Connell, 1987; Kandiyoti, 1988).

In this chapter, I examine an issue of male involvement in birth control
from a feminist political-economic perspective. Arguably, this is a symptomatic case of new backlash against feminist struggles. Firstly, I briefly
describe the development of a new agenda in international population
policy. Secondly, I examine the debate over men's role in fertility decline in
Turkey and my study of varying men's attitudes to birth control in Eastern
Turkey. Lastly, I attempt to unravel the intricate relations between men's
involvement and women's empowerment in the sphere of reproduction. A
feminist political-economic account of reproduction seeks to understand
patriarchal relations of reproduction under certain socioeconomic and
political conjunctures. It attempts to demystify reproduction and women's
subordination. Feminist perspectives are indispensable to a study of
reproduction, yet the early second-wave feminism in North America often
dealt with biological reproduction as a material base of women's subordination and hardly went further to situate it in specific historical realities.
Reproduction is, however, socially embedded and differentiated by one's
gender, class, race, ethnicity and geographical positions within rapidly
globalizing political-economic systems. A feminist and political-economic
approach pays attention to the interconnection of the systems of inequality
(especially patriarchy), historical contingencies and personal troubles.

Ambivalence about Male Involvement: Sharing Responsibility or Male Intrusion?

In retrospect, the 1994 International Conference on Population and
Development (ICPD) was a strange turning point in the history of women's
rights movement (Petchesky, 2003). It was the authorization of feminist
conceptualization of gender inequalities and the beginning of indefinable
reversal of the feminist achievement at the same time. After long-term
debates, lobbying and intense negotiations, the term 'reproductive
rights' was included in the official document. Gender equality and women's
empowerment were stressed as important issues to be tackled. The

right-based perspective finally replaced the idea of overpopulation — an alienating view which treats women's reproductive capacity as an instrument of population control. After the Conference, international population policy moved away from the myopic view of birth control as a women's issue to the more inclusive approach of reproductive health as a gender issue. It advocated male participation in a wide range of reproductive activities for a recognition that '(m)en play a key role in bringing about gender equality since, in most societies, they exercise preponderant power in nearly every sphere of life' (United Nations, 2014, p. 36). Studies, particularly feminist studies, had been pointing out the limitation of family planning programmes which targeted solely women by showing a range of patriarchal constraints on women across cultures. Global policymakers were convinced about men's critical role as the decision-maker in families and communities. It was considered that men's cooperation would contribute to more effective family planning and sexual and reproductive health promotion. It was even argued that women's empowerment without men's involvement would create conflictual gender relations in society (Sternberg & Hubley, 2004).

A new agenda of male involvement stimulated debates about men's role in reproductive decision-making and practices but also raised some concerns (Greene & Biddlecom, 2000). For instance, it is not clear how men's reproductive rights are to be defined, whether they include a biological father's right to tell a woman to give or not to give birth to a child, how women feel about their partners' involvement (Mundigo, 2000) and whether men's involvement actually help women's empowerment (Sternberg & Hubley, 2004). Sternberg and Hubley (2004) examined the published evaluations of projects which targeted men in different Asian and African countries. They see that men tend to welcome the projects and their participation seems to increase contraceptive use in general. Regarding its implication for women's empowerment, the authors refer to an evidence of men's increased power over women's fertility observed in Middle Eastern family planning programmes yet only carefully state the need for more researches. In the following sections, I examine men's role in reproductive decision-making in Turkey for its quality of presenting another evidence about the relations of men's involvement in birth control with women's empowerment.

Men's Role in Turkey's Fertility Decline

Turkey's fertility rate reached replacement level in the 1990s. The history of Turkey's population policy is, however, a curious process of constant fertility decline and inconsistent implementations of family planning programme. Turkey launched antenatal policy in the 1960s in the context of the rise of neo-Malthusianism — a zealous promotion of contraception against overpopulation — in international politics (Franz, 1994). As in other developing countries, Turkey's family planning programme focused on promoting female modern contraceptives, especially intrauterine device (IUD). As a matter of fact, Turkey's birth rate had already started declining as early as the mid-1930s when pronatalist laws were still enforced in the country. According to Shorter's estimation (1968, p. 16), total fertility rate declined 9% between 1935 and 1960. The population growth of the post-WWII era, which scared neo-Malthusian policymakers, resulted from decreased mortality rate and increased longevity. In their study of family formation in the early 20th century, Duben and Behar (2002) demonstrate that the desire and attempts for limiting births were existent among urban people in Istanbul, who were reasonably considered as the trendsetter, long before the 1965 legalization of contraceptive devices. The authorization of birth control may have reinforced people's attempts in forming smaller families. Yet it was largely realized by traditional methods of withdrawal, folk barrier methods and induced abortion. In 1978, only 3% of married women of reproductive age were using IUD while the number of abortions per 100 pregnancies more than doubled in 15 years (Akin, 2007). Overall, contraceptive usage increased considerably in the 1980s but the use of modern methods was still slightly behind that of traditional methods — principally withdrawal — at the end of the 1980s (Ergocmen, Koc, Senlet, Yigit, & Roman, 2004).

After the introduction of 'involving men' approach in international and national population policies, a high rate of withdrawal practice and men's role in family planning in Turkey drew attention of researchers from different disciplines like public health, demography and sociology. The reported usage of withdrawal went up from 10% to 25% between 1963 and 1983 (Akin, 2007; Ergocmen et al., 2004). Since then the rate remains constant until today (HUIPS, 2014), and is among the highest in the world (Ergocmen et al., 2004). Several scholars, especially in public health, highlight men's direct (practicing withdrawal) and indirect (influencing wives' use and choice of contraceptive method) involvement in birth control and advocate an informed integration of men in family planning programme (e.g. promotion of condom) (Mistik, Naçar, Mazicioğlu, & Çetinkaya, 2003; Özvaris, Doğan, & Akin, 1998; Pirinçici & Oguzöncül, 2008; Yanikkerem, Acar, & Elem, 2006). Gender relations are, however, an intricate matter. Demographic and sociological studies of reproductive decision-making process demonstrate conflicting views. Some studies show the husband's dominant role in reproductive decision-making while others stress the prevalence of joint decision-making among couples.

Ergocmen et al. (2014) indicate the husband's critical role in birth control. Their analysis of multiple nationally representative data of Turkey observes that reliance on withdrawal appears common particularly among socioeconomically disadvantaged women (e.g. farmers, unpaid workers and workers without social security). However, multivariate analysis shows that the husband's education is the most significant predictor of withdrawal use. It is likely in case that the husband is uneducated regardless of the wife's educational status; it tends to be low when the husband is educated, again, regardless of the wife's education. This study supports Cindoğlu, Sirkeci, and Sirkeci's (2008) analysis of Turkish Demography and Health Survey (TDHS) data of multiple periods. Women in urban areas with better educational and socioeconomic status are unlikely to rely on withdrawal to prevent pregnancy. Men's educational attainment reduces the chance of sex without contraception, and every early educational year increases the likelihood of using withdrawal in a very small but statistically significant way.

Another study finds that male factory workers in a town of the Marmara region described their choice of withdrawal as 'act[ing] honourably like a man' (Ortayli, Bulut, Ozgurlu, & Çokar, 2005, p. 171). They were proud of being responsible caring husbands by protecting their wives from the risks of IUD and controlling the number of children. They defined withdrawal by a version of masculinity — powerful, in control and protective. Some studies however confirm the conventional view of alienated men. Save et al. (2004), for example, report that the men they interviewed in a low-income district in Istanbul support birth control but see family planning as a women's business.

Meanwhile, Angin and Shorter (1998) defend the dynamics of joint decision-making as a neglected aspect in the study of reproductive behaviour. From an ethnographic research in working-class communities in Istanbul, they present invaluable analysis of the multiple ways in which wives and husbands negotiate in making contraceptive decisions. The authors are uncomfortable with the 'uncritical' emphasis that many studies give on male domination in Turkish family and critical of studies which advocate women's empowerment assuming their subordination. They assert that the use of male methods is not necessarily a manifestation of male control, and question 'the idea that the 'empowerment' of women by the processes of 'modernization' is an important, even necessary, societal change to bring about reductions in fertility' (Angin & Shorter 1998, p. 563). Kulczycki (2008) likewise finds the concurrence between wives and husbands regarding the idea and practice of birth control in his analysis of the couple-level data from the 1998 TDHS. But these same data indicate the widespread acceptance of the wife's subordination to the husband. Kulczycki (2008) recognizes profound gender inequalities especially in the sexual sphere in society. While pointing out a possibility of social desirability bias, he concludes that Turkish couples' reproductive decision-making is rather egalitarian.

Olson-Prather (1976) finds the contextual effectiveness of women's autonomy in gender-segregated society by analysing the 1968 Turkish national survey data to explore husband—wife agreement about contraception. She finds that in rural areas as well as small towns contraceptive use is high when husband—wife concurrence is strong; but in metropolitan areas it is highest when a couple agrees not at all or fully. Because of physical distance to healthcare services, women's lack of access to cash and gender segregation in society, the husbands' active commitment is indispensable to rural women's contraceptive use. However, for many metropolitan women, 'such cooperation is relatively unnecessarily; in fact, both discussion and companionship between spouses may actually limit women's freedom' (Olson-Prather, 1976, p. 385). Urban women rather exploit gender segregation and make relatively autonomous contraceptive decision. Olson-Prather (1976) thus challenges a model of effective family planning in spousal interaction and stresses the importance of family planning programme which is directed to improve the availability and accessibility of contraceptives for all women rather than to modify spousal attitudes.

Birth Control and Empowerment

Conflicting views on spousal reproductive decision-making in Turkey may be related to the differences in husband's socioeconomic status and views of masculinity. My research on reproductive practices among Kurdish women in Van, a city of eastern Anatolia where socioeconomic development and fertility trend considerably lagged behind the other regions in the country, suggests two different attitudes among husbands and their consequences on birth control. I conducted in-depth interviews with 40 women selected by snowball sampling in one of the rural—urban migrant neighbourhoods in 2008. The main finding of the research was the lone struggle of socioeconomically and linguistically disadvantaged women under various patriarchal constraints (Suzuki Him & Gündüz Hoşgör, 2011). Women explained that their husbands wanted birth control because of economic hardship but hardly cooperated in accessing healthcare services and practicing contraception despite many obstacles women face: strict gender segregation, women's lack of experience in the public sphere and communication with strangers including health workers, and recurring health problems related to contraceptive use. Majority of women tried contraceptives but frequently stopped using them because of misunderstandings, difficulties in regular access, side effects and unexpected pregnancies. Most of the women were still seeking an effective and healthy contraceptive method.

Among many stories of unsuccessful birth control, however, there were eight Kurdish women in the study who were successfully using contraceptives. These women did not become pregnant for a year or more, had no health problems related to contraceptive usage, and were satisfied with the methods they were using. Most of these women knew the Turkish language but five women were illiterate. Only three of them went to school and only one completed primary education. The rest had no schooling at all. All women but one married in their teens. In short, these women were not particularly different from the other participants in the study in terms of socioeconomic statuses. But they differ from other women because their husbands were actively involved in birth control. These women went to a clinic with their husbands or the husbands went to a clinic to get an information about contraception and chose a method. In the case of those women who chose a condom, their husbands were going and getting condoms. In the case of IUD, the husbands took their wives to a clinic. These involved husbands were different from the other husbands in terms of educational attainment as well. While the participants' husbands went to school for three years on average, all the involved husbands completed primary education and two of them were high school graduates. These men had regular income and managed to fulfil their role as breadwinners, which many men in the neighbourhood failed to do.

Kurdish women who participated in the research were also aware of the effect of husbands' involvement. One participant said, 'Some men, who love their wives very much, use balloons (condoms)'. The women who experienced contraceptive failures complained their husbands' lack of involvement. Meanwhile, the women who were successfully preventing pregnancy praised their husbands' active involvement and related it to their educational attainment. A young Turkish-speaking but illiterate woman stated:

> I hate pills, coil (IUD), and that sort of things. My husband said, 'You don't use. I'll use (condoms)'. My husband is very good. He's an educated person. So he's understanding of course.

Yet, the husband's involvement has a paradoxical aspect. One of the 'successful' contraceptive users wanted more children. After having four children, her husband took her to a clinic:

> My husband said, 'Enough. I don't want anymore. Get a coil'. I want seven children. I love kids. Some can die, some would work. When my husband wants, (I'll remove the coil). If he doesn't want, how do I have children […].

Bargaining with Patriarchy for Birth Control

Negotiation and joint decision-making are prevalent in the case study of Kurdish women, too. Both attitudes of husbands indicate male-led spousal relationship. The participants who were struggling for effective contraception also discussed about birth control with their husbands, and they both wanted it. Yet their husbands just told them off to find a solution. In case of the women who successfully controlled fertility, their husbands, who were integrated into modern educational system, labour market and modern masculinity, aspired to be responsible and caring fathers. Contraceptive use seems to be high, consistent and effective among women whose husbands are involved in contraception in a social setting where women's independent access to the public sphere is constrained. Husband's education is particularly significant in his attitude towards conjugal negotiation over birth control.

Women in explicitly patriarchal social relations I studied were never passive in contraceptive decision-making process. Yet, they as well as many spouses in Turkey, I argue, live in male-led relationship although it might be non-confrontational (Isvan, 1991) and increasingly benevolent and paternalistic. In patriarchal society, even democratic spousal negotiations turn out rarely against what husbands want. Hence, the promotion for male involvement in Turkey would convince the remaining traditional segment of alienated men for active participation in birth control and simply reinforce the tendency of male-led reproductive relations unless, as Correa and Petchesky (2003) convincingly argue, the programme is consciously designed as part of the more comprehensive project aiming at changing larger issues about gender inequalities and creating enabling conditions for women to control their own reproductive capacity. For women who live in non-confrontational spousal relationship in gender-segregated society, autonomy is one of the few effective means to realize their goals (Isvan, 1991). Enabling conditions for women may be created in a way of supporting their autonomy rather than promoting spousal cooperation in the sociocultural setting of Turkey.

Folbre (1983) aptly points out the shift of patriarchal material interests in women's reproductive capacity in capitalist society. Men realized the economic benefits of family planning promoted by the state and demanded by women as the costs of childrearing surpassed the material benefits of having children in the process of modernization. Probably, Turkey's fertility decline was driven by an increase of aspiring modern fathers who desired small families that they can manage to provide with their meagre wages. In other words, Turkey's fertility decline was realized despite women's little empowerment in the sphere of reproduction. It was possible because men, as well

as the state, wanted it. At the same time, men's involvement did not necessarily contribute to women's empowerment; or, it might have deprived
women the opportunity in controlling their reproductive capacity and
empowering themselves. Many Kurdish women who struggled with contraception in the study proudly talked about how they learned to visit a clinic
by themselves; how they dealt with bureaucratic procedures in hospital; and
how they could now take their children to a doctor when they, not their husbands, considered necessary. These women earned a sense of empowerment
through bitter but valuable experiences in the public sphere.

Experiences of Kurdish women are valuable from a feminist standpoint.
It is hard to judge what is good for women: male-led birth control without
troubles or female-led birth control with social obstacles, failures and
health risks. After all, Kurdish women desired their husbands' sharing of
responsibilities although from feminist perspectives such demand would
undermine the basic right of women to control their own fertility (Correa &
Petchesky, 2003). It can be postulated that a great number of women in
Turkey made a pragmatic choice of effective fertility control by accepting
the husbands' benevolent control over their reproductive bodies: they
bargained with patriarchy (Kandiyoti, 1988). In Turkey, women's empowerment was not necessarily required for fertility decline (Angin & Shorter,
1998). Yet, a kind of birth control that helps women's emancipation
certainly requires women's empowerment.

Conclusion

While several studies show the influence of international policy trends on
Turkey's population policy (Akin, 2007; Franz, 1994; Levine, Üner, &
Altıok, 1978; Özberk, 2003), they had limited effects on the country's fertility decline. The fundamental driving force of demographic transformation
was micro-level changes in the modernizing society: integration to market
economy and men's increasing desire for small families. However, as Angin
and Shorter (1998) advocate, a closer examination of gender dynamics is
imperative. It is important to distinguish the standpoint which takes heed
of women's empowerment for their emancipation from the approach which
defends women's empowerment for fertility decline. The former is often
mistaken and discarded with the latter. By doing that, patriarchal order is
reset to the state of mind before the 1994 ICPD conference. Indeed, gender
relations are power relations continuously deployed in forms of domination, compliance, and resistance. Women are by no means the passive
subject in any patriarchal society but they struggle against and/or bargain
within insidious constraints. Nonetheless, the rise of women's strength,

intelligence and subjectivity should not lead to an argument that women's empowerment is unnecessary, or feminism has ended, because patriarchy has not ended.

Since the late 2000s, Turkey's population policy has made another shift to benign pronatalism in response to the prediction of future population aging. Fragmented but consistent information indicate that family planning services are gradually downsized as part of health sector reform (Acar & Altunok, 2013; Çiçeklioğlu, 2010; Güner, 2006). At a meeting held in 2006, the Minister of Health justified the state's withdrawal from family planning programme by the liberalization of international policy from birth control to reproductive health (Güner, 2006). Recep Tayyip Erdoğan, the former Prime Minister and President since 2014, habitually urges the public, as 'worried brother', to have at least three children to preserve young Turkish population, which Western countries try to wipe out (Ntvmsnbc, 2008). The policy change might be a sensible measure that any state which faces population decline would take. Yet it is legitimized by paternalistic anti-imperialist rhetoric and implemented under a neoliberal health sector reform. Women and men are morally persuaded to be mothers/fathers and have more children for the sake of the nation. There is neither an attempt for sociological understanding about why women and men have less and less children nor a hint of defence for women's reproductive rights against the previous population control programme. The latest report of the 2013 survey is alarming: a very slight increase of fertility rate; more than 5-point decrease of induced abortion; and 3.5-point increase of miscarriage despite the rapid socioeconomic developments of the country (HUIPS, 2009, 2014). Feminist critics are concerned that the figures could be an indication of the decreased availability of contraceptive services and safe abortions (Sosyalist Feminist Kolektif, 2014). Amidst all these, it is time to reintroduce more articulate, better-founded and more inspiring visions and policies which produce enabling socioeconomic and moral conditions for women to defend bodily integrity and assert their reproductive rights against the new backlash of benevolent patriarchy.

References

Acar, F., & Altunok, G. (2013). The 'politics of intimate' at the intersection of neo-liberalism and neo-conservatism in contemporary Turkey. *Women's Studies International Forum, 41*, 14–23.

Akin, A. (2007). Emergence of the family planning programme in Turkey. In W. C. Robinson & J. A. Ross (Eds.), *The global family planning revolution: Three decades of population policy and programs* (pp. 85−102). Washington, DC: The World Bank.

Angin, Z., & Shorter, F. C. (1998). Negotiating reproduction and gender during the fertility decline in Turkey. *Social Science & Medicine, 47*(5), 555−564.

Çiçeklioğlu, M. (2010). Sağlık reformlarının kadın sağlığına etkisi [The impact of health reform on women's health]. In S. Solmaz (Ed.), *II. Kadın hekimlik ve kadın sağlığı kongresi: kadını görmeyen bilim ve sağlık politikaları* [The 2nd conference of women physicians and women's health: Science and health policies which do not see women] (pp. 84−87). May 20−23, Ankara, Turkey. Ankara: Rulo Ofset Matbaacılık

Cindoğlu, D., Sirkeci, I., & Sirkeci, R. F. (2008). Determinants of choosing withdrawal over modern contraceptive methods in Turkey. *The European Journal of Contraception and Reproductive Health Care, 13*(4), 412−421.

Connell, R. W. (1987). *Gender and power: Society, the person and sexual politics.* Stanford, CA: Stanford University Press.

Correa, S., & Petchesky, R. (2003). Reproductive and sexual rights: A feminist perspective. In C. R. McCann & S. K. Kim (Eds.), *Feminist theory reader: Local and global perspectives* (pp. 88−125). New York, NY: Routledge.

Daly, M. (1978). *Gyn/ecology: The metaethics of radical feminism.* Boston, MA: Beacon Press.

Duben, A., & Behar, C. (2002). *Istanbul households: Marriage. family and fertility, 1880−1940.* Cambridge: Cambridge University Press.

Ergocmen, B. A., Koc, I., Senlet, P., Yigit, E. K., & Roman, E. (2004). A closer look at traditional contraceptive use in Turkey. *The European Journal of Contraception and Reproductive Health Care, 9*(4), 221−244.

Firestone, S. (2003). *The dialectic of sex: The case for feminist revolution.* New York, NY: Farrar, Straus and Giroux.

Folbre, N. (1983). Of patriarchy born: The political economy of fertility decisions. *Feminist Studies, 9*(2), 261−284.

Franz, E. (1994). *Population policy in Turkey: Family planning and migration between 1960 and 1992.* Hamburg: Deutsches Orient-Institut.

Greene, M. E., & Biddlecom, A. E. (2000). Absent and problematic men: Demographic accounts of male reproductive roles. *Population and Development Review, 26*(1), 81−115.

Güner, H. (2006). Sağlık bakanı'nın gündeminde aile planlaması yok! [There is no family planning in the agenda of ministry of health!]. *Medimagazin, September 16.* Retrieved from http://www.medimagazin.com.tr/authors/haldun-guner/tr-saglik-bakani8217nin-gundeminde-aile-planlamasi-yok-72-9-877.html

Hacettepe University Institute of Population Studies (HUIPS). (2009). *Turkey demographic and health survey 2008 preliminary report.* Ankara, Turkey: Hacettepe University Hospitals Press.

Hacettepe University Institute of Population Studies (HUIPS) (2014). *Turkey demographic and health survey 2013.* Ankara, Turkey: Elma Teknik Press.

Isvan, N. (1991). Productive and reproductive decisions in Turkey: The role of domestic bargaining. *Journal of Marriage and the Family, 53,* 1057−1070.

Johnson, A. G. (2005). *The gender knot: Unravelling our patriarchal legacy.* Philadelphia, PA: Temple University Press.

Kandiyoti, D. (1988). Bargaining with patriarchy. *Gender and Society*, 2(3), 274–290.

Kulczycki, A. (2008). Husband-wife agreement, power relations and contraceptive use in Turkey. *International Family Planning Perspectives*, 34(3), 127–137.

Levine, N., Üner, S., & Altıok, E. (1978). The development of a population policy and its implementation. In N. Levine & S. Üner (Eds.), *Population policy formation and implementation in Turkey* (pp. 53–74). Ankara, Turkey: Institute of Population Studies, Hacettepe University.

Mistik, S., Naçar, M., Mazicioğlu, M., & Çetinkaya, F. (2003). Married men's opinions and involvement regarding family planning in rural areas. *Contraception*, 67, 133–137.

Mundigo, A. I. (2000). Re-conceptualizing the role of men in the post-Cairo era. *Culture, Health and Sexuality*, 2(3), 323–337.

Ntvmsnbc. (2008). *Başbakan'dan kadınlara '3 çocuk' mesajı* [A message of '3 children' from prime minister to women]. Retrieved from http://arsiv.ntvmsnbc.com/news/438418.asp.

O'Brien, M. (1981). *The politics of reproduction*. Boston, MA: Routledge & Kegan Paul.

Olson-Prather, E. (1976). Family planning and husband-wife relationships in Turkey. *Journal of Marriage and the Family*, 38(2), 379–385.

Ortayli, N., Bulut, A., Ozgurlu, M., & Çokar, M. (2005). Why withdrawal? Why not withdrawal? Men's perspectives. *Reproductive Health Matters*, 13(25), 164–173.

Özberk, E. (2003). *Nüfus politikaları ve kadın bedeni üzerindeki denetim* [Population policies and control over women's body]. Unpublished master's thesis, Ankara University Ankara, Turkey.

Özvaris, Ş. B., Doğan, B. G., & Akin, A. (1998). Male involvement in family planning in Turkey. *World Health Forum*, 19, 76–88.

Petchesky, R. P. (2003). *Global prescriptions: Gendering health and human rights*. London: Zed Books.

Pirinçici, E., & Oguzöncül, A. F. (2008). Knowledge and attitude of married Turkish men regarding family planning. *The European Journal of Contraception and Reproductive Health Care*, 13(1), 97–102.

Rich, A. (1986). *Of woman born: Motherhood as experience and institution*. London: W.W. Norton & Company.

Save, D. C., Erbaydar, T., Kalaca, S., Harmanc, H., Cal, S., & Karavus, S. (2004). Resistance against contraception or medical contraceptive methods: A qualitative study on women and men in Istanbul. *The European Journal of Contraception and Reproductive Health Care*, 9, 94–101.

Shorter, F. C. (1968). Information on fertility, mortality, and population growth in Turkey. *Population Index*, 34(1), 3–21.

Sosyalist Feminist Kolektif. (2014). *Türkiye nüfus ve sağlık araştırmaları raporunda öne çıkan bulgular* [Primary findings in Turkey demography and health survey report]. Retrieved from http://www.sosyalistfeministkolektif.org/emegimiz/39-kadinlar-icin-sosyal-haklar/922-tuerkiye-nuefus-ve-sagl-k-arast-rmalar-rapor-unda-oene-c-kan-bulgular.html.

Sternberg, P., & Hubley, J. (2004). Evaluating men's involvement as a strategy in sexual and reproductive health promotion. *Health Promotion International, 19*(3), 389–396.

Suzuki Him, M., & Gündüz Hoşgör, A. (2011). Reproductive practices: Kurdish women responding to patriarchy. *Women's Studies International Forum, 34*(4), 335–344.

United Nations. (2014). *Programme of action—Adopted at the International Conference on Population and Development Cairo, 5–13 September 1994: 20th Anniversary Edition.* New York, NY: United Nations Population Fund.

Walby, S. (1990). *Theorizing patriarchy.* Oxford: Blackwell.

Yanikkerem, E., Acar, H., & Elem, E. (2006). Withdrawal users' perceptions of and experience with contraceptive methods in Manisa, Turkey. *Midwifery, 22*, 274–284.

Chapter 15

Intimate Partner Violence and Poverty: Malaysian Indian Women in Penang, Malaysia

Premalatha Karupiah and Parthiban S. Gopal

Abstract

Poverty and stress associated with it have been identified as key contributors to intimate partner violence. This chapter explores intimate partner violence experienced by Malaysian Indian women living in poverty in Penang. Data for this study come from in-depth interviews of 12 women who were categorized as hard-core poor, ordinary poor and vulnerable poor. Most participants experienced some form of violence from their husband; some experienced physical, emotional and verbal abuse, while some experienced only verbal abuse. Low income was the main reason for material deprivation in these households which became worse with substance abuse and extra marital affairs by male partners. Both violence and poverty is part of a vicious cycle, and some male children are following in their father's 'footsteps'. Violence is closely tied to patriarchal values and gender relations in family relationships showing how notions of hegemonic masculinity and emphasized femininity play out in everyday life.

Keywords: Traditional femininity; Tamil; domestic violence; Malaysia; poverty; urban poor

Introduction

In Malaysia, studies on domestic violence is scarce even if it accounted for almost 50% of reported violence against women between 2000 and 2010

Global Currents in Gender and Feminisms: Canadian and International Perspectives, 225–236
Copyright © 2018 by Emerald Publishing Limited
All rights of reproduction in any form reserved
ISBN: 978-1-78714-484-2/doi:10.1108/978-1-78714-483-520171021

(Abdul-Ghani, 2014). According to the 1994 Domestic Violent Act (DVA), domestic violence is defined as acts[1] by a person against his/her spouse, former spouse, a child, an incapacitated adult or other family members. It is not seen as a specific crime but attached to the Penal Code under definitions and procedures for hurt, criminal force and assault (Awang & Hariharan, 2011).

One of the biggest studies on violence against women in Malaysia was conducted by Women's Aids Organization (WAO) in 1995. This study involved 1221 respondents nationwide which reported that 36% of the respondents experienced intimate partner violence (Abdul-Ghani, 2014; Shuib et al., 2013). Another study which involved 3440 female respondents from West Malaysia showed that 15% of 2640 respondents (who have or have had a partner) had experienced intimate partner violence (physical, sexual or emotional) at some point in their life (Shuib et al., 2013). Even if these studies do not specifically report ethnic variations in the prevalence of intimate partner violence, other smaller studies, which did not use a nationwide sample, have indicated a high prevalence of domestic violence among Malaysian Indians (Awang & Hariharan, 2011; Wong & Othman, 2008).

This chapter which focuses on intimate partner violence in a minority and disadvantaged community in Malaysia is an outcome of a study which focused on material and non-material deprivation experienced by Malaysian Indians who are living in poverty. Penang has a level of urbanization of 90.8% (Department of Statistics, 2010b) which, is a suitable place to study the experiences of poor urban women.

Poverty, Masculinity and Violence

Poverty and issues related to poverty has been identified as one of the main contributors to intimate partner violence. Even though intimate partner violence occurs in all socio-economic groups, it has been reported in many countries that it is more severe among lower income groups (Jewkes, 2002). Scholars have argued that, while poverty may not directly cause intimate

---

[1]These acts include placing, or attempting to place, the victim in fear of physical injury; causing physical injury to the victim; compelling the victim by force or threat to engage in any conduct or act, sexual or otherwise, from which the victim has right to abstain; confining or detaining the victim against the victim's will; causing destruction or damage to property with intent to cause or knowing that it is likely to cause distress or annoyance to the victim (DVA, 1994). The Domestic Violence (Amendment) Act 2012 also included causing psychological abuse and causing the victim to suffer any delusion by using any intoxicating substance (DVA, 2012).

partner violence, the influence may be mediated by notions of masculine identity (Gelles, 1974 as cited in Jewkes, 2002). Intimate partner violence is more likely to occur when men's sense of masculinity is challenged. This may explain the higher rates of intimate partner violence among those who live in poverty (Anderson, 2005). In families living in poverty, the inability to provide for the family challenges the sense of masculinity of the male partner, hence violence is used as another way of exerting control over his spouse (Anderson, 2005).

Feminists have long argued that intimate partner violence is a way in which patriarchal power is manifested in everyday life (Anderson, 2005). However, this view has been contested using findings of sex-symmetry in the way violence is committed by spouses (Anderson, 2005; Renzetti, 1994) and this has challenged the feminists' understanding of intimate partner violence as a problem of gender and power (Anderson, 2005). While such view is problematic for feminists' struggle to get the needed attention on domestic violence, it cannot be denied that the meaning and the experience of domestic violence is different in different parts of the world. Fernandez's (1997) analysis of 15 case studies of domestic violence from Bombay showed violence against a married woman can be perpetrated not only by her husband but also his family members. Older women (such as mother-in-law and sister-in-law) may assist in the violence on younger women who marry into their family. Therefore, violence is not only caused by male dominance but is 'a product of interlocking systems of gender and life-cycle-based hierarchies in the Indian family' (Fernandez, 1997, p. 451). Older women have the power to abuse younger women because of their relationship with the men in the family.

In most society, masculinity is associated with power and domination while femininity is associated with being weak and submissive. Violence and aggression are often seen as characteristics of the idealized form of masculinity in a society; therefore, it can be used to perform masculinity in everyday life, that is 'to show others that one is a "real man"' (Anderson, 2005, p. 857). Violence particularly in intimate relationships has been used by men to control their female partners and display their masculinity. Hegemonic masculinity is a cultural ideal which refers to the most valued way of being a man in a particular community (Connell & Messerschmidt, 2005). Connell (1995) defines hegemonic masculinity as:

> [...] the configuration of gender practice which embodies the currently accepted answer to the problem of legitimacy of patriarchy, which guarantees (or is taken to guarantee) the dominant position of men and the subordination of women (p. 77)

When discussing hegemonic masculinity, Connell (1987) emphasized that hegemony 'does not refer to ascendancy based on force, [but] it is not incompatible with ascendancy based on force' (p. 184). She explained further that ascendancy embedded in religious doctrine or practices and mass media is a form of hegemony. In the case of domestic violence, religious and cultural ideologies are often used to justify violence against female partners (Anderson & Umberson, 2001). Femininity, on the other hand, is constructed in the context of subordination of women to men and emphasizes compliance, nurturance and empathy as womanly virtues. The most valued form of femininity is referred to as emphasized femininity and it describes social relations that involve subordination to men, and accommodates their interests and desires (Connell, 1987). Emphasized femininity has many similar expectations as traditional femininity in Tamil culture in which the self-sacrificing, caring and submissive wife is often celebrated as the 'ideal' wife. These qualities are the most valued and cherished quality of femininity.[2] In addition to this, the notion of *karpu* (chastity) is the most celebrated virtue for a Tamil woman (Sivakami, 2004). *Karpu* in Tamil culture does not only refer to physical chastity but it includes devotion to one's husband. The notion of *karpu* is so glorified in Tamil literature that it gives sacred power to women who abide by these norms (Ramaswamy, 2010). The notion of *karpu* by default gives ascendancy for the husband in a husband and wife relationship. In addition to this, marital status often gives different kinds of status to a woman. The existence of words such as *vazhavetti* (separated) and *vithavai* (widow) for women, without equivalent terms for men, is a reflection of this. Both words have negative connotation and are associated with some level of inauspiciousness.

In this chapter, the manifestation of hegemonic masculinity and emphasized femininity can be seen in the experiences of urban poor Malaysian Indians in Penang. The perpetrators of violence are all males while the victims are all females. From the narratives of these women we are able to see how the notion of femininity and masculinity are constructed in their everyday lives. The understanding of how these constructions are related to the problem of intimate partner violence is important for feminist researchers and activists in influencing policy and support programme for victims. It is also important to ensure that front-line service provides do not reiterate traditional biases related to domestic violence (e.g. domestic violence as a family matter; men will be men; violence is a norm) to ensure that more women can come forward in their struggle against intimate partner violence.

---

[2]See Karupiah (2015) for a detailed discussion on traditional feminine ideals in Tamil culture.

Malaysian Indians and Urban Poverty

Malaysian Indians are people of Indian origin who are Malaysian nationals. They constitute around 7.3% of the total population (Department of Statistics, 2010a). Most are Hindus, but there are also some Malaysian Indians who are Christians or Muslims. Most Malaysian Indians are descendants of migrants from South India, particularly from Tamil Nadu. There have been a few waves of migration to Malaysia from India (Gopal & Karupiah, 2013). Most migrations happened during the British colonial times, when Indians were brought to Malaysia (then Malaya) to work in rubber plantations (Sandhu, 1993). While most of the Indian labourers were brought in to work on the plantations, a fair percentage were also located as labourers in other service sectors like road construction, railways, telecommunications and port activities. Many of this latter group of labourers reside in urban areas (Lim, Gomes, & Rahman, 2009).

At present, the Indian community in urban areas in Malaysia rank as one of the poorest groups in the urban sector. Many of them moved to the urban areas when the plantation economy gave way to development projects. The environment in the plantation was hardly conducive for them to attain a decent education or acquiring critical skills that are needed in the modern sector of the economy. These displaced people with low levels of education and skills were largely unemployable. They not only found themselves competing with foreign workers for low-paying jobs, but also competing in informal sector activities to earn a living, thus perpetuating their cycle of poverty (Nair, 2007).

Methods, Data and Results

Data for this study come from in-depth interviews of 12 poor women living in Penang. Interviews allow these women to express and describe their experiences about issues related to poverty, and give voice to women in a minority community in Malaysia. Equal numbers of participants were selected from three categories of poverty, that is ordinary poor, hard-core poor and vulnerable poor. Ordinary poor refers to a household with monthly income below RM 763 (≈US$183) which is the poverty line income (PLI). Hard-core poor refers to a household with a monthly income of less than RM 620 (≈US$155), while vulnerable poor refers to a household with monthly income that is more than the PLI. This PLI is for Peninsular Malaysia and is based on the Tenth Malaysian Plan (Economic Planning Unit, 2010). All the participants spoke Tamil for most parts of the interviews, sometimes used Malay and English words or phrases during their interviews. Data from the interviews were transcribed and translated to English. After going through the transcripts for familiarization, the researchers coded the data to describe participants' experiences of domestic violence and the causes of violence and poverty in their households.

In this study, participants were between the ages of 31 to 78 with a majority of them in their 30s. All the participants had monthly income less than RM 1000 ($\approx$US\$250). All participants (except one) had children. Most were single mothers either because their husband has passed away or they were de *facto single* mothers.[3] Most participants have experienced intimate partner violence at some point in their married life, and the type of violence they experienced may differ. Almost all participants shared experiences of verbal abuse. For some, this was experienced with physical and emotional abuse. While participants highlighted that lack of social support, fate, lack of educational qualification and skills may be responsible for their condition, substance abuse particularly alcohol addiction and extra marital affairs are the main causes of violence they experienced.

Substance Abuse, Extra Marital Affair and Violence

Substance abuse has been identified as one of the causes of both poverty and violence. In some households, for example, up to 50% of their monthly income was spent on alcohol, hence, they had very little money to spend on other necessities. Kanaga shared her experience:

> [...] because of his heavy drinking habit he [my husband] spends more than 50% of his earnings on alcohol and smoking [...] neglecting me and the kids [...] This kind of habit has made us poorer [...] If I try to advise him he will beat me [...] My other fear is that my kids would follow the footsteps of my husband and become a drunkard.

Meena explained how her husband's involvement with another woman added strain to their family well-being and financial situation at home:

> Another reason my family have become poor because my husband has the heart to leave the family and cohabit or live with another woman [...] even though he has many children with me. He has 7 kids with me and now he goes to other

---

[3]This includes adult children.

women [...] How is he going to support both of us? At the moment, he is only giving us RM200 [≈US$50] per month [...] do you think it is enough? He is worse than an animal.

Malar, a single mother described her experience living with her husband who is an alcoholic:

When I ask him to stop drinking and be responsible [...] each time I question him, he scolds, shouts and beats me [sobbing] [...] The children were small and they would just watch him beating and scolding me using vulgar words. As I couldn't stand the daily torture, I would go and stay with my mother and will take my children with me. He will come there and create more havoc, scolds and beats me in front of my mother and starts framing me that I go to my mother's house because I have an affair with someone. So, he doesn't allow me to go to my mother's house at all.

Malar's and Kanaga's experiences showed that they have been suffering from physical, emotional and verbal abuse for a long time. Meena, on the other hand, did not clearly talk about physical violence but her experience suggested that she has been suffering from some form of emotional abuse. For Malar, her husband's accusation on infidelity added stress to her relationship and everyday life. Here, 'infidelity' has been used as a 'tool' to limit her movement and stop her from going to her parents' house. This made her feel alone and isolated because she lost the only family support in her life. Her experiences highlighted how the notion of *karpu* is being used by her husband to limit her mobility and strain her relationship with her parents. When her *karpu* was challenged she was put in a position where she was expected to defend or prove her loyalty and devotion to her husband. In her narratives, she used the word 'allow' which clearly shows the hierarchy in their relationship. Her husband has the 'power' to control and discipline her, while the wife is expected to play her role as a carer and nurturer regardless of how she was treated.

From the experiences of these women, power lies in the hands of the male partner; he uses violence to maintain this power. Women remain rather submissive in the context (even if they can find some income on their own) of their relationship, and are controlled by violence and traditional expectations of femininity. This situation manifests hegemonic masculinity and emphasized femininity in their lives.

Lakshmi is a 38-year-old housewife who lives in a low-cost house in Penang. She has some formal education, but did not complete her secondary education. She also experienced physical, emotional and verbal abuse:

> My life is full of hardship [...] because my husband is an irresponsible guy who creates havoc with the children and becomes a nuisance after drinking [...] He always end up beating me if I tried to advise him to avoid all this vices. I don't have any peace because of him [in tears] [...] My jewelleries are all gone. He would beat and pester me daily for money to drink. I just wish someone could help me, just give me RM500 [US$125]. I don't have help from anyone at all. He will shout at us using vulgar words. My youngest child would watch and ask why his father is talking like that. I tell him [my son] that the father is not in his senses due to his drinking habit. I used to send him to the neighbour's house to prevent him from listening to the quarrels, beatings, vulgar words etc. Even the children's education was affected in this way [...] I have a lot in my heart to try to control and improve the condition of my husband and my two spoilt sons [in tears].

Lakshmi's experience highlighted not only the violence she faced but her fear about the future of her children. She is worried that the violence witnessed by her children at home would influence them to engage in violence outside their home. She also feared that her children, particularly male children, would be addicted to drugs and alcohol. Malliga shared similar experiences:

> *My husband's drinking samsu*[4] habit is the biggest culprit that brought us to be in this state [...] and he spends his half of earnings on illicit samsu [...] as a result, the main source of income for the family is affected. I'm so stressed as to how to feed all the children and to look into their education. The eldest child is 24 years old now. But I also don't get any help from him [...] as parents would expect. Another son is involved in gangsterism. The eldest son is on drugs. He has fallen into a pit and I don't have any hope that he can be redeemed. For all these, I blame their father who did not

---

[4]*Samsu* is a distilled potent spirit with an alcohol content of between 37% and 70%. It is often consumed by consumers from the lower income category (World Health Organization [WHO], 2004).

navigate the family. He is so arrogant and wouldn't want to listen to our advice. The second son drinks daily [...] following his father's footstep [...].

Malliga and Lakshmi felt that their children, particularly their sons, have been most affected by the violence and substance abuse of their fathers. Their children are now addicted to various substances such as drugs and alcohol, and act violently.

The narratives of urban poor Malaysian Indian women in Penang often emphasized how much they contributed to the caring and maintenance of the household with limited or no support from other family members. They clearly articulated their role as the nurturer of the family, responsible in taking care of family members including their abusive husbands. However, substance abuse (particularly alcohol) and violence is used by male partners to 'perform' masculinity which is often constructed as being powerful and being in control (Jewkes, 2002; Peralta, Tuttle, & Steele, 2010). Their narratives show the sacrifices they make in their everyday life, and their effort to closely fulfil traditional gender role expectations in Tamil society in Malaysia. Other than caring for the family, many participants also work to earn a living to manage the financial demands of the family. While these women are rather independent in their ability in finding some form of income for the family, they often still succumb to traditional gender roles in a heterosexual relationship where they show acceptance and submission to male dominance, particularly their husbands.

In Malaysia, traditionally, intimate partner violence has been viewed as a private matter. This has slowly changed with much effort from various women's organizations and non-governmental organizations in the early 1980s. These organizations played a major role in creating awareness and establishing intimate partner violence as a public issue in Malaysia, which eventually led to enactment of the Domestic Violent Act in 1994. Because of this legal development, front-line health workers and NGO groups further lobbied for the establishment of a formal service protocol to support victims. This eventually led to the establishment of a pilot One Stop Crisis Centre (OSSC) in 1996. Since then, more OSSCs have been set up in hospitals to respond to violence — domestic violence, sexual violence and child abuse (Colombini, Ali, Watts, & Mayhew, 2011). OSSCs provide medical, counselling, police and legal services in hospitals, and the services are provided by medical staff from these hospitals supported by other agencies such as non-governmental organizations, police, Legal Aid and the Welfare Department (OSSC, 2016). The OSSCs allow an active role of NGOs in supporting domestic violence victims. Even if there are issues in running these OSSCs, it is a positive step in assisting victims of domestic violence (Colombini et al., 2011).

Any effort in advancing women's rights in Malaysia needs to consider not only the cultural and religious diversity but also other demographic differences such as age and class. For example, the struggle towards the enactment of the Domestic Violent Act had to take into consideration the fact that family matters are under the jurisdiction of the *Syariah* laws for Muslims and the civil law for non-Muslims (Lai, 2012). As well, there are many social constructs such as the meaning of violence, family honour, faith and karma becoming barriers for victims in the process of seeking help (Othman, Goddard, & Piterman, 2014). Therefore, understanding the experiences of women from all walks of life is very important in designing policies and programme to support victims of intimate partner violence. People who actively work with victims such as feminist researchers, women organizations, front-line health and legal service providers are responsible in bringing forward the complexities experienced by victims to provide better support for them.

Conclusion

Issues related to intimate partner violence are rather serious in the lives of urban poor Malaysian Indian women in Penang. Substance abuse further contributes to this form of violence. The imbalance of power in marital relationship among these women clearly illustrates hegemonic masculinity and emphasized femininity in their everyday lives. Aside from the deleterious effects of violence on women, there is also the intergenerational effect of intimate partner violence because children tend to display similar behaviour in adult life. While this study provides a glimpse of intimate partner violence among Malaysian Indian women, it is not a gauge to address the seriousness of the problem among the urban poor in Penang or to generalize intimate partner violence in Malaysia. While there has been much progress in the struggle against intimate partner violence in Malaysia, particularly involving severe physical violence, much work needs to be done on other aspects of abuse such as verbal and emotional. Furthermore, awareness of the rights of women both in public and private spheres are important for feminist researchers and activists alike to address and combat intimate partner violence.

References

Abdul-Ghani, M. (2014). *Exploring domestic violence experiences from the perspective of abused women in Malaysia*. PhD Thesis, Loughborough University.

Retrieved from https://dspace.lboro.ac.uk/dspace-jspui/bitstream/2134/14620/3/ Thesis-2014-Abdul-Ghani.pdf

Anderson, K. L. (2005). Theorizing gender in intimate partner violence research. *Sex Roles, 52*(11−12), 853−865.

Anderson, K. L., & Umberson, D. (2001). Gendering violence: Masculinity and power in men's accounts of domestic violence. *Gender & Society, 15*(3), 358−380.

Awang, H., & Hariharan, S. (2011). Determinants of domestic violence: Evidence from Malaysia. *Journal of Family Violence, 26*(6), 459−464.

Colombini, M., Ali, S. H., Watts, C., & Mayhew, S. H. (2011). One stop crisis centres: A policy analysis of the Malaysian response to intimate partner violence. *Health Research Policy and Systems, 9*(1), 25.

Connell, R. W. (1987). *Gender and power*. Oxford: Polity Press.

Connell, R. W. (1995). *Masculinities*. Berkeley, CA: University of California Press.

Connell, R. W., & Messerschmidt, J. W. (2005). Hegemonic masculinity rethinking the concept. *Gender & Society, 19*(6), 829−859.

Department of Statistics. (2010a). *Population and Housing Census, 2010, Malaysia*. Retrieved from http://www.statistics.gov.my/

Department of Statistics. (2010b). Population distribution and basic characteristics 2010. Retrieved from https://www.statistics.gov.my

DVA. (1994). *Domestic Violence Act 1994*. Retrieved from https://www.wcwonline. org/pdf/lawcompilation/malaysia_DVact1994.pdf

DVA. (2012). *Domestic Violence (Amendment) Act 2012*. Retrieved from http:// www.federalgazette.agc.gov.my/outputaktap/20120209_A1414_BI_JW001762% 20Act%20A1414(BI).pdf

Economic Planning Unit. (2010). *Tenth Malaysia Plan 2011-2015. Putrajaya*. Retrieved from https://www.pmo.gov.my/dokumenattached/RMK/RMK10_Eds.pdf

Fernandez, M. (1997). Domestic violence by extended family members in India interplay of gender and generation. *Journal of Interpersonal Violence, 12*(3), 433−455.

Gopal, P. S., & Karupiah, P. (2013). Indian diaspora and urban poverty: A Malaysian perspective. *Diaspora Studies, 6*(2), 103−122.

Jewkes, R. (2002). Intimate partner violence: Causes and prevention. *The Lancet, 359*(9315), 1423−1429.

Karupiah, P. (2015). Have beauty ideals evolved? Reading of beauty ideals in Tamil movies by Malaysian Indian youths. *Sociological Inquiry, 85*(2), 239−261.

Lai, S. Y. (2012). The women's movement in Peninsular Malaysia, 1900−99: A historical analysis. In M. Weiss & S. Hassan (Eds.), *Social movement in Malaysia* (pp. 45−74). London: Routledge Curzon.

Lim, T. G., Gomes, A. G., & Rahman, A. A. (2009). *Multiethnic Malaysia: Past, present and future*. Petaling Jaya: Strategic Information and Research Development Centre.

Nair, S. (2007). Poverty in Malaysia: A new look at old problem. In S. Nambiar (Ed.), *Reassessing poverty in Malaysia* (pp. 22−78). Kuala Lumpur: Wisdom House Publications.

One Stop Crisis Centre. (2016). Retrieved from http://www.osccmy.org/

Othman, S., Goddard, C., & Piterman, L. (2014). Victims' barriers to discussing domestic violence in clinical consultations: A qualitative enquiry. *Journal of Interpersonal Violence, 29*(8), 1497−1513.

Peralta, R. L., Tuttle, L. A., & Steele, J. L. (2010). At the intersection of interpersonal violence, masculinity, and alcohol use: The experiences of heterosexual male perpetrators of intimate partner violence. *Violence Against Women, 16*(4), 387–409.

Ramaswamy, V. (2010). Chaste widows, cunning wives, and Amazonian warriors: Imaging of women in Tamil oral traditions. *Asian Ethnology, 69,* 129–157.

Renzetti, C. M. (1994). On dancing with a bear: Reflections on some of the current debates among domestic violence theorists. *Violence and Victims, 9*(2), 195–200.

Sandhu, K. S. (1993). The coming of Indians to Malaysia. In K. S. Sandhu & A. Mani (Eds.), *Indian communities in Southeast Asia* (pp. 151–189). Singapore: Institute of Southeast Asian Studies.

Shuib, R., Endut, N., Ali, S. H., Osman, I., Abdullah, S., Oon, S. W., … Shahrudin, S. S. H. (2013). Domestic violence and 'women's well-being in Malaysia: issues and challenges conducting a national study using the WHO multi-country questionnaire on 'women's health and domestic violence against women. *Procedia-Social and Behavioral Sciences, 91,* 475–488.

Sivakami, S. (2004). Women in Tolkappiyam. *Journal of Tamil Studies, 66,* 93–106.

WHO. (2004). *WHO global status report on alcohol.* Retrieved from http://www.who.int/substance_abuse/publications/en/malaysia.pdf

Wong, Y.-L., & Othman, S. (2008). Early detection and prevention of domestic violence using the Women Abuse Screening Tool (WAST) in primary health care clinics in Malaysia. *Asia-Pacific Journal of Public Health, 20*(2), 102–116.

Chapter 16

Becoming a 'Real Man' is a Feminist Issue

Sigal Oppenhaim-Shachar

Abstract

The growth of the pick-up industry all over the world and in Israeli society in recent years has been called 'reverse sexism'. This phenomenon reflects how young men in hierarchical and competitive culture suffer from what they perceive to be fragile or partial masculinity, and are misled by the pick-up industry to learn and practice aggressive seduction techniques. All to improve their ability to gain sex and, therefore, to become 'real men'. The discourse, language and concepts taught in these pick-up courses echo the traditional approach of hegemonic masculinity and patriarchy, reinforcing rape culture on the one hand, and the vulnerability and suffering of these men on the other.

Keywords: Israel; patriarchy; pick-up industry; rape culture; backlash; hegemonic masculinity

Introduction

Recent academic literature about 'masculinities' has focused for the most part on ways men abandon hegemonic masculinity in favour of new masculinities. Yet the pendulum has also swung in the opposite direction, with a backlash against various waves of the feminist movement. One

Global Currents in Gender and Feminisms: Canadian and International Perspectives, 237–250
Copyright © 2018 by Emerald Publishing Limited
All rights of reproduction in any form reserved
ISBN: 978-1-78714-484-2/doi:10.1108/978-1-78714-483-520171022

counter-reaction is found in arenas such as pick-up companies[1] that invite men to experience the opposite process of regaining traditional patriarchy (Connell, 1995) and reinforce their masculinity, covertly and overtly strengthening the 'rape culture' (Buchwald, Fletcher, & Roth, 1993). There is a great importance for feminist work with men involved with the pick-up industry because the messages conveyed continue to influence men, particularly those with fragile masculine identity. While these messages lead men to mistreat women they seek to conquer, they also mistreat themselves in the process.

This chapter describes parts of a research which traced attempts to change traditional perceptions concerning masculinity in an Israeli pick-up company. As the manager of *Please Touch*, my former student had become disillusioned with the pick-up community's modus operandi referred to as the 'Game' (Strauss, 2005) and had begun to understand the personal and social price paid by young men, his customers, for the claims he imparted in his courses. The company's traditional pick-up course was modified and new contents were added to encourage men to abandon, or at least examine, their hegemonic perception of masculinity, to understand many masculinities or more than one model of 'being a man' (Connell & Messerschmidt, 2005),[2] and that dominance is not a prerequisite for building an intimate relationship. Perhaps not surprisingly, the new course, known as 'the process', attracted fewer customers than the previous workshop which had taught aggressive seduction techniques. The new course was, therefore, discontinued due to lack of participants and financial viability.

Study and Methodology

I served as the academic advisor of the new workshop, 'the process' of the Israeli pick-up company, *Please Touch*, from 2011 to 2013. During this time, I also attended the workshop and conducted a study of its effect on the company's employees and workshop participants through conversations

---

[1]Companies which offer intensive courses that teach young men the correct and proper way to harass women and young girls, and even intrude and invade their space to 'be dominant' (Strauss, 2005).
[2]In the pick-up industry, a 'real man' is perceived through the lens of evolutionary psychology and has certain characteristics that attract women. These characteristics are not pre-determined and can be acquired, including through training and practice. The "making hegemonic masculinity" project is at the heart of the becoming process (Mystery, 2007), and fits hand in glove with the notion of the 'self-made man' which is one of the foundations of the capitalist approach (Almog, 2016).

and interviews, in addition to feedback provided after the course. Participants of this study were: (a) 3 company managers, (b) 3 company sales managers, (c) 6 dominant customers who had become part of the small *Please Touch* pick-up group and (d) 11 new customers, mainly young men.

The study defined three negotiated responses to examining masculinity through a dialogue with 'the process' and its contents, some grounded in feminist ideology. Data collected were decoded and analysed based on grounded theory (Strauss & Corbin, 1990) to examine how men positioned themselves in relation to constructions of masculinity and how, through increased personal and social awareness, they created a new (or maintained their old) dialogue with their own masculinity. Their interpretations of this process were also examined to distinguish and conceptualize the social process (Strauss & Corbin, 1990) as an identity positioning process. The initial analysis indicated three distinct negotiated responses to 'the process' and its contents: repelling (seven men), cautious negotiation (seven men) and consenting (nine men). Those who chose the repelling response rejected the opportunity to conduct a dialogue about masculinity and their masculine identity. The negotiated response of those in the cautious category was heedful and hesitant. The men whose response was consenting were willing to conduct a dialogue with the nature and construction of masculine identity, its price and privileges.

This chapter focuses on the consenting negotiation response and maps its three significant stages. It describes a reverse process of entrenchment in the hegemonic masculine identity which repelled the contents of 'the process'. Although the negotiated response is outside the scope of this chapter, it is primarily characteristic of young men with a pronounced need to reaffirm their masculinity on the backdrop of the convergence of oppression identities such as social class, national or ethnic origin and race (Lingard & Douglas, 1999). To demonstrate and underscore the possible outcome of feminist work in 'the process', I chose to focus on men's ability and choice to change their socially structured masculine position and locate themselves in a less oppressive position towards women and themselves.

Journey towards Masculinity

Masculinity is commonly viewed as a becoming process that never ends (Gilmore, 1990) during which a boy turns into a 'real man' (Kimmel, 2008). This ultimate reward of becoming a 'real man' is important that men appear willing to undergo a gruelling journey of initiation to earn it. The primary reason is that denying or invalidating a man's hegemonic male identity is experienced as a severe social sanction that can deny power and privilege (Connell & Messerschmidt, 2005). Hegemonic masculinity, as an organizing ideational model, is embodied in social—institutional—individual interactions in which masculine identities negotiate myriad types of relations, among them cooperation, subordination, comparison or rebellion (Connell, 1995).

Courting relations are a key component of the social construction of hegemonic masculinity, which is why sexual achievements with women, and the conflicts that arise in men when they do not meet expectations, are of utmost significance (Connell, 1995). This significance turns the pick-up industry into an arena that reinforces, encourages and cultivates the image of 'hegemonic masculinity'[3] particularly callously. It also relates to the fact that male ideology has not been transformed (Kimmel, 2008) and still requires young men to adhere to traditional myths (Connell, 1995). These myths require them to be dominant and active in all daily interactions with women, mainly because the latter are expected to be passive and seducible (Connell & Messerschmidt, 2005). As part of the process of becoming and being a 'real man', men must adopt behaviour that is sexual, flirtatious and offensive (Kimmel, 2008; Lingard, Martino, Mills, & Bahr, 2002).

Culture of Pick-Up Industry

The research literature about pick-up industries has attempted to map, understand and track the way they represent itself as a supporting community,[4] uses hegemonic masculinity and its supposedly 'natural' messages to explore what need they seek to satisfy, and how they go about it (Almog, 2016). Most pick-up companies in Israel and around the world are founded on the notion of 'men for men' support communities that seek to affirm their members' masculinity within the supportive homosocial community (Grazian, 2007). This support is reflected, among other things, in developing a language of power that often espouses terminology from spheres such as 'the battle of the sexes, power games and conquests' (Almog, 2016). The community also uses a universal lexicon that in effect turns women into a

---

[3]This is about hegemonic culture defined by Kimmel (2008) as 'Guyland'. This masculinity is hedonistic and less committed and responsible than traditional masculinity, yet similar to its emphases on power, achievement and conquest.

[4]This industry takes advantage of fragile masculinity, encouraging men to believe that by practicing dominant seduction techniques they will make good progress towards the desired ideal of masculinity. Using a discourse of support, this industry exploits these young men financially, causing them to believe that they need more mentoring and practice, even after the course, as part of their 'becoming' process.

threat that must be brought to surrender so they can be taken advantage of, or so that men will no longer be afraid (Strauss, 2005). To this end, the men must learn to seduce, court and defeat women to fulfil their need for sexual and other forms of excitement.[5]

Pick-up companies usually conduct intensive marathon weekends (boot camp) where men (mostly young) learn how to pick-up women (Strauss, 2005). The weekends begin with theoretical studies, acquaintance with the 'Game' and its techniques and working on the use of dominant words from the community's universal lexicon. It is only during the second stage that the participants go out into the field to practice the techniques, more or less aggressively, with the aim of invading women's space, and, if possible, also their bodies (Mystery, 2007). The underlying assumption of this method is that aggression, perceived as an expression of masculine dominance that marks the alpha male's position — his degree of power and importance — will cause women to be attracted to him (Strauss, 2005).

Dramatic Turnabout: New Contents from a Feminist Perspective

Discussion about 'masculinities' from a feminist perspective tends, for the most part, to centre on the desire to encourage and engender change in the construction and positioning of masculine identity by working with young men and adolescent boys (Kimmel, 2009). The aim is to foster a different socialization experience that is not grounded in structural gender disparity and complex social power relations (Lingard & Douglas, 1999; Lingard et al., 2002).

The attempt to change the approach in a pick-up company is complex and daring. A new course had to be designed, contents developed and the previous curriculum overhauled. The manager of *Please Touch* faced the challenge of convincing and rallying his business partners to agree to the company's new direction. Furthermore, the company's organizational culture had to be re-defined, beliefs and attitudes replaced, among them the 'alpha male' ideal in a hierarchical culture. This meant that employees did not only have to agree to the radical change, but they had to actively participate in the newly developed culture — by changing their language,

---

[5]Few of the men who attend these courses seek to equip themselves with the tools that will enable them to meet the special One and not just an abundance of women, as most of the companies highlight. This goal changes the nature of the dialogue these men conduct with the course contents of 'the process', as it explicitly aims to improve ways to meet women to build an intimate relationship rather than to strengthen the image of their masculinity.

dialogue and work methods. The final challenge was to market the new course and attract customers to 'the process'. This involved a different target audience of men seeking, or at least willing to examine, male empowerment based on values and principles that were not grounded in the hegemonic masculinity discourse. And, this had to be accomplished while the company competed with traditional-content pick-up companies.

In contrast to the previous course, the 'Game', that was shorter and focused on quick courting that promised (but did not fulfil) immediate results, 'the process' offered an approach that required time and different positioning of masculinity. 'The process', conducted as a workshop, invited men to acquaint themselves with more than one type of masculinity (Connell, 1995; Connell & Messerschmidt, 2005), and to identify the practices they had developed or adopted that had either strengthened or weakened the masculine identity and image they sought. In effect, the workshop invited participants to critically examine the need to be a 'real man', to recognize its implications and to deal with its impact in all areas of life. The goal was to offer the participants the choice to free themselves, at least in part, from its coercive and tyrannical gaze.

Using the sharing circle method, the men discussed their intimate experiences of failure and non-success and were given legitimacy to express the social shame (Brown, 2006) they felt in the face of their non-successful or failed experiences as 'real men'. This method adopted the principles and followed in the footsteps of the feminist tradition of consciousness-raising groups. Exposing vulnerability became an integral part of 'the process' contents which challenged masculine ideology that requires men to conceal weaknesses and vulnerabilities (Kimmel, 2009; Lingard et al., 2002). The transition to practicing a culture of empathy (Brown, 2006) transformed what had been considered shameful, and had marked them as less masculine (Connell, 1995; Kimmel, 2009) into a legitimate and even worthy experience; a signifier of the 'new man'.

Men and Masculinity: Engaging Feminist Ideology

Lingard and Douglas (1999) classified men's possible responses towards feminism into four responses, examining various junctures at which masculine identity is mediated between feminist ideology and the hegemonic conception of masculinity. Two responses, on one side of the continuum, range from strengthening the traditional conservative conception of masculinity to developing a discourse of men's rights — responses more characteristic of those who experienced a convergence of oppressions (class, economic and social) under varied circumstances. According to Lingard and Douglas (1999), this confluence may drive men to validate their sense of worth by reinforcing and strengthening their hegemonic masculine identity.

The two other responses found at the other end of the continuum — masculinity therapy and the development of a pro-feminist masculinity — were characterized by awareness, openness and flexibility and the ability to validate a sense of worthiness with the help of additional identity positions. Given the fact that masculine identity has not been transformed particularly in varied groups in the Israeli society, especially compared to the demands of feminist approaches (Connell & Messerschmidt, 2005; Kimmel, 2009; Lingard & Douglas, 1999), it was interesting to examine the responses that would emerge from the clients of the pick-up company after 'the process'. This is pertinent since the pick-up industry reflects or represents 'reverse sexism'[6] (Lingard & Douglas, 1999) that in certain arenas strengthen gender inequalities.

Lingard and Douglas (1999) present alternatives that can be promoted, mainly through the education system, to mitigate the toxic effects of the underlying assumption of reverse sexism. This assumption is that, faced with situations in which they find it difficult to live up to the hegemonic model, men will not develop a different ideal and identity position, but will choose instead to do everything they can to demonstrate that they do not belong to the minority group (Kimmel, 2009).

In her book, *Joining the Resistance* (2011), Carol Gilligan asks rhetorically why we are still dealing with gender issues, as she presents crimes of patriarchy against boys and girls, men and women. It is the process of initiation, under the force of binary culture that encourages everyone, in different ways, to disconnect, to split and to feel alienated. She urges the need to resist and fight using diverse feminist ways of thinking and interpretation.

Challenging Masculinity: Sharing and Showing Vulnerability

'The process' invited the workshop participants to share their vulnerabilities and to strengthen their sense of belonging to the group, based on commonly shared social shame (Brown, 2006) that they are not 'real men' or 'not man enough' (Connell, 1995). It appears that the experience of sharing and listening to others was of vital importance and value as it reinforced

---

[6]Men believe that women are stronger than men, and that many times women will even seek to oppress and weaken them.

men's understanding that their difficulties are primarily social rather than personality-based. According to Leonid, a client:

> I feel that for me 'the process' is like a close friend that comes and offers you a hand and hears the things that up until then were concealed in the vaults of the heart. We opened the wounds that had scabbed over and we tended to them and healed them throughout the course slowly, gently and tenderly, and throughout the course these wounds mended and continue to heal. (Leonid, 24, feedback)

The opportunity to share experiences perceived as diminishing masculinity, and, therefore, hidden and repressed, replaced boasting stories of conquests. Sharing anxieties, fears and concerns, feelings of helplessness and failure elicited support that up until then was apparently unavailable. This recuperative masculinity (Lingard & Douglas, 1999), allows this type of vulnerable dialogue. As Yigal, a client, described:

> I began to share things with my friends. I told them what a hard time I was having [...] how difficult it was for me [...] what I am afraid of [...] and I can't believe I was so secretive with them all this time! It just created a sense of alienation and misunderstanding between us, and that is why the friendship between us before was also not entirely genuine [...] and it was immediately evident to me that this step only increased my worth in their eyes [...] it also created an amazing emotional connection, that also brought them to tell me things that I would have never thought about them, and did not believe I would ever hear from them. (Yigal, 29, feedback)

Sharing revealed repressed emotions and created a transformative experience that weakened the dominance and power of the ideal of hegemonic masculinity. As participants understood that this ideal is only suited for a minority of men, and not necessarily because only few can realize it, and that reality is more complex, some acknowledged that they were wasting their time in futile pursuit of excitement to alleviate a sense of social shame. These men recognized the value of sharing that they now perceived as a possible and legitimate element of masculinity. Moreover, it became an imperative of a genuine and legitimate masculinity, offering a complex dialogue between values and discourses. By granting legitimacy to share and reveal feelings and weaknesses in 'the process', men could now construct a masculinity that incorporated feelings and practices up until then attributed only to women.

Price of Hegemonic Masculinity

Men pay the price when they are required to be 'real men' all the time and in all circumstances. In this stage, men reflect on such recognition. Hanan, an employee recounted:

> I thought that a man is someone who is silent [...] over the years I carried a huge load of things that had happened to me and I continued on and simply did not speak about them, maintained appearances. During the course, when we sat in class and began to talk, I felt how I was taking this load that had not enabled me to move on because of its weight, and removing a weight, and then another one, until at some point I began to feel lighter, free, I felt that I could charge on ahead. (Hanan, 24, interview)

It appears that the legitimacy to show vulnerability in the workshop context, to share it and give it presence, can bring people close together, develop a sense of belonging and increase the option to share, and to reconnect to themselves (Gilligan, 2011). It also sanctions interpretations that deviate from the accepted conception of masculinity as experienced by different groups in Israeli society. By doing so, it paves the way to free oneself from the enslaving hegemonic image of the 'real man'. Ron, an employee, explained:

> I got tons of phone numbers every day, you can't imagine how many [...] they just lay there in the drawer. I was simply proud of every telephone number I got, it proved my power. From time to time I went out with some of them [...] but now I understand that it is so insignificant. What did I achieve? I didn't build a real relationship with them. I thought I was a king and I was a slave. A real slave. (Ron, 25, interview)

Almog (2016) maintains that by training and practicing seduction, the pick-up industry adheres to the code of the self-made man. This is the same code that requires men to work hard to advance themselves on the socially sanctioned scale — in this case, the seductive courting scale, to be considered a 'real man' (Gilmore, 1990; Kimmel, 2008). Relinquishing this stance through awareness and understanding can liberate men from what they experience as unending 'slavery'. It also supports the argument that pick-up companies do not only directly affect women who are victims of harassing men performing in an abusive culture, but also harm and exact a price

from the men. Consciousness raising and change may lead to a transformation in other areas of life, as demonstrated by Roy, a client:

> [...] now I even manage my business differently. I don't have
> to be authoritative and dominant all the time at work as well.
> I share, ask, consult. I discovered a whole new world. It not
> only has to do with an intimate relationship, this whole story
> of masculinity, it pertains to everything. Absolutely every-
> thing. (Roy, 32, interview)

Alongside the understanding that his attitude towards women had been
based on exploitation, aggression and control, Roy now recognized that
the ability and legitimacy to share and seek advice could liberate him from
the burden of the previously desired image of invincible masculinity. Just as
important, he understood that this new freedom affected every area of life.

New Definition of Masculinity

In this stage of 'the process' the participants deconstruct the narrow and
limiting conception of masculinity they had known and adopted up until
then. They could now choose a broader and multi-dimensional masculine
identity and reposition themselves with respect to their masculinity, not
necessarily in conformity with hierarchic and hegemonic definitions and
limitations set in traditional myths. Benny, an employee, described this:

> It always seemed to me that sharing, asking and requesting
> clarification was a sign of weakness. Suddenly I discovered
> their power. Today I no longer think they belong to the
> world of the nerds, but rather to the world of those who are
> sure of themselves. (Benny 22, informal conversation)

This quote shows how the notion of universal 'macho man' model
(Connell & Messerschmidt, 2005) that reflects a man's primal nature is
deconstructed into a different and varied image of masculinities that are,
even if only to a certain extent, unencumbered by the power of hegemonic
conception and hierarchy. The interpretation of the distinction between
strength and weakness, still present in the language used in the pick-up
industry and outside of it, as well, is also reversed in the eyes of men who
chose the consenting response and were willing to examine their own conceptions of masculinity. What they had up until recently defined as 'hegemonic' was no longer perceived to be worthy in their eyes, and vice versa.

Ronen, a client, describes how 'the process' changed not only his perceptions and feelings, but also his actions:

> Until I participated in the course I lived my life as an Israeli man that doesn't do much except for sitting with the guys and sometimes going out to meet new girls. I discovered that there is more to life and we can make our hobbies come true [...] not just alcohol and women [...] because after all, when you feel good about yourself, others feel it and, put simply, you don't walk around like a 'dog in heat'. For example, the day after the course I signed up for a hand to hand combat class that I had put off for a very long time [...] It also helps me a great deal to feel satisfied like a person that has a girlfriend even when he doesn't, because life is full of interesting things. (Ronen, 26, feedback)

Participants in 'the process' defined a new set of values for themselves, expanding the concept of the 'Israeli man'. This is in line with Lingard and Douglas (1999) who maintained that it is possible to strengthen additional identity positions, enabling a shift in the way men perceive their masculine identity. This relieves them of the need to continuously prove their masculinity by walking around like a 'dog in heat', as Ronen stated in his narrative.

Danny, a client, describes the understanding he gained from 'the process' about his previous perception and experience of social expectations about being a man:

> Society taught us what a man is within clear-cut boundaries. A man is someone who has women. It doesn't matter how rich you are [...] if you don't bring 78 different young women a month you can be many things, but a man you are not [...] In 'the process' we learned that everyone is a man in his own way. You don't have to be a crazy womanizer to be considered a man, you can simply be yourself and be seen as a man your way, not according to any dictates which our society imposes. (Danny, 28, interview)

In saying 'not according to any dictates', Danny means ignoring the existing hierarchical order and assigning new value to what hegemonic discourse perceives as inferior. This may appear to be a subversive strategy, but in fact reflects a critical re-evaluation of values and a conscious choice among men. Danny describes the way he deals with the external definitions on his path to redefining himself and redrawing the boundaries of his masculine identity.

Conclusions

This chapter focused on the consenting negotiated response to 'the process'. This workshop was designed to create a safe space where participants could examine their own conceptions and experiences about masculinity, and, based on a new understanding, choose whether to position themselves differently including its consequences. The goal was to demonstrate how masculine identity is a fluid category and that, given the suitable opportunity and social space along with proper mediation, men can position themselves differently in relation to masculine identities. Tracing the stages experienced by men in a pick-up company during 'the process' highlights the possibility and the hope that masculine ideology can be reshaped in a space that affords more choice. Up until the workshop the men had invested in perpetual attempts and practices to demonstrate that they were 'real men' by conquering women, and hoped to gain recognition as such. After 'the process', they seek to win a new recognition and sense of worthiness with practices that reflect a different perception and positioning. This may undermine the existing structure of power relations (Connell, 1995), especially in traditional societies. But it may also foster a space that lessens women's vulnerability to become victims in a 'rape culture' (Buchwald et al., 1993).

Through the prism of the negotiated responses proposed by Lingard and Douglas (1999) to describe engagement with feminist ideology, 'masculinity therapy' was very prominent in 'the process', similar to its prominent presence in educational spaces (Kimmel, 2009; Lingard et al., 2002). In the case of 'the process', the same need arose to adopt values of containing and sharing without relinquishing the privileges of 'masculinity'. This response is easier to embrace as it minimizes the need to preserve hegemonic masculinity and limits situations of gender inequality (Lingard & Douglas, 1999). It even may drive men to adopt a victim discourse without taking responsibility for the possibility that by doing so they may be victimizing others. Hence, despite men's changing attitudes, women's place as subjects is lacking and they remain objects in patriarchy.

In planning the contents and activities of 'the process', we assumed that to persuade young men to abandon traditional beliefs of masculinity would be through a role model with specific characteristics. A man who had been where they were had undergone a consciousness-raising process, and, as a result, had changed his perspective and practices. In other words, someone with a proven record as a 'master pick-up' and therefore an 'alpha male' who is well-versed in the language, contents, scene, social arena of the 'Game' in the pick-up culture. This role model perceived as reliable and trustworthy revealed the big bluff of masculinity after experiencing 'the process' himself as well as recognizing the pain and price of hegemonic masculinity. Ironically, only 'real man' could convince young men to relinquish their aspirations to achieve such a position, and they would be less willing to listen, let alone to believe and follow a woman, not to mention a feminist woman.

The use of a male role model may have reinforced the absence of women and their pain, such that it ultimately remained a homosocial project (Almog, 2016). In 'the process' workshop, as in reality, women are neither the issue nor the focus, nor are they subjects having shape or form. Furthermore, as the focus is on the pain and price experienced by men deceived by the desired image of masculinity, who now seek to free themselves from the illusory and fallacious concept of masculinity, a critical discussion of men's privileges and their social implications is also lacking.

The consumer discourse in the competitive pick-up industry preserves, and even encourages, differences between men and women, and even more so between men. It is, therefore, necessary to strengthen the use of 'change agents' within these companies reinforcing masculine discourse, and to use their position and status as mediators to raise men's awareness about traditional myths and disparities in existing power relations in society. At the same time, ensure that change agents themselves, using continuous feminist work, can also conduct a critical discussion about hegemonic masculinity not just through their own pain, but a new vision of really 'becoming a real man'.

References

Almog, R. (2016). The seduction community as an expression of contemporary youth culture. Unpublished PhD thesis, Bar-Ilan University.

Brown, B. (2006). Shame resilience theory: A grounded theory study on women and shame. *Families in Society: The Journal of Contemporary Social Services, 87,* 43−52.

Buchwald, E., Fletcher, P. R., & Roth, M. (1993). *Transforming a rape culture.* Minneapolis, MN: Milkweed Editions.

Connell, R. (1995). *Masculinities.* Cambridge: Polity Press.

Connell, R. W., & Messerschmidt, J. W. (2005). Hegemonic masculinity: Rethinking the concept. *Gender & Society, 19*(6), 829−859.

Gilligan, C. (2011). *Joining the resistance.* Cambridge: Polity Press.

Gilmore, D. (1990). *Manhood in the making: Cultural concepts of masculinity.* New Haven, CT: Yale University Press.

Grazian, D. (2007). The girl hunt: Urban nightlife and the performance of masculinity as collective activity. *Symbolic Interaction, 30,* 221−243.

Kimmel, M. (2008). *Guyland: The perilous world where boys become men.* New York, NY: Harper Collins.

Kimmel, M. (2009). "What about the boys?" What the current debates tell us — and don't tell us — about boys in school. *Michigan Feminist Studies, 14,* 1−28.

Lingard, B., & Douglas, P. (1999). *Men engaging feminisms: Pro-feminism, backlashes and schooling*. Buckingham: Open University Press.

Lingard, B., Martino, W., Mills, M., & Bahr, M. (2002). *Addressing the educational needs of boys—Strategies for schools*. Canberra: Commonwealth Department of Education, Science and Training.

Mystery (2007). *The mystery method: How to get beautiful women into bed*. New York, NY: St. Martin's Press.

Strauss, A., & Corbin, L. (1990). *Basics of grounded theory methods*. Beverly Hills, CA: Sage.

Strauss, N. (2005). *The game: Penetrating the secret society of pick-up artists*. New York, NY: Reagan Books.

Part Five

Sports and Bodies

Global Synthesis

Glenda Tibe Bonifacio

Bodies are sites of representation, oppression and resistance. Bodies are constructed in different cultures and societies as normative ideals of masculinity and femininity. Women's bodies inscribe nationalist ideals and values, and are subject to more scrutiny and regulation than men. Proper attires in public to show modesty, codes for physical expressions of identity and affection, acceptable fashion and comportment to belong, ability and self-confidence are some of the issues associated with bodies. With the spread of western pop culture to other parts of the world, a new globalizing beauty ideal of whiteness contributes to the rise in cosmetic surgeries and proliferation of bleaching products in some predominantly non-white populations in the world. Bodies are central to notions of inclusion and exclusion, with parameters based on a complex intersection of materialism and social psychology together with other context-specific variables. In sports, certain body types and gender are perceived to ideally inhabit athletic spaces in basketball, gymnastics and the like. But the introduction of inclusive sports enabled the participation of more diverse bodies today, and growing. Awareness into the many ways in which human bodies are able to express strength, agility, flexibility or simply for fun have motivated further moves for inclusion by sports organizations regardless of gender. As body constructs change with time and place, so are the ways of engagement and negotiation. And, while these continue to be contested by particular interest groups we have broaden our understanding of bodies and its autonomy.

Chapter 17

Ghostly (Dis)Appearances: Sport, Gender and Feminisms in Canada

Carly Adams and Jason Laurendeau

Abstract

Since the 1970s there have been extraordinary changes and growth in Canadian sport in terms of access, opportunity and recognition. Yet, the gains and successes of girls and women's sport are often written, told and retold as uncomplicated success stories, as progress, with the battles fought and the complex negotiations of the past eerily absent. In this chapter, we turn to the work of feminist poststructuralist Avery Gordon to consider gender, feminisms and sport in the Canadian context. We do this by putting various moments in time in conversation with one another and considering our current moment in light of what has come before but is often forgotten, overlooked or even suppressed. We argue that the need for feminist praxis remains significant in Canadian sport and it is imperative that we continue to shed light on ghostly (dis)appearances in narratives of sport in Canada.

Keywords: Sport; histories; feminisms; Canada; ski jumping; ice hockey

On Triumphant Feminist Tales

Sport has long been viewed as a sexist, discriminatory, male-dominated, male-centred institution, a 'masculinizing project' (Hall, 2016, p. xv). Moreover, it is an institution in which broader gender relations are not

Global Currents in Gender and Feminisms: Canadian and International Perspectives, 253–263
Copyright © 2018 by Emerald Publishing Limited
All rights of reproduction in any form reserved
ISBN: 978-1-78714-484-2/doi:10.1108/978-1-78714-483-520171024

simply reflected, but actively produced (Connell, 2008a, 2008b). The ways gender is (re)constructed, negotiated and contested in sport and physical activity constitute a central part of broader configurations of gender in Canadian society (and more broadly, of course).

In the context described above, women athletes have achieved many successes and gains. Ideologies and discourses of gender equality and social justice work to position girls and women's sport as a 'triumphant feminist tale' (Messner, 2011, p. 152). Arguably it is. In Canada, for example, there have been dramatic increases in the numbers of girls and women playing sport. Since the 1970s there have been extraordinary changes and growth in Canadian sport in terms of access, opportunity and recognition. Yet, as we engage with contemporary sport as researchers, participants, spectators and parents we are struck by the normative ways that Canadian sport gets storied and remembered. While there is much to be celebrated in Canadian sport and the changes and growth over the past four decades, as Schultz (2014) reminds us, we need to 'cheer with reserve' (p. 187). The gains and successes of girls and women's sport are often written, told and retold as uncomplicated success stories, as progress, with the battles fought and the complex negotiations of the past eerily absent (Adams & Leavitt, in press). What is lost or forgotten in narratives of Canadian women's sport is that the history of women's sport is also a 'history of cultural resistance' (Hall, 2016, p. xv).

Ghosts and Histories

To understand the silences highlighted above, we turn to the work of feminist poststructuralist Avery Gordon. Gordon's (2008) call to listen to and take notice of the ghostly, that which is suspiciously absent, encourages us to examine what is there but *not there* by putting different moments/events in conversation with one another. By considering historical moments and their connection to the present, we can begin to disrupt dominant narratives of Canadian sport to consider how the 'past and present ignite each other, resemble each other, articulate with one another, figure meaning in one another' (Brown, 2001, p. 165). In other words, we draw on 'a methodology that is attentive to … what appears to be in the past, but is powerfully present' (Gordon, 1990, p. 493). In this chapter, we consider gender, feminisms and sport in the Canadian context by 'writing a history of the present' (Gordon, 2008, p. 195). We do this by putting various moments in time in conversation with one another and considering our current moment in light of what has come before but is often forgotten, overlooked or even suppressed. Gordon suggests that 'to write a history of the present requires stretching toward the horizon of what cannot be seen with ordinary clarity yet' (Gordon, 2008, p. 195). Stretching towards this horizon or even beyond it, according to Gordon (2008), requires a particular kind of perception where the transparent and the shadowy confront each other.

We take the importance of histor(y/ies) as our starting point, not only in our research but for understanding contemporary moments and considering the unimagined future (Brown, 2001; Gordon, 2008). We argue that the language of past, present and future becomes difficult to sustain if we understand the future as an (un)imagined possibility of the past and present and the present as the once-imagined future. Too often the complexities of the past remain 'absent' from the contemporary stories of Canadian sport. As Gordon (2008) suggests, these haunting presences are *unseen* because they are systematically rendered invisible. In sport scholarship, we (too) often construct narratives that rest on an underlying set of assumptions about linear notions of history. But, as Hall (2016) reminds us, history is never linear; it is messy and complex, and does not flow from moment to moment. As we consider gendered notions of sport in Canada and feminist activism that has pushed boundaries and helped to shape the Canadian sport context, we aim to blur categorical notions of history to construct the kind of 'history of the present' for which Gordon (2008, p. 195) calls. Moreover, we seek to contribute to 'a field that gives notice to structures of exclusion and that does not enclose the landscape in only what can be seen' (Gordon, 1990, p. 498).

Feminisms and Sport Scholarship

It is important to recognize the various feminist approaches to studying sport. Early scholarly work on gender and sport in Canada provided a critique of male dominance with much of the focus on women and sport (see, e.g. Hall, 1996). Despite the many advances in sport outlined above, women still do not have as many opportunities to compete as men, with observably fewer medals and professional sport pathways and unequal funding. Since the 1960s, liberal feminists in sport have focussed on issues of access, opportunity, socialization, discrimination and gender stereotyping with the underlying assumption 'that sport is fundamentally sound and represents a positive experience to which girls and women need access' (Scraton & Flintoff, 2013, p. 97). While the continuing initiatives of liberal feminist sport activists are productive and needed to continue to put women's sport on organizational agendas and consider opportunity, access and issues of equality/equity, Scraton and Flintoff (2013) argue that these superficial changes in Canadian sport have 'simply hidden more complex gender inequalities that continue to impact many women and some men' (p. 97). In other words, when we consider questions of access, we must constantly ask the question: 'access to what?' (Laurendeau & Sharara, 2008). One of the continuing critiques of liberal feminist activism in Canadian sport is that it treats girls and women as a homogenous group with little regard for difference (Adams & Leavitt, in press). With a focus on reform, this approach posits that the current system — a system that continues to serve the needs of boys and men — needs to change; it is not enough to challenge particular inequities in Canadian sport.

In contemporary scholarship examining the sport/gender nexus, the emphasis has shifted from 'women in sport' to 'gender in sport' as scholars critically engage discourses of masculinities and femininities in sport (Vertinsky, 1994). Most recently, as Scraton and Flintoff (2013) suggest, in critical sport scholarship, more emphasis has been placed on identities, bodies, empowerment and the significance of difference. This poststructuralist perspective forefronts a complex understanding of gender as performative, contingent, contradictory and inextricably intertwined with knowledge, power and identity (e.g. Laurendeau, 2014). From this poststructuralist perspective, (hetero)sexuality is seen as a major site of men's domination over women (Scraton & Flintoff, 2013). This approach sees compulsory heterosexuality, whereby heterosexuality is constructed not only as *normative*, but as the only culturally intelligible *choice*, as a form of social and sexual control (Sykes, 2006). Arising out of the critical poststructuralist work described above, there has been a push to celebrate women and develop a separatist philosophy through consciousness raising. Stevens and Adams (2013), for example, explore the Ontario Women's Hockey Association's push for a separatist philosophy in women's hockey. Radical feminists in sport are concerned with structural power relations, patriarchy and the domination of men over women within and through sport (Scraton & Flintoff, 2013). Further radical feminist research on lesbianism and homophobia in sport explores the strategies taken up by sporting groups to negotiate and resist mainstream sport thereby creating spaces for the queering of sport (Cahn, 1994; Cunningham, 2012). Canadian activist organizations such as the Canadian Association for the Advancement of Women in Sport (CAAWS) are often charged with providing 'a liberal response to a radical issue' (Scraton & Flintoff, 2013, p. 99). Scholars have taken up poststructuralist and Marxist/socialist approaches to challenge liberal understandings of sex, gender and sexuality (Sykes, 2006) and to address gender inequality as it relates to capitalism, class and economic exploitation (Thompson, 1999). Scholars have also examined the privilege men experience through sport due to unequal gender relations by examining sport through the lens of historical constructions of masculinity (Connell, 2008a, 2008b; Messner, 1992).

We argue that while embracing the cultural, visual, linguistic and reflexive turns in sport studies and considering new feminist questions, it is, as Scraton and Flintoff (2013, p. 105) remind us, 'important not to lose sight of the 'old' questions' that still have relevance. Feminist sport history points to a past of 'women being denied opportunities, of being restricted and excluded from participation, of having our accomplishments ignored or ridiculed, or hearing our efforts being used as male forms of derision, of having our labour and our bodies exploited in the name of sport' (Thompson, 2002, p. 106). We need to consider the past as it is revealed — the negotiations, challenges and achievements — to interrogate how it haunts our current moment. We need to take this approach to infuse the Canadian sport system with renewed political activism. We see the past everywhere as we seek to engage with and understand contemporary moments in Canadian sport. As we look more closely into 'how that which appears to be absent can indeed be a seething presence' (Gordon, 2008, p. 17), we have come to understand that analyzing hauntings and disrupting normative narratives leads to a more complex understanding of the historically embedded social actions that impact contemporary moments in Canadian sport in ways that are seen and unseen. To do this we turn to two case studies of contemporary Canadian sport that are haunted by a lost but not forgotten past.

'Jumping Like a Girl'

The International Olympic Committee (IOC) has long been criticized by feminist sport scholars for its exclusionary practices, entrenchment of gender differences, and for contributing to the construction of men's sport as 'real' sport and women's sport as less-than (Hargreaves, 1994; Laurendeau & Adams, 2010; Lenskyj 1986; Smith & Wrynn, 2008). Yet in 2008, Richard Pound, long time IOC member from Canada problematically suggested that 'gender equality had all but been achieved' in the Olympics (Pound, 2008, p. 2). A claim like this suggests that 'we have arrived', at least with respect to gender equity. More importantly, in terms of this chapter, it constructs the present as the imagined future of the past, one in which women compete on a level playing field with men. For this kind of claim to be intelligible, however, moments from the past and the present must never be brought into close conversation with one another, lest such a conversation shatter the illusory triumphant tale being conjured. Our task here is to foster such a conversation in the case of women's ski jumping.

In 2014, women's ski jumping was, for the first time, included as part of the Winter Olympic programme. This was heralded as a major achievement in women's sport, an event '90 years in the making' (Loney, 2014). Almost a century after men's ski jumping was introduced as part of the Olympic programme, women were finally to be included, despite considerable foot-dragging from the IOC (Laurendeau & Adams, 2010). Canadian women figured centrally in this story, many of them front and centre in a lawsuit filed against the Vancouver Organizing Committee in the lead up to the 2010 Olympic Winter Games.[1]

The Canadian women involved in the lawsuit, as well as those who competed in the 2014 Olympic ski jumping event, are quite rightly part of the story. Media coverage of women's inclusion in the 2014 Olympic ski jumping event emphasizes the reluctance of the IOC to include the event in earlier Olympiads, the recent organized efforts of women to resist this discriminatory ruling, and recent statements by senior officials that seem to question whether women's bodies can handle the rigours of the sport (Clarke, 2013; Laurendeau & Adams, 2010; Loney, 2014). Another Canadian woman, however, is also part of the story, though in a more ghostly form (Gordon, 2008), and it is to her story that we turn our attention.

In 1922, Canadian Isabel Coursier earned the title of 'Women's Amateur Champion Ski Jumper of the World' (Canadian Olympic Team Handbook, 2006). Coursier, born in British Columbia in 1906, showed an interest in, and aptitude for, skiing as a young child, recalling: '... I was always in the out-of-doors sliding on something either on my seat or a pan or a shovel or a piece of linoleum'.[2] As a youngster, Coursier joined a fledgling group of ski jumpers called the 'glider girls' (Porter, 2002, p. 66). In her teens, Coursier became a star, winning ski jumping competitions and touring widely to compete in venues across North America. What is more, from 1922 until 1929, Coursier's jump of 84 feet at Revelstoke Ski Club stood as the record for the longest ski jump by a woman (Porter, 2002).

Coursier is by no means the only, or earliest, notable woman ski jumper in history (Laurendeau & Adams, 2010). But we consider her ghostly presence here to shed additional light on the contemporary 'success' story of women's ski jumping. Coursier's story beckons us to reconsider the recent struggles over the place of women's ski jumping in the Olympic programme. If we consider the present as the once (un)imagined future from the perspective of the past, it seems hard to fathom that Coursier and her contemporaries might have envisioned a future in which organized resistance would be at

---

[1]For more information about the lawsuit and the implications for women's sport, see Vertinsky, Jette, and Hofmann (2009).
[2]Interview with Isabel Patricia Coursier, by Christina Mead and Gertrude Leslie, 22 February 1977, transcripts at Revelstoke Museum and Archives, Revelstoke, British Columbia.

all necessary for women's ski jumping to be taken seriously. More striking still is that the lengthy history of women's involvement in ski jumping is rendered all but invisible in contemporary coverage of the 'victory' with respect to Olympic inclusion, even in stories written with a more critical eye (see, e.g. Clarke, 2013). Coursier's ghostly presence calls our attention to a much longer history of women's involvement in the sport than is generally acknowledged, and shatters the IOC's recent claims that women's ski-jumping was simply not 'mature' enough to be included in the Olympic programme (Laurendeau & Adams, 2010). Moreover, it raises serious questions about the continued gender segregation of the sport, with women's competition sanctioned on only the smaller ski jumps. At the Sochi Games, for example, men competed on both the 'large' (90m/K120) and the 'normal' (70m/K90) hills, whereas women were only permitted to compete on the 'normal' hill. This segregation continues to construct women's bodies as fundamentally different — even inferior — to men's bodies, and thus perpetuates the myth upon which so much contemporary gender segregation in sport rests.

Codes of (Mis)Conduct

Similarly, moments in contemporary women's hockey are haunted by a forgotten but seemingly always present past. While aggression and violence is accepted, romanticized and in many cases encouraged in men's hockey, in women's hockey bodily comportment is more controlled through rules and public scrutiny. In January 2015, a women's hockey match between Boston Blades and Brampton Thunder in the Canadian Women's Hockey League made the news, not for the hard-fought match and the skills of the teams but because of a fight that broke out on the ice between two players. News outlets made sure to clarify that Monique Lamoureau and Jamie Lee Rattray, the combatants featured on social media videos, were not 'goons' but women (Kennedy, 2015).

The rules of men's and women's hockey are similar, but with one particularly striking difference: body checking is prohibited at all levels in women's hockey. Ostensibly based on reasons such as the possibility of violence and/or injuries, and the importance of protecting women's bodies, the codified rules of hockey (not to mention the informal norms) place women's bodies under paternalistic protection in troubling ways (Adams, 2014; Theberge, 2000; Weaving & Roberts, 2012). As Adams and Leavitt (in press) remind us, this ongoing process of social control through the rules and regulations of sport sends meaningful messages to the players, spectators and coaches: 'their practice of hockey is "inferior" and "different" (p. 13). It was not always this way, however.

Women have been playing hockey in Canada since the 1890s and by the early 1920s it was widespread across the country. Early on, it had the reputation of being a hard-fought sport where rough play, aggression and occasional injuries were commonplace (Adams, 2009; Kidd, 1996). Press reports from the period describe 'Hockey Amazons in Fistic Display' (1936) where 'tempers flared, sticks and fists flew in reckless abandon' (Gibb, 1935, p. 16). These reports suggest that 'some women were as willing as men to put themselves in harm's way on the ice rink' and they were enabled to do so then through the codified rules of the game (Adams, 2014, p. 209). This participatory violence, however, tends to be framed in popular discourse only within men's hockey of the past and present (Adams, 2014). From the outset, men's hockey was recognized and celebrated as a violent, physical sport (Lorenz & Osborne, 2006; Morrow & Wamsley, 2013). In hockey, 'women embraced the codes of conduct established for the men's game, making the rink their own space for the embodiment of aggressive, physical, and skilful comportment' (Adams, 2014, p. 2010). Yet, despite women's hockey in the 1920s being played under the same rules as the men with body checking, fighting and aggression, there was moral panic among sports leaders and social critics about women moving their bodies in these ways (Adams, 2014; Hall, 2016). When women's bodies move in aggressive, skilful, and rough ways in a place that has typically been male-dominated, it 'brings on a state of disorientation' (Puwar, 2004, p. 14). Thus, contemporary moments of physicality in women's sport, such as the fight between Lamoureau and Rattray, are haunted by past moments when aggression and fighting were commonplace in women's hockey, yet were criticized by social and moral reformers. These past moments ignite present debates about physicality in women's hockey, fundamentally undermining the all-too-convenient narrative that women simply *can't take a hit* the way men can (Weaving & Roberts, 2012). The parallels between the social responses to such physicality (or even the prospect thereof) also shed light on the ways women's hockey continues to be constructed as secondary, as a derivation of the men's game, which is so often produced as 'real hockey' in the cultural imaginary.

Histories of the Present

To borrow from Cahn (1994), the two case studies we have considered in this chapter point to the 'dominant culture's view of sport as inherently masculine and of women athletes as, therefore, charming but temporary imposters, freakish anomalies, or threatening transgressors of sexual and gender binaries' (pp. 599–600). Moreover, they highlight the importance of sport as a space for the cultural production of particular ideas about masculinities, femininities, bodies and identities. What is at stake, we would suggest, is much more than simply the outcome of any particular athletic contest. Rather, what is at stake is the social fabric and the ways we think about gender, sexuality and numerous other systems of alterity.

In light of the above, the need for feminist praxis remains significant in Canadian sport. Not least, it is imperative that we continue to shed light on ghostly (dis)appearances in narratives of sport in Canada. It is simply not good enough, for example, to content ourselves with histories of sports that begin (somewhat magically, it seems) with the sanctioning of a particular sport by an international federation, and thus erase a much longer and richer history, one likely characterized by important moments of cultural resistance and struggle that connects the past with the present. Nor should we allow women's sporting achievements to be constructed (directly or indirectly) in relation to men's sport and sporting achievements *rather that as extensions of women's own earlier achievements and political struggles.* Instead, we must push to write — and insist upon — histories of the present. These histories will shed important light on the sporting experiences of different groups of women — indigenous women, queer women, women with disabilities and many more. We must settle for nothing less as we contribute to the broader feminist project(s) in which we are engaged.

References

Adams, C. (2009). Organizing hockey for women: The Ladies Ontario Hockey Association and the fight for legitimacy, 1922–1940. In J. C. Wong (Ed.), *Coast to coast: Hockey in Canada to the Second World War* (pp. 132–159). Toronto: University of Toronto Press.

Adams, C. (2014). Troubling bodies: The Canadian girl, the ice rink, and the Banff Winter Carnival. *Journal of Canadian Studies, 48*(3), 200–220.

Adams, C., & Leavitt, S. (in press). 'It's just girls' hockey': Troubling progress narratives in girls' and women's sport. *International Review for the Sociology of Sport.* doi:10.1177/1012690216649207

Brown, W. (2001). *Politics out of history.* Princeton, NJ: Princeton University Press.

Cahn, S. (1994). *Coming on strong: Gender and sexuality in twentieth-century women's sport.* New York, NY: Free Press.

Canadian Olympic Team Handbook, Turin. 2006. Retrieved from http://www.olympic.ca/EN/media/2006_handbook/skijumping/intro.shtml

Clarke, L. (2013). Sochi 2014: Women's ski jumping ready to prove their Olympic mettle. *The Washington Post*, February 3. Retrieved from https://www.

washingtonpost.com/pb/sochi-2014-womens-ski-jumpers-ready-to-prove-their-olympic-mettle/2014/02/03/eb45f3ac-8aa5-11e3-916e-e01534b1e132_story.html

Connell, R. (2008a). *Gender and power: Society, the person and sexual politics.* Cambridge: Polity Press.

Connell, R. (2008b). Masculinity construction and sports in boys' education: A framework for thinking about the issue. *Sport Education and Society, 13*(2), 131–145. doi:10.1080/13573320801957053

Cunningham, G. B. (Ed.). (2012). *Sexual orientation and gender identity in sport.* College Station, TX: Texas A&M University Press.

Gibb, A. (1935). Sticks and fists fly freely as girl hockeyists battle. *The Toronto Daily Star*, March 26, p. 12.

Gordon, A. F. (1990). Feminism, writing, and ghosts. *Social Problems, 37*(4), 485–500. doi:10.2307/800577

Gordon, A. F. (2008). *Ghostly matters: Haunting and the sociological imagination.* Minneapolis, MN: University of Minnesota Press.

Hall, M. A. (1996). *Feminism and sporting bodies.* Champaign, IL: Human Kinetics.

Hall, M. A. (2016). *The girl and the game: A history of women's sport in Canada* (2nd ed.), Toronto: University of Toronto Press.

Hargreaves, J. (1994). *Sporting females: Critical issues in the history and sociology of women's sports.* New York, NY: Routledge.

Hockey Amazons in Fistic Display. (1936). *The Toronto Daily Star*, February 20, p. 16.

Kennedy, R. (2015). Women's hockey fight: *Monique Lamoureau vs Jamie Lee Rattray. The Hockey News*, January 20. Retrieved from http://www.thehockey-news.com/blog/womens-hockey-fight-monique-lamoureux-vs-jamie-lee-rattray

Kidd, B. (1996). *The struggle for Canadian sport.* Toronto: University of Toronto Press.

Laurendeau, J. (2014). 'Just tape it up for me, ok?' Masculinities, injury and embodied emotion. *Emotion, Space and Society, 12*, 11–17. doi:10.1016/j.emospa.2013.03.010

Laurendeau, J., & Adams, C. (2010). 'Jumping like a girl': Discursive silences, exclusionary practices and the controversy over women's ski jumping. *Sport in Society, 13*(3), 431–447. doi:10.1080/17430431003588051

Laurendeau, J., & Sharara, N. (2008). 'Women could be every bit as good as guys' Reproductive and resistant agency in two 'action' sports. *Journal of Sport & Social Issues, 32*(1), 24–47. doi:10.1177/0193723507307819

Lenskyj, H. (1986). *Out of bounds: Women, sport and sexuality.* Toronto: Women's Press.

Loney, H. (2014). Women's ski jumping makes historic Olympic debut, *Global News*. Retrieved from http://globalnews.ca/news/1142320/womens-ski-jumping-makes-historic-olympic-debut/

Lorenz, S., & Osborne, G. (2006). 'Talk about strenuous hockey': Violence, manhood and the 1907 Ottawa Silver Seven-Montreal Wanderer rivalry. *Journal of Canadian Studies, 40*(1), 125–156.

Messner, M. (1992). *Power at play: Sports and the problem of masculinity.* Boston, MA: Beacon Press.

Messner, M. (2011). Gender ideologies, youth sports, and the production of soft essentialism. *Sociology of Sport Journal, 28*(2), 151–170. doi:10.1123/ssj.28.2.151

Morrow, D., & Wamsley, K. (2013). *Sport in Canada: A history* (3rd ed.). Don Mills: Oxford University Press.

Porter, A. (2002). *Honour: Canadian skiers of distinction*. Woodbridge: Ski Canada.

Pound, R. W. (2008). The future of the Olympic movement: Promised land or train wreck. In R. K. Barney, M. Heine, & K. B. Wamsley (Eds.), *Pathways: Critiques and discourse in Olympic Research* (pp. 1–19). London: International Centre for Olympic Studies, The University of Western Ontario.

Puwar, N. (2004). *Space invaders: Race, gender and bodies out of place*. New York, NY: Berg.

Schultz, J. (2014). *Qualifying times: Points of change in US women's sport*. Champaign, IL: University of Illinois Press.

Scraton, S., & Flintoff, A. (2013). Gender, feminist theory, and sport. In D. L. Andrews & B. Carrington (Eds.), *A companion to sport* (pp. 96–110). London: Wiley-Blackwell.

Smith, M., & Wrynn, A. M. (2008). *Women in the 2000, 2004 and 2008 Olympic and Paralympic Games: An analysis of participation and leadership opportunities*. East Meadow, NY: Women's Sport Foundation.

Stevens, J., & Adams, C. (2013). "Together we can make it better": Collective action and governance in a girls' ice hockey association. *International Review for the Sociology of Sport, 48*(6), 658–672.

Sykes, H. (2006). Queering theories of sexuality in sport studies. In J. Caudwell (Ed.), *Sport, sexualities and queer/theory* (pp. 13–32). London: Routledge.

Theberge, N. (2000). *Higher goals: Women's ice hockey and the politics of gender*. Albany, NY: SUNY Press.

Thompson, S. (1999). *Mother's taxi: Sport and women's labor*. Albany, NY: SUNY.

Thompson, S. (2002). Sport, gender, feminism. In K. Young & J. Maguire (Eds.), *Theory, sport, & society* (pp. 105–127). Oxford: Elsevier.

Vertinsky, P. (1994). Gender relations, women's history and sport history: A decade of changing inquiry, 1983–1993. *Journal of Sport History, 21*(1), 1–24.

Vertinsky, P., Jette, S., & Hofmann, A. (2009). Gender justice and gender politics at the local, national and international level over the challenge of women's ski jumping. *Olympika, 18*, 43–74.

Weaving, C., & Roberts, S. (2012). Checking in: An analysis of the (lack of) body checking in women's ice hockey. *Research Quarterly for Exercise and Sport, 83*(3), 470–478. doi:10.1080/02701367.2012.10599882

Chapter 18

Physical Education in Israel: Teachers' Talk of Girls' Bodies

Ornit Ramati Dvir and Orly Benjamin

Abstract

The view that physical education (PE) positively affects students' perception of their own body efficacy and self-esteem is not often seen as related to issues of gender equality. Nevertheless, PE classes leave many girls with a negative physical experience, of weakness, clumsiness and heaviness. Although the ways in which the beauty myth undermines girls' self-esteem and body image are quite known, until recently researchers in the field of PE have not focused on the possibility that PE teachers also play a role in disciplining girls' bodies and subjectivities. Consequently, studies in this area tend to marginalize the covert exclusionary mechanism potentially exerted on girls who find their bodies unsuitable for PE. This study is the first to examine PE in Israel from a gender perspective. Some PE teachers in Israel are already aware to a certain extent of their educational role in legitimizing diversity in girls' body shapes. How then do PE teachers negotiate this awareness with regard to the dominant discourses related to girls' bodies? To explore this question, we conducted in-depth semi-structured interviews with 15 PE teachers. The analysis revealed two key features of PE teachers' talk about girls' bodies: acceptance of body shape diversity, and awareness of girls' issues about their bodies. Our findings suggest that these progressive aspects of teachers' perspectives on girls' bodies are negotiated against older forms of girls' body disciplining.

Keywords: Physical education (PE); gender; adolescent girls; girl bodies; body pedagogies; exclusion

Global Currents in Gender and Feminisms: Canadian and International Perspectives, 265–277
Copyright © 2018 by Emerald Publishing Limited
All rights of reproduction in any form reserved
ISBN: 978-1-78714-484-2/doi:10.1108/978-1-78714-483-520171025

Introduction

In many countries, including Israel, physical education (PE) in schools is formally associated with the socialization and empowerment of adolescents. The official PE policy is of equality in terms of gender, sexual preferences, race, social class, etc. (Galily, Lidor & Ben-Porat, 2009; Penney & Evans, 2002). Research shows that while for some girls PE classes provide positive physical experiences and increased feelings of efficacy and success, for many others the physical experience is negative (e.g. Clarck, 2012). Studies that have applied a gendered perspective to the exploration of the disparity between the stated aims of PE and girls' experiences have not considered PE teachers' point of view. Thus, the notion that PE teachers as women are likely to have encountered feminist ideas and may try to support girls in their struggles with their body perception has not received sufficient attention. This chapter examined the ways PE teachers perceive girls' bodies, with the primary assumption that teachers' perceptions are part of the interactions with their students (Davies, 2000), and therefore may contribute significantly to the ways in which girls' experience of PE classes and their perception of their bodies are shaped.

Adolescent Girls and Bodies

The body is a central arena for adolescent girls. This involves physical changes the body goes through, the development of sexuality and the awakening of awareness of the body as a symbol of femininity (Frost, 2001a, 2001b). The girls act within the dominant 'Feminine Proper Body Discourse' which implies that the body should be thin and firm, well-shaped, delicate, nice-smelling and smooth (Bordo, 1993). Teenage girls perceive their bodies and their physical appearance as critical factors in their social status and future success (Budgeon, 2003; Lemish, 1998; Peshkin, 2000). They internalize the external masculine gaze on themselves (Aapola, Gonick & Harris, 2005), start viewing their own body as an object that needs repair and put increasing efforts into improving their appearance (Wolf, 1992).

A girl's body can be seen as 'an entity in the process of becoming', a 'project' that she needs to conduct and perform (Shilling, 2003, p. 4). The emerging body can serve simultaneously as a source of pleasure and power, and as a source of difficulty and weakness. PE classes can empower girls and enhance their self-efficacy or weaken them and prompt feelings of failure, dissatisfaction with the body and self-criticism. To address the discursive order in PE teachers' world, we unfold below common forms of scrutinizing girls' bodies.

Body Pedagogies

The educational system is one of the social institutions that reproduces body-related discourses. Learning about the body takes place in a formal, official manner during cognitive learning about the body (Evans, Rich & Allwood, 2008; Shilling, 2010), but in practice, it takes place during every single moment of the school day since culturally dominant body-related discourses are embedded in the school atmosphere, in its culture, norms and values. Thus, alongside the declared official school curriculum, there is a hidden curriculum that deals with pupils' bodies (Carey, Donaghue & Broderick, 2010; Rønholt, 2002; Webb, Quennerstedt & Öhman, 2008). In the school context, the proper body does not refer to appearance alone but also to proper activities, nutrition, personal hygiene, appropriate clothing and even to physical aspects of relationships (Shilling, 2010). Both the official and hidden curricula adhere to this broad meaning of what is a 'Proper Body'.

PE — A Field of Inequality

In many Western countries, the official PE policy is of equality (e.g. Galily, Ronnie & Ben-Porat, 2009; Penney & Evans, 2002). Criticism of PE as a space of gender inequality has been voiced since the 1980s (Flintoff & Scraton, 2001; MacDonald, 1997). Initially, this criticism focused on the resources allocated to girls' PE classes in comparison to those allocated to boys (Leaman, 1984). More recent criticism has dealt with the characteristics of the field such as the curriculum, teaching practices and teachers' perceptions that make the field of PE gendered (Hunter, 2004). With regards to teachers' views, research shows that the sociocultural discourses of PE itself, gender, and gender relations are embedded in teachers' discursive practices and have a significant impact on the implementation of the curriculum in PE classes (Beckett & Martino, 2007; Rønholt, 2002). These studies have mainly dealt with teachers' views on the curriculum, and their ideas about femininity and masculinity. In the last 10 years more emphasis has been placed on the intersection of gender and other axes of inequality, and the claim has been made that the field is not open to diversity (Flintoff & Scraton, 2001). Broadening earlier endeavours to investigate teachers' attitudes towards girls, we add a focus on teachers' stances towards girls' bodies, aiming at mapping the diversity among them.

Research Design

This chapter is based on in-depth semi-structured interviews with 15 female PE teachers working in different secondary schools in Israel. All teachers are bound by the central guidelines and supervision of the Ministry of Education. All are Jewish, and all but one are secular. They differ in age, experience and training with careers ranging from 40 to only one year. They attended three different PE colleges in Israel. Six teachers out of the 15 were athletics trainers during their compulsory military service. Five were professional athletes while at school. The teachers interviewed in our study mentioned their own experiences in PE classes. They remember themselves as excellent students, and in their mind, PE classes are strongly linked to a very positive experience. The interviews took place from 2013 to 2015, and were recorded and transcribed. Themes were extracted and subjected to Interpretive Content Analysis (Glaser, 2002; Shkedi, 2003), a method based on tracing repeated themes that emerge both inductively from the interviews and deductively from the research question. The analysis aims at understanding the subjective meanings interviewees give to the themes. On the basis of the analysis of themes, a social process is extracted in ways that allow shedding new light on the field. The themes reflect the ways teachers view girls and how they negotiate with dominant body-related discourses. All names used in this chapter are pseudonyms.

PE Teachers' Talk about Girls

During the interviews the teachers shared their views on today's teenage girls, the nature of their relationships with their students, their challenges as well as their good experiences and satisfaction. On the basis of earlier research and in order to deepen the understanding of teachers' diverse stances on girls' bodily disciplining, we distinguish three groups of teachers. The first group includes teachers who reinforce dominant hegemonic discourses such as the 'Tyranny of Slenderness' (that raises the demand that women be thin) and the 'Capable Body' (that associates the feminine body with physical incapability) (Hunter, 2004). The second group includes ambivalent, somewhat moralistic teachers, who see the recognition of different girls' bodily experiences as their ethical obligation, but concurrently view these experiences as deserving various forms of exclusion (Williams & Bedward, 2002). The third group is comprised of open-minded teachers who are willing to see the broad range of girls' bodies and resist other hegemonic discourses related to girls' bodies (O'Sullivan, Bush, & Gehring, 2002). We organized the analysis around these discursive stances which we classified as hegemonic, ambivalent or resisting.

Hegemonic Stance towards Girls' Bodies

When talking to the teachers, we asked for their view on the preferred body for PE classes. Some replies revealed the presence of the dominant Thin Discourse. These teachers even considered themselves responsible for motivating the girls to diet and supporting them to achieve a thin body. According to Lea,

> If this is a bad place for me [being unsatisfied with my body] I need to do something about it [...] Now, you just need to figure out where you want to be [...] want to lose weight? OK, let's move on and do it together.

In another case, the grade in PE was linked to weight loss. Tsili said,

> I called her and suggested that we make a plan together. I wrote out her a diet plan and a monitoring process. I promised her a good grade if she was able to lose weight.

The weight loss in this case was defined as a motivator to get a better grade in PE. The dominance of the Thin Discourse can be explained not only by its dominance in the Western culture but also by the dominant performative school culture that promotes physical appearance (Evans et al., 2008; Shilling, 2010). It can also be explained by the low value attributed to school PE which is often the least appreciated subject in school, and PE teachers rank lowest in the school hierarchy. To signify added value and commitment, teachers often intentionally or unconsciously adopt dominant school discourses like the 'Thin discourse'. Another possible explanation is the teachers' solidarity with those students who, from their perspective, do not fit the hegemonic visual model and the teachers' desire to best prepare them to be members of society, that is to help them lose weight.

Other views of the preferred body in PE class linked body shape to physical abilities. For Lea,

> This girl [the overweight one], she can't do a handstand. It doesn't matter how hard I try, it's pathetic. Normally there are four or five fat awkward girls in a class.

The teacher's stance about the overweight girls' incapability represents the hegemonic view that physical ability is weight sensitive (Brabazon, 2006), that is Lea expects the overweight girls to be unable to do certain exercises. This view is a hidden, probably even an unconscious form of exclusion. When the teachers talked about the preferred body in PE class, they also referred not only to PE classes but to the preferred body in general. Lea states,

> It's not just in PE class [that it's better to be thin]. Also on the beach. And at parties. And on a daily basis at school. And in the summer you sweat less, you don't get rashes, etc. Every given minute is better and easier for the skinny girl. It's the same in the bathroom in front of the mirror.

Lea addresses the entire being of a thin girl in various areas. She voices the common view of associating the thin body with happiness (Brabazon, 2006). Another is the equation of body shape with well-being (Brabazon, 2006), where the heavy body is portrayed as a barrier to happiness. Furthermore, not wanting to change the body shape is seen as morally wrong. Lea notes,

> They [the overweight girls] give up on themselves. Those who do not look good, with low self-esteem, give up on themselves. They are willing to accept themselves like this.

The thin body reflects self-control, restraint and strength, and being overweight is a symbol of weakness, passivity and avoidance of the struggle towards self-improvement. Physical appearance seems to stand for inner virtues and it mirrors the soul (Brabazon, 2006). However, other interpretations suggest that being overweight is genetic, or that it reflects the girls' preferences to internalize the motto of 'accept yourself as you are'. Being overweight can also be regarded as a social problem that stems from consumer culture. These alternative views apparently have yet to impact Israeli PE teachers.

When we asked the teachers to describe their students' experience of PE, they used the verbs 'dislike' and 'avoid'. They suggested that this is related to the girls' refusal to 'fix' their bodies, and referred solely to girls. Nati comments,

> I can tell you I have encountered lots of different bodies — fat and thin, tall and short, each girl has her own issues — large breasts, small breasts, being overweight [...] I think it has to do with their motivation, their will [...] I believe when there's a will, there's a way.

PE is seen as a body-shape neutral space, and success in PE is a function of girls' will and effort. This view represents the neoliberal hegemonic approach that places responsibility on the individuals and withdraws responsibility from the other parties involved (Aapola et al., 2005; Duits,

2008), including PE training schools, the Ministry of Education and the teachers themselves.

Ambivalent Stance towards Girls Bodies: Diversity and Body Disciplining

PE teachers with ambivalent stance towards girl bodies are aware of its implications in terms of social status. They also seem to be aware of diversity of body shapes and how bodies change during adolescence. They expressed empathy and sympathy towards the girls. Ravit said,

> Those who used to be excellent runners became slow. Because of [...] because of the body changes. All of a sudden, she can't run as fast as she could. These are the physical changes that slow her down. I remember myself — I used to run very fast, I used to be good at high jump, and when I got my period at the age of 13 and a half, 14, it all changed.

Michal also states,

> For a big-breasted girl, I suggest walking [instead of running with the class]. This year I approached one of the students and suggested she stopped running and said she could walk instead.

Alongside care and sensitivity to girls' emotional bodily experience, these PE teachers expressed essentialist views of the body. This included assumptions such as the feminine body is less adequate to physical activity than the masculine body, and that a boy-like build is better adapted to PE classes than a curvy feminine shape (Brabazon, 2006). If this stance is embedded in class interactions, it constitutes another kind of exclusion which affects overweight students. Thus, body shape constitutes an inequality axis between and within genders.

PE teachers with ambivalent views referred to the physical obstacles related to body growth and changes as well as to the social context of the PE class. Gal said,

> The changes related to puberty [...] for some girls the activity is really more difficult. You are more cumbersome and heavy. I can't understand it [looking down at her own body and smiles] but it definitely disrupts. It might be frustrating — how come I can't do what I used to do? I often hear these kinds of remarks [...] It slows them down, encumbers their motion [...] they want to know when the boys are leaving the space. They don't want to run when the boys are looking. They don't want

to be seen running. These are probably the ones who are not comfortable with their bodies and prefer not to be seen. Some girls actually do want that.

Gal expressed the essentialist view on the impact of puberty on physical abilities which 'definitely disrupts' girls' bodies. However, she also describes the social challenges some girls face while asked to run in front of boys and be the object of their gaze and ridicule. She accepts body shape diversity and is aware of girls' various relationships with their bodies. Thus, while voicing empathy for the changes in physical behaviour, she remains focused on capabilities, and seems to be certain that helping the girls who do not want to be seen would be to help them remain invisible. Her empathic response runs the risk of reinforcing their bodily shame and embarrassment.

Another teacher referred to the social context of the class and described her way of addressing it. Varda notes,

> Generally speaking, they love ball games — basketball, volleyball, and we play them. They hate sweating; they are nervous when the boys are around; they don't want to be seen doing PE. So we take them out to the nearby park. They love it, we walk and run and play. They prefer being there than being in the gym at school […] out of a class of 37 students, 4—5 girls distance themselves from the class. They are afraid of the ball. They are very delicate. One of them is tiny, very small, but the others are actually normal. I think it is embedded in the body. If you are asking me, it is inborn.

Varda describes her students with sincere empathy and care. She appears to be really attentive to them, understand and respect them, and design her PE classes in a way that meets their needs and desires. She legitimizes different body shapes and acknowledges the differences among girls. This explains her view that some girls do not like ball games. She believes that avoiding ball games is related to certain girls' physical inborn inabilities, and is not aware of the fact that embodied practices are acquired and can be relearned even in adolescence. In any case, Varda is apparently not aware of girls' experiences when excluded from the class. She does not offer these girls an alternative that would better meet their needs and better suit their bodies.

Open-Minded Stance towards Girls' Bodies

Three of the teachers resisted hegemonic discourses, and accepted diversity of body shapes. Two of them teach at the same school, together with two of the teachers with ambivalent views. Each of the four PE teachers in the same school uses different didactic techniques and strategies. At the beginning of the semester, each student chooses which of the four classes to join. When we inquired about the objectives of PE classes we learned that they refer mainly to the emotional experience of the students. According to Rachel,

> In my classes the key thing is to relax, feel released and free, and step by step eliminate inhibitions and remain me, only me, as I really am, and joyfully, without too much thinking about how I look, who is looking [...] it's a real liberation [...] Many of the overweight girls come to my class. Also the big-breasted girls. And thin and shy girls.

Rachel is aware of the dominant performative school culture (Cale & Harris, 2013; Duits, 2008) and the Thin Discourse, and resists them. She tries to work with her students in a way that lets them concentrate on their feelings rather than on their appearance. By doing so, she expands their view to be inside-out, not only outside-in, as it commonly is (Grosz, 1994), that is to pay attention to the way the body feels and the emotions it awakens in addition to the awareness to the way the body is seen by others.

Another teacher mentioned a touching case that gave her great satisfaction. For Tony,

> I had a student who used to be very quiet, with low body image, low self-esteem and was very insecure. At the end of the year she came up to me and said: 'you changed the way I see myself'. You know, it was worth working my entire life for this moment [...] We hugged and I told her this was the greatest compliment I could hope for.

In this case, Tony realized that one of her students changed the way she feels about herself. For her, this was a very exciting moment. Tony, as well as other teachers, talked about their educational role in legitimizing diversity. Irit, for example, notes,

> My message to the girls is that everyone has a different body, with unique characteristics, and what suits one body does not suit someone else. Every girl needs to find what's best for her. How to reach balance, because when the body is balanced you keep smiling, you feel the joy and fun [...] and this is what's right for you.

The teachers who belong to this group do not only legitimize diversity, but also express a stance that has not been voiced by the other teachers: they talk about each girl's inner agency (Aapola et al., 2005; Brown & Gilligan, 1993) and knowing what is best for her. In addition, they talk about pleasure and enjoyment. This voice was missing in the talk of most teachers in the other groups.

Openness to Diversity

Earlier research on PE teachers sought to document teachers' attitudes towards PE classes and the PE curriculum but paid little attention to their stances concerning the body. Thus feminist approaches to the ways in which teachers help reproduce the social 'other' in PE classes have tended to be overlooked. Clearly, the teachers we interviewed love PE and care for their students. They all view PE classes as a place of equality and believe that any girl, with any body shape, can acquire the values embedded in these classes. They all negotiate with the hegemonic discourses related to girls' bodies; namely the 'Thin Discourse' that reproduces the 'Tyranny of Slenderness' and leads many girls to self-criticism and hatred of their own body (Bordo, 1993; Frost, 2005), the 'Body as a Mirror to the Soul Discourse' that associates body shape with character and emotional state, and the 'Capable Body Discourse' that associates the feminine body with cumbersomeness, heaviness and slowness (Brook, 1999) while ignoring the cultural aspects of being an adolescent girl (Young, 2005), and hence not addressing girls' issues in PE classes.

Our analysis of the data suggested that teachers position themselves through continuous negotiation with these disciplining discourses which demand bodily repair. Both the hegemonic and the resisting stances remain relatively marginal, and the third, ambivalent stance appears to be more attractive to teachers allowing them to experience themselves as sensitive to the girls even when they give up on some of them. Teachers who hold the ambivalent stance are more permeable to various body shapes, but at the same time see the curved feminine body as a barrier to success in PE, and thus, they reproduce dominant discourse of thinness and help the overweight girls remain invisible. They understand the social challenges girls have to face in PE classes but maintain PE routines that do not take the girls into account. They are aware of physical characteristics when explaining issues girls have in PE classes, but nevertheless their understanding is not translated into tolerating bodily diversity in their school. The teachers care for their students but unconsciously exclude some of them from the class and thus curtail their right to develop bodily efficacy.

Davies (2000) argued that a person's stance regarding different social discourses can be explained by the concepts one has, and that these concepts are related to the person's unique positions. Teachers' positions shape their worldview and the way they negotiate these body-related discourses. Each teacher's position incorporates the dominant social, political and cultural discourses and norms, as well as her own training and career. The position also includes her personal bodily experience as teenager and as young woman, and to her memories of her own PE classes and PE teachers. The teachers who have ambivalent stance take a progressive liberal stand which is aligned with current educational and cultural discourses. These views reflect the 'child in the center' educational philosophy and the encouragement of diversity. However, they are sometimes blind to girls' experience and to the exclusionary mechanisms they enforce. This is not related to lack of will or concern but to a lack of knowledge. As stated, these teachers incorporate the hegemonic cultural perception of the body, their own experience and what they learned during their training to become PE teachers in teachers' colleges. They remember their PE classes as a safe space that enabled creation, with the body as a means of expression. Thus, their view of bodily experiences in PE class is positive. The training they have gone through prior to becoming PE teachers did not provide progressive knowledge of girlhood and the sociology of the body. And, their stances do not constitute a coherent progressive whole.

Nevertheless, teachers' stances can change over time as a function of their experiences in class and professional development. Therefore, we suggest broadening teachers' knowledge and views on girls and their bodies by modifying the curriculum in teachers' colleges and professional training. This could lead to changes in their position and expand the concepts available to them into a more inclusive diversity of body shapes. One outcome might be a greater ability to resist hegemonic discourses in PE classes, thus giving more girls the opportunity to experience their bodies as a source of expression, pleasure and power.

In conclusion, not enough feminist attention has been drawn to the extent to which PE is a site in which girls struggle for gender justice, and need feminist support and action. We showed how specifically courageous teachers shoulder the project of turning PE space into a more inclusive space. At the same time, it is clear that without the backing of the feminist movement and progressive initiatives to modify PE their voice cannot be heard and become influential enough.

References

Aapola, S., Gonick, M., & Harris, A. (Eds.). (2005). *Young femininity: Girlhood, power and social change.* New York, NY: Palgrave Macmillan.

Beckett, L. M., & Martino, W. (2007). Schooling the gendered body in health and physical education: Interrogating teachers' perspectives. *Sport, Education and Society, 9*(2), 239–251.

Bordo, S. (1993). *Unbearable weight: Feminism, western culture, and the body.* Berkeley, CA: University of California Press.

Brabazon, T. (2006). Fitness is a feminist issue. *Australian Feminist Studies, 21*(49), 65–83.

Brook, B. (1999). *Feminist perspectives on the body.* London: Longman.

Brown, L. M., & Gilligan, C. (1993). Meeting at the crossroads: Women's psychology and girls' development. *Feminism & Psychology, 3*(1), 11–35.

Budgeon, S. (2003). Identity as an embodied event. *Body & Society, 9*(1), 35–55.

Cale, L., & Harris, J. (2013). 'Every child (of every size) matters' in physical education! Physical education's role in childhood obesity. *Sport, Education and Society, 18*(4), 433–452.

Carey, R., Donaghue, N., & Broderick, P. (2010). 'What you look like is such a big factor': Girls' own reflections about the appearance culture in an all-girls' school. *Feminism & Psychology, 21*(3), 299–316.

Clarck, S. (2012). Being 'good at sport'—Talent, ability and young women's sporting participation. *Sociology, 6*(46), 1178–1193.

Davies, B. (2000). *A body of writing, 1990–1999.* Walnut Creek, CA: Altamira Press.

Duits, L. (2008). *Multi-girl-culture: An ethnography of doing identity.* Amsterdam: Amsterdam University Press.

Evans, J., Rich, E., & Allwood, R. (2008). Body pedagogies policy health and gender. *British Educational Research Journal, 34*(3), 387–402.

Flintoff, A., & Scraton, S. (2001). Stepping into active leisure? Young women's perceptions of active lifestyles and their experiences of school physical education. *Sport, Education and Society, 6*(1), 5–21.

Frost, L. (2001a). Adolescence and body hatred. In L. Frost & J. Campling (Eds.), *Young women and the body: A feminist sociology* (pp. 60–81). New York, NY: Palgrave.

Frost, L. (2001b). Sexuality and body hatred. In L. Frost & J. Campling (Eds.), *Young women and the body: A feminist sociology* (pp. 108–130). New York, NY: Palgrave.

Frost, L. (2005). Theorizing the young woman in the body. *Body & Society, 11*(1), 63–85.

Galily, Y., Ronnie, L., & Ben-Porat, A. (2009). *The playing field: Sport in society in the early 21th century.* Tel-Aviv, Israel: Open University of Israel.

Glaser, B. (2002). Conceptualization: On theory and theorizing using grounded theory. *International Journal of Qualitative Methods, 1*(2), 23–38.

Grosz, E. (1994). *Volatile bodies.* St Leonards: Allen & Unwin.

Hunter, L. (2004). Bourdieu and the social space of the PE class: Reproduction of doxa through practice. *Sport, Education and Society, 9*(2), 175—192.

Leaman, O. (1984). *Sit on the sidelines and watch the boys play: Sex differentiation in physical education.* London: Longman for Schools Council.

Lemish, D. (1998). Spice Girls' talk: A case study in the development of gendered identity. In S. A. Inness (Ed.), *Millennium girls: Today's girls around the world* (pp. 145—169). New York, NY: Rowman & Littlefield Publishers, Inc.

MacDonald, D. (1997). The feminisms of gender equity in physical education. *Journal Cahperd, 63*(1), 4—8.

O'Sullivan, M., Bush, K., & Gehring, M. (2002). Gender equity and physical education: A USA perspective. In D. Penney (Ed.), *Gender and physical education: Contemporary issues and future directions* (pp. 163—189). London: Routledge.

Penney, D., & Evans, J. (2002). Talking gender. In D. Penney (Ed.), *Gender and physical education: Contemporary issues and future directions* (pp. 13—23). New York, NY: Routledge.

Peshkin, A. (2000). The nature of interpretation in qualitative research. *Educational Researcher, 29*(9), 5—9.

Rønholt, H. (2002). 'It's only the sissies …': Analysis of teaching and learning Processes in physical education: A contribution to the hidden curriculum. *Sport, Education and Society, 7*(1), 25—36.

Shilling, C. (2003). Introduction. In M. Featherstone (Ed.), *The body and social theory* (3rd ed., pp. 1—16). New York, NY: Sage.

Shilling, C. (2010). Exploring the society—body—school nexus: Theoretical and methodology issues in the study of body pedagogics. *Sport, Education and Society, 15*(2), 151—167.

Shkedi, A. (2003). *Words of meaning. Qualitative research: Theory and practice.* Tel-Aviv: Ramot, Tel Aviv University.

Webb, L., Quennerstedt, M., & Öhman, M. (2008). Healthy bodies: Construction of the body and health in physical education. *Sport, Education and Society, 13*(4), 353—372.

Williams, A., & Bedward, J. (2002). Understanding girls' experience of physical education: Relational analysis and situated learning. In D. Penney (Ed.), *Gender and physical education: Contemporary issues and future directions* (pp. 146—159). London: Routledge.

Wolf, N. (1992). *The beauty myth.* New York, NY: Harper Collins.

Young, I. M. (2005). Throwing like a girl: A phenomenology of feminine body comportment motility and spatiality. *Human Studies, 3*(1), 137—156.

Chapter 19

Basketball Diary

Jocelyn Thorpe

Abstract

I have played basketball for almost three quarters of my life. It is a sport I love and it taught me young that sexism exists and feminism matters. By paying close attention to the local and particular — playing basketball for almost 30 years in various gyms in Ontario, Newfoundland and Manitoba — I demonstrate in this piece how politics of gender, race and sexuality infuse our everyday lives and connect to larger themes of societal inclusions and exclusions. The piece is written as a series of fictionalized diary entries, beginning in 1987 when I was 10 and first started to play basketball, and ending in 2014 when I wrote the chapter. Learning to play the game came along with navigating life as a girl on a team of boys who passed the ball to one another but not to me. The tone and content of the diary entries change as I grow up and understand the world better, but the theme of passing the ball, and what it might mean to live in a world where we passed the ball more often and differently, remains central to the story. I chose to write a short story rather than an essay because form matters for how content is delivered and received. One thing I have learned from my students is that academic writing often communicates that the 'we' who produce it want merely to sound clever and not actually to communicate with the 'you' who try to make sense of it. Here I take seriously students' concerns by writing in an engaging and accessible way, thus following a feminist politics of inclusion rather than alienation.

Keywords: Basketball; sexism; Audre Lorde; personal as political; feminism; sports

Global Currents in Gender and Feminisms: Canadian and International Perspectives, 279–289
Copyright © 2018 by Emerald Publishing Limited
All rights of reproduction in any form reserved
ISBN: 978-1-78714-484-2/doi:10.1108/978-1-78714-483-520171026

Introduction

I have played basketball for most of my life and taught women's and gender studies for a much shorter time. I love both, and am glad to be able to bring them together in this chapter, one that reinforces the feminist adage that the personal is the political. In my years of teaching, I have noticed (and have been repeatedly reminded by students!) that academic writing can exclude students, making them feel uninspired to learn about a topic, even when, as is the case with feminism, the topic matters in their everyday lives. When I first noticed that academic writing gets in the way of real communication between writers and readers, I laughed it off as merely one of life's ironies. But the more I thought about it, and the more I taught — and therefore grappled with translating to students amazing ideas wrapped up in inaccessible language — the more I began to think it was no joke. Writing is not separate from theory and methodology, and feminist scholars would do well to remember that we want to welcome people into our work, not exclude them from it. I do not mean to suggest that we attempt to 'dumb down' complex ideas, but rather that we write about ideas in ways that encourage people to keep reading.

Anti-racist feminist poet and scholar Audre Lorde (1984) draws readers in not only because of her brilliant ideas, but because she writes those ideas beautifully, often heartbreakingly so. She pulls readers into her writing, and in so doing pulls them also into feminist theory. The writing is a big part of the *how* of Lorde's work, her methodology, and I suspect that her *how* has as much to do with the enduring influence of her work as does her *what*, or theory. More importantly, the *how* and the *what* of Lorde's work are inextricably connected. Readers access her thoughts through her writing, and her writing is a central part of the work she does to convince us to live towards the beautiful world she envisions and makes real on the page.

I wrote 'Basketball Diary' inspired by Lorde. Like her work, 'Basketball Diary' is personal, and yet I hope resonates with readers who grew up in different times and places than I did, and who played sports or did not. I hope the piece is accessible and engaging and that it does the theoretical work of showing that gender and feminism still matter today. For me, feminism is about creating a different kind of world, one that puts all people and the planet first and eliminates oppression and greed. I invite readers to consider whether it is possible to play basketball towards that different world.

'Basketball Diary' is a journal of my thoughts over the years between 1987 and 2014 about playing basketball. In real life, I didn't write a basketball diary, but all the stories I tell in the diary are true. You will notice while reading that sometimes I skip over years without an entry, so please pay attention to the dates while you are reading. You will notice as well that both the tone and the content of the diary change as I grow up and grow to understand the world better, but the theme of passing the ball, and what it might mean to live in a world where we pass the ball more often and differently, remains central to the story. I hope you will notice the political in this personal account, that you will understand this chapter as a narrative approach to 'doing' feminism, and that you will add to the story's power by adding your own basketball (or other sport) diary, deepening my analysis by tying it to your own.

30 September 1987

I got this diary for my birthday. Even though my birthday was in the summer, this is the first time I am writing in my diary. Hello, Diary. My name is Jocelyn Thorpe and I am 10 years old. I have two sisters and two parents and a cat and I am in grade 5. I don't exactly understand the point of a diary, except that you can tell your secrets to it because it has a lock. Here is my secret: my diary is kind of ugly and I don't like it that much because it has puffy white material on the outside and it says 'Diary' in frilly blue writing. Sorry, Diary. I do appreciate getting it as a gift from my Aunt Heather and I do find the key part really cool because it is tiny and silver. The puffy part is very, very ugly. But, Diary, I will try to write in you about my new sport of basketball, even though you are puffy and you are also me in a way because you are not actually alive. Weird.

I have the sport of basketball to write about because I picked it as my new activity to try this year. There is some programme called Youth Basketball Canada that's happening at my school in the evening. Since I wasn't really into Guides (so boring!!!), my mom said I can do this instead.

15 October 1987

We had our first basketball practice tonight and it was fun. Our coach is named Rhonda. I'm the only grade 5 on the team (everyone else is in grade 6), the only one from my school (even though practices are in my school gym), *and* the only girl (other than Rhonda). Our team shirts are green with a little hoop and ball and they say 'YBC'. Mine has the number 11 on the back.

We practiced passing by doing a game called the Three-Man Weave, which is a pretty funny name for passing the ball and then running behind the person you passed to. Then we did a game called Bump where the first person had to get a shot in before the next person in line or we would get bumped out. I bumped everybody and I won! (I know I am not supposed to be excited about winning because the point is to have fun, but I can't help it. I love winning! Winning *is* fun.)

10 November 1987

Tonight, we had our first real game against the maroon team. We won 20 to 14 and I scored 6 points! Yay! It is so cool to watch the ball swish through the net. I have noticed something annoying, though. At practice when we are scrimmaging (which means playing a pretend game), the boys don't pass me the ball unless Rhonda makes them. She says things like, 'Look! Jocelyn is wide open!' and then sometimes they pass.

But in the real game, no one passed me the ball at all, even though I kept on being open! All my points came from rebounding my teammates' missed shots. Maybe I need to practise my rebounding. Or maybe I could work on my ball handling and become a point guard instead of a forward. But Rhonda says I should be a forward because I'm tall. A point guard's job is to dribble the ball up the court and then to make good passes and plays. Our point guard is Miles and he likes not to pass the ball and instead to dribble and dribble until he shoots. I get it that it's fun to score, but I wish he would pass sometimes.

Still, basketball is really fun. I don't mean to sound like a complainer. I told my mom about Miles and the other boys not passing to me and she said that sometimes boys have a problem called 'not passing to girls', but that it's the boys' problem, not mine. I don't know if Miles has that problem or just the problem called 'not passing at all'.

3 December 1987

The blue team has a girl on it! So far, it's the only other team with a girl on it. She is really, really good. Definitely better than me. Well, maybe. She sure had the ball a lot. Actually, she was kind of a ball hog, like Miles. Maybe it's not just boys who have a passing problem! Or maybe she knows if she gives it away, she'll never get it back. She scored a lot of points, maybe 12 or 14. I keep scoring 6, every single game.

I can't decide if I like practices or games better. In practices, I get to take more shots, but in games it's exciting because everyone is watching.

25 September 1989

I found this old diary again and read it. Some things I noticed: (1) My handwriting has gotten better. (2) I still think the diary is quite ugly. It's maybe puffy because it's trying to look like leather, which it is not. (3) I still love basketball! And guess what?! I made the school team! It's for grade 7s and 8s. Only two grade 7s made it, and I am one! Oh, and this time it is only girls, not like my YBC team. The boys have their own school team. I guess probably that means I will get the ball more often on this team.

12 October 1989

Our coach gives us an Astro Pop every time we make a foul shot in a game. I have a lot of Astro Pops. They are delicious and pointy, but mostly I like looking at them in my desk at school. I also like giving them to my friends, because who can eat that many Astro Pops? Our coach is Mr. Collins. He is very serious about basketball, but also very fun. Astro Pops, for example, are fun. *But* if we miss an easy shot in a game, we have to get 10 in a row in at the beginning of our next practice. Also, we have to pass to each other all the time. If someone is a ball hog, that someone ends up sitting on the bench and not playing (which sometimes actually happens, especially with Sarah). We have certain plays, which involve working together to get open and to have our team score. Mr. Collins reminds us a lot that there is no 'I' in 'team', which is obvious but smart. This school basketball is *way more fun* than YBC because of all the passing and teamwork, but I think YBC helped me make the team and not be scared of the ball. Also, it helped me get good at passing and shooting and dribbling. So really I have Rhonda and YBC to thank for all my Astro Pops. And also Mr. Collins, of course.

Basketball is pretty much the most fun thing I get to do. And I like swimming. And reading. And school, especially English. But if somebody said pick one thing to do forever, I would say basketball. Well, I might get tired after awhile. But if I lived on a desert island with only one sport to play, I would definitely choose basketball. It's hard to explain. I love all the parts — how the ball feels, the squeaky-shoe sound on the floor, everyone cheering. When you say it's a game where you try to put a ball in a net, it sounds very boring. But I could shoot and pass and play all day, and never get bored.

10 September 1991

I made the grade 9 girls' team! *And* I even get to practice with the senior girls' team sometimes, because their coach invited me. Yay, yay and *yay*!

19 November 1991

My mom says I can't be a prima donna about basketball. But we lost the game all because of me. I missed almost every single one of my shots. I even missed a foul shot! And then in the car on the way home, my mom was all, 'If you're going to be a prima donna about it, then you can't continue to play. The point is to have fun'. Blah blah blah. I'm not even allowed to be upset for one minute on the way home about the worst game *ever* when I disappointed the *whole* team and the *whole* school. My mom is the worst! I am going to bed.

19 June 1993

I didn't get MVP this year. Funny because when I have gotten it in the past, it hasn't seemed like a very big deal. It's like it makes sense because I'm the only one on my school team who was asked to play on the city team. My mom says awards are political, whatever that means. At awards night, I tried to be happy for Megan. She is a great player, and she's my friend. But inside I just kept feeling sad. When I got home, I lay on the couch and cried. That's when my mom said the thing about how awards are political. She also said that *she* thinks I'm the best player, which did kind of make me feel better, even though she's my mom and so she probably has to say that. MVP is a weird award now that I think about it. Most Valuable Player. I thought there was no 'I' in 'team'.

Anyway, I know that awards aren't the most important thing, or at least I know I'm not supposed to think they're the most important thing. But when you win them, people think you're good. I should just be confident and say that it doesn't matter. I am good at basketball. Just not the best.

1 August 1996

I decided not to try out for the university team. I'm not sick of basketball, exactly. I'm just sick of going away every weekend and eating at Taco Bell or Kelsey's and sleeping in a full hotel room. Plus, I don't really want to work out all the time, which you have to do to play university basketball. I want to have friends who don't play basketball and I want to make sure I have time to do well in university, because everyone says it is way harder than high school. Is this just a way of saying I want to have a life? Two coaches 'recruited' me, I guess. But I can't imagine choosing where to go to school based on which coaches asked me to play on their team. I guess it is about what is serious. Basketball has always felt serious to me, I mean in a fun way, but serious like it matters. But it's not like I'm going to be a professional basketball player. Would I think differently if I were a guy? My parents think that school is important and sports are for fun. Is that what I think too? It feels strange to write all this down.

5 March 2003

Ha! I guess I really do think that school is important. I can't seem to stop the habit. I haven't written in this thing for years, and I've been in school the whole time. I just finished my M.A. and I'm starting a Ph.D. in the fall. Basketball has definitely taken a back seat, though I've been playing for fun ever since high school. Actually, I was laughing to myself about it the other day when I remembered once watching a bunch of 'old women' play basketball after one of our high-school practices. The gym was empty except for the old women and me, and I remember thinking from the stands, 'Why do they even bother? No one is watching, no one cares, and they're not very good'. According to my (embarrassingly arrogant) teenage definition, now *I* am an old woman who plays when no one is watching. I'm finding, though, that age has its advantages. For one thing, I know that while no one is watching and I might not be very good, *I* care. It matters to me. And I keep noticing beauty in the little things. A perfect pass and finish. A clean block. I get to play this game I love. That is the gift, the part that matters.

I could definitely not say these kinds of things out loud to my teammates. Almost all of them played university basketball at some point, and now here we are playing together on the other side of that decision. It's funny to think about how seriously I once took this game (it's even called a game!), and how serious many of my teammates still seem. I wonder whether my decision not to play in university helps me now to enjoy the game part of basketball. Tonight, one of my teammates was in a terrible mood all game because her shot was off. It was hard not to channel my mom and say that her attitude rather than her shot was ruining our game. To be fair, though, as a culture we do send out some strange messages, for example the message that winning matters more than playing well together. It is possible, likely even, that my teammate did not have my mom, the world's most persistent parent, to counter that message. These days, I'm really glad about that mom of mine. She didn't have much patience for what she considered prima donna behaviour, but she taught me that basketball (like life?) isn't really about winning games or awards. It's more about getting to play, and maybe even about playing well with others.

29 January 2004

My sister roped me into playing with a bunch of grad students and profs in her faculty. It's pretty fun, actually — just a lunchtime league. I haven't played co-ed basketball for years, and it's giving me hope about the world, cheesy as that is to say. It seems... regular. Maybe this is another advantage of age. Everyone passes to everyone, and we get on with the game. But maybe there's something to be said, too, for a critical mass. There are a lot of women playing, not just one or two girls like in YBC days. And now that I think about it, the women who play are very experienced, have played for years. The guys for the most part are not basketball players, but are happy to play whatever sport is happening. I wonder why more women don't just play, whether or not they know how. I see it all the time at the Y too, pick-up basketball with lots of guys of varying abilities. If there are women there (which is rare), they are always skilled players. I'm sure the answer is sexism somehow, I just don't get exactly how, or what would make it better. Are there women wanting to play who feel they can't, or have women internalized the 'throw like a girl' nonsense to the extent that they don't want to try throwing anything for fear of being teased? Maybe it just comes down to women being scrutinized, including by themselves, more than men. Everyone knows you can't get better without practicing, but it's hard to practice if everyone is watching you, or if you think they are watching. Arg. Sexism. I'm so over it.

8 September 2010

What a whirlwind. This is what I have learned so far about academic life: there is a lot of moving around. In three cities, my partner and I have managed to finish two Ph.Ds. and two postdocs (one of each for each of us), find one tenure-track job (for me), and add two members to our family (a daughter and a cat). Today I learned something else: there's a lunchtime basketball league at the university, mostly faculty and staff! I haven't gotten to play much since grad school, and so I'm extra excited. It might be foggy and windy here in St. John's, but, hey, there's lunchtime basketball! I'm so excited. Did I say that already? The lunchtime part is perfect. I'm finding life with this kid to be wonderful, of course, but it's not the easiest thing to fit everything of life into the hours of life. If I didn't ride my bike to school, I don't know that I would get any exercise at all. With basketball at lunchtime, I can teach and then take a break to run around before my next class. Life–work balance, here I come!...

17 September 2010

… Or maybe not. It was just 'the boys' and me, which was fine until they did not pass me the ball for the entire game. I wish I were kidding. It does feel like a kind of unfunny joke. Ha. At one point, I blocked someone's shot and all the other guys laughed and made fun of him.

'*Dude!* She blocked your shot!'

To his credit (and he was the one who invited me to lunchtime basketball in the first place), he ignored them. 'Nice block', he said. Still, the whole experience reminded me a little too much of grade 5.

Part of me wants to go back next week and give it another chance, to keep playing until they get used to me and start playing with me. But another part of me, perhaps the larger part, doesn't see the point. Who has that kind of time? I have a job, a kid, a partner, people to call, a bike to ride, laundry to wash, friends to make, a city to get to know…

Maybe I should start running at lunchtime, since that's effectively what I did anyway. But running, ugh. I couldn't help but smile at the irony as I got changed in my office after lunchtime basketball, and showed up sweaty to teach intro to gender studies.

6 August 2014

It's hard to believe we have lived in Winnipeg for two years now. Toronto to Vancouver to St. John's to Winnipeg. A baby born on each coast, and now here we are in the centre, finally, *finally* with two jobs. Somehow it seems to fit. And good news! I just called our community centre and the woman on the phone agreed that I could organize a pick-up basketball league. It was so easy. Just one phone call. I've been missing basketball since we moved here. After the terrible lunchtime experience (I never did go back), I found a great women's league in St. John's. The people on my team were so funny and welcoming, and I surprised myself by realizing how much playing basketball with them made me feel at home there. After kid number two was born, I came back to play as soon as I could. I think he was six weeks old. He spent many early evenings of his life cuddled into the arms of one sweaty player after another on the bench as we alternated between playing and holding him. Thinking about it makes me miss St. John's.

For Winnipeg basketball, I just have to decide whether in the community centre advertising to call it women's or co-ed. What I want to say is this: 'We're playing basketball. It doesn't matter how you identify in terms of gender (or anything else), but it matters that you're willing to pass the ball to everyone. The point is to have fun. The point is for *everyone* to have fun'.

But the community centre person says I can't say all that. Here is the phone conversation we just had:

Me: 'Could we please put 'queer and trans positive' in the advertising somewhere?'

Her: 'Clear and trans positive? Okay. Sure... What's that?'

Me: 'Queer, not clear. I want people to know that they can play no matter their gender identity or sexual orientation'.

Her: 'Okay. Right. I'll check with my boss and get back to you'.

13 August 2014

Her boss said we had to keep it simple, so did I want co-ed or women's in the ad? Simple isn't simple, I wanted to say. Co-ed doesn't quite capture it. If only there were a just-want-to-play box. Instead, I chose women's. A cop-out? I didn't want it to go the not-passing way, and I wasn't sure what else to do. There aren't enough boxes. Or perhaps there are too many. Now I'm trying to make up for it by talking to everyone I know in this city about Sunday basketball and how everyone can play.

'Not everyone who signs up will look like a woman', I told the community-centre person.

'Of course', she said. 'We don't want to exclude anyone'.

Jaxon says he'll play and I'm glad because he's just so great (in life, but I think at basketball also). He's looking more and more like a young man these days. I was avoiding gendered pronouns until my kids started calling him 'he' and I asked what he preferred, and he said he is fine. So, he. I feel grateful that my kids get to know him and that he is in the world helping to redefine what it means to be a man. I hope our son also will be a redefiner. So far, he is a real gender defier, although I don't think he quite knows that. He just thinks he looks beautiful in dresses, and is young enough to be unaware of the fact that not everyone thinks that beautiful, dresses and boy can go together in a sentence, or on a body. I'm not sure it's necessary to know the rules in order to change them. He is, though, interested in the rules these days, asking his big sister and arbiter of all things in his world, 'I'm a boy, right? I'm a brother and you're a sister?' I hope and hope and hope that we are helping him become the ball passing kind of kid, even if basketball is only a metaphor.

12 September 2014

I've been thinking about it: Is basketball a metaphor for life, or is it life itself? I mean, there's the question of what kind of game we are playing.

I want to play the game called 'survive on Earth without killing each other or the planet'. In that game everyone matters, and 'winning' means passing the ball to everyone and getting to keep playing, at least for our time. Basketball can stand in for a game of life like that, where the point is somehow beyond the object of the game. It's the moments of beauty. It's the working together. The teams and hoops and ball are just the things that allow the real thing to happen. That's what I wish Sunday basketball could be.

But the world often seems very different from that, as though the purpose is to win at all costs. Basketball works as a metaphor for that life too: score the most points, beat the other team, be the best, win. Heh. I guess that is the point of the game. No wonder the world is in this state. What I wonder about basketball beyond the metaphor is this: does playing *actual* basketball help make the world? Perhaps more importantly, does how we play that game shape how we play the not-game of life?

14 September 2014

We had our first Sunday basketball today. As I put on my shoes, my stomach turned in a familiar excited and nervous way, the same feeling I've had hundreds of times on hundreds of courts. It's kind of cool to have a thing your body knows how to do, even if age and lack of practice create a gap between the knowing and the doing. I have played this game for 27 years, almost three quarters of my life. I love the fact that all of us who showed up today still play, or want to learn to play. I love that we don't know each other, we are not like each other, and yet the whole point of doing this (I hope!) is to play together. A part of me wishes it could be more, that we could end sexism, racism, homophobia and so on just by playing together, by passing the ball. I need to remember that it's only Sunday basketball. Still, Sunday basketball is at the very least a part of life, and I can't help but think that how we play matters. Today was really good. And for now, I will hold onto the idea that we can play towards a different kind of world. I'll let you know how that goes!

Reference

Lorde, A. (1984). *Sister outsider: Essays and speeches*. Freedom, CA: The Crossing Press.

Index